The Sports
SCHOLARSHIPS
Insider's Guide

GETTING MONEY FOR COLLEGE AT ANY DIVISION

DION WHEELER

SOURCEBOOKS, INC.
NAPERVILLE, ILLINOIS

Published by Sourcebooks, Inc.
P.O. Box 4410, Naperville, Illinois 60567-4410
(630) 961-3900
FAX: (630) 961-2168
www.sourcebooks.com

Originally published in 2000.

Library of Congress Cataloging-in-Publication Data

Wheeler, Dion.
The sports scholarships insider's guide : getting money for college at any division / by Dion Wheeler.
    p. cm.
Includes index.
ISBN 1-4022-0376-4 (alk. paper)
1. Sports--Scholarships, fellowships, etc.--United States. 2. Universities and colleges--United States--Admission--Planning. I. Title.

GV351.W475 2005
796'.079'73--dc22

2005003152

To all the track animals I ever coached.
You gave me infinitely more than I ever gave you.

Contents

Acknowledgments vii

Introduction 1

Recruiting Myths 5

Chapter 1: Understanding the Recruiting Process 7

Chapter 2: Recruiting and Financial Aid 15

Chapter 3: Preparing for College and the Future 25

Chapter 4: Your Education and Athletics 31

Chapter 5: Academic Requirements 35

Chapter 6: Constructing the Profile 43

Chapter 7: The Cover Letter 55

Chapter 8: The Videotape 59

Chapter 9: Sending Credentials 61

Chapter 10: Organize, Organize, Organize 67

Chapter 11: Critical Documents 71

Chapter 12: Communication Activities 79

Chapter 13: The Visit 83

Chapter 14: Visit Questions 87

Chapter 15: Why Prospects and Families Get Hurt 93

Chapter 16: Awarding of Athletic Financial Aid 97

Chapter 17: Negotiating Guidelines 107

Chapter 18: Financial Aid Limits 113

Chapter 19: Solving the Division III Athletic
Financial Aid Mystery 121

Chapter 20: Interdepartmental Communications 131

Chapter 21: Division III's Pleasant Surprise 139

Chapter 22: Negotiate, Negotiate, Negotiate 141

Chapter 23: The Ultimate Negotiating Weapon 145

Chapter 24: How Do I Contribute to
My Future Success? 149

Glossary of Recruiting Terms 153

Appendix 1: Additional Resources 159

Appendix 2: Institution Contact Information 163

Appendix 3: Women's Sports 205

Appendix 4: Men's Sports 275

Appendix 5: Mixed Sports 339

Index 341

About the Author 343

Acknowledgments

With Special Thanks To:

Sy Kessler, without whom I would have never thought about using my experience to help overlooked prospects be successfully recruited.

Al Perres and Ed Niziol, who not only rescued me in my darkest hour, but introduced me to the power of self-belief and persistence.

Peter Lynch, who believed in this project and required that it be complete.

Jill Amack, whose professional editorial work discovered its errors, offered sensible advice, and supported my effort.

Betsy Lancefield Lane—my light at the end of the rejections.

Introduction

The confluence of two seemingly unconnected and important aspects of collegiate culture combine to create an interesting phenomenon: the distribution of financial aid for athletic ability by a huge majority of America's colleges. Soon after athletic competitions between schools began, it became clear that the student bodies of the schools took the contests quite seriously and they preferred winning as opposed to losing, no matter how much sportsmanship the athletes on the fields of competition exhibited. And they didn't want to win occasionally; they wanted victories on a consistent basis. The winning formula became obvious: when your team has better players, your team dramatically increases its chances to win these important contests. The obvious question followed, "How can the best players on the field be wearing our school's colors?" Athletic Scholarships (having little to do with scholarship) were created and the rest is Recruiting History.

Is your dream to exploit this situation so you can continue your athletic career and simultaneously have your athletic ability be rewarded with a reduced financial burden while competing and earning your college education? Is that why you are here? If so, you've come to the right place.

This book is designed to help your son or daughter become a successfully recruited high school student athlete. It is constructed to provide you with the tools, devices, and strategies to give you the best opportunity to continue an athletic career in college and to receive financial aid based upon your athletic ability. For the purposes of this book, the term *financial aid* will include scholarships, grants, low-interest loans, or any combination of the above. In short, *The Sports Scholarships Insider's Guide* is intended to give you an advantage over the equally qualified student athlete who dreams your dream.

I am uniquely qualified to lead you through the tangled web of recruiting confusion, duplicity, and unfairness. For twelve years I coached at a NCAA member university. One of the primary responsibilities in my position was recruiting high school student athletes.

I coached at three high schools in two Midwestern states over a fourteen-year period. Much of this time was spent working with college recruiters, as well as the parents and prospects of those who were being recruited. I have two grown children who were both successfully recruited: one by a Division I state university and the other by a private Division III college. One was an All-American and the other's career was cut short by injury.

I empathize with the positions that all the parties involved find themselves in. I know intimately what each one is going through during all phases of the recruiting process, especially the crucial and fragile negotiating prior to an offer of athletic or other financial aid and a roster position. I owned a college prospect recruiting service. My clients were academically and athletically qualified student athletes wanting expert help in becoming professionally exposed to college coaches. I contacted and often negotiated with coaches and recruiters on behalf of my clients. My recruiting service had a 94 percent success rate for my clients, who were offered roster positions and significant financial aid packages.

You are about to use the inside knowledge I have accumulated, sometimes painfully, over many years of experience as the parent of recruited student athletes, a high-school coach, a recruiting service owner, and as a college coach/recruiter. Effectively using the information in this book requires that you have discipline, courage, and persistence (fundamental traits of successful athletes). If you closely follow the suggestions and techniques and are in fact qualified to compete in college (either a four- or a two-year school), both in the classroom and in your sport, you can look forward to being successfully recruited and receiving significant financial aid for athletic ability.

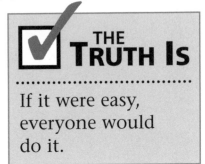

THE TRUTH Is

If it were easy, everyone would do it.

Throughout, you will find statements, which give you the facts: the truth. As is so often the case, the truth has a hard edge. Usually the truisms located in this book are hard-edged. Often you will not want to hear them. Why? Because they will force you to clearly recognize that a journey toward your athletic and academic dreams will not be convenient or easy.

Many college coaches/recruiters aren't going to like that you will know their recruiting secrets. Their vested interest in recruiting as many good athletes as they can for the least amount of money is jeopardized. Because they know the secrets, they can keep you confused. Your confusion benefits them. You are about to slash through the confusion so you can get what you want and deserve. So a word of caution: when communicating with coaches or the NCAA, be very discreet.

Recruiting Myths

1. Division III schools don't offer financial aid for athletic ability.

   This myth is shattered on page 121.

2. If a prospect is good, the coaches will find him or her.

   This myth is shattered on page 11.

3. If a coach wants a prospect, a coach can get him/her enrolled even if he/she has poor grades.

   This myth is shattered on page 35.

4. A prospect can trust everything the coach says and promises.

   This myth is shattered on page 11.

5. A prospect can wait until his/her senior year to find financial aid based on athletic ability.

   This myth is shattered on page 149.

6. Most athletic scholarships are "full-rides."

   This myth is shattered on page 12.

Chapter 1

Understanding the Recruiting Process

This chapter shatters Myth #2 and Myth #4 (see page 5 for a list of myths). The recruiting process is fundamentally unfair. It is unfair for many reasons; but the primary ones are money and winning. This unfairness impacts college coaches, prospects and their families, and high-school coaches. College coaches have to win to keep their jobs. No matter how this fact is shaded, colored, coated, nuanced, veiled, or denied—it is fundamental.

It is the wellspring of the unfairness in the recruiting process. College coaches coach for a reason; they do it because they love it. There may be a few exceptions, but not many. Very, very, very few coaches make the big money of the highly visible basketball and football coaches you hear about.

No matter what sport they coach, when their team competes against another team, the score of the contest is kept. The winner and loser are easily identified. If the coach's team loses too often, the coach will be dismissed (fired). If a coach is fired, it usually means he/she will no longer have the opportunity to enjoy the experience of coaching. He/she will no longer get paid (usually for much less than what they are worth) for doing what he/she loves to do. The pressure on coaches to win is as intense today as it has ever been in college athletics. (Note the scandals that continuously rock colleges from all three divisions. To see the extent of prohibited activity, log on to the NCAA website and access the violations link. *U.S. News & World Report* has done admirable reporting on NCAA violations as well as college financial aid issues.) That pressure may be disguised better than in the past as the NCAA trumpets its laudable attempts to raise the academic standards for college prospects. Recently, the *NCAA News* has been running small strips declaring that winning isn't everything. Look at the facts. You decide.

To its credit, the NCAA is demanding academic integrity from the nation's colleges, along with raised academic entrance standards in an effort to coerce them to pay greater attention to their student athletes' education. The NCAA has successfully reduced the influence of supporters of athletic programs from participating in the recruiting process (although the recent Ohio State football scandal makes one wonder). The penalties can be very severe. Just ask the University of Michigan's Basketball Program or the University of Wisconsin's Football Program. Yet most administrators would agree that they are under some pressure from the supporters of athletic interests (usually alumni and local businesses that benefit from game attendance) to develop and maintain winning programs. While many administrators try to resist overt pressure from boosters, it's difficult to resist the influence of donations (money) to institutional programs by boosters. When programs don't meet the expectation of boosters, something gives—usually the coach's job or a reduction in the amount of donations. It doesn't take a rocket scientist to figure out which one gives first. In the article "College Sports" from the March 2002 issue of *U.S. News & World Report,* the authors, Gordon Witken and Jodi Schneider, state that the system's toughest problems arise from commercialization. In the same article, Maureen Devlin of the Knight Commission says, "The analogy is that money is an arms race that nobody will win and that we need multilateral disarmament." In other words, every institution has to give up the money and play by the same rules or violations will continue. How likely is that to happen? You decide.

At the opening business session on January 8 of the 2005 NCAA Convention in Dallas, Myles Brand delivered a wide-ranging speech in which he forthrightly discussed the status of money and winning on institutions' and coaches' motivations for recruiting. He revealed his disappointment after he repeated a quote from a coach, "I was hired to win; I wasn't hired to graduate student athletes." He went on to say, "...in fact the security of his future employment is based on winning..."

THE TRUTH Is

A significant minority of college coaches violate the NCAA recruiting rules and regulations in order to stay competitive—and in order to keep their jobs.

Why is winning so important? Because, as Brand went on to explain, the money that is used to fund investments for new building on campus is "paid by projected future athletics-generated revenues." This means that the more they win, the more money should pour in, which "has resulted in an inflated need to increase wins." And all this comes back on the coaches' recruiting motivations.

When coaches get fired, it is painful. It hurts. To avoid losing their jobs, they try to find ways to ensure that they win.

Coaches who win usually don't get fired. One of the best ways to ensure a winning program is to have athletes on their team that are better than the athletes on opposing teams. Because most coaches don't want to be fired, they try to find ways to enroll superior athletes.

How do coaches get better athletes? They recruit them. They know that other coaches are recruiting for the best athletes, too. They also know that competing coaches are recruiting for their financial and professional lives. They know that the competition is vicious. If they are to be successful in the recruiting battle, they must be prepared to do everything possible to recruit the best athletes.

Green Influence

The December 20, 2004, *NCAA News* quotes Doug Williams, former NFL quarterback with the Washington Redskins and current college coach, "We may say it's about black and white, but in the end it's green. The big-time boosters and alumni are out there and the [college] presidents and athletic directors are afraid to make a decision that might irk some of their big-time boosters."

We hear of violations primarily in the highly visible, Division I, revenue-producing sports, but coaches in other sports and other divisions violate and/or stretch the limits of the NCAA rules, regulations, and bylaws, as well. Remember the value (and therefore the importance) of booster donations to college athletic programs and the influence on college administrators that those donations create. Booster donors can be found influencing institutions at every division level. Some may say the foregoing is an exaggeration. The truth is, it's not. Because recruiting is so intense, vicious, and unfair, many people get hurt along the way. It is unlikely that any coach intentionally hurts a prospect, yet because of the mechanics of the recruiting process and the high stakes involved, prospects and their families get hurt.

As an example, if a coach follows the recommendation of the *Ultimate Recruiting Seminar*, three of four prospects for every recruited position are being strung along. I confess that during the recruiting year 1998–1999, I strung along four athletes while my number one, must-have choice considered which of the many offers she would accept. She accepted our program's offer late into the recruiting season. I then had to call the others to tell them the bad news. You can imagine the response to my apology and my offer that the prospect could walk on and that I'd try to get them athletic aid the next year. My ears continue to ring.

What Does This Mean to You?

Despite our best efforts, it is likely that you will experience some pain. It goes with the territory. However, this book provides you with the understanding and the tools required to be successfully recruited by a college with a program and a coach that is best for you.

First, by following *The Sports Scholarship Insider's Guide,* you will be found. Why? Because every college coach your profile is sent to will know who you are, where you are, what you can do, and what they can expect from you when you begin competing in college. Many qualified prospects are overlooked because coaches can't be everywhere or see everything. You will not be overlooked.

Second, very few colleges have the budgets or the scouts to be able to locate all the prospects who would be qualified to compete in their program. It's that simple. No college coach can possibly know where every potential prospect for his or her program is.

The number of qualified prospects a coach learns about depends on the size of the college, the program, interested alumni, number of assistants, and the recruiting budget. Coaches of small- and medium-sized colleges and programs want to locate qualified prospects just as desperately as coaches in larger institutions. Unfortunately, smaller schools don't have adequate budgets or personnel to compete. They need help. You need help. By sending your credentials, you provide them with the help they need and, ultimately, you help yourself.

Other than the largest Division I revenue-producing programs, very few programs have a sufficient level of funding to make full-ride athletic financial aid offers to the prospects they are recruiting. This is especially true for Division II and III colleges (the bogus assertions concerning no financial aid based on athletic ability at Division III colleges require a separate section, which follows).

Consequently, these restrictions cause the coach to be very careful about which prospects are offered athletic scholarships or financial aid awards. The less money spent to recruit one prospect (which could be you) means there are more funds available to recruit other prospects. The cheaper a coach can recruit higher-quality prospects, the more funds are available to recruit additional good prospects. This means coaches increase their chances to have better athletes than their competition and ultimately, they can produce a winning program and keep their jobs.

Essential Companion Guide

To be able to follow the suggestions in this guide, you must obtain an essential companion guide, the *NCAA Guide for the College-Bound Student-Athlete.* You can get a free copy from your guidance counselor or athletic director. If a copy is not obtainable, call the NCAA and request a copy. The NCAA number is (800) 638-3731. The Internet address is www.ncaa.org.

Get prepared. Get moving. Get recruited.

Chapter 2

Recruiting and Financial Aid

While it is not my intention to provide you with a course on comparative recruiting philosophies of different colleges, some discussion of why colleges recruit is necessary. You need some information about the basics of recruiting philosophy in order to understand why and how the suggestions made in this guide can help you achieve your athletic and academic goals.

Colleges offer athletic financial aid and other types of financial aid for many reasons, some more obvious than others. Many big-time Division I programs offer "full-ride" athletic scholarships for the most obvious reason: money. These programs sign and enroll "blue-chip" student athletes so that they can have powerful, winning programs.

Generally, powerful, winning programs in Division I football and basketball generate substantial revenue for their institutions. Very few other programs generate enough revenue to even be self-sustaining and are subsidized by the institution itself. However, most other colleges want to have winning programs, too, but they have additional reasons for recruiting student athletes and offering financial aid based on athletic ability.

Even though coaches may be from programs that are not as powerful, they too must recruit as hard and as smart as they can. But often these coaches are forced to recruit with three additional burdens placed on them:

- The institution's financial aid award packaging formula,
- The recruiting objectives of the coach, and
- The combined recruiting and enrollment philosophy of the institution for which they coach.

Colleges Operate Like Businesses

Most institutions use the awarding of financial aid as a tool to encourage potential students to enroll at their college. Financial aid is a powerful marketing tool used to remain or become competitive in the bidding war among colleges for worthy students. Fundamentally, here's how it works: each institution creates a budget (which, by the way, very few colleges publish) that is required to deliver the level of educational services desired by the institution's administrators. The institution's administration calculates how much money is required to deliver the desired educational services while keeping the college solvent. Generally, college administrators fashion tuition policies to accomplish those two interwoven objectives.

The money required to keep the college operating on a sound financial basis comes from a number of different sources. In addition to other sources of funding, the most important source of funds related to the mission of this guide: tuition, fees, room, board and other expenses charged to students enrolled in any college.

Most institutions calculate non-student funding resources (i.e., endowment, state funds, if applicable, billable use of facilities, donations, etc.) available to the institution in the fiscal year. The amount of non-student funding is subtracted from the budget. The remainder of the budget must be generated from the tuition, fees, and other related charges from the college's student body.

Generally, figures are calculated that define the number of students required to enroll and what enrollment will cost the students. The calculation of the number of students multiplied by the cost per student is structured to allow the institution to remain financially stable. For a number of reasons, some understandable, others not so understandable, many colleges announce inflated costs for attending the college for that year. The final, inflated cost published by the institution is called the "sticker price," which is somewhat analogous to a new car sticker price. In other words: sticker price = pretend price.

The largest groups of colleges that discount the sticker price are private colleges with substantial sticker prices. Less expensive private colleges provide less financial aid/discounted tuition. Often state colleges and universities have their tuition levels written into law. This type of restriction fundamentally disallows the college from using the flexibility accorded to the director of financial aid to use professional judgment, which means that in the judgment of the financial aid director a financial aid package can be adjusted based upon factors regarded as important by the director. And that judgment is not necessarily bound by the parameters of the institutions recruiting or financial aid regulations, in order to discount the "sticker price." However, state taxes help keep state college's tuition lower than most private schools and therefore constitute invisible tuition discounts.

According to a College Board survey done during the 2003–2004 school year, almost 70 percent of students attending four-year colleges paid less than $8,000 for tuition and fees for the school year. So don't allow yourself to be intimidated by the "sticker prices."

A March 1997 *U.S. News & World Report* article, "America's Best Colleges," which recommended methods for cutting the costs of college education stated, "And 'pretend' is the operative word. There just aren't enough people with enough money. Nowadays, after acceptance letters go out, a season of souk-like haggling and price-cutting begins. The actual cost of a private college education is at least 30 percent less than the 'sticker price.'" That is to say: $19,700 × 70 percent = $13,790.

Apparently, the institution's administrators hope to attract as many students who will pay the full tuition (known as "full-freight" students) and other costs as possible. Those students will then not only be paying for the cost of their education, they also provide funds to help cushion the cost of enrolling students who the administrators decide shouldn't have to pay or can't afford to pay the full tuition and fees. The more "full-freight" students a college can enroll, the more flexibility the institution has, thus enabling it to provide financial aid relief to those "can't pay" and/or "shouldn't have to pay."

THE TRUTH Is

When colleges talk about money, need can mean many things.

How to Get Financial Aid

It would take three chapters to explain the convoluted and tortured reasons why some students, especially the "shouldn't-have-to-pay" category of students, are provided relief from paying full tuition and fees. Generally though, discounts are provided because of: merit (pretend and real), academic potential or achievement, athletic ability, special circumstances (to

But someone is paying the interest. That someone is the federal government. They are willing to risk paying interest on $3,300 (the freshman year maximum) for the next four years to give you an opportunity to attend college and play your chosen sport. They also risk nonpayment by the student athlete because they guarantee the loan. When you begin repayment, the government continues to subsidize the interest rate on your loan, keeping it well below market rates. Most students who accept loans subsidized by the Department of Education are also required to participate in the federal work-study program. Students usually work at on-campus jobs, are usually paid minimum wage, and normally work 10 to 15 hours per week.

Many states offer education loans at below-market rates. Check with your state's treasurer's office to see if a state loan is available.

It doesn't require a brain surgeon to recognize that a grant (money given to you that you don't have to repay) is a better deal than a loan. But it is quite probable that a loan will be part of a financial aid package. Loans are pretty good deals.

Credits and Deductions

A helpful reduction of the financial burden of a college education is the Hope Tax Credit. It can be used during a student's freshman and sophomore year to a maximum of $1,500. One dollar in tax credit means a one-dollar savings in federal tax. Another available credit is the Lifelong Learning Credit. It is calculated on the first $10,000 and awards 20 percent of that total to a maximum of $2,000. It is means-tested with a maximum income for families of $83,000 for full credit and $103,000 the disqualifying income level. Certain politicians have decided that those who earn these levels of income are wealthy. The politicians decided those earners should be penalized for their earning power and are disqualified. Income limits on singles is $41,000 and $51,000; again such income levels designate wealthy taxpayers who are evidently worthy of the disqualification penalty. So there. That will teach you to own an alarm clock.

(continued)

> You can claim up to $3,000 of tuition as a tax deduction. But you can't claim both a credit and a deduction. Remember that a deduction only reduces income that is eventually taxed. The average taxpayer can anticipate a savings of about $800.

That's why last year students borrowed over $28 billion in subsidized loans, about 60 percent of all student financial aid.

Loan Update

Since 2001 you can deduct $2,500 of college educational costs from federal income taxes. And still more good news: if you choose to work for a charitable organization or some type of governmental body, you could have your loan forgiven with no tax consequences. Who said that Congress isn't interested in helping Americans with the spiraling costs of higher education?

Many student athletes, competing in all three NCAA divisions, are receiving some federal and/or state financial aid. In addition, many students are awarded institutional financial aid, in addition to federal and state aid that is loaded into a student athlete's total financial aid package.

Another Financial Aid Consideration

You may win a scholarship from an entity outside the college's regular financial aid sources. If you do, most colleges ask that you report or even send the award to the school's financial aid office. Typically, the financial aid office will reduce your financial aid package by the amount of the award. This saves the school money, but won't improve your overall financial aid package. Ask the organization to give the award directly to you so the school won't reduce your financial aid package by the outside entity's award amount.

Pell Grants

After you have completed the FAFSA form and sent it in to the Department of Education, its computers will decide if you are in need of federal financial aid grant. If so, it awards the grant based on a sliding scale. The maximum award is $4,050 and is renewable each year that you are in good academic standing. The award is made directly to the institution and credited to your total financial aid package.

Awarding Financial Aid

There exist a number of methods and means for institutions to award financial aid for athletic ability. Institutions attempt to fashion financial aid packages in such a manner that the recruited student is satisfied with the package and that the institution's objectives are met while recruiting and providing financial aid to that student.

The awarding of financial aid to students with proven athletic ability is generally awarded in four ways:

1. "Full-ride" athletic scholarships—Division I and II
2. Partial athletic scholarships—Division I and II and NAIA
3. Combination financial aid awards, including partial athletic scholarship—Division I and II and NAIA
4. Combination financial aid, not to include scholarships related to athletic ability—Division III and NAIA

Please note that NCAA rule #15 requires that Division III colleges are obliged to tell you that they do not offer athletic scholarships. (Chapters 17, 18, and 19 reveal the truth about this bogus assertion.)

Chapter 3

Preparing for College and the Future

The future is where you will spend the rest of your life. Do you wish to be in control of your future so that you get from it what you want and deserve? Is your answer yes? If it is, you must grasp this fact: it is highly unlikely that you will get what you want from the future unless you know what it is that you want. Before reading another word, close the book and take at least five minutes to consider what kind of future you want for yourself.

The more specific you are as to what you want to own, what experiences you would like to enjoy, what accomplishments you wish to achieve, what career and/or occupational goals you have, the more valuable this imaging activity is. As you discover each element, item, or aspect of your desired future, write it down. Do that now.

_____

_____

_____

_____

_____

_____

_____

_____

_____

_____

_____

_____

_____

_____

_____

_____

_____

_____

_____

_____

_____

_____

_____

_____

_____

_____

_____

Welcome back. If you have completed discovering your future—great. If you chose not to consider your future, you have made a colossal error. If you were traveling to a destination to which you had never been, you certainly must know you'd be a fool to try to get there without a map or directions, right? The most important place you are going is into your future.

Is it smart to journey somewhere without a clue about how to get there or how you'll know when you've actually arrived at your destination? You know the answer.

If you haven't done the imaging activity, demonstrate some discipline, go back, and do it now.

You have one more activity to accomplish before we move on to the issue that caused you to purchase this book. You have identified the fundamental elements of a future you wish for yourself. For each element, you must identify in writing what you know you must achieve, acquire, and do and are prepared to do, acquire, and achieve to secure the future you have described.

THE TRUTH Is

If you don't know where you're going, you'll probably end up somewhere else.

Review the elements of your desired future. Now focus on the goal of becoming successfully recruited. You are about to begin the process of turning this most important goal from a fantasy—a dream—into reality.

Complete the following steps:

1. **State your exact goal.** (State your goal clearly and precisely. Do this in order to visualize your exact goal.)

2. **State the date.** (Indicate the future date by which the goal will be accomplished. Use the month and year. Specifically

targeting the exact date for the accomplishment of your goal helps you avoid procrastination.)

_____

_____

_____

_____

_____

_____

THE TRUTH Is

There is no worthwhile goal that can be achieved without effort, discipline, and sacrifice.

3. **Determine what you will sacrifice.** (What will you personally sacrifice to achieve your goal?

Be sure you understand what it is that must be sacrificed and what you will sacrifice. If what you intend to sacrifice is less than what you know is required to achieve your goal, it is highly unlikely you will achieve it.)

_____

_____

_____

_____

4. **State your plan of action.** (The great Olympic sprinter, Michael Johnson, tells of his father always asking him, "How do you plan to do that?" whenever he told his dad that he wanted to get something or achieve something important. He credits the discipline of planning as essential to his determination to sacrifice as he prepared for achieving Olympic immortality.)

_____
_____
_____
_____
_____

Is your plan worth the discipline and sacrifice it takes to commit it to paper? By writing down the plan, you have created something tangible upon which your thoughts and ideas are recorded. You can then refer to the plan on a regular basis.

The more you want, the more you must be willing to sacrifice.

Writing your action plan organizes your goal-oriented direction and activities, makes them more understandable, more real, and therefore more doable. Referring to the plan as you move toward your goal provides you the information you need to make any mid-course corrections that may be required.

You must constantly reinforce your visual image; if not, your desire, your belief, or your plan will wither and die. You will experience almost immediate results if you read your plan daily.

This goal-planning strategy works not only for achieving successful recruitment; it works for achieving any important goal you might have.

Sample Goal

1. I want to be on a college swim team at a school where I can receive a great education, compete, and receive a large financial aid award.
2. I will be successfully recruited by April 2007.

THE TRUTH Is

If something is easy, everyone will be doing it.

Easy Button

- It's easy to be lazy.
- It's easy to let others take care of you.
- It's easy to whine about how tough life is.
- It's easy to not try something challenging, and therefore avoid disappointment.
- It's easy to blame your disappointment on others.
- It's easy to blame others for your lack of accomplishment.
- It's easy to blame circumstances for a lack of achievement.

It's important to remember, as you proceed toward the future, the only place that cheese is free is in a mousetrap.

3. I will make successful recruitment my priority. If I must miss time with friends or must choose between other things or activities and pursuing my goal, I will pursue my goal. I will devote 100 percent of the time and effort necessary to achieve my goal.

4. I will:

- Create an irresistible profile.
- Send profiles and cover letters to 50 college swimming coaches in Division II and III.
- Organize a communications log and file folder holder.
- Respond immediately to every request for information from any coach until I know I don't want to attend that college.
- Visit at least three colleges.
- Gain acceptance into at least two colleges.
- Negotiate with the coach for the best financial aid package at the school of my choice.
- Use the *The Sports Scholarships Insider's Guide* suggestions and processes.

I know it won't be easy, but I can and I will discipline myself and make sacrifices to accomplish my goal.

Chapter 4

Your Education and Athletics

Hopefully, acquiring a good education is one of the goals you listed in the previous activity. While the goal of this book is to help you be successfully recruited by a college coach and receive financial aid for your athletic ability, its mission is to help you obtain the best possible education you can.

That means the academic portion of your high school work is more important to your preparation for future success and fulfillment than your athletic activities.

THE TRUTH Is

You will do much more important things in your life than compete in athletic contests.

You may be one of the many young athletes who dream of a career in professional sports. You may have been told by others that nature has wired you up well enough that if you work hard you could in fact become a professional athlete.

While many young American athletes dream of careers in professional tennis, golf, softball, soccer, and track and field, most student-athlete dreamers wish to be professional baseball, football, or basketball players. The truth is:

• On average, fewer that 225 rookies earn a position on a professional football team in any one year.

- Over 280,000 seniors will play high-school football in that same year. 225 ÷ 280,000 = .00080
- A professional football player can expect an average pro career of about 3.5 years.
- Professional football players sometimes end their careers financially broke, live on average less than 60 years, and have many more personal problems than the general public.

Basketball has equally disturbing statistics:
- Over 150,000 high-school seniors play boy's basketball each year.
- Approximately 1 in 30 high-school seniors playing basketball will play in the NCAA. 1 ÷ 30 = .0333
- About 50 rookies make pro teams each year. 50 ÷ 150,000 = .00033

While basketball players appear to live longer, their personal problems seem to be even greater than football players.

And baseball:
- Approximately 1 in 20 high-school baseball players will play in the NCAA.
- Approximately 1 in 200 high-school baseball players will be drafted by (notice that no one said "play on") a major league team.
- Baseball players seem to enjoy lives more similar to normal Americans.

I'm not advocating that young athletes not aspire to be professional athletes, it's a worthy goal. But the following chart of sobering statistics concerning opportunities to compete in athletics after high school is worth very serious study.

Do the Math

Student-athlete participation	Football	Baseball	Men's basketball	Women's basketball
High school	980,000	450,000	550,000	457,000
High-school seniors	280,000	130,000	157,000	130,000
Total NCAA	56,000	26,000	16,000	14,000
NCAA freshmen	16,000	7,000	4,500	4,000

Certainly, your athletic preparation and performance are very important. You will not be recruited unless the recruiter/coach feels that you can contribute to the success of his/her program. So, for the rest of your high-school career, you must seriously and with the greatest amount of discipline prepare yourself for college competition: both in the classroom and in your sport. Your academic credentials will be just as important to your successful recruitment as your athletic credentials.

So this can't be stated forcefully enough: *the authentic value of a college athletic scholarship is the opportunity it provides its recipient to prepare for a future of success and fulfillment by acquiring a college education.*

Reality Check

The hope, even the expectation, that a high-school athlete has of becoming a professional athlete must be tempered by the foregoing statistics. Too many prospects regard athletics as the only path to achievement, wealth, and fame. This is particularly true of minority prospects, as Harry Edwards, author and a famous counselor to minority student athletes, notes as he writes about this issue in the *Lexington Herald Leader*, "Big-name athletes who tell black kids to 'practice and work hard and one day you can be just like me' are playing games with the future of black society... [African Americans] have a principal responsibility to understand that sports must be pursued intelligently and the [African American's] involvement in sports is no game."

Chapter 5

Academic Requirements

This chapter shatters Myth #3. The academic requirements to be eligible as a freshman continue to become tougher. To be eligible at a Division I or II institution you must complete, with a 2.0 average in a core (required) curriculum of at least 14 academic units, or full-year courses, which must include the following units:

- 4 English;
- 2 social sciences;
- 2 math, including Algebra I or higher;
- 2 science (at least one lab course, if a lab course is offered at your high school);
- 3 or more in any of the above or in foreign language, computer science, philosophy, or nondoctrinal religion; and
- 1 more from among English, math, and natural or physical science.

To be eligible for Division I competition, you must accomplish the following:

- Graduate from high school;
- Successfully complete 14 core courses listed above; and
- Have a core course GPA combined with an SAT score or an ACT sum score based on the 14 core GPA/Test score index.

The NCAA has developed a sliding scale in order to

accommodate variations in GPA in combination with either the SAT or ACT scores you might achieve. The sliding scale can be located in your *NCAA Guide for the College-Bound Student-Athlete*. In 2008, the number of core courses will increase to 16. To be current with any academic eligibility rule, log on to www.ncaa.com/NCAA/student/index/student.html and check out the list.

Division II schools have no sliding scale. To be eligible at D-II institutions:

- You must earn a 2.0 GPA on a 4.0 scale in 14 courses in the core curriculum; and
- You must earn a combined score of 820 on the SAT or a composite score of 68 on the ACT.

Division III has no eligibility requirements.

Because of NCAA regulations, Division III schools must claim they don't award financial aid based on athletic ability, and therefore aren't bound by the constraints of Bylaw 14.3.

THE TRUTH Is

Your future success will be determined more by what you achieve in the classroom than in any sport.

The institution, conference, and other NCAA regulations govern eligibility for financial aid and roster positions.

Check all eligibility information against your *NCAA Guide for College-Bound Student-Athletes*. It is absolutely essential to discuss your transcript and core courses with your high-school counselor to be certain that you meet all the NCAA Bylaw 14.3 requirements. The NCAA Clearinghouse is demonstrating a very tough attitude about student athletes meeting the core-curriculum requirements.

NCAA General Recruiting Rules

Contacts

You become a prospect when you enter ninth grade. You become a recruited athlete if a college coach contacts you or a member of your family about either: attending the school or participating in an athletic program. Coaches are not allowed to contact* you until September 1 of your junior year, then by letter only. Other than football and basketball, you may not be contacted by telephone until after July 1 prior to your senior year of competition. Consult your *NCAA Guide for the College-Bound Student-Athlete* for telephone football and basketball contact rules. You or your parents may contact a coach at any time. After the aforementioned July 1 date, if available, you may contact a coach via a provided toll-free number. No student or athlete from the school may make a recruiting call to you, but you can call them after the July 1 date.

* * *

*Be sure to consult with your *NCAA Guide for the College-Bound Student-Athlete* for the precise definition of the contact rules. You can examine the *Guide* by going online at www.ncaa.org/eligibility/cbsa/index1.html.

Evaluations

An evaluation is "any off-campus activity used to assess your academic qualifications or your athletic ability, including a visit to your high school (during which no contact occurs) or watching you practice or compete at any site." Sound confusing? It can be. That's why it's important to own a *NCAA Guide for the College-Bound Student-Athlete* so that you can refer to it on an as-needed basis.

Contacts and evaluations are both considered by the NCAA as "recruiting opportunities." All sports other that football and basketball must limit recruiting opportunities to seven. Basketball has a limit of five and football three. And with many sports contacts and evaluations are limited to certain calendar dates. Other times are designated as "dead time." Again the need to consult your *NCAA Guide for the College-Bound Student-Athlete* becomes essential to be successfully recruited.

There are many other Byzantine restrictions and regulations explained in the *Guide*. Each school can require even more robust standards than the NCAA, if they choose.

NAIA Eligibility Rules

The number of scholarships available for any sport at an NAIA college is unlimited. The school alone decides how many to award and the amounts per award. Rarely does a NAIA institution award a full grant-in-aid, also known as a "full ride."

To be eligible you must qualify in two of three standards:
• Graduate in the top half of your graduating class;
• Score a minimum of 18 on the ACT or 860 on the SAT; or
• Achieve a high-school GPA of 2.0 on a 4.0 scale.

Once accepted and competing you must:
• Be in good academic standing according to school standards;
• Make normal progress toward graduation according to school standards;
• Be enrolled in 12 credits during your season of competition;
• Accumulate a minimum of 24 credits the two previous terms (repeated courses don't apply to that 24);

- As a junior, you must have achieved a GPA of 2.0 on a 4.0 scale; and
- In your second competitive season, you must have accumulated a minimum of 24 semester hours of credit (that number is factorial for years three and four).

There is no eligibility clearinghouse in the NAIA. Also, you may transfer among NAIA colleges with no "sit out" penalty. You may have a campus tryout for a team and not be penalized.

Why Are You Here?

By purchasing this book, you have shown the desire and have the dream of continuing your athletic career in college; you want to compete in your chosen sport. The foregoing information should make it very clear that if you don't take your academic preparation as seriously as your athletic preparation, you are most certainly jeopardizing your dream.

As was discussed previously, if your dream is to tolerate college athletics as a short, unwanted stopover before becoming a professional athlete, you are making a colossal error. Research indicates that high-school athletes who harbor this dream-poisoning attitude very often don't even graduate from high school, much less become either college athletes or (what a joke) professional athletes.

THE TRUTH Is

You will have a large, even unfair advantage over the many, many other qualified prospects who have the same dream as you.

By using the exposure strategies and techniques in this book, you will generate massive, national exposure or regional exposure—whichever you want.

The advantage will mean nothing if you don't demonstrate to the college coaches that you are constantly developing and improving, both academically and athletically. If you delude yourself into thinking that the exposure you receive will be all that is required for you to being successfully recruited, you are in for a huge disappointment.

THE TRUTH IS

The future is never inherited; it is created. Create your future now. Your future is where you will spend the rest of your life.

While exposure is the only strategy that accomplishes successful recruitment, coaches won't recruit student athletes who may have a difficult time staying eligible or who fail to demonstrate continuing improvement in their sport. The best way to avoid problems is to be the finest student and dedicated athlete you know how to be. *You must: study, hustle, think, practice, believe in and discipline yourself, and compete as hard as possible.*

Another valuable exposure technique is enrolling in top-level summer camps in your sport. Be sure college coaches are either running the camp or are teaching at the camp. Camps provide instant exposure. By making these commitments, you can reach the dream of playing your sport at the collegiate level and receive financial aid from the college for which you compete.

Unfortunately, there are many prospects that want the recruiting process to be easy. They are uncomfortable with, some even hostile to, the expectation that they must perform in the classroom, sacrifice during practices, and execute on the field of competition. They don't want to make disciplined choices for themselves that may interfere with having fun and hanging out with friends. They refuse to let their sport or their education interfere with their social life. If this describes you, you must reorder your priorities.

Doesn't it make sense to be well prepared for the rest of your life? If it was easy, everyone would be recruited. It's not. And few are. So be prepared to be tough on yourself. Almost everyone has a will to win. Everyone has heart during the last ten meters of the race. Too many athletes call upon their will to win only

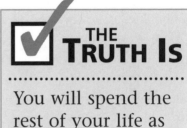

THE TRUTH Is

You will spend the rest of your life as an adult.

at the instant of competition. Winners have the will to prepare to compete.

If anyone tells you the recruiting process will be easy, they are mistaken. As you will discover, it is fundamentally unfair. You'll also learn that every effort you make will generate substantial benefits.

You now have an opportunity to do what very few young people do: take control of your future. If you hold tightly to your goals and use the suggestions to follow, you can obtain what you want.

Chapter 6

Constructing the Profile

To be successfully recruited you must create maximum exposure for yourself and your ability. You must make yourself known to the greatest number of coaches that might be interested in recruiting you as possible. You need a device that creates specific, usable information for a coach to evaluate and you need that device in the hands of at least fifty coaches. The most useful exposure tool is the personal profile.

A profile is simply a structured compiling of data about you and your athletic and academic record of accomplishments. It is organized in an arrangement that allows an interested coach the opportunity to quickly evaluate your potential to contribute to the coach's athletic program. A properly created profile can generate tremendous interest in you as a student athlete. As you will learn, a thoughtful, well-designed profile will create many benefits for you. A sloppy profile filled with hot air and information that is useless to recruiters or coaches will be promptly discarded.

The guiding principle to building an effective profile is simple to understand, yet often difficult to do. Be truthful.

You and your parents have a lot at stake concerning your college education. The emotional intensity generated by the considerations of money and pride can (and too often does) cause people to inflate the accomplishments of the prospect. Student athletes, parents, and high-school coaches must overcome the understandable urge to oversell the potential, achievements, statistics, and coachability of a prospect. However, some "selling" should take place in your cover letter, which will be covered in the next chapter.

THE TRUTH Is

Lying on the profile will most certainly destroy your chances to be successfully recruited.

Recruiters and coaches have experienced many snow jobs and are alert for them. Most coaches will check the accuracy of the information you have provided if they sense that you are trying to deceive them.

Your profile should contain the following information:

- Name
- Address
- Phone number (include area code)
- Email address
- High school
- Enrollment
- Conference
- High school phone number
- Date of birth
- Height/weight
- 40-meter-dash time (depending on sport)
- Bench press (depending on sport)
- Squat (depending on sport)
- Vertical jump (depending on sport)
- NCAA Clearinghouse PIN number (to be covered later)

- FAFSA/SAR report and EFC number (to be covered later)
- Academic statistics: graduation date, SAT/ACT score(s), intended major or undecided, NCAA core-course GPA, class rank, current courses, significant academic honors (honor roll; National Honor Society; school, local, regional or national awards; but avoid listing *Who's Who*)
- Athletic statistics: all customary statistics (see following list) for the most recent season related to the sport for which you wish to be recruited and other significant athletic awards and honors.
- Coach's evaluation

Personal Profile

Joe Smith
1370 Deforest Rd.
Anywhere, OH 53111
(216) 555-5467

Sport: Track
Position: 800M/CC
Birth Date: 7/25/86
Height: 6' 1"
Weight: 155 lbs.
Speed: 40 Yds. 4.6
Strength: Bench: 160 lbs. Squat: 300 lbs.
Other sports: Cross-country
Anywhere High School
Coach: Jack Simpson 216-555-1234

Academic Statistics: Graduation Year 2005
149/322 ACT: 19 GPA: 2.76
Intended Major: Education
Current courses: Geometry, English 3, US History, Zoology, Intro. to Computers

Athletic Statistics: 800M 1.57.9, 400M 49.8, 200M 23.6, 100M 10.7, 1600M 4:35.1, 3000M (CC) 16.51

Honors/Awards (Athletic): Conference Champion 2004–800M, Regional Qualifier, 2003, 04–800M, Sectional Champion 2004–800M, MVP (CC) 2003, 04, State Qualifier (CC) 2003, 2004, Placed 31sr.

Honors/Awards (Academic/Extracurricular): B Honors, Key Club

Coach's scouting evaluation: Joe's greatest strength is an ability to concentrate on relaxing when he is in pain at the end of a race. While other runners are tying up, he is able to maintain good running mechanics, often edging out competitors who are stronger than him. He has learned to run very tactical, smart races, often deceiving his opponents and then surging past them and breaking their will at critical points in the race. "Joe is an athlete who knows what he wants to do in track, does whatever it takes to prepare to accomplish his goals, and leaves nothing of himself at the end of a race. His determination to win is inspiring." He needs to continue increasing his distance base and weight lifting to get even stronger, especially in the upper body.

His coach and your recruiter project him to be a small Division I 800M & cross-country prospect.

Videotape available.

Customary Athletic Statistics and Guidelines by Sport

Your profile should include the following statistical and skill information pertaining to your sport.

Basketball:

- assists
- field-goal percentage—2-point/3-point
- free-throw percentage
- rebounds
- steals
- minutes-per-game average

Division I Women's Guidelines:

Position	Height	Skills
Center	6'2"+	aggressive/powerful rebounder, 8'6" jump/touch, quick first step, set solid pick, accurate shooting with shots beginning with back to basket and face up, maintain post position under pressure, fearless, 60 percent free throws
Power Forward	6'0"+	good rebounder, accurate shooter (both perimeter and inside), aggressive defender, creative/accurate passer, 70 percent free throws
Small Forward	5'10"+	high shooting percentage (both perimeter and inside), aggressive defender, creative/accurate passer, good penetration ability, 70 percent free throws
Point Guard	5'4"+	exceptional ball handler/passer, leader, good speed, great court sense, creative/accurate passer, good penetration ability, 70 percent free throws
Shooting Guard	5'6"+	excellent perimeter shot, excellent ball handler, creative/accurate passer, quick off pick, excellent catch and release shooter, 75 percent free throws

Division I Men's Guidelines

Position	Height	Skills
Center	6'9"+	aggressive/powerful rebounder, 10'6"' jump/touch, quick first step, set solid pick, accurate shooting with shots beginning with back to basket and face up, maintain post position under pressure, fearless, 60 percent free throws
Power Forward	6'7"+	good rebounder, accurate shooter (both perimeter and inside), aggressive defender, creative/active passer, 65 percent free throws
Small Forward	6'5"+	high shooting percentage (both perimeter and inside), aggressive defender, creative/active passer, good penetration ability, 70 percent free throws
Point Guard	6'0"+	exceptional ball handler/passer, leader, good speed, great court sense, creative/accurate passer, good penetration ability, 75 percent free throws
Shooting Guard	6'2"+	excellent perimeter shot, excellent ball handler, creative/accurate passer, quick off pick, excellent catch and release shooter, 75 percent free throws

Baseball
- batting average: .350+
- earned run average (ERA): pitchers–2.1+
- extra base hits
- fielding average
- throwing speed (pitchers): 87–92+/D–I, 84–87+/D–II
- pitches–fastball, curve/slider, change up
- speed–60 yard: 6.7–7.2
- runs batted in (RBI)
- stolen bases
- win/loss record (pitchers)

Cross-Country
- distance and times
- places: conference, invitational, regional, state
- 3200 meters D–I men: 8:30–9:10; women: 10:10–11:00
- 5000 meters D–I men: 15:15–16:00; women: 16:50–17:30

Diving
- dives, degree of difficulty, best score
- places: conference, invitational, regional, state

Football
- attempts and completions
- assists and tackles
- field goals: attempts and goals, longest, average
- fumbles recovered
- interceptions

- kickoffs: attempts, longest, average
- receptions: number, total yards, average yards, touchdowns
- sacks
- tackles: solo
- yards rushing: attempts, average, total yards

Position	Acceptable	Preferred	Speed
QB	6'2"/200'	6'4"/225'	4.7/40
RB	5'11"/205'	6'0"/215'	4.4/40
FB	6'0"/215'	6'2"/230'	4.8/40
WR	6'0"/175'	6'2"/185'	4.5/40
OL	6'2"/250'	6'4"/265'	5.0/40
DL	6'1"/250'	6'5"/275'	5.1/40
LB	6'2"/215'	6'3"/245'	4.7/40
DB	5'9"/170'	6'0'/185'	4.5/40
FS/SS	5'10"/180'	6'2"/200'	4.5/40

Golf

- handicap D-I men: 0–3 women: 0–7; D-II men: 3–7 women: 5–9; D-III men 8–12 women: 8 - 13
- average 18-hole score: D-I men: 70–74 women: 71–80; D-II men: 74–82 women: 78–84; D-III men: 79–84 women: 82–90
- medalist number
- places: conference, invitational, regional, state

Gymnastics

- event scores: average and best
- places: conference, invitational, regional, state

Soccer
- assists
- blocked shots
- goals

Softball
- batting average
- ERA (pitchers)
- extra base hits
- fielding average
- throwing speed (pitchers)
- RBI
- stolen bases
- win/loss record (pitchers)

Swimming
- event: distance and best time
- places: conference, invitational, regional, state
- 100-Free men: 50.5–54.3; women: 55.6–62.3
- 100-Back men: 59.4–64.0; women: 61.6–70.8
- 100-Breast men: 1:08.8–1:16.6; women: 1:10–1:20
- 100-Fly men: 59–68.5; women: 60.4–70
- 200-IM men: 1:53.5–2:04.8; women: 2:05–2:17

Tennis
- position: singles and doubles
- handedness
- record
- places: conference, invitational, regional, state

Track and Field: Division I
- 100-meters men: 10.2–11.0; women: 12.0–13.0
- 200-meters men: 20.5–22.5; women: 23.5–24.7
- 400-meters men: 44.5–49.0; women: 52.0–57.2
- 800-meters men: 1:51–1:55; women: 1:58–2:03.5
- 100-meter hurdles men: 13.0–14.3; women: 13.5–14.9
- 300-meter hurdles men: 37.5–41.0; women: 41.5–47.0
- high jump men: 6'6"+; women: 5'8"+
- long jump men: 2'8"+; women: 18'+
- shot put men: 52'+; women: 37'+
- discus men: 150'+; women: 130'+
- pole vault men: 15'+; women: 10'5"+
- event and personal best
- places: conference, invitational, regional, state

Volleyball
- aces: number and average
- assists
- blocks
- digs
- kills

Division I
Middle/Outside
- height: 5'10"+
- jump touch 10'0"+
- strong shoulders
- good arm speed
- pass and defend
- handle ball skillfully

Setter
- height 5'8"+
- jump touch 9'0"+
- strong hands and fingers
- quick and agile
- team leader

Wrestling
- record and weight
- escapes
- near falls: 2-point and 3-point
- reversals
- pins and falls
- takedowns
- places: conference, invitational, regional, state

Speak to your high-school coach about your goals and your exposure action plan. Unfortunately, some high-school coaches do little or nothing to help their athletes with the recruiting process. While their support isn't essential for you to be successfully recruited, it can be very helpful.

If your coach is willing to make a comment for your profile, be sure it is short and hard-hitting. It should be about attitude, practice habits, coachability, etc. Keep the comments to one short paragraph. The paragraph should be the last item on your profile.

Also, you should affix a picture to the top right hand corner of the profile. A high-school graduation or similar picture is the best. One in uniform is okay, but it should be close enough for your face to be easily seen. A picture often creates a subtle, psychological familiarity between the coach and you. You are no longer just a name or a list of statistics.

Your profile must be clean and neat, grammatically correct, all words spelled correctly, and typed or computer generated. Ask someone who is qualified (an English teacher is a good choice) to check and edit the components of your profile.

Sending profiles that don't follow these rules greatly reduces your chances to be successfully recruited.

Chapter 7

The Cover Letter

You will have opportunities to meet and communicate with those who can help you realize your goal of being successfully recruited: college coaches. You must present yourself so that a coach will not only be interested in your abilities as an athlete, but your character as a mature person.

Below are important factors for a good presentation:

1. **Confidence.** Have confidence in the skills and abilities you have developed in your sport. Present those skills and abilities demonstrating your confidence that they are equal to the task of positively contributing to the team's success.

2. **Respect.** Demonstrate your respect for the coach/recruiter and the institution he/she represents. Few things destroy a prospect's chances to be offered an athletic tender or a financial aid award letter more quickly than a prospect who appears verbally or mentally undisciplined. These prospects are regarded as not coachable. The consequences are obvious.

3. **Humility.** You must be proud of your accomplishments and achievements; you have worked hard and persistently to reach the level of skill you have achieved. While many people are ignorant of the price you have paid, you and the recruiter know that the level of ability you possess is no accident. Remember, the recruiter knows, so there's no need to brag—demonstrate humble pride.

Even though your home phone number is included in the profile, you should provide it in the cover letter as well. Tell coaches when the best time is to call either you or your parents. If your high-school coach is willing to have coaches call him or her at home, mention the coach's number (including area code), as well as the best contact times.

The same editing, grammar, and spelling rules apply to your cover letter as those recommended for your profile. Keep your cover letter to one page.

If your cover letter appears to be mass-produced, it is likely that it will receive less serious attention. The following devices will ensure that the coach knows the letter is written specifically to him or her:

- Use the college name.
- Use the college address.
- Use the team name.
- Use the coach's name.
- Keep it to one page.

By using the first four suggestions, it quickly reveals that you have done research on the school and athletic program that you are making contact with. Comments about a team or athlete success gleaned from the school's website can make a valuable first impression. Use a small item like that in your cover letter.

A sample cover letter follows.

Sample Cover Letter

May 28, 2006

Mr. Clyde Wienerschnots
Head Track Coach
Vogelheimer University
6676 West Benchbottom Street
Athletica, NH 04111

Dear Coach Wienerschnots,

I would like to introduce myself to you. I am currently a junior sprinter and long jumper at Einars High School. I have spoken to a number of coaches and other qualified people concerning the Laser Track Program. They all say it's a good track program.

Last year I qualified for the state meet in each event. While I didn't make it to finals, I have already improved on the performances this season. I am determined to win state meet medals in June. My personal best in the 100 meters is 10.64 achieved at the Spring Valley Invitational. My 200 meters personal best is 22.12, achieved during a home dual meet on May 4, 2006. I jumped 22' 9" at the Porker Relays. I expect my performances to continue to improve.

I scored a 23 on the ACT, have a 2.9 GPA in the 14 NCAA core courses, a 3.1 cumulative GPA, and I rank 61 in a class of 233. I plan to take the ACT again.

I believe my performance and my continued development demonstrate that I could contribute to your program. I would like to continue my track career at Vogelheimer, as well as pursue my educational and career goals.

I have enclosed my profile and videotape of some of my recent competitions. I've also included next season's meet schedule so that you can evaluate me, if time permits. Please send me whatever materials are required for me to be further considered as a prospect for Laser Track and Field.

My home phone number is (502) 555-2573. I should be available on weekdays after 6:00 p.m. My coach, Bobo Otendoten, invites you to call him at school (502) 555-2200. I look forward to hearing from you in the near future.

Sincerely,

Horace T. Bunkerschnives

Enclosures

Chapter 8

The Videotape

Team sport coaches almost universally ask for videotape. It is a quick and effective way to evaluate your skill, ability, intelligence, and intensity. Even some individual-event coaches request videotape (e.g., track, wrestling, swimming). A well-produced videotape can generate great benefits for you. A poorly produced one, while not a kiss of death, does not help you accomplish your objective.

The best videotapes include five sections:

1. **Video profile.** An opening 30-to-40-second still shot of the top section of your profile (but don't include the picture).

2. **Personal introduction.** You, on camera, introducing yourself, giving a few personal statistics (name, age, high school, height, weight, graduation date, position/event, high school coach's name, ACT/SAT score, NCAA core-course GPA, etc.), and a short statement similar to the following. Practice the statement—out loud.

"Hi, I'm Morsly Horsefeather. I play defensive tackle and fullback for Homefield High School. I weigh 207 pounds and am 6'1" tall. I graduate in June of 2007. My ACT score is 21 and my core-course GPA is 2.6. My coach is Bobo Otendoten. I want to be considered as a prospect for Rumbler football. I hope you will agree that this tape shows that my level of play qualifies me to make a solid contribution to your program. Thanks for your time and consideration."

3. **Competition.** You competing in games, matches, or meets.

   a. **Team sport competitors.** Two of your best games, start to finish. Don't be tempted to cut or splice out poor performances. The coaches will detect it and wonder what it is that you're trying to hide. The consequences of creating suspicion should be obvious. Remember, coaches know that nobody plays a perfect game.

   b. **Event competitors.** Two to ten performances, depending on the event length (500 meter free style, 1600 meter run) and technical requirements (hurdles, diving, parallel bars).

4. **Highlights.** Ten to fifteen of your season highlight plays or performances. These plays should demonstrate athletic ability, effort, versatility, and intensity, and not just dramatic episodes (ten slam dunks or five goals scored against an inferior goalkeeper won't help you). Highlights always follow game/performance sections.

5. **Final profile.** End your tape with another 15/20-second segment of your profile.

Try to get help in editing, splicing, dubbing, and special effects for your videotape. You may even want to use a professional or experienced videographer. Sometimes, all the help you need may be found in your high-school media department. However, if you can't find help or can't afford it, still send the best video you can if a coach requests one.

Chapter 9

Sending Credentials

Where should I send my credentials? Before you can answer this question, you must ask and answer a few preliminary planning questions:

1. Am I willing to attend a college far from home or am I willing only to attend local or regional institutions? And are my parents/guardians willing to let me attend a college far from home or would they prefer me to stay close to home?

2. Do I want to attend small/large or public/private schools?

3. At what level of competition do I realistically believe I can successfully compete? (Division I, II, III, NAIA I, II, or 2-year junior college?)

4. Is my choice of a major course of study more important than where I compete?

THE TRUTH Is

If you are a senior currently competing in your sport season and you haven't been recruited by Division I schools, it is highly unlikely that you will be offered an athletic scholarship by a Division I coach.

The answers to these questions can provide a frame of reference for you as you decide which coaches to send your profile to. That's right—you send your profile to a specific coach of your sport at the college receiving your profile.

Use the list in the last section of the book to locate the information you need. If you use the foregoing suggestions, you should receive an excellent response; that is, unless you send profiles to only Division I programs. Then you can anticipate only limited responses.

You may however, be offered an invited "walk-on" status, perhaps with an inducement that if you do well your freshman year that you might get a scholarship the following year.

In most cases the reality is that "walk-on" status in Division I usually means you will get to *practice* your sport for four years. You will rarely, if ever, compete in an intercollegiate contest.

But if you're satisfied with being a practice opponent (often known as a "scout," "gray," or "hamburger squad") for the team's regular players, then go for it. That is, unless your parents need your help in reducing the financial burden they bear in helping you get a college education and an opportunity to continue your athletic career.

Sometimes a degree from a certain institution (Stanford, Notre Dame, Northwestern, etc.) is sufficient motivation to walk on. And some walk-ons do receive scholarships in later years. A painfully small percentage of walk-ons do receive scholarships and create for themselves an opportunity to play regularly.

Remember, having a substantial part of your college education paid for is no small accomplishment for you and no minor detail for your parents. If significant financial aid is a priority, you should strongly consider NCAA Division II and III and NAIA colleges.

How Many Colleges Should Receive My Credentials?

The greater your exposure, the greater your chances to be successfully recruited. Depending on your sport and your realistic appraisal of your ability, you should be exposed to a minimum of 30 colleges. A good number is 50. Even if your realistic appraisal causes you to conclude that you are a D-I prospect, you should send many profiles to D-II and D-III institutions. Fifteen to each is good.

"But I want to compete in a glamorous or prestigious program," you say. Meaning of course, Division I. You truly may be qualified to compete at Division I, but the truth is, if you were a solid Division-I prospect, a Division-I program probably would have recruited you by now and you wouldn't be studying this book.

Thirty or more colleges? Absolutely. Here's why: coaches recruit prospects that fit their coaching philosophy, system, and style of play. Your abilities and objectives may not fit the coach's requirements. Also, coaches just aren't recruiting for every position or event every year, so there may be no need for a prospect in your position or event.

Even if you interest coaches with your credentials and they make contact with you, you may be low on the recruiting depth chart. You may not move up high enough on the chart to be recruited. Conversely, the more depth charts you are on, the better your chances to move up and eventually be recruited.

If you follow the suggestions in this guide, your credentials will be in the hands of 30 or more coaches in the various divisions. This will produce the results you want and deserve. Very

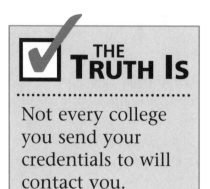

THE TRUTH IS

Not every college you send your credentials to will contact you.

often, this part of the recruiting process is a numbers game. So you must generate sufficient numbers to overwhelm the odds.

Credential Evaluation

When college coaches and recruiters receive your profile, cover letter, and video, they will look at them in a manner similar to the way prospective employers look at resumes. Once the profile has been evaluated, coaches then consider their individual needs to determine their interest in you. Factors such as the number of graduating seniors on their roster, the players playing your position and competing in your event, and available financial aid, in addition to the previously mentioned academic and athletic criteria, all contribute to the degree of interest coaches will have in you as a prospect.

Interested Coach?

If they are interested, most colleges will send you an introductory letter and/or questionnaire. The questionnaire is an important first step. You must understand, however, that its function is more of an elimination process as compared to the selection process. Remember, the only time you are technically offered a scholarship is by an athletic tender or a financial aid award letter.

The questionnaire sent by colleges serves several purposes; but, very importantly, it is a tool with which the coach determines your interest in the college and in his or her program. An important factor considered by the coaches is how quickly you respond to any contact, be it a letter/questionnaire/phone call. (If you have any interest in a college, send the information requested immediately.)

Do whatever is requested quickly and accurately. Often, when a coach must choose between student athletes who are similar academically and athletically, they most often choose the one who has demonstrated discipline and maturity in his/her communications with the coach.

Some recruiting services recommend that a prospect staple a copy of a personally created questionnaire. That is a colossal error. When a coach receives a stapled questionnaire returned from a prospect that has made the first contact by sending a profile, it demonstrates that the prospect is fishing for scholarships and has no special interest in the coach's program. Some coaches may not care if they receive mass-produced and stapled questionnaires to their questionnaire, but many feel exploited and don't pursue that prospect.

Chapter 10

Organize, Organize, Organize

As you can appreciate, if you are contacted by each college you send your profile to, you will be receiving a lot of information. In the early stages of recruiting there will be a process of elimination both by you and by a number of the coaches you are communicating with. For you to make a wise decision you need to have as much information about each school, program, and coach that you can find. It is essential that you record the content of each of your conversations with all coaches as you begin your personal elimination process. It is so easy to forget what was discussed and equally easy to confuse one discussion with another.

If you choose not to organize all information, you will eventually confuse programs and coaches and/or lose important information from phone calls, letters, or documents. Demonstrate some discipline. Get organized.

You must have a filing system for each college to which you send information. Manila file folders are a good beginning. On the tab place the name of the college. On the left inside cover place the address and each coach's name and phone number. A very detailed review of the initial contact between you and the coach/recruiter is very helpful. All contacts should be recorded on a communications log.

Record each contact from the institution: letter, document, visit (college coach at your high school, your college visit(s), or college coach that comes to your home), or phone call. Each phone call or visit must be recorded. The discipline you demonstrate doing this important task will be a powerful asset toward your successful recruitment. The recording should include date, time, coach/recruiter name, and the content of the conversation and any planned next step in the process. Be prepared to be a great listener and a great note taker. Keep your logs clipped in chronological order. The communications log that follows can and should be photocopied.

It is very important to send a thank-you note to each coach expressing your gratitude to him/her for taking the time to speak with you and to consider you for the program. Making an impression as a mature and intelligent prospect is always in your best interest.

Communications Log

1. Date: _____   Time: _____
2. Type of contact: ☐ letter   ☐ personal note
   ☐ questionnaire   ☐ phone call
   ☐ face-to-face visit at home
   ☐ face-to-face visit at high school
   ☐ face-to-face visit at a college campus
   ☐ sent newspaper clippings
3. Initiated by whom? ☐ me   ☐ coach
4. Recruiter/coach and college:_____
5. Content of discussion:_____
6. Next step: ☐ by coach   ☐ by me
7. Thank-you note sent? ☐ yes   ☐ no
8. Date sent: _____

Organizing your recruiting communications intelligently and efficiently is crucial to your success. Truly, you are creating your first major business deal. This deal could be worth $100,000 or more over four or five years. The earning power of a college graduate as compared to a person with a high-school education has recently been pegged at $1,700,000 over a lifetime. (Yes, that's more that one million dollars.)

THE TRUTH Is

Most student athletes do not appreciate the value of their college education.

Chapter 11

Critical Documents

Because of NCAA Clearinghouse regulations, Department of Education regulations, and institutional requirements, you can anticipate a request for a number of documents to be sent to the:

1. Coach/recruiter: athletic information
2. The institution's Admissions Department: academic transcripts and special requirements
3. The institution's Financial Aid Department: financial aid information
4. The NCAA: eligibility information

Many shattered dreams lie strewn on the road to successful recruitment because prospects decide to wait until tomorrow to act on requests to send documents.

The documents requested are normally required for admittance to the college, required by the financial aid office to begin awarding financial aid or required to certify your eligibility to practice and/or participate in NCAA competition.

THE TRUTH Is

Coaches are looking for prospects with inner motivation and mature responsibility; prospects who are self-starters. Procrastination is championship stupid.

Document List

This list may not include all the documents required by the institutions you are considering. Any additional documents requested by the coach, admissions office, financial aid office, or the NCAA must be responded to immediately.

1. **Application form.** No financial aid will be awarded to you unless this form is completed and received by the admissions office. Financial aid offices are forbidden to generate awards until the admissions department has accepted the prospect. It is likely that the admissions form will request that you send an application fee.

   Call the coach and tell him/her that you can't handle the admission fee right now. Ask if he/she can help you get the fee deferred until you enroll. In many cases, they can. Often they will suggest you send the application directly to them. Then the coach will deliver the form to the admissions office. As you will appreciate, if you follow the suggestions of this book and seek acceptance at a number of colleges, sending a check of between $15 to $75 along with each application can become quite expensive. Your goal should be to pay an application fee only to the college in which you ultimately enroll. If you are fortunate enough to receive a scholarship, usually the application fee is waived.

2. **Free Application for Federal Student Aid (FAFSA).** This form can be found in your high-school guidance office. Ask your counselor for it. When you receive it, immediately complete it with the help of your parent(s) or guardian(s). Be certain to complete all sections of the form. If it is incomplete, you will be asked to complete it by the U.S. Department of Education and the enrolling

college before any financial aid other than an athletic scholarship can be awarded to you. Mail it in the enclosed envelope.

Some parents don't complete the FAFSA. They may believe they will not qualify for any type of aid because their income is too high. As stated earlier: assume nothing. Others may determine that they won't divulge the personal and tax return information requested on the FAFSA. While I appreciate a desire for privacy, it is probably foolish to be stubborn in this circumstance. The requested information is very similar to that on your tax return. It is a mistake not to complete and mail the FAFSA. Unlike the IRS, which wants to take your money, colleges use the information on the FAFSA to award you money.

Factors other than income influence eligibility for federal

THE TRUTH Is

Many families with incomes in the six-figure range are receiving need-based financial aid. No kidding. And no cheating.

or state financial aid. And state financial aid is almost always calculated based on the formula (called Federal Methodology) the Department of Education's computers use to evaluate the information provided on the FAFSA. And state financial aid standards are often less harsh than the federal financial aid standards. Your financial aid forms are sent to a central processing unit in Illinois. Computers crunch the data and determine how much you can afford to pay. Personal, family, financial, or employment issues are not part of the calculation executed by the computer program. Many families miss opportunities to reduce the financial burden of a college education because they choose not to complete and mail the FAFSA.

Many colleges award institutional grants (discounts from the announced tuition, room, and board) and other financial aid based on the information generated by the FAFSA. When information from the FAFSA is used as a baseline for awarding financial aid, it is called Federal Methodology. While this aid is from the college's financial aid budget, it was calculated with Federal Methodology. And often a college's need-based financial aid awarding standards are less rigid than either the state or federal standards. When an institution uses it's own unique formula for calculating student need and consequently determining which students will receive tuition and/or room and board discounts, this is called Institutional Methodology.

If there is no baseline data like that generated from the FAFSA, very often the conclusion drawn is that you should be a "full-freight" student. You didn't buy this book in order to become a "full-freight" student, did you?

3. **CSS profile.** Over 800 colleges require incoming freshmen to complete a form called a profile. The profile questions provide the institution information that the FAFSA doesn't ask. These colleges use the information on the profile to help the director of financial aid determine how much of a discount (Institutional Methodology) from the sticker price you should receive. Like all other requests for documents from a college, complete it and send it immediately.

4. **Student Aid Report (SAR)**. This report is generated by the Department of Education's computers. The SAR is based on the information you provide on the FAFSA. Your parent(s) or guardian(s) will receive a copy of this report. A number of the colleges you are interested in will receive a copy of the SAR. You will have directed, by naming them in section G of the FAFSA, which colleges will receive a copy of the SAR on the FAFSA form completed by you and your parent(s). When you receive your SAR (sometimes called Blue Forms, even though the colors of the forms are often not blue), examine it—there may be mistakes on it that could cost you plenty. Also, call immediately to request another free copy of the SAR at (319) 337-5665.

> **Student Aid Report (SAR) To Do List**
>
> • Keep your copy in a place where it will remain neat and clean. You may have to make a number of photocopies of the SAR.
>
> • Take a SAR with you on each visit you make to a college, even if you think the college has already received a copy.
>
> • Give a copy of your SAR to any coach/recruiter or admissions counselor who visits you at school or at your home.

You will discover a number called the Expected Family Contribution or EFC. The college's financial aid office will calculate (Federal Methodology) the federal and state financial aid available to you from the EFC# and other information found in the SAR.

5. **High-school transcript**. The process of sending your transcript to a college is the responsibility of your high-school guidance counselor. Even if you haven't finished high school, you should request that transcripts be sent to the

admissions department of the colleges that interest you. Final transcripts will be sent upon your graduation. Your grade point average (GPA) in the core course requirements, as identified by the NCAA and presented earlier in the book, plays an important role in your eligibility to practice and compete.

Many types of financial aid are awarded based on your high-school GPA. Doesn't it make sense to be a good high-school student and focus on achieving as high a GPA as possible?

6. **ACT/SAT scores.** To be NCAA eligible, you must sit for the ACT/SAT on one or more of the National Testing Dates. Your counselor can give you the dates and locations of these tests. You can take the ACT/SAT as often as you want (on a National Testing Date) to achieve a better score, which will help you to be NCAA eligible. (Refer to the academic eligibility section in your *NCAA Guide for the College-Bound Student-Athlete.*)

As with your high-school transcript, your high-school counselor sends your ACT/SAT scores to the college admissions department. Like your GPA, your ACT/SAT scores play an important role in your eligibility to practice and compete. (Refer to the academic eligibility section of your *NCAA Guide for the College-Bound Student-Athlete.*) Also, like your GPA, many financial aid awards are based on the scores of these tests. Some colleges will allow you to retake the ACT or SAT test on the college campus to give you an opportunity to improve your score in order to increase your academic financial aid award. Ask the college admissions office if they offer this opportunity.

Remember, sitting for an ACT/SAT test on the college campus can't change an ACT/SAT score for the purposes of NCAA eligibility because it isn't given at a National Testing Date location. The ACT/SAT scores that the NCAA recognizes for the purpose of determining your eligibility are those scores earned on the National Testing Dates only.

7. **Financial Aid Estimator.** Many Division II and III colleges use an FAE to provide preliminary information from which they can estimate the amount of financial aid you might need to be able to attend that institution. A coach/recruiter or admissions counselor may send you an FAE. This document helps the coach make preliminary recruiting decisions based on the results of yours and other prospects' FAEs. As you can appreciate, if the coach receives a requested FAE from a prospect who has similar academic and athletic qualifications as you and doesn't receive your FAE, guess who's going to be offered a scholarship. This isn't brain surgery, is it?

8. **Institutional Financial Aid Application Form.** An institution may ask you to complete a Financial Aid Application Form even though you also have completed a FAFSA and a CSS Profile. Private schools often have financial aid available for special circumstances. Having a special circumstances category adds to the flexibility of a director of financial aid to award discounts. Examples are: alumni-sponsored scholarships and major field of study scholarships (i.e., nursing, engineering, elementary education, or a religious institution that awards members of its faith).

9. **NCAA Clearinghouse Form "Making Sure You Are Eligible to Participate in College Sports."** This form must be completed and sent to the NCAA. There is an $18 registration

fee. The Clearinghouse certifies your eligibility to participate in practices and competition. You're not eligible in Divisions I or II without Clearinghouse certification, even if you meet the eligibility standards.

Coaches rarely offer any kind of financial aid to students who haven't been certified eligible by the NCAA Clearinghouse. You can get the form free from your guidance counselor, athletic director or coach. If its not available, call the NCAA Clearinghouse at (319) 337-1492 or (800) 638-3731 or www.ncaa.org for a free form.

You and the college coach will receive notice of your eligibility certification from the NCAA. You will be given a Personal Identification Number (PIN). On the NCAA Clearinghouse form, you will be asked which colleges you wish to be notified. The NCAA will notify those colleges you identify of your eligibility status.

Chapter 12

Communication Activities

If a college coach/recruiter that you are interested in calls or sends you an email, you should immediately write or email a short letter thanking him/her for "your interest in me as a recruit for your program." Tell him/her of your interest in both the college and the athletic program. If there is additional information (awards won, recent performances, etc.) about yourself you want to share, do it at this time. This is also a good time to include your upcoming competition schedule. Be prepared with some questions, too. Some of the questions located in the chapter "The Visit" can be asked over the phone. Another source of good questions is the NAIA's *Guide for the College-Bound Athlete*. A coach to whom you sent nothing might contact you. Don't be shocked; word of good prospects can travel quickly.

As indicated previously, you may receive more than one phone call or email from the same person or other people related to a program. This is no accident. Additional calls or emails are very good signals, but you haven't been recruited yet. You must continue to do your part. After a few contacts by the coach/recruiter, you will detect a pattern of questions that indicate an increasing level of interest and/or concerns:

- Asking for videotape of last game or performance.
- Asking for your coach's home phone number.
- Asking if you plan to retake the ACT/SAT.
- Asking if you have applied for admission.
- Asking if you have sent transcripts and ACT/SAT scores to Admissions.
- Asking about recent injury.
- Asking if you'd be willing to change playing positions in college.
- Asking you to send a SAR to him/her.
- Asking you to visit their institution.
- Asking if you would be willing to walk on.
- Asking if you would commit to their program if you get a partial scholarship.
- Asking how much financial aid it will take for you to enroll.

Try to anticipate questions. Write down what you feel are the kind of answers you want to give and practice them—out loud. As the recruiting season progresses, you'll discover that the questions will begin to change. Some coaches will stop calling or returning your calls or emails (in this case, you've probably been strung along). Others may begin sending you handwritten notes or emails (a very positive sign). By following the suggestions in the "Organize" section, you will be prepared for the changes and be ready to answer critical questions.

Communications That You Initiate

Whenever you are cited in the newspaper or other media, send another note to the coach ("Coach, I thought you might be interested in this article," etc.) that includes a photocopy (or referencing that he/she should visit your profile and add it to your personal information) of the article that presents you favorably. Or send it as an email attachment.

If you aren't home when a coach calls, it is wise to return the coach's call as soon as possible. You may telephone (at your expense) and email a college coach as often as you wish. Keep communicating. A coach may conclude that you've lost interest if he/she doesn't hear from you. You may visit a college campus (unofficial visit) as often as you wish. However, you must avoid creating the impression that you can be recruited with little or no financial aid or that you will accept loan-type aid only or that the financial aid office can GAP you (offer you less financial aid than your certified need as indicated with the EFC# on the SAR). You should never pay more than EFC# amount.

Chapter 13

The Visit

If a coach is really serious about recruiting you, he/she will ask you to visit the campus. Always ask if they will be "handling" (don't say "paying") the expenses for the visit. Remember, there are certain restrictions concerning official—that is to say, paid—visits. Refer to your *NCAA Guide for the College-Bound Student-Athlete*.

Remember, you can make as many unofficial visits to a campus as you wish. That means you handle (pay) your expenses. You may take one "official visit" per school and five total official visits.

Be sure you visit only colleges in which you are interested. It's unfair to waste other people's time, but even more important, don't waste your own time. An official visit must always be followed by a sincere thank-you note, no matter if you're recruited by that college or not. After all, the program has invested time and financial and personnel resources in you.

On your visit you must try to speak with faculty and staff in many different departments of the college, in particular:

- Admissions Office
- Financial Aid Office
- Housing
- Athletic Department
- Department head of your intended major field of study

Be certain to examine all the facilities that will directly impact your life on that campus:

- dorms
- athletic facilities
- dining facilities
- laboratories
- classrooms
- student union
- library

Get a feel for the campus ambiance, as well.

Recruiting Can Be Unfair

While being asked to visit is a very positive step toward being successfully recruited, a cold dousing of reality is needed here. As you now know, the coach is almost surely recruiting more than one prospect for any one position. You should be aware that it is highly unlikely that the coach will successfully recruit each prospect that is his/her first choice for a position or event. In order to protect themselves, most coaches have back-up recruit lists. These lists are usually referred to as depth charts.

The problem is that you may be a back-up recruit, low on the depth chart, and never know it. You may well experience the same kind of reception and may be told the same things as the recruit who is #1 on the coach's depth chart. This is known as being *strung along*.

At a recent *Ultimate Recruiting Seminar* designed for college coaches and recruiters, the following suggestion was part of the seminar content: "For every scholarship you have, you should be recruiting four prospective student athletes." In other words, effective recruiting requires that the recruiter/coach string along three prospects. This is the harsh reality. To ignore this reality is championship stupid.

That's why it is so important for you to never, never ever place your college future in one coach or college. You must have some options available to you until you are asked to commit to a college. The coaches will be shopping for prospects and keeping their options open; so you must shop for coaches and programs keeping your options open, too. Remember, the recruiting process is often a numbers game—you must play the game, too. Overwhelm the odds with massive numbers. College coaches commonly have five hundred or more potential recruits on their initial mailing lists.

Chapter 14

Visit Questions

The wise prospect seeks answers to many important questions. While the coach/recruiter of the college will be your primary source for answers, be aware that other sources are also available. These include: other athletes (usually met while visiting the campus), college-produced introductory reading material, catalogs, college Internet websites, and observations made on the campus. Arm yourself with this book by keeping it conveniently located at your telephone and with you (but out of sight) at all times when visiting a campus.

A word of caution: be careful not to appear that you are investigating the coach. However, be sure to get the answers as they can provide you with the information from which you can make an informed and therefore, good decision. While a coach may string you along, it is quite rare that a coach will lie when asked a direct question.

It is very important that you get satisfactory answers to each of the following questions before you commit to a coach or college. Some of these questions will be better asked in-person while on a visit. As your conversation proceeds with the coach, you will get an idea what questions you should ask while on the phone and which questions to ask when you visit the college.

Go over the questions (pages 88–91) with your parent(s)/guardian(s) and highlight a few of the questions which are most important to get answers to so you can generate a level of interest in the coach, his/her program, and the school.

Most of your conversation will be spent listening. The coach will spend a lot of time telling you about his/her program and selling you on his/her school. Be patient and be a good listener. There will be time to ask your questions.

The following four topics encompass most of the experiences you will have as a student athlete at any school. You should know which school appears to be the best fit for you in all four areas.

Put your questions on 3 × 5 cards. It is not a good idea to let any school official see you using this book.

Athletic

1. How much time is spent in practice?
2. When does the season begin? End?
3. Are there additional training periods?
4. What are practice hours?
5. What are my off-season responsibilities?
6. Can I compete in other sports?
7. What is the team's past record?
8. What conference and division does the team compete in?
9. How many games/meets per season?
10. How often does the team travel?
11. Can he/she describe the athletic facilities? (If not, wait and observe during the visit.)
12. What is the coach's philosophy?
13. What are my chances of regularly competing and when?

14. What position/event/class am I being considered for?
15. How many freshmen at your position are being recruited?
16. What position am I on the recruiting depth chart?
17. Will I be redshirted?
18. What are the housing arrangements for athletes?
19. Have you seen me play or compete?
20. Do my skills fit into your program?

Academic

1. Are my career goals compatible with the college's majors and programs?
2. Am I allowed time to make up classes and tests missed because of the competition schedule?
3. Am I qualified to meet admission standards?
4. Are tutors provided for athletes?
5. What percent of freshmen graduate? Graduate with their class?
6. What is the college's policy toward student athletes during summer session?
7. Will I have an academic advisor?
8. Will the coaches provide any guidance if I have academic problems?
9. How many hours of studying per day is average for my major?
10. Do professors teach?

Legal

1. Do I receive a written contract/tender?
2. If I get injured or become sick, will I lose my financial aid?
3. What medical expenses does the college cover?

4. a. How many credits are required for me to be eligible to compete?

4. b. How many credits are required for me to keep my financial aid?

5. What is the status of the college's relationship with the NCAA?

Financial

1. Is there academic or need-based financial aid available?

2. What is the amount of financial aid being offered?

3. How many years is it being offered?

4. What criteria is used to determine renewal of aid?

5. What portion of the total (yearly/semester) cost is covered by the financial aid I will receive?

6. What expenses does the financial aid cover (tuition, room, board, books, special assessments, supplies, etc.)?

7. What sources and types of financial aid will be included in the total financial aid package? (state, Pell, USEOG, institutional, special awards, grants, loans, etc.)

8. Am I eligible for additional financial aid now? In future years?

9. If I need five years to graduate, will I continue to receive the same amount of financial aid as the other four years?

After the Visit

After your visit, you should review the visit by asking yourself the following questions:

1. Did the coach/recruiter say negative things about other schools in an attempt to persuade me to attend his/her college?

2. Were the coaches interested in my academic success?
3. What was the attitude of the players toward their coaches?
4. Does the institution satisfy my requirements?
5. Would I attend this college if I weren't going to be an athlete?
6. Can I play in games here or will I be a member of the "gray" squad?
7. Was I offered benefits or enticements that I realize were sleazy?

Chapter 15

Why Prospects and Families Get Hurt

Prospects and families get hurt because they don't understand their value in the recruiting marketplace. They don't know how to interpret the meaning (both obvious and hidden) of all the calls, letters, promises, and other communications from college recruiters. They don't know when they are being strung along or when they are being told the truth.

You can be intensely recruited with letters, personal notes, and phone calls for months and suddenly hear nothing because you were being strung along. It goes with the territory.

Protect yourself with the following counterforce of knowledge and strategies to level the playing field:

1. Until you have an offer in writing (award letter, contract, or tender) and until you make a commitment to a coach; you must always create the impression that you are considering other colleges' offers. In fact, you should always have at least one backup in case of an unpleasant surprise. Why? Sometimes, if a coach believes that you are being recruited by other coaches and you are at or near the top of his/her recruiting depth chart, the coach (or some other official at the college) may offer additional incentives (financial aid) for you to choose his/her program. If a coach believes you have no other options, often he/she will try to

recruit you for as little as possible. In that way, he or she can use the unused resources that you didn't receive for some other recruit who is bargaining more effectively than you are.

2. Remember, ask if the coach is recruiting other athletes for the same position. Why? This question signals the coach that you have a grasp of a fact basic to recruiting: that most coaches are recruiting (and usually saying the same things to) more than one prospect. (Someone's being strung along here. Is it you?) If the coach really wants you, he/she will know that you understand the foregoing facts and may be eager to make you an offer that is satisfactory to you.

3. Gain admittance to several colleges that you have visited that have the right ingredients for you to be a successful student athlete. Why? If you are admitted to a number of institutions that are recruiting you, you have two very important benefits:

   • The coach can begin working early with other departments (admissions, financial aid, athletic, housing, etc.) in order to insure that you receive all the financial aid and other benefits to which you are entitled.

   • You can honestly tell any coach that you have been accepted at other colleges that are recruiting you. With this weapon you can bargain from a position of strength.

Sleazy Recruiting Tactics

While the majority of college coaches are people who wish to be a positive influence on the student athletes they coach and are fundamentally honest, a minority of them have little interest in you beyond your helping them have a winning program and thus keeping their jobs. These are harsh comments about some in the coaching ranks, but it is sadly the truth. Be alert for them.

The following points can help you recognize sleazy recruiting tactics and therefore, the coaches to avoid:

1. A coach who has a "booster" contact you or tells you that a "fan" will contact you about the program. The NCAA is making a concerted effort to eliminate from the recruiting process those persons who have "an interest" in the program. Even if they offer you nothing, which is highly unlikely, you are in violation of the NCAA guidelines.

   Even though the NCAA often looks the other way on many violations, to its credit it severely punishes those who violate the "booster" rules. Even if you just talk to a "booster," you jeopardize your future with the NCAA. Refer to the *NCAA Guide for College-Bound Student-Athletes.*

2. A coach who promises that your "best friend" can walk on. This coach has no interest in you or your friend. He is manipulating you by dangling a false hope in front of your friend.

3. A coach who promises you a starting position your freshman year. Or one who guarantees that you will be an All-American, national champion, or have a professional career in sports primarily because you compete for him/her. (Remember, there is a difference between a guarantee and a statement about your potential.)

4. Coaches who "trash, slam, or bum raps" other colleges, programs, or coaches. If coaches can't persuade you to join their program because of its qualities and their coaching abilities, you'd be a fool to enroll. Be especially alert for this sleazy tactic.

5. Some coaches may tell you that the academic program in the field of study you plan to pursue is the "best in the nation" at their college or some similar hyperbole. Consult with your high-school counselor, or there are a number of publications, easily accessed on the Internet, to check the accuracy of that statement. It is usually a sleazy recruiting tactic.

6. Some coaches may promise you easy courses, easy professors, and no academic pressure. These coaches have little concern about your future beyond helping their program. By making your academic requirements easy, the coaches have done you no favors. After all, you are going to do more important things in your life than compete in athletic contests. You'll need a good education that requires you to rise to high standards if you are to be successful in those more important things.

7. Student guides that invite prospects to parties where alcohol, drugs, or sexually provocative activities are unfortunately, not uncommon. There are many reports of these sleazy recruiting tactics in Division I football and basketball, but there is anecdotal evidence of this sleazy tactic being employed at other divisions and other sports. If you experience this on a visit, you know that the coach has sunk to odious recruiting depths and has no interest in your success or welfare as a student athlete.

An Important Word of Caution

If you or your parents accept money or any kind of gift from a school representative, you will be declared ineligible to compete in the NCAA.

Chapter 16

Awarding of Athletic Financial Aid

Virtually all colleges that sponsor a sport that competes on the intercollegiate level want that sport program to be successful (to be a winning program). To enjoy the benefits of a winning program, some level of recruiting is required. The level, intensity, directness, and operation of collegiate recruiting by any particular school is affected by a number of factors.

As you have learned, NCAA Division I and II offer designated athletic scholarships of some monetary value applied toward the cost of the tuition and/or fees of the institution awarding the financial aid. Division I schools often offer full rides, although they sometimes split some athletic scholarships up and offer partial rides. Division II programs offer full rides much less often than does Division I. They split up their athletic scholarships more often than Division I. As you now know, NCAA rules restrict the number of athletic scholarships in each sport for both Division I and II. And Division II is allowed fewer athletic scholarships in nearly every sport than Division I.

When you are being recruited by a Division I or II college, the recruiters and coaches will discuss financial aid in terms of athletic scholarships. Usually Division II coaches will discuss additional financial aid opportunities in other terms, as well, like: need-based, academic, special-talent, minority, merit, leadership, institutional grants, or loans (Stafford, Perkins, PLUS, etc.).

Division II institutions (more often than Division I institutions) try to combine one of the foregoing types of financial aid with an athletic scholarship in order to increase the total amount of financial aid to a prospect. The greater the nonathletic financial aid, the greater the chance of recruiting the prospect. However, unlike Division III institutions, Division I and II colleges usually don't negotiate an increase in the nonathletic categories of financial aid. The category left open for negotiations is usually the athletic award.

As you discuss/negotiate financial aid, paying very, very close attention to your financial aid arithmetic, be sure you are combining all types of financial aid in order to calculate the total financial aid package. When you and the coach agree upon the athletic scholarship, he/she and the athletic director will notify the college financial aid office of the amount offered. This is accomplished by sending an initial Athletic Tender (that must be signed by you, the athletic director, and the coach) to the institution's financial aid office. The NCAA requires this so that the total amount of financial aid being offered in that sport can be monitored. It's required so that all athletic tenders offered are compatible within the allowable limits of total athletic financial aid for that particular program.

The financial aid office then combines the athletic scholarship with the financial aid you will be awarded in the other categories previously noted. You will receive two documents indicating the awarding of financial aid:

1. **Award Letter.** This document itemizes each financial aid award (in every category i.e., athletic, academic, work-

study, loan, institutional, grant, etc.) you will receive if you choose to attend that college. You will be asked to confirm your decision to attend by accepting the award letter or signing a letter of intent or both. You may receive competing and similar offers from two or more schools. Try the worksheets from www.collegeboard.com in order to carefully compare the offers.

Financial Aid Award Letter

Bunkerschnives University
Financial Aid Award

March 21, 2007
ACCEPT/DECLINE (Circle One)

Morsly Horsefeather
1 Prospect Street
Athletica, PA 12345

Dear Morsly,
Bunkerschnives University is pleased to offer you financial assistance for the academic year 2007–2008.

This award is not official until this form is completed and returned to the Office of Financial Planning.

Please read the enclosed Information for Financial Aid Recipients before accepting any part of this award.

Congratulations,

Financial Aid Director
Bunkerschnives University

Information for Financial Aid Recipients

Bunkerschnives University Grant $7,500	☐ Accept	☐ Decline
Founders Grant $1,000	☐ Accept	☐ Decline
Leadership Award $500	☐ Accept	☐ Decline
Religious Service Award $500	☐ Accept	☐ Decline
Alumni Grant $500	☐ Accept	☐ Decline
Diversity Grant $1,000	☐ Accept	☐ Decline
Pell Grant $2,000	☐ Accept	☐ Decline
Federal Work-Study (potential earnings) . .$1,500	☐ Accept	☐ Decline
Federal Stafford Student Loan–if needed . .$2,500	Please Apply	

The white copy of this form must be signed and returned to the Office of Financial Planning by April 16, 2007.

After this date, Bunkerschnives University cannot guarantee the receipt of any funds offered in this award. Deadline extensions may be granted upon written request until May 1.

For more information, please contact the Bunkerschnives University Office of Financial Planning.

Statement of Educational Purpose

I understand my rights and responsibilities. I declare that I will use any funds I receive under the Pell Grant, SEOG, College Work-Study, Perkins Loan, Stafford Student Loan, PLUS Loan, or any funds administered by the Bunkerschnives University Financial Planning Office solely for the expenses contacted with attendance at Bunkerschnives University. I further understand that I am responsible for repayment of the prorated amount of any portion of payments made which cannot be attributed to meeting educational expenses related to attendance at Bunkerschnives University.

You will not receive Title IV financial aid unless you complete the following statement:

☐ I certify that I am not required to register with the Selective Service, because (check one):

　☐ I am a female.
　☐ I am in the armed services on active duty (Note: members of the National Guard are not considered on active duty).
　☐ I have not reached my eighteenth birthday.
　☐ I was born before 1960.
　☐ I am a permanent resident of the Trust Territory of the Pacific Islands or the Northern Mariana Islands.

☐ I certify that I am registered with Selective Service.

I accept the awards above, and hereby authorize Bunkerschnives University to directly credit my account with the applicable state, federal, college, and/or outside agency funds, as, and when appropriate, in accordance with current regulations. I further certify that I am not in default on any educational loan and that I do not owe a refund on any grant funds previously received to attend Bunkerschnives University. I certify that if I receive a Pell Grant, as condition of my Pell Grant, I will not engage in unlawful manufacture, distribution, dispensation, possession, or use of a controlled substance during the period covered by my Pell Grant.

I further understand I must maintain full-time enrollment (12 hours or more) each semester to receive the Bunkerschnives Grant, Recognition Award, Sibling Grant, Alumni Grant, Diversity Grant, and International Award. I will refer to the Bunkerschnives Undergraduate Bulletin for refund policies pertaining to state, federal, and institutional financial aid, should I withdraw or go less than full-time.

Signature: _____ Date: _____

2. **Athletic Tender.** This document has two purposes:
   a. To describe the type and amount of athletic financial aid (and only the amount of athletic financial aid) you will receive if you choose to attend that college.
   b. To secure your attendance at the institution and to bar you from competing at any other NCAA institution.

You can sign the Award Letter, and even though it is unethical, you could still decide to attend a different institution. However, if you sign the Athletic Tender, you can compete only at that NCAA institution. Do not sign one without knowing the contents of the other. If you do sign one without knowing the contents of the other, you lose virtually all your negotiating leverage. The best insurance is to only sign the two of them at the same time.

Athletic Tender of Financial Assistance

Bunkerschnives University
Athletic Tender of Financial Assistance

_____
Name of Applicant

_____
Street Address

_____
City

_____
State, Zip

_____
Date of Entrance

_____
Sport

_____
Date

☐ Initial   ☐ Renewal

_____Academic Year

_____
In University

1. This Tender represents all commitments to you by Bunkerschnives University and is subject to:
   a. Fulfillment of the admissions requirements of Bunkerschnives University;
   b. Fulfillment of NCAA academic eligibility requirements; and
   c. Fulfillment of financial aid requirements set forth by the NCAA and Bunkerschnives University.

2. This Tender covers the following as checked:
   ☐ a. Full Grant: Includes tuition and all fees, standard room (double occupancy), and board (meal plan 1).
   ☐ b. Partial Grant of _____

3. You will be eligible for a year-to-year renewal of the Tender according to this University's renewal policies at the end of the academic year. Should you fall below the academic eligibility GPA requirement, you will be allowed a one-semester probation period to increase your GPA to the required status.

4. If you wish to accept this Tender, please return four (4) signed copies of this form to the Athletic Office no later than _____

Signed

_____   _____
Director of Athletics   Financial Aid Director

ACCEPTANCE

THIS TENDER IS CONTINGENT UPON THE SUBMISSION OF THE FINANCIAL
AID FORM (FAF)

I accept this Tender of Financial Assistance. In doing so, I certify that I have not
accepted any other Tender of Financial Assistance from another school.

I understand that:
a. The value of this Tender shall not exceed the value of the permissible Bunkerschnives University and NCAA expenses applicable to ISSC and Pell Grant
   awards.
b. The aid provided in this Tender will be canceled if I sign a professional sports
   contract of accept money for playing in an athletic contest.

Signed

_____   _____   _____
        Student   Date   Social Security Number

Signed

_____   _____
  Parent or Legal Guardian   Date

A Letter of Intent is a contract that binds you to compete for the institution and binds them to the level of financial aid stated on it as long as the prospect fulfills the obligations cited in the contingency section. Sign the Letter of Intent at the same time that you sign the Athletic Tender, otherwise you lose all negotiating leverage.

Letter of Intent

Fighting Prospects
Bunkerschnives University
123 Main Street
Anywhere, FL 12345

National Soccer Letter of Intent

Athletic Aid Agreement: Expected Behavior; Practices and Games

This is to say that Joe S. Athlete will be awarded as much as $2000.00 in athletic aid for the year of 2007–2008 ***

Awards are contingent of the following:
1. Attendance at all practices.
2. Attendance at all games.
3. Maintaining academic eligibility and full-time student status.
4. Appropriate conduct to avoid being dismissed from the athletic team.
5. Completion of all required financial aid applications on a timely basis.
6. Official acceptance by the College of Admissions Department.
7. Other: Exceptions to numbers 1 and 2 will be determined by the coach: for example, illness or extenuating circumstances. Also, do not sign this contract unless you have received acceptance by the College of Admissions Department. Please notify the Athletic Department if you have not yet been accepted.

Pledge: I understand that I must fulfill the above obligation and any infraction could lead to a loss of my athletic aid for one or all semesters.

<u>   </u>   <u>   </u>

    Signature of Athletic Director   Date

<u>   </u>   <u>   </u>

    Signature of Student Athlete   Date

*** Athletic aid cannot be awarded over and above the total bill of your education for the year and, if you are awarded full government aid, athletic aid may have to be reduced.

On the previous pages are examples of what you will receive from a college offering you athletic financial aid: A National Letter of Intent and an Athletic Tender of Financial Assistance. Please note that both of these samples include a line item with a $ sign. This is the amount (or value) you will receive in athletic financial aid. Some Division III institutions also issue a National Letter of Intent, even though NCAA regulations require that Division III colleges claim they offer no athletically related financial aid. This is normally done to "lock in" the prospect so that he/she can only compete at that institution. (More on this bogus claim later.)

Chapter 17

Negotiating Guidelines

In order for a prospect to receive the maximum amount of financial aid for athletic ability, he/she must be prepared to negotiate for that maximum. If you have examined any college's "sticker price," you know the enormous cost, other than most junior colleges, of a college education. The more you attempt to reduce the cost of a college education from the sticker price, the more you increase the pressure on the institution's financial aid officer to resist further reductions. Because of the flexibility of "professional judgment" combined with the desire of an institution to enroll a prospect, one rarely knows how much of a reduction can be secured. The only strategy that delivers the reductions you want and deserve is negotiation. If negotiating is a dialogue that makes you so tense that you choose not to do it, you must be ready to accept the inevitable financial consequences. Many uncomfortable parents have left thousands of dollars on the table because they failed to deal with their anxiety about negotiations and potential confrontation. Don't you be one of them. The money you didn't negotiate for will go to someone who did. Practice using the following strategies, tools, and devices, and you will dramatically increase the chances of getting what you want and deserve.

Negotiations (never use this term with financial aid officers—they hate it!)require some careful balancing and delicate control. Use the following guidelines to ensure that you are in control:

- Be sure the coach always knows that the amount of the financial aid award will be a critical factor in choosing a college. A parent might say, *Coach, I don't mean to be audacious, but it's important to me that you know I need/expect financial aid for my son/daughter.*

- Be sure the coach knows that no commitment will be made until an award letter, tender, or contract is forthcoming. *Coach, I mean no offense, and I'm confident you understand when I say that we can't make a final commitment to you until we receive the award letter [Division III] or athletic tender [Division I or II]. Is that fair?*

The importance of asking "Is that fair?" Are you kidding? You've been telling me that the recruiting process is unfair. Guess what: it is.

This seemingly innocuous sales technique has a powerful effect on the receiver of its message. (If the recipient of that question says no then that person is unfair.) This subtle psychological device is very powerful because the receiver usually perceives him/herself as a fair person and instinctively wishes to maintain that perception with a "yes" answer. (Meaning: I am a fair person.) Also, the question is unexpected in an emotionally intense situation giving the recipient less psychological room to gather his/her thoughts and respond in his/her best interests and not respond to the protection of their image of being fair.

THE TRUTH IS

Very few people, including coaches, enjoy being perceived as unfair.

(I know it's tough, but you need to be tough. Tough on yourself and your opponent.) You may wish to use synonyms for the word fair. Try: reasonable, decent, square, evenhanded, principled, above-board, straight, appropriate, all right, okay, equitable, satisfactory, etc. to reduce the ferocity of the question.

- Always tell the coach that his/her institution is your number-one choice. *Coach, as you know, you are our number-one choice, but it's very important to us that all the issues, including financial aid, get satisfactorily resolved.*

If you must have more aid, or feel you can negotiate for more, do it with the coach/recruiter. The basis for further negotiation should be the athletic tender. The objective is to increase the amount of the athletic tender. *Coach, I apologize, but after carefully calculating the total financial aid package offered in the award letter, I'm going to need a little more help. I need another $500/$1,000/$2,000. Can you handle that additional amount?*

Then be quiet. The first one who talks after the question is asked, loses.

Negotiating Is Selling

The coach and the institution are generally in a position to put psychological pressure on you. They recognize that they are in a position of power and control and are usually quick to take advantage of the psychological stress you feel. You need a psychological counter-force to level the playing field.

Successful salespeople know what devices to employ when they want to put the ball into the customer's court: that is to say, make them buy the product or service they are selling. That device is one of the most powerful psychological stressors known to man: silence.

A salesperson will ask a closing question like, "Would you like to take the shoes home?" When the customer doesn't answer right away, say fifteen seconds, the timid salesperson can't stand the pressure of no one talking and breaks the silence. The moment he or she starts talking, the sale is lost.

The wise and courageous salesperson remains silent and forces the customer to talk first. When the customer talks, often he or she says yes.

Sometimes the coach will ask a question. This is a good sign.

- It demonstrates the coach's interest in you.
- It provides you the opportunity to ask another closing question.

A coach may ask a question similar to "I can't go $2,000. If I could increase the award letter by $1,000 would that be okay?" Now the coach has asked a closing question. That is to say, he wants you to say yes. That's in his/her best interest.

Only you know the answer to this or a similar question. If your answer is no; say no. Now the ball is back in the coach's court. If you sense the coach is bluffing with that type of question, be quiet.

Colleges give away close to $11 billion of their own funds for financial aid each year. If you want more money (a discount on tuition) than what you are initially offered, you must ask for it. Otherwise your financial aid package will not be increased. And if there is additional financial aid available, it will go to someone else who did ask for it.

If the coach suggests that you sign either of the documents (Athletic Tender or Financial Aid Award Letter) you must decline. "Well, go ahead and sign the award letter and I'll see what I can do."

Your answer should be, *Coach, I don't mean to be offensive, but it's important to me to see if you can secure the increase with a new Financial Aid Award Letter. If you can, I'll sign both the award letter and the athletic tender at the same time. Is that fair?* OR *Coach, I mean no disrespect, but I'd rather sign an Award Letter and the Athletic Tender that both show the additional amount as awarded. Is that fair?* Then be quiet.

If the coach refuses to budge, you've lost nothing. Don't be afraid that the coach will become angry or withdraw the offer. (You have the documents in your hands. Signing them legally compels the institution.) Most coaches expect people to negotiate and usually respect those that negotiate aggressively, yet fairly.

Belligerence and threatening will accomplish nothing. Many parents don't realize that it's important to a financial aid counselor whether you attend the institution as it may affect him or her keeping his or her job. Some admission counselors have to generate certain predetermined numbers. If they don't, jobs can be lost.

Sometimes you may have to appeal the financial aid package with a financial aid officer. If you feel that you've not been offered an amount that the institution should reasonably handle or if you can cite new or changed financial circumstances that change your ability to pay, usually a financial aid officer will hear an appeal. If the appeal is for the former, normally, the coach recruiting you will prepare you for the appeal interview. If it is the latter, normally you would handle this yourself.

Remember that the awarding of financial aid is a marketing tool used to increase or sustain enrollment. If a small- to medium-sized private college is recruiting you, the following bold question often provokes outstanding results. *Isn't it better for the college to have a student enrolled who is receiving enhanced financial aid rather than having an empty seat or an empty bed?* Then be quiet. Pleading and groveling are counterproductive.

You must always be reasonable and calm, yet in control. As you can appreciate, there will be certain schools where negotiations will be less productive than at others. There is a waiting list at many prestigious schools so they don't need to give discounts to attract students.

Chapter 18

Financial Aid Limits

The NCAA limits financial aid for each sport in both Division I and Division II. The NCAA counts athletic financial aid in two categories:

1. **Head-Count Sports.** Used for some Division I sports. Any athlete who receives institutional financial aid, no matter the amount of aid, is counted as one. Head count limit sports are only in Division I. Most, but not all, head count awards are full grant-in-aid (full-rides).
   - I-A Football: 85
   - I-AA Football: 63
   - Men's Basketball: 13
   - Ice Hockey: 30 counters/18 equivalencies
   - Women's Basketball: 15
   - Women's Gymnastics: 12
   - Women's Tennis: 8
   - Women's Volleyball: 12

2. **Equivalency Sports.** Any sports not listed above are considered equivalency sports. Generally, this means that one full grant-in-aid (full-ride) can be divided among more than one student athlete. Each college publishes the cost for a student to enroll in that institution. That cost is used as the benchmark for one full grant-in-aid athletic scholarship.

That benchmark scholarship number multiplies the equivalency number assigned to a sport. The product of that multiple determines the actual dollar amount available to award to athletes in the sport being considered. The number of athletes receiving athletic financial aid is irrelevant; only the total amount of dollars in aid given matters in equivalency sports.

Equivalency Limits for Division I Sports

Men's Sports	Women's Sports
Baseball 11.7	Archery 5.0
Cross-Country/Track 12.6	Badminton 6.0
Fencing 4.5	Bowling 5.0
Golf 4.5	Cross-Country/Track 18.0
Gymnastics 6.3	Fencing 5.0
Ice Hockey 18.0	Field Hockey 12.0
Lacrosse 12.6	Golf 6.0
Rifle 3.6	Ice Hockey 18.0
Skiing 6.3	Lacrosse 12.0
Soccer 9.9	Rowing 20.0
Swimming 9.9	Skiing 7.0
Tennis 4.5	Soccer 12.0
Volleyball 4.5	Softball 12.0
Water Polo 4.5	Squash 5.0
Wrestling 9.9	Swimming 14.0
	Synchronized Swimming 5.0
	Team Handball 10.0
	Water Polo 8.0

Some Division I institutions offer cross-country but not track and field.

These institutions may offer 5.0 equivalencies for men and 6.0 equivalences for women in cross-country.

Equivalency Limits For Division II Sports

Men's Sports	Women's Sports
Baseball 9.0	Archery 5.0
Basketball 10.0	Badminton 8.0
Cross-Country/Track 12.6	Basketball 10.0
Fencing 4.5	Bowling 5.0
Football 36.0	Cross-Country/Track 12.6
Golf 3.6	Fencing 4.5
Gymnastics 5.4	Field Hockey 6.3
Ice Hockey 13.5	Golf 5.4
Lacrosse 10.8	Gymnastics 6.0
Rifle 3.6	Ice Hockey 18.0
Skiing 6.3	Lacrosse 9.9
Soccer 9.0	Rowing 20.0
Swimming 8.1	Soccer 9.9
Tennis 4.5	Softball 7.2
Volleyball 4.5	Squash 9.0
Water Polo 4.5	Swimming 8.1
Wrestling 9.0	Synchronized Swimming 5.0
	Team Handball 2.0
	Tennis 6.0
	Volleyball 8.0
	Water Polo 8.0

All Division II sports are considered equivalency sports.

Football, Basketball, and Baseball Special Considerations

Football, basketball, and baseball are the three sports that dominate the American media's attention. These sports all originated in America and each has a rich history of great players, great plays, great games, and zealous fans. Because of their traditions and histories, each of the games is experiencing intense media coverage that in no small part motivates young people with athletic interest to aim for participation, if not glory, by competing in one of the sports.

Not long ago, basketball and football players aspiring to the professional leagues learned and perfected their craft while in college. Aspiring baseball players developed their major-league skills at the minor-league level. Few college baseball players went on to become major-league stars.

While professional football leagues have wisely maintained (except in a few highly publicized instances) their policy of drafting players from college, professional basketball leagues have begun drafting high-school players who are college-basketball prospects. Both sports allow college underclassman to announce their availability for their sport's draft. More baseball players are emerging from the college ranks, although the best prospects are inundated with offers of money to forego their college education and continue their development in the minor leagues.

Football, basketball, and baseball are securely woven into the sports culture of America and are the goals for most aspiring American athletes. Because of this, special attention must be paid to the necessary preparation required to become a prospect and to the recruiting circumstances unique to each.

Football

Many high-school football players who are college prospects get strung along as they seek roster positions and financial aid. Remember, coaches aren't trying to harm any prospect; their priority is fielding a winning team.

Good college football coaches create a prospect depth chart for the positions for which they are recruiting (computer software is available that helps coaches organize both a depth chart and a prospect chart). Their preference would be to recruit the prospect that is their first choice (number one on the position depth chart). They know, however, that often they will lose their first choice to another college, so they need to have a second and third choice, perhaps even more.

To be certain that coaches keep all the prospects on the depth chart strongly considering their programs, they usually treat all prospects as if they were their first choice. If you happen to be the coach's third or fourth choice, you may think you're as good as successfully recruited because of the way the coach talks to you. But more likely than not, the phone calls and promises will abruptly stop because the coach has successfully recruited a prospect higher on the position depth chart.

You must never allow yourself to be strung along. You must ask early in the recruiting process where you are listed on the recruiting depth chart for your position. Coaches rarely deceive a prospect when asked a direct question. If you are listed as number three, for example, but you really want to join that program, tell the coach that you want him or her to continue considering you for the roster position. You also want to increase your leverage in the process. *Coach, I appreciate that you think there might be another player that can play my position better than me. Your program is my first choice, and*

I look forward to demonstrating that I'm the type of player you're looking for. I'm talking to (two, three) other coaches about their programs, so if you choose not to include me in your plans, would you please let me know so I can sign with another college? Then, be quiet.

While your profile is important, football coaches rarely recruit players without first seeing videotape of them playing. That is why the creation of a video is so vital to your being successfully recruited. Refer back to the section concerning creating an effective videotape.

Many football coaches sponsor or attend football camps or combines. Be sure you know which coaches will be working or attending the combine or camp you attend. Combines are usually organized around a number of activities that allow attending coaches to evaluate speed, power, courage, and strength of prospects. Camps are designed with football skill development as the primary objective. Many coaches attend the best camps in search of prospects. The wise football prospect will be certain to attend at least one camp and one combine.

Basketball

Basketball is the toughest recruiting challenge for a prospect. Why? There are fewer roster positions and scholarships available than in most other major sports.

If it is important to you to play intercollegiate basketball (as opposed to practicing as the "scout squad" against your school's real team), you will want to maintain a higher level of flexibility in your negotiations with the coach. Because of the number of scholarships available, wise prospects have three to four potential programs they are negotiating with in order to ensure a roster position and a solid financial aid package.

As with football, videotape is an essential ingredient to your successful recruitment. Create yours carefully, using the suggestions provided in the videotape section.

Include in your video episodes of ball-handling drills; demonstrate your shooting ability, using every shot you have developed. This is especially important to centers and power forwards as they need to demonstrate they can face the basket and score as well as possess shots that begin with their backs to the basket. Players in these positions must also demonstrate that they can and will score in the face of an opponent.

As with football, participation at prestigious or elite camps is essential to creating massive exposure. Shoot-outs are also great venues for basketball exposure. If your coach doesn't enter your team in a summer shoot-out, ask him or her to enter one in your area.

Coaches like shoot-outs for scouting purposes as it gives them the opportunity to observe their prospect really playing basketball with all its intensity and skill, demanding the best of the players. Try to learn which coaches will be scouting the shoot-outs you attend.

Baseball

No matter how accomplished you are in the field, no matter your speed from home to first or in the outfield, no matter how strong or accurate your throwing arm (unless you are a pitcher), if you can't hit the baseball, you won't be recruited. Learn to hit. If you can hit, learn to hit better. Batting cages, baseball camps that emphasize hitting, hitting coaches, hitting instructional videos and books, batting tees, and wiffle balls should be a part of your preparation to be a successfully recruited baseball prospect.

Baseball camps and summer leagues are a must for the aspiring intercollegiate baseball prospect. Your video must emphasize your hitting ability. If you are a pitcher, you must emphasize the speed of your fastball as well as its location.

Chapter 19

Solving the Division III Athletic Financial Aid Mystery

This chapter shatters Myth #1: NCAA Regulations and Bylaws disallow Division III institutions from awarding financial aid based on athletic ability. However, it is important to recognize that the vast majority of students participating in sports at the Division III level are receiving substantial financial aid packages. Very many of these financial aid awards are at or near full-ride levels, which means that Division III colleges are funding the education of student athletes. How they accomplish that funding is the focus of this chapter.

The NCAA Regulations impacting the types and amounts of financial aid that Division III colleges can award student athletes, by rule, must also be available to all students. The regulations of NCAA rule 15.4.9 states: "The composition of the financial aid package offered to a student athlete *shall be consistent with the established policy* of the institution's financial aid office for all students..." [italics mine]

Rule 15.4.9(c) states: "The financial aid package for a particular student athlete cannot be *clearly distinguishable from the general pattern* of all financial aid for all recipients (of financial aid) at the institution..." [italics mine]

Rule 15.4.9(a) states: "A member institution *shall not consider athletics ability* as a criterion in the formulation of the financial aid package..." [italics mine] (Rules 15.49, 15.49(c), and 15.49(a) are from *NCAA Manual*, NCAA, 1996, p. 219).

After receiving a profile from one of my clients, a Midwest Division III private college basketball coach contacted her and said she was interested in having her play basketball for the school and asked if she would come to campus for a visit. Prior to the visit, all the pertinent documents were sent to the admissions and financial aid offices. She and her father visited the school, which was not too far from their home. They met the coach, who they liked, and explored the campus with a student guide who was also a basketball player. My client was able to ask questions of the guide, the coach, the athletic director, and others at the admissions office. The tour ended at the financial aid office. The officer presented a financial aid package that I felt was quite generous, filled with impressive grants, awards, and loans, but no athletic scholarship. Her father knew not to expect any, but knew from our discussions that he should negotiate if he felt that she should receive more aid. They both knew that this college was their first choice even though they had two others with whom they were in serious discussions.

He reviewed the award letter in front of the officer and declared that it was close to what he had hoped but that he "needed a little more help to get the package to match another college's offer that interested his daughter, as well." The officer asked which college, and found that it happened to be in the same conference. "How much more have you been offered?" It was approximately $1,000. The officer said that she would review the package with the financial aid director and get back to them the following day, which she did. "We can give you an additional $500 in your academic award." As suggested, he replied, "I'm sorry, but that is $500 that will be very difficult for me to raise, isn't there anything else that can be done?" The officer said that she didn't have the authority to offer any more and suggested that he call the women's basketball coach. He did and explained what had transpired with the financial aid office and that even though her school was their first choice she would be attending the other school and playing basketball for them. The coach asked him to give her another day before the oral commitment to the other school was made so she could have time to "modify the offer." The athletic director called an hour later and explained to the father that if his daughter would send a short essay on why she wanted to attend and would discuss the essay with him, he would be able to award her an "Interview Scholarship" of $500. She received a great education at that school and played basketball there for four years.

NCAA Division III coaches or recruiters are obliged to tell you that they can't/don't offer scholarships for athletic ability (i.e., athletic scholarships). Still, substantial financial aid will very often be awarded to a prospective student athlete. A potential financial aid award for a prospective student athlete by an NCAA Division III school will never be discussed with you in terms of athletic scholarships or athletic ability. Many of these institutions have learned how to use the scholarship "name game." Play along.

Financial aid will likely be discussed in terms of merit awards, leadership awards, academic and honors awards, loans, employment, "awards of circumstance," and institutional awards. Institutional awards have many names, some of the more common names are: presidential award, founders grant, trustees award, leadership scholarship, etc.

Most colleges offer an institutional grant. Some offer more than one, each grant being given different names. This institutional grant, no matter what name the college chooses to give it, is a discount on the "sticker price" of that college. The grant often has the college's name as part of the grant title, but some colleges use very creative names.

The meaning is clear. Many NCAA Division III institutions award financial aid to prospects because of athletic ability; but invent an award name so that it appears that the award is for some other criteria.

Very simply, that's the method used by NCAA Division III institutions that decide to circumvent Rule 15.4.2 and thereby makes scholarship money available to students with athletic ability.

If a college offers institutional grants, they are often described in the scholarship description section of the college catalog. The description of the grants may be similar to the following statement: "The (Beezer Benchbottom) Presidential Grant—given to students to meet their gift eligibility as determined by their financial need and the [name of the college/university's] Assistance Packaging Formula." Or "Institutionally funded financial aid offered to students to help defer their cost of an education." (Both use Institutional Methodology.) Or as the *U.S. News & World Report* article cited previously states, "Aid officials look at their own school's 'need' (that is, how badly they want you to attend based on your academic accomplishments or other talents) [could they possibly mean athletic ability?] before deciding how much...financial aid...they'll actually award." It goes on to further illuminate the issue, "the first lesson in college economics: financial need is in the eye of the beholder."

ILLICIT FINANCIAL AID CASTS SHADOW ON DIVISION III
from the *NCAA News*

The Division III subcommittee of the NCAA President's Commission is presently considering restructuring in the areas of governance, membership, and championships, in addition to strengthening Division III transfer-eligibility legislation.

After reading the August 2, 1996, memorandum from the chair of the subcommittee, it is apparent that a sizeable part of its agenda deals with providing fair competition within the Division III membership. Though the committee's structural proposal for governance does include a "committee on eligibility and infraction," there was no mention of any emphasis on eliminating a major cause of our tilted playing field, that cause being illegal financial aid given to Division III student athletes.

Whether it is because there are no television contracts or no large amounts of money involved, there seems to be either a naïve assumption that financial aid violations do not occur at the Division III level or a lack of desire to resolve or even acknowledge the problem.

Well, there is a problem. It is of significant dimensions and not much is being done about it.

The regulations concerning financial aid for student athletes are defined clearly in the NCAA Manual. Bylaw 15.01.10 states that Division III institutions shall award financial aid to student athletes only on the basis of financial need shown by the recipient. Bylaw 15.4 delineates the situations in which athletic ability is not allowed to be a criterion for awarding financial aid.

Yet, in the name of winning, some Division III coaches and administrations are sacrificing their personal and professional integrity, as well as putting the reputation of their schools at risk, by awarding excessive financial aid to student athletes under the guise of leadership, merit, or presidential (or other inventive titles) scholarships.

No matter what the competitive level or reward for winning, these violations of the financial aid rules have no justification. The present Division III administrative restructuring process provides the NCAA with a great and timely opportunity to increase the emphasis on dealing with these violations and those who commit them.

It is also our responsibility as coaches and administrators to deal with the rule breakers. We are supposed to be builders of character, examples of commitment, and role models for the acceptance of responsibility.

We know violations are occurring. Many of us know some who are guilty. Yet, for some reason closely akin to the misguided principle of "honor among thieves," we have allowed and abetted behavior we would not accept from our players or children.

Chris Murphy,
Head Basketball Coach
Maine Maritime Academy

Often financial aid is awarded based on need. Where financial aid money is concerned, need can mean almost anything. Technically though, this type of award is meant to be based on the financial need of the student. But it has become quite obvious that many Division III institutions have used their unique Assistance Packaging Formula to broaden the meaning of need to mean nearly anything that accommodates perceived needs that are designated and defined, openly or secretly, by the institution and arbitrarily protected by the formula. We need rebounds.

This formula, while usually having financial aid award elements consistent with other institutions is uniquely designed to meet the needs—we need pass receptions—of the particular institution and its students. The institution alone decides what its needs—we need strikeouts—are. The institution alone decides how it will structure its assistance packaging formula. If the college's need—we need sprinters—happens to be powerful or improved athletic teams: well, this isn't brain surgery, is it?

In other words, the institutions are free to structure their assistance packaging formulas so they have considerable flexibility. The institution is also free to name the financial aid grants they award any student or student athlete for the purpose of either enhancing or concealing the real purpose of the financial aid award. The director of financial aid is the staff member responsible for accomplishing the institution's enrollment goal. S/He normally has great latitude to be flexible in deciding which prospective student gets what level of assistance and from what category according to the assistance packaging formula. This latitude, literally written into the enabling federal legislation, is called "professional judgment." A financial aid director using "professional judgment" can change the rules whenever it suits his/her purpose. (We need Iron Crosses.)

College administrators, usually directors of financial aid, decide which prospects "meet" (qualify) the "established criteria" of the financial aid assistance packaging formula. Just as importantly, these administrators also get to decide the meaning for measuring the qualifying terms such as, "consideration, clearly distinguishable, consistent, and general pattern" in designing the institution's award packaging formula. They are also given the freedom, enabled by federal legislation, to use their professional judgment.

The coach of a powerful Division III athletic program stated in an alumni newsletter "If private schools choose to be marginal in their ethics when it comes to awarding scholarships and grants, they can have a pretty good financial aid package." And Fredrick Starr, former president of Oberlin College stated, "There are many gray areas in the aid formulas. And increasingly, colleges are using aid to shape their classes to ensure that they include students with all the backgrounds and talents the schools are seeking." I'll let you decide what the backgrounds and talents might be for any particular school. The fact is an ever-increasing number of colleges are luring talented

THE TRUTH IS

A great minority of Division III institutions use institutional needs, professional judgment, assistance packaging formulas, and other devices, gimmicks, and methods to circumvent or bend NCAA recruiting rules and regulations.

freshmen with special inducements like grants and loans based on academic merit, leadership ability (you, like college admission officers, can interpret that term to fit certain needs), and special skills. (We need takedowns.)

A confidential study by the National Association of College and University Business Officers Director of Research Robin Jenkins says, "The price warfare is beginning to resemble the frequent-flier programs in the airline industry."

As recently as August 2004, the NCAA's Executive Committee has approved a rule requiring institutions to file, by December 2004, with the NCAA their individual and conference recruiting regulations in an additional attempt to force colleges to comply with the recruiting rules. Violators would face NCAA sanctions.

* * *

After receiving a profile from one of my clients, a Division III state university contacted him to ask if he would come in for a visit to discuss playing football at the school. As it was a relatively small college with an unremarkable football program, I encouraged visiting because he might be able to start as a freshman, which was important to him. He had mediocre grades and a 17 on the ACT and would have been unable to attend any Division I or II institution other than as a partial qualifier, yet was told by the coach that that wouldn't be a problem. I called the school and had a catalog sent to him. We met before he and his mom went on the visit, that was to a neighboring state. It was no surprise to me, although it was a shock to his mother and him, that according to the catalog he would be required to pay out-of-state tuition to the tune of $1,965 per semester. They knew they couldn't afford that amount; as a matter of fact, the prospect could only afford to go to a school where a financial aid package equaled nearly a full ride. The mom was reluctant to spend the money to go on a two-day college visit with little hope of her son being accepted. I called the coach, who of course knew that the prospect was on my service, and shared with him the prospect's mother's reluctance and asked him if he would "handle" the trip. He agreed to make it an official visit. I never spoke to him again.

I prepared the mother for the visit in the same manner the book prepares you for a college visit. We especially focused on the out-of-state tuition. During the interview with the coach, the mother expressed her inability to handle the costs of the prospect's education at that institution. The coach replied by asking her not to make any decision until he had talked with the people in admissions and financial aid. He explained to them that he couldn't accompany them to either office because of recruiting rules, but he was confident that her son would be offered a good package. When they were finished being presented with the financial aid package, he told them to ask the officer to call him and he would come to get them to take them to lunch. To their astonishment, they found that they were eligible for a full Pell Grant, a hefty academic award, a Stafford Loan, a minority/diversity grant (the prospect was Hispanic), a Leadership Award, and a waiver of the out-of-state tuition. Their out-of-pocket expenses were $785 per semester, which they could cover.

Even though my client struggled academically for the first year, he not only snagged the roster position; he was a starter after the second game of the season. He accepted the academic challenge his sophomore year, became a small college football hero, and graduated with honors.

Chapter 20

Interdepartmental Communications

NCAA rule 15.4.2 states: "All forms of financial assistance for student athletes shall be handled through the regular college agency or committee that administers financial aid for all students" (*NCAA Manual*, NCAA, p. 217).

Division III recruiting regulations forbid a coach, an athletic director, or for that matter, any person who as an interest in a particular athletic program or from the athletic department to have communications with the college's Financial Aid Department concerning financial aid for any prospective student athlete. This restriction is created to prevent athletic department representatives (coaches) from influencing or manipulating acceptance, enrollment, or a financial aid package on behalf of any prospect. A great concept.

Coaches recruit top prospects knowing full well that they can designate to the financial aid director those prospects who should be granted large financial aid packages that are sometimes nearly "full-rides."

THE TRUTH Is

A majority of Division III institutions tolerate this type of communication.

THE TRUTH Is

Some schools in fact encourage these types of communications or give permission to certain coaches within an athletic department to recruit top high-school prospects.

Many metaphorical terms are given to the recruiting practice whereby Division III coaches can recruit top prospects, promise them excellent financial aid packages, and know that the financial aid director will use his or her professional judgment to award that prospect what the coach has already promised. The most common term is called "chipping." This chipping has nothing to do with golf or potatoes. This is chipping as in "blue chip."

Some football coaches have been known to "move the goalpost" for a highly prized prospect. Some softball coaches have recognized the benefits of "shading the pole" for a pitcher who will take her team to the next level. Be alert the next time you watch a professional athletic contest. Listen for the athlete's names and colleges being announced prior to the battle. From time to time you'll hear the name of a college that may be unfamiliar to you. Find that college's home page on the Internet and visit the athletics link. Very often you will learn the NCAA Division of that college is Division III or an NAIA institution.

Division III, as well as NAIA (National Association of Intercollegiate Athletics) schools are often very competitive with many Division II and even some Division I programs. It is no accident that some of the nation's finest athletes can be found at these schools. Large financial aid packages (usually based on need, the prospect's financial need, or—we need home runs—

often play a crucial role in a student athlete's enrollment in an NCAA Division III or NAIA institution.

So if you are convinced you are a Division I prospect, but you feel you are being overlooked or are being strung along, your best choice for continuing your education and your athletic career, as well as receiving financial aid for your athletic ability, may well be at Division III or NAIA.

Twins were cut from a cheerleading squad as seniors in high school, even though they had been members since they were freshman. Rather than spend a lot of emotional energy on feeling sorry for themselves, they decided that they wanted to do something at school to replace the busy lives they led as cheerleaders. The school had a nascent swimming program so the sisters decided that they would try swimming, as it was a long winter season that was similar to the cheer season. With no prior competitive experience, the two of them quickly became the best team swimmers and team leaders, and they were rewarded with trip to the state swim meet. However, they were barely recruited.

The Division III school closest to their home (although just across the state border) that showed the most interest in them invited the twins and their parents for a visit. The twins loved the coach, the school, and the swim-team guides they met. In the interview with the coach after the campus tour and before their visit to admissions, the coach told them plainly that she wanted both girls on the team. The family discussed with her the cost of sending the twins to the college. Even though the family had been frugal and owned a modicum of assets, the father made it clear that he couldn't afford to send them without considerable help. The twins were not his only children.

The coach encouraged the family to join her in a trip to the admissions and financial aid offices (their admission and financial documents had already been received by the school). During the meeting at the financial aid office, the coach explained that she would be pleased if both girls could join the swimming program, but that the costs for both of them to attend would be prohibitive. The financial aid officer asked the father what it would take for both girls to come to the college. "Two for one," was his answer and then he remained quiet. After a short silence, the admissions officer replied, "We can do that."

The twins have graduated and are both successful teachers.

Other Benefits for Student Athletes

Student athletes often receive preferential treatment regarding admissions. You may not be quite as competitive academically as other students applying for admission and still be admitted to many Division III or NAIA colleges. Your status as an athletic prospect (we need goals) may cause you to receive a "waiver" of the academic entrance standards (SAT/ACT scores, GPA, class rank, etc.) required of other entering students. Because Division III offers no financial aid based on athletic ability, the NCAA allows Division III institutions to set their own admission standards. If a Division III college determines that a certain needy student (we need stuck dismounts) requires a loosening of the admissions requirements, the magic of professional judgment solves the problem.

Some athletic departments conform a little more closely to the regulations, yet still make their wishes known concerning financial aid awards and waivers for good prospects. They inform the admissions department or a counselor concerning what the financial aid requirements are for enrolling a hot or blue-chip prospect. Admissions passes the information on to financial aid so that it can work the magic of financial aid flexibility based on institutional methodology.

Sometimes a list of desirable prospects mysteriously appears on the desk of the appropriate financial aid officer. Then the assistance packaging formula can, with proper professional judgment flexibility, be fortuitously applied to those prospects' total financial aid packages. If an institution is found to be significantly violating recruiting rules and regulations, to its credit, the NCAA will deal with the violating institution in a severe manner. But:

The NCAA requests that violations be "self-reported," to the NCAA. Most often these self-reported violations are minor in nature and are usually followed by perfunctory NCAA action or no action taken.

Are there any Division III institutions that obey the recruiting regulations? Yes. Of course. You can find them—they are consistently at the bottom of their conference's standings.

THE TRUTH IS

The NCAA hasn't yet perfected the resources and it appears to have little desire to monitor Division III intensely enough to discover and punish the institutions that are intentionally violating the rules.

Some coaches of these obedient institutions write guest editorials in the *NCAA News*, a weekly newspaper sent to all NCAA members, pleading that the violations stop, asking that the playing field be level for all Division III institutions. The violations continue.

THE TRUTH IS

Most major violations are reported to the NCAA from outside the athletic program or by student athletes within the program.

As you have learned, many Division III programs do violate the spirit, if not the actual bylaws of the NCAA. You are now aware of this tendency to violate. And you also know how to use the strategies I've created to exploit the systemic violations of NCAA rules and regulations by Division III institutions.

You learned earlier from a letter from a Division III coach to the NCAA News that financial aid violations are regularly taking place. In the past, it appeared that the NCAA either couldn't or didn't want to enforce its own Division III recruiting regulations. Some coaches had accused the NCAA of simply denying that any infractions were occurring. But a long train of complaints and highly publicized violations combined with the potential of new technology has evidently brought the apologists and deniers out of their delusions.

At this writing, the violations continue. But on January 12, 2004, the NCAA Division III President's Council decided to consider a number of proposals. Some were agreed to and are to be implemented. Three of the proposals the council agreed to have a direct bearing on Division III recruiting and awarding of financial aid to Division III student athletes as reported in the NCAA News.

Also the Division III Management Council recommended to the Division III President's Council that institutions reporting no Level II (minor infractions) violations at the end of an academic year be required to certify that no violation occurred. This appears to be a thinly veiled attempt to force Division III institutions to improve their self-monitoring and self-reporting obligations to the NCAA.

So there's good news and bad news. The bad news is that violations are very common. The good news is that if you know the system, you can exploit it so that you get what you want and deserve.

One Exception

There is one minor exception in Division III that provides for athletic financial aid awards based on athletic ability. "The one exception is for endowment funds that Division III institutions received before January 1, 1979, and established specifically for student athletes. You can offer awards with these funds, so long as you comply with the other polices related to financial aid" (*Guide to Financial Aid*, NCAA, 1996, p. 162).

Proposal #55. Financial Aid-Athletic Endowments—which intends to stop the use of funds, endowed prior to January 1, 1979, to an institution specifically for recruiting student athletes. The effective date of this regulation is August 1, 2008.

The institutions included in the endowment group are: Clarkson College, Colorado College, Hartwick College, John Hopkins University, State University College at Oneonta, Rensselaer Polytechnic Institute, Rutgers, the State University of New Jersey, Newark, and St. Lawrence University.

It should be clear that the NCAA is attempting to regulate financial aid awards to student athletes enrolling in Division III institutions. It should be equally as clear that student athletes enrolling in those colleges can and do receive financial aid. The NCAA creates the parameters within which Division

III colleges are supposed to operate. Within those parameters, each institution makes its own individual, unique financial aid award decisions. Very often, decisions to award financial aid dramatically stretch and often break the recruiting rules and regulations.

Chapter 21

Division III's Pleasant Surprise

As the foregoing has noted, Division III institutions state that they don't (with the one designated endowment exception) offer financial aid based on athletic ability. You have learned that all divisions (including Division III) have great flexibility in packaging financial aid awards.

You have also learned that many students attending Division III colleges are playing sports and receiving substantial financial aid. Athletic scholarships awarded by Division II and I are usually awarded on a year-to-year basis. The coach is very often the person who decides if your athletic financial aid is renewed.

Usually, the only way you can lose your financial aid when enrolled in a Division III institution is because your academic performance doesn't meet the institution's publicly announced standards. That standard is normally related to a student's grade point average.

Poor performance during an athletic season isn't supposed to be used as a reason or excuse for reducing the amount of a financial aid package. In fact, you should be able to quit the team and maintain your financial aid package as though you were still on the team. After all, if you weren't awarded any financial aid because of your athletic ability, how can you lose financial aid because you choose to no longer participate in athletics? Your Division III financial aid had nothing to do with you being a recruited student athlete. Right?

Chapter 22

Negotiate, Negotiate, Negotiate

You too can and should use the very same flexibility that Division III assistance-packaging formulas provide the college's financial aid director. Deciding to negotiate, but never using that term, and knowing on what basis and what strategies to negotiate with can produce substantial benefits.

Remember, Division III coaches are obliged to tell you, and will always tell you, that the college doesn't offer athletic scholarships. After the coach has made his obligatory comment concerning no athletic scholarships, listen carefully to the next comments.

If those comments indicate that the college "creates excellent financial aid packages," or "works very hard to be sure that our athletes get every dollar they're entitled to," or "we have lots of financial aid available" or "nobody can give you more financial aid than we can" or "we have a strong recruiting program" or "we'll match any financial aid package you're offered" (many financial aid departments will actually request that you send a copy of your financial aid award letter from another school for the purpose of matching it) or similar comments, let the negotiations begin. Each of the foregoing comments have been made to my clients when they talked to Division III coaches that were interested in them.

Start your part of the initial negotiations with something like this: *Coach, you're our first choice, so I'm happy to hear that about financial aid, because the amount of financial aid my son/daughter gets will be crucial in the enrollment decision we make.*

Remember, when discussing financial aid with a Division III coach you must avoid using the term "athletic scholarship" or any similar terms. This creates real difficulties for the coach. He/she may feel that it's not in the program's best interest to recruit you.

As you negotiate a financial aid package with a coach, recruiter, or financial aid officer, be sure you are prepared for the discussion by reviewing the paragraphs and scripts from chapters 10, 11, 13, and 15. Have your questions ready.

Many parents make the unfortunate mistake of immediately asking, "How much financial aid is my son/daughter going to get?" This is a colossal error because it immediately puts the coach on the defensive. The coach probably has a good idea of what you can contribute to his/her program, but knows nothing about your EFC# or other pertinent factors used in determining your financial aid package.

Ask first about academics, housing, cost per credit hour, instructor-to-pupil ratio, major fields of study available, food plan, percentage of program athletes who graduate in four/five years, etc. Remember, the coach is interested in the quality of his/her program, not about the financial aid concerns of any one prospect. It's likely that he/she is recruiting between two and four prospects for the position you want.

Most coaches and financial aid departments are in no position to tell you how much financial aid will be forthcoming on the occasion of your first contact with them. They need transcripts and ACT/SAT scores provided to the Admissions

Office and the Student Aid Report (SAR) made available to the Financial Aid Office.

Only after these documents are in the hands of both admissions and financial aid counselors can they begin to determine the financial aid implications for you and your parents. Only then do they have the data to create a financial aid package using federal and state government grants and loans (federal methodology) and institutional grants and scholarships (institutional methodology). Be persistent, but be patient.

Chapter 23

The Ultimate Negotiating Weapon

Your ultimate negotiating weapon is provided to you free of charge by the college's Financial Aid Office, sometimes called the Office of Financial Planning or Financial Planning Office. That weapon is the Financial Aid Award Letter. It is a letter or form from the college, which states by line item what financial aid awards, grants, loans, work study, etc. you are being offered. See sample Financial Aid Award Letter on page 99.

As you can see, the form is structured in such a way that you can indicate whether you accept or decline each item in the financial aid award package. The form identifies a date by which the completed form must be returned. If the financial aid offered on the Financial Aid Award Letter is not acceptable, or not what you agreed to with either the coach, admissions counselor, or financial aid officer, you must return it.

But first send a photocopied form to the coach with a note indicating why you've returned the letter or form and ask him/her to help you get what you want and deserve. If the coach wants you on the team, it is highly likely that someone from the institution's Financial Aid Office will be contacting you shortly to review your financial aid package. Probably they will revise the financial aid award to better meet your needs.

This is typically the type of situation for serious negotiation. You must be ready to use all your negotiation strategies and techniques presented to you in chapters 10, 11, 13, and 15. Generally, what you receive with the first Financial Aid Award Letter is your individual sticker price. It's the price that institution hopes you will settle for. The sticker price can often be changed through negotiations. Remember the "souk-like haggling" mentioned in chapter 1? This is when very serious haggling happens. Be prepared to negotiate.

Here are some suggestions for your negotiation opener:

I'd love for my son/daughter to come to your college, it's his/her first choice and ours, too. For him/her to go there, we need a little more help than what is in the award letter. Could you take a look at the package and see if my son/daughter can be awarded an additional $500/$1,000/$3,000 or more?

or

We've nearly got a deal here. We need an additional ($750) for my son/daughter to be able to attend the university. Can you review the package and see if in your professional judgment the amount of the award could be increased?

or

I'm sorry, but I was under the impression that my son/daughter would qualify for ($12,500) in financial aid. The award letter only provides for an ($11,000) package. My son/daughter won't be able to attend unless he/she receives that level of help. That will be a shame because you are our first choice.

On the other hand, if the coach can't get additional financial aid or doesn't want to ask the Financial Aid Office for more aid, he/she will contact you. By his/her explanation you will know that you have been awarded all you will receive from that institution. Then it's time to decide to accept the package or move on to another program's offer. (You are negotiating with more than one college, aren't you?)

Once you have made your decision about which college you will attend, it's very important that you notify the other institutions that you've been negotiating with that you will be attending another school. This may well provide someone who is being strung along an opportunity to be recruited and receive financial aid based on his/her athletic ability.

Whether it is called a scholarship, grant, financial aid, or any other name (except a loan), this is an amount of money that you or your parents will not have to pay "out of pocket." Many student athletes receive financial aid that is called or titled everything from a Presidential Grant to a Room Grant to a Leadership Grant, or whatever. Don't get caught up in the semantics of what these funds are called.

THE TRUTH Is

Few colleges refuse to reconsider award letters. A substantial majority of American colleges are under extreme pressure to enroll students. They discount tuition and accommodate other needs whenever possible.

Remember this: Talk is cheap, if you don't have it in writing you have nothing. Get it in writing; it will come in the form of an award letter or a similar format.

Chapter 24

How Do I Contribute to My Future Success?

It's easy. Easier said than done. But you can ensure the kind of future you want for yourself by understanding that those who are the most successful in life recognize that there is no substitute for the will to prepare.

You first prepare by planning. As you know, very few high school athletes continue their athletic careers in college. Just to remind you, less than 10 percent of high-school football players will play in college. Less than 5 percent of high-school basketball players will play in college. Even if you receive a questionnaire from a college coach, the odds are better than 50 to 1 against you receiving a roster position on that college team. So you must prepare for more important things than competing in athletic contests. You must prepare academically to be successfully recruited, as well as being prepared for the more important things coming in your future. Here's how:

Freshman Year
- Get a physical examination from a doctor; present the results to your school's athletic department.
- Meet with your counselor; tell him/her of your goal of playing college sports.

- Ask for an academic plan that prepares to meet the core curriculum requirements that includes courses that can make you an attractive prospect.
- Meet again to discuss your sophomore schedule to be certain you are taking courses that meet the NCAA standards.

Sophomore Year

- Prepare for the ACT/SAT by taking the PACT/PSAT. Take the test at least twice, and more often if possible.
- Watch the NCAA video–*ABC's of Eligibility for College-Bound Student-Athletes*. Your counselor or athletic director should have a copy.
- Meet with your counselor at the end of the first semester to review your transcript and plan your junior courses.

Junior Year

- Tell your coach you want to continue your athletic career in college.
- Take PSAT/PACT again for a final practice before taking the test at the National Testing Site.
- Get a copy of *NCAA Guide for the College-Bound Student-Athlete*. Be certain you are complying with all the regulations. Discuss the *Guide* with your parents.
- Attend your school's college search day. Talk with all schools in which you have any interest.
- Send profiles to at least 50 colleges during the early part of your second semester.
- Sit for the SAT or ACT on the National Testing Date in the winter. Be sure to see your score as soon as possible. If you're not satisfied with the score, sit for the test on the spring National Testing Date.

- Begin recruiting activities as recommended in this book.
- Begin visiting colleges.

Senior Year

- Meet with your counselor during the first month of school. Review your transcript to be certain you will meet the NCAA Clearinghouse requirements.
- Meet with your coach. Ask his/her advice about improving your chances to continue your athletic career in college and recommendations for schools to consider.
- Begin mailing college applications.
- You have three more National Testing Days for the ACT/SAT. Take the test until you are satisfied that you have attained your best score.

How do you continue to prepare? By committing to yourself, every day, that you will be the best student and the best athlete you can be. How can you accomplish that? You must think, hustle, study, practice, concentrate, persist, focus, and win. You must always believe in yourself. Remember: winners never quit and quitters never win.

Usually when a book of this type ends, the reader is wished good luck. Sorry.

Consider yourself lucky if you're not lazy. Consider yourself lucky if you don't quit. Consider yourself lucky if you believe in yourself.

THE TRUTH Is

Luck will have very, very little to do with your becoming successfully recruited. Luck will also have little to do with your success and fulfillment as an adult.

Create your own luck. Follow the suggestions of *The Sports Scholarships Insider's Guide* so you can be successfully recruited, continue your athletic career, and receive financial aid for your athletic ability. Good courage, good skill, and good preparation.

Glossary of Recruiting Terms

athletic scholarship: A discount or grant-in-aid, based on athletic ability, subtracted from the announced tuition and fees of a college.

blue-chip prospect: A student athlete who has demonstrated during high-school competition that he/she has exceptional ability and will likely have an immediate impact on a top-level Division I program.

booster: Any person who demonstrates an interest in a specific sport or in the athletic program of any NCAA college. NCAA prospects or student athletes will lose all NCAA eligibility if found to respond to any direct contact of a booster, including phone calls, mail, or in person.

campus visit: *Official Visit*—A visit that is paid for by the recruiting institution, including: transportation, food, lodging, and entertainment for the prospect. *Unofficial Visit*—A visit that is paid for by the prospect. A prospect can have an unlimited number of unofficial visits to a campus.

combine: A series of tests, measures, and drills used by college coaches to determine the potential of many prospects at one time.

contact: Any face-to-face meeting among a prospect, his/her parents, and any representative (official or unofficial) of a recruiting institution.

core courses: Fourteen required courses in which a prospect must earn a C average. Generally, the courses include: 4 years of English, 2 years of math, 2 years of science, 2 years of social science, and an additional 4 courses drawn from any of the other categories.

division: The NCAA has three divisions: I, II, and III. The NAIA has two divisions: 1 and 3. Recruiting rules vary by division and association.

early signing period: A one-week period in November during which prospects other than football players may sign a National Letter of Intent that commits an athlete to a specific school.

financial aid: Discounts of tuition, fees, and other associated costs that are not based on athletic ability. Athletic ability is likely to be an important factor in the granting of financial aid. Conference and association rules vary, but many schools who claim that they don't offer athletic scholarships still provide substantial financial aid to students who are athletes too.

gender equity: Colleges are required to provide athletic opportunities for women in proportion to the school's population.

graduation rate: The number and percentage of student athletes who have graduated from a college within a six-year period.

JUCO: An acronym for the term "junior college." It identifies two-year junior and community colleges.

Letter of Intent: A document that binds a prospect to a particular institution when signed by the student athlete. The college is bound to provide an agreed-upon athletic scholarship.

NAIA: The National Association of Intercollegiate Athletics is an association of close to 400 small to medium colleges. They sponsor 26 sports for men and women.

23500 West 105th Street

Olate, KS 66051-1325

(913) 791-0044

www.naia.org

Member Institutions

www.naia.org/local/memberschools.html

NCAA: The National Collegiate Athletic Association is an organization consisting of member institutions that create rules and regulations governing eligibility, recruiting, and all aspects of competition for its over 800 members.

700 West Washington St.

P.O. Box 6222

Indianapolis, IN 46206-6222

(317) 917-6222

www.ncaa.org

NCAA Initial Eligibility Clearinghouse: The Clearinghouse is a department of the NCAA that gathers prospects' test scores and transcripts. It provides eligibility information to both colleges and the prospect.

The NCAA provides a brochure, "Making Sure You Are Eligible to Participate in College Sports," that has a Student Release form. It can be obtained from either your high-school counselor or from the NCAA at their Internet website, www.ncaa.org, or by calling and requesting a form at (319) 337-1492.

Proposition 48: The proposition that created the NCAA regulation that requires prospects to score at least minimum scores on standardized tests and achieve at least a C in the core courses as identified by the Clearinghouse.

prospect: A student athlete who has entered at least ninth grade and has drawn the interest of college recruiters.

qualifier: A prospect that has achieved the grade requirements in the core courses while achieving the minimum acceptable score on the ACT or SAT.

questionnaire: A document that asks a prospect for personal, academic, and athletic information.

recruiting: The process of identifying, contacting, evaluating, persuading, and signing prospects.

Recruiting Calendar: The annual sequence of periods during which coaches may contact prospects by mail or telephone and make home visits, and when prospects can officially visit a college and sign a Letter of Intent.

Recruiting Service: A company that offers to help a prospect by either locating schools that may match the prospect's interests or provide athletic and academic information about prospects to college coaches.

redshirting: The practice of holding a player out of competition for a year. The athlete may still practice with the team. Coaches typically redshirt student athletes so they can add size, strength, or skill, or be in a better depth-chart position for the next season. Injured athletes are sometimes redshirted.

representative of athletic interests: Anyone, whether or not they have an official connection with a school, who supports or assists the school in its recruiting efforts.

scholarship athlete: A student athlete who has been given some form of financial aid based on athletic ability.

signing day: The NCAA designates a day that starts the period when prospects can sign Letters of Intent. Most sports sign in April except for football, which signs in February or during the Early Signing Period in November.

sport camp/clinic: Fee-based sessions during which participants are to receive intensive and qualified coaching in their particular sport. Too often these sessions are used to attract college coaches to evaluate blue-chip talent, with the result that the other participants receive little coaching attention.

strung along: When a prospect is not the number-one choice of a recruiting coach but receives the same treatment as the prospect who is number one.

tape: A videotape that illustrates a prospect's athletic performance or skills.

test scores: An NCAA Division II prospect must score a 700 on the SAT or a 17 on the ACT. NCAA Division I prospects' tests must be combined with their GPAs to determine eligibility. There is a sliding scale, which can be found in your *NCAA Guide for College-Bound Student-Athletes*. For the NAIA, the requirements are 18 ACT or a 740 SAT + 2.00 GPA.

tryout: Practice episodes that demonstrate athletic potential by measuring, weighing, or timing a prospect. They may engage in practice-type games or scrimmages as a part of the tryout. In NCAA divisions, only Division II can hold tryouts. NAIA schools can also hold tryouts.

verbal commitment: The announced intention of a prospect to accept a scholarship from a particular school. Verbal commitments are not binding on prospects.

walk-on: A prospect who opts to try out for a roster position with a college team without receiving an athletic scholarship.

Appendix 1

Additional Resources

Statistical Inventory

Approximate Number of Student Athletes by Division

Division	Men	Women	Total
I	85,800	62,800	148,600
II	45,300	29,500	74,800
III	79,900	57,900	137,800
Total	211,000	150,200	361,200

NCAA Women's Sports Sponsorships

Division	I	II	III
archery	3	0	0
badminton	0	0	3
basketball	325	276	422
bowling	29	15	2
cross-country	321	252	367
equestrian	13	0	0
fencing	25	3	15
field hockey	76	26	153
golf	225	99	142
gymnastics	64	6	15
ice hockey	30	2	40
lacrosse	77	32	149
rifle	11	0	2
rowing	85	16	42

NCAA Women's Sports Sponsorships *(continued)*

Division	I	II	III
rugby	1	0	1
skiing	16	9	18
soccer	295	203	398
softball	265	254	389
swimming	187	68	232
synchronized swimming	3	1	3
tennis	312	210	357
track (indoor)	289	108	219
track (outdoor)	294	156	252
volleyball	312	260	407
water polo	30	10	18

NCAA Men's Sports Sponsorships

Division	I	II	III
baseball	286	227	352
basketball	327	278	390
cross-country	306	224	340
fencing	20	3	13
football	238	151	229
golf	290	192	263
gymnastics	17	1	2
ice hockey	58	7	69
lacrosse	54	29	129
rifle	4	0	4
skiing	14	8	17
soccer	199	157	373
swimming	143	52	191

tennis	269	166	307
track (indoor)	247	106	208
track (outdoor)	264	151	243
volleyball	23	15	43
water polo	21	9	16
wrestling	86	39	98

Financial Aid Information Resources

Websites

Finaid: Financial Aid Information Page at www.finaid.com

Worldwide College Scholarship Directory at www.800headstart.com

College Costs and Financial Aid at www.collegeboard.org

SallieMae Student Loans at www.salliemae.com

FAFSA Information at www.fafsa.ed.gov

Merit Scholarships and Essay Contests at www.fastweb.monster.com

Essay Writing Tips at www.supercollege.com

Other Scholarships at www.wiredscholar.com

More information at www.CollegeSource4u.com

Federal Student Aid Programs at www.studentaid.ed.gov

Scholarship Announcements at www.scholarshipamerica.org

Other Scholarship Strategies at www.studentrewards.com

General Financial Aid Information at www.usnews.com and www.petersons.com and www.collegemoney.com

Financial Planning Calendar, Financial Aid Glossary, and a To Do List for Juniors at StudentLoanXpress.com

Books

Kaplan Scholarships 2003 (Kaplan, 2002)

The Complete Scholarship Book (Sourcebooks, 2000)

College Board Scholarship Handbook 2004 (2003)

1001 Ways to Pay for College (Supercollege)

Recommended Recruiting Service

National Recruiting Service at www.nationalrecruits.com

Appendix 2

Institution Contact Information

All colleges and universities have Internet websites. Connect to the athletics link and you will be presented with the information you'll need to contact any person in the Athletic Department. You can also research any information you wish.

Abilene Christian University
Abilene, TX
(325) 674-CATS x2287
www.acu.edu

Adams State College
Alamosa, CO
(719) 587-7402
www.adams.edu

Adelphi University
Garden City, NY
(516) 877-4240
www.adelphi.edu/

Adrian College
Adrian, MI
(517) 264-3972
www.adrian.edu

Agnes Scott College
Decatur, GA
(404) 471-6170
www.agnesscott.edu

Alabama A&M University
Normal, AL
(256) 372-4001
www.aamu.edu

Alabama State University
Montgomery, AL
(334) 229-4464
www.alasu.edu

Albany State University (Georgia)
Albany, GA
(229) 430-4673
asuweb.asurams.edu/asu/

Albertus Magnus College
New Haven, CT
(203) 773-8579
www.albertus.edu

Albion College
Albion, MI
(517) 629-0900
www.albion.edu

Albright College
Reading, PA
(610) 921-7535
www.albright.edu

Alcorn State University
Alcorn State, MS
(601) 877-6500
www.alcorn.edu

Alderson-Broaddus College
Philippi, WV
(304) 457-6262
blue.ab.edu

Alfred University
Alfred, NY
(607) 871-2193
www.alfred.edu

Allegheny College
Meadville, PA
(814) 332-2824
www.allegheny.edu

Alma College
Alma, MI
(989) 463-7279
www.alma.edu

Alvernia College
Reading, PA
(610) 796-8374
www.alvernia.edu

Alvernia College
Reading, PA
(610) 796-8374
www.alvernia.edu

**American
International College**
Springfield, MA
(413) 205-3939
www.aic.edu

American University
Washington, DC
(202) 885-3001
www.american.edu

Amherst College
Amherst, MA
(413) 542-2274
www.amherst.edu

**Anderson College
(South Carolina)**
Anderson, SC
(864) 231-2029
www.anderson-
college.edu

**Anderson University
(Indiana)**
Anderson, IN
(765) 641-4483
www.anderson.edu

**Angelo State
University**
San Angelo, TX
(325) 942-2091 x222
www.angelo.edu

Anna Maria College
Paxton, MA
(508) 849-3447
www.annamaria.edu

**Appalachian State
University**
Boone, NC
(828) 262-4010
www.appstate.edu

Arcadia University
Glenside, PA
(877) 272-2342
www.arcadia.edu

Arizona State University
Tempe, AZ
(480) 965-6360
www.asu.edu

**Arkansas State
University**
State University, AR
(870) 972-2082
www.astate.edu

**Arkansas Tech
University**
Russellville, AR
(479) 968-0345
www.atu.edu

**Armstrong Atlantic
State University**
Savannah, GA
(912) 921-5849
www.armstrong.edu

Ashland University
Ashland, OH
(419) 289-5441
www.ashland.edu

Assumption College
Worcester, MA
(508) 767-7279
www.assumption.edu

Auburn University
Auburn, AL
(334) 844-4750
www.auburn.edu

Augsburg College
Minneapolis, MN
(612) 330-1241
www.augsburg.edu

**Augusta State
University**
Augusta, GA
(706) 737-1626
www.aug.edu

**Augustana College
(Illinois)**
Rock Island, IL
(309) 794-7223
www.augustana.edu

**Augustana College
(South Dakota)**
Sioux Falls, SD
(605) 274-4335
www.augie.edu

Aurora University
Aurora, IL
(630) 844-5111
www.aurora.edu

Austin College
Sherman, TX
(903) 813-2499
www.austincollege.edu

**Austin Peay State
University**
Clarksville, TN
(931) 221-7904
www.aspu.edu

Averett University
Danville, VA
(434) 791-5701
www2.averett.edu

Babson College
Babson Park, MA
(781) 239-4528
www3.babson.edu

Baldwin-Wallace College
Berea, OH
(440) 826-2184
www.bw.edu

Ball State University
Muncie, IN
(765) 285-5131
www.bsu.edu

Baptist Bible College
Clarks Summit, PA
(570) 585-9256
www.bbc.edu

Bard College
Annandale-on-
Hudson, NY
(845) 758-7531
www.bard.edu

Barry University
Miami Shores, FL
(305) 899-3550
www.barry.edu

Barton College
Wilson, NC
www.barton.edu

Bates College
Lewiston, ME
(207) 786-6341
www.bates.edu

Bay Path College
Longmeadow, MA
(413) 565-1244
www.baypath.edu

Baylor University
Waco, TX
(254) 710-1222
www.baylor.edu

Becker College
Leicester, MA
(508) 791-9241 x464
www.beckercollege.edu

Bellarmine University
Louisville, KY
(502) 452-8380
www.bellarmine.edu

Belmont Abbey College
Belmont, NC
(704) 825-6809
www.bellmontabbey-
college.edu

Belmont University
Nashville, TN
(888) 9-BRUINS
www.belmont.edu

Beloit College
Beloit, WI
(608) 363-2229
www.beloit.edu

**Bemidji State
University**
Bemidji, MN
(218) 755-2941
www.bemidjistate.edu

Benedict College
Columbia, SC
www.benedict.edu

**Benedictine
University (Illinois)**
Lisle, IL
(630) 829-6150
www.ben.edu

Bennett College
Greensboro, NC
(336) 517-2256
www.bennett.edu

Bentley College
Waltham, MA
(781) 891-2256
www.bentley.edu

**Bernard M. Baruch
College**
New York, NY
(646) 312-5040
www.baruch.cuny.edu

**Bethany College
(West Virginia)**
Bethany, WV
(304) 829-7240
www.bethanywv.edu

Bethel University
St. Paul, MN
(651) 638-6396
www.bethel.edu

**Bethune-Cookman
College**
Daytona Beach, FL
(386) 481-2215
www.cookman.edu

**Birmingham-Southern
College**
Birmingham, AL
(205) 226-4936
www.bsc.edu

Blackburn College
Carlinville, IL
(217) 854-4321
www.blackburn.edu

Bloomfield College
Bloomfield, NJ
(973) 748-9000 x363
www.bloomfield.edu

Bloomsburg University of Pennsylvania
Bloomsburg, PA
(570) 389-4050
www.bloomu.edu

Bluefield State College
Bluefield, WV
(304) 327-4208
www.bluefield.wvnet.edu

Bluffton College
Bluffton, OH
(419) 358-3227
www.bluffton.edu

Boise State University
Boise, ID
(208) 426-1826
www.boisestate.edu

Boston College
Chestnut Hill, MA
(617) 552-8520
www.bc.edu

Boston University
Boston, MA
(617) 353-4683
www.bu.edu

Bowdoin College
Brunswick, ME
(207) 725-3327
www.bowdoin.edu

Bowie State University
Bowie, MD
(301) 860-3588
www.bowiestate.edu

Bowling Green State University
Bowling Green, OH
(419) 372-2401
www.bgsu.edu

Bradley University
Peoria, IL
(309) 677-2670
www.bradley.edu

Brandeis University
Waltham, MA
(781) 736-3663
www.brandeis.edu

Bridgewater College (Virginia)
Bridgewater, VA
(540) 828-5476
www.bridgewater.edu

Bridgewater State College
Bridgewater, MA
(508) 531-1352
www.bridgew.edu

Brigham Young University
Provo, UT
(801) 422-4837
www.byu.edu

Brigham Young University, Hawaii
Laie, HI
(808) 293-3764
www.byuh.edu

Brooklyn College
Brooklyn, NY
(718) 951-5366
www.brooklyn.cuny.edu

Brown University
Providence, RI
(401) 863-1086
www.brown.edu

Bryant College
Smithfield, RI
(401) 232-6070
www.bryant.edu

Bryn Mawr College
Bryn Mawr, PA
(610) 526-5364
www.brynmawr.edu

Bucknell University
Lewisburg, PA
(570) 577-1232
www.bucknell.edu

Buena Vista University
Storm Lake, IA
(712) 749-2253
www.bvu.edu

Buffalo State College
Buffalo, NY
(716) 878-6534
www.buffalostate.edu

Butler University
Indianapolis, IN
(317) 940-9878
www.butler.edu

C.W. Post Campus/Long Island University
Brookville, NY
(516) 299-2288
www.cwpost.liu.edu

Cabrini College
Radnor, PA
(610) 902-8571
www.cabrini.edu

Caldwell College
Caldwell, NJ
(973) 618-3260
www.caldwell.edu

California Institute of Technology
Pasadena, CA
(626) 395-6146
www.caltech.edu

California Lutheran University
Thousand Oaks, CA
(805) 493-3402
www.clunet.edu

California Polytechnic State University
San Luis Obispo, CA
(805) 756-2924
www.calpoly.edu

California State Polytechnic University, Pomona
Pomona, CA
(909) 869-4631
www.csupomona.edu

California State University, Bakersfield
Bakersfield, CA
(661) 664-2188
www.csub.edu

California State University, Chico
Chico, CA
(530) 898-6470
www.csuchico.edu

California State University, Dominguez Hills
Carson, CA
(310) 243-3893
www.csudh.edu

California State University, Fresno
Fresno, CA
(559) 278-2643
www.csufresno.edu

California State University, Fullerton
Fullerton, CA
(714) 278-2777
www.fullerton.edu

California State University, Hayward
Hayward, CA
(510) 885-3038
www.csuhayward.edu

California State University, Los Angeles
Los Angeles, CA
(323) 343-3080
www.calstatela.edu

California State University, Northridge
Northridge, CA
(818) 677-3208
www.csun.edu

California State University, Sacramento
Sacramento, CA
(916) 278-6481
www.csus.edu

California State University, San Bernardino
San Bernardino, CA
(909) 880-5011
www.csusb.edu

California State University, Stanislaus
Turlock, CA
(209) 667-3016
www.csustan.edu

California University of Pennsylvania
California, PA
(724) 938-4351
www.cup.edu

Calvin College
Grand Rapids, MI
(616) 526-6169
www.calvin.edu

Cameron University
Lawton, OK
(580) 581-2460
www.cameron.edu

Campbell University
Buies Creek, NC
(910) 893-1327
www.campbell.edu

Canisius College
Buffalo, NY
(716) 888-2972
www.canisius.edu

Capital University
Columbus, OH
(614) 236-6528
www.capital.edu

Carleton College
Northfield, MN
(507) 646-4056
www.carleton.edu

Carnegie Mellon University
Pittsburgh, PA
(412) 268-2346
www.cmu.edu

Carroll College (Wisconsin)
Waukesha, WI
(262) 524-7319
www.cc.edu

Carson-Newman College
Jefferson City, TN
(865) 471-3396
www.cn.edu

Carthage College
Kenosha, WI
(262) 551-5931
www.carthage.edu

Case Western Reserve University
Cleveland, OH
(216) 368-6517
www.cwru.edu

Castleton State College
Castleton, VT
(802) 468-1365
www.csc.vsc.edu

Catawba College
Salisbury, NC
(704) 637-4474
www.catawba.edu

Catholic University
Washington, DC
(202) 319-5286
www.cua.edu

Cazenovia College
Cazenovia, NY
(315) 655-7142
www.cazenovia.edu

Cedar Crest College
Allentown, PA
(610) 606-4634
www.cedarcrest.edu

Centenary College (Louisiana)
Shreveport, LA
(318) 869-5275
www.centenary.edu

Centenary College (New Jersey)
Hackettstown, NJ
(908) 852-1400
www.centenarycollege.edu

Central College (Iowa)
Pella, IA
(641) 628-5310
www.central.edu

Central Connecticut State University
New Britain, CT
(860) 832-3035
www.ccsu.edu

Central Michigan University
Mount Pleasant, MI
(989) 774-3046
www.cmich.edu

Central Missouri State University
Warrensburg, MO
(660) 543-4250
www.cmsu.edu

Central State University
Wilberforce, OH
(937) 376-6681
www.centralstate.edu

Central Washington University
Ellensburg, WA
(509) 963-1914
www.cwu.edu

Centre College
Danville, KY
(859) 238 5485
www.centre.edu

Chadron State College
Chadron, NE
(308) 432-6344
www.csc.edu

Chaminade University
Honolulu, HI
(808) 735-4790
www.chaminade.edu

Chapman University
Orange, CA
(714) 997-6691
www.chapman.edu

Charleston Southern University
Charleston, SC
(843) 863-7678
www.csuniv.edu

Chatham College
Pittsburgh, PA
(941) 236-51650
www.chatham.edu

Chestnut Hill College
Philadelphia, PA
(215) 248-7060
www.chc.edu

Cheyney University of Pennsylvania
Cheyney, PA
(610) 399-2287
www.cheyney.edu

Chicago State University
Chicago, IL
(773) 995-2295
www.csu.edu

Chowan College
Murfreesboro, NC
(252) 398-6468
www.chowan.edu

Christian Brothers University
Memphis, TN
(901) 321-3370
www.cbu.edu

Christopher Newport University
Newport News, VA
(757) 594-7217
www.cnu.edu

City College of New York
New York, NY
(212) 650-7550
www.ccny.cuny.edu

Claremont McKenna-Harvey Mudd-Scripps Colleges
Claremont, CA
(909) 607-3562
cms.claremont.edu

Clarion University of Pennsylvania
Clarion, PA
(814) 393-2079
www.clarion.edu

Clark Atlanta University
Atlanta, GA
(404) 880-8123
www.cau.edu

Clark University (Massachusetts)
Worcester, MA
(508) 793-7160
www.clarku.edu

Clarke College
Dubuque, IA
(563) 588-6462
www.clarke.edu

Clarkson University
Potsdam, NY
(315) 268-6622
www.clarkson.edu

Clayton College & State University
Morrow, GA
(770) 961-3465
www.clayton.edu

Clemson University
Clemson, SC
(864) 656-2114
www.clemson.edu

Cleveland State University
Cleveland, OH
(216) 687-4539
www.csuohio.edu

Coastal Carolina University
Conway, SC
(843) 347-3161
www.coastal.edu

Coe College
Cedar Rapids, IA
(319) 399-8622
www.coe.edu

Coker College
Hartsville, SC
www.coker.edu

Colby College
Waterville, ME
(207) 872-3258
www.colby.edu

Colby-Sawyer College
New London, NH
(603) 526-3609
www.colby-sawyer.edu

Colgate University
Hamilton, NY
(315) 824-7572
www.colgate.edu

College Misericordia
Dallas, PA
(570) 674-6294
www.misericordia.edu

College of Charleston (South Carolina)
Charleston, SC
(843) 953-8251
www.cofc.edu

College of Mount St. Joseph
Cincinnati, OH
www.msj.edu

College of Mount St. Vincent
Riverdale, NY
www.cmsv.edu

College of New Rochelle
New Rochelle, NY
(914) 654-5315
www.cnr.edu

College of Notre Dame (Maryland)
Baltimore, MD
(410) 532-3588
www.ndm.edu

College of Saint Elizabeth
Morristown, NJ
www.cse.edu

College of Saint Rose
Albany, NY
(518) 454-5158
www.strose.edu

College of St. Benedict
St. Joseph, MN
(320) 363-5301
www.csbsju.edu

College of St. Catherine
St. Paul, MN
(651) 690-8771
www.stkate.edu

College of St. Scholastica
Duluth, MN
www.css.edu

College of Staten Island
Staten Island, NY
(718) 982-3160
www.csi.cuny.edu

College of the Holy Cross
Worcester, MA
(508) 793-2571
www.holycross.edu

College of William and Mary
Williamsburg, VA
(757) 221-3330
www.wm.edu

College of Wooster
Wooster, OH
(330) 263-2500
www.wooster.edu

Colorado Christian University
Lakewood, CO
(303) 963-3185
www.ccu.edu

Colorado College
Colorado Springs, CO
(719) 389-6475
www.coloradocollege.edu

Colorado School of Mines
Golden, CO
(303)273-3095
www.mines.edu

Colorado State University
Fort Collins, CO
(970) 491-3350
www.colostate.edu

Colorado State University-Pueblo
Pueblo, CO
(719) 549-2711
www.colostate-pueblo.edu

Columbia Union College
Takoma Park, MD
(301) 891-4195
www.cuc.edu

Columbia University
New York, NY
(212) 854-2548
www.columbia.edu

Columbia University-Barnard College
New York, NY
(212) 854-2548
www.columbia.edu

Columbus State University
Columbus, GA
(706) 565-3531
www.colstate.edu

Concord College
Athens, WV
(304) 384-5347
www.concord.edu

Concordia College (New York)
Bronxville, NY
www.concordia-ny.edu

Concordia College, Moorhead
Moorhead, MN
(218) 299-4440
www.cord.edu

Concordia University (Illinois)
River Forest, IL
(708) 209-3192
www.curf.edu

Concordia University (Wisconsin)
Mequon, WI
(262) 243-4404
www.cuw.edu

Concordia University at Austin
Austin, TX
(512) 486-1162
www.concordia.edu

Concordia University, St. Paul
St. Paul, MN
(651) 641-8854
www.csp.edu

Connecticut College
New London, CT
(860) 439-2550
www.conncoll.edu

Converse College
Spartanburg, SC
(864) 577-2057
www.converse.edu

Coppin State College
Baltimore, MD
(410) 951-3737
www.coppin.edu

Cornell College
Mt. Vernon, IA
(319) 895-4257
www.cornellcollege.edu

Cornell University
Ithaca, NY
(607) 254-8706
www.cornell.edu

Creighton University
Omaha, NE
(402) 280-5810
www.creighton.edu

Curry College
Milton, MA
(617) 333-2216
www.curry.edu

D'Youville College
Buffalo, NY
(716) 881-8131
www.dyc.edu

Dallas Baptist University
Dallas, TX
(214) 333-5524
www.dbu.edu

Daniel Webster College
Nashua, NH
(603) 577-6498
www.dwc.edu

Dartmouth College
Hanover, NH
(603) 646-2465
www.dartmouth.edu

Davidson College
Davidson, NC
(704) 894-2000
www.davidson.edu

Davis and Elkins College
Elkins, WV
(304) 637-1251
www.davisandelkins.edu

Defiance College
Defiance, OH
(419) 783-2342
www.defiance.edu

Delaware State University
Dover, DE
(302) 857-6030
www.dsc.edu

Delaware Valley College
Doylestown, PA
(215) 489-2268
www.devalcol.edu

Delta State University
Cleveland, MS
(662) 846-4300
www.deltastate.edu

Denison University
Granville, OH
(740) 587-6428
www.denison.edu

DePaul University
Chicago, IL
(773) 325-7503
www.depaul.edu

DePauw University
Greencastle, IN
(765) 658-4934
www.depauw.edu

DeSales University
Center Valley, PA
(610) 282-1100 x1351
www.desales.edu

Dickinson College
Carlisle, PA
(717) 245-1320
www.dickinson.edu

Dominican College (New York)
Orangeburg, NY

Dominican University (Illinois)
River Forest, IL
(708) 524-6556
www.dom.edu

Dowling College
Oakdale, NY
(631) 244-3019
www.dowling.edu

Drake University
Des Moines, IA
(515) 271-2889
www.drake.edu

Drew University
Madison, NJ
(973) 408-3648
www.drew.edu

Drexel University
Philadelphia, PA
(215) 895-1416
www.drexel.edu

Drury University
Springfield, MO
(417) 873-7222
www.drury.edu

Duke University
Durham, NC
(919) 668-5700
www.duke.edu

Duquesne University
Pittsburgh, PA
(412) 396-5589
www.duq.edu

Earlham College
Richmond, IN
(765) 983-1483
www.earlham.edu

**East Carolina
University**
Greenville, NC
(252) 328-4600
www.ecu.edu

**East Central
University**
Ada, OK
www.ecok.edu

**East Stroudsburg
University of
Pennsylvania**
East Stroudsburg, PA
(570) 422-3642
www3.esu.edu

**East Tennessee State
University**
Johnson City, TN
(423) 439-4646
www.etsu.edu

**East Texas Baptist
University**
Marshall, TX
(903) 923-2228
www.etbu.edu

**Eastern Connecticut
State University**
Willimantic, CT
(860) 465-5169
www.easternct.edu

**Eastern Illinois
University**
Charleston, IL
(217) 581-7058
www.eiu.edu

**Eastern Kentucky
University**
Richmond, KY
(859) 622-2120
www.eku.edu

**Eastern Mennonite
University**
Harrisonburg, VA
(540) 432-4646
www.emu.edu

**Eastern Michigan
University**
Ypsilanti, MI
(734) 487-1050
www.emich.edu

**Eastern Nazarene
College**
Quincy, MA
(617) 745-3638
www.enc.edu

**Eastern New Mexico
University**
Portales, NM
(505) 562-2153
www.enmu.edu

Eastern University
St. Davids, PA
(610) 341-1785
www.eastern.edu

**Eastern Washington
University**
Cheney, WA
(509) 359-2461
www.ewu.edu

Eckerd College
St. Petersburg, FL
www.eckerd.edu

Edgewood College
Madison, WI
(608) 663-3249
www.edgewood.edu

**Edinboro University
of Pennsylvania**
Edinboro, PA
(814) 732-2776 x223
webs.edinboro.edu

**Elizabeth City State
University**
Elizabeth City, NC
(252) 335-3388
www.ecsu.edu

**Elizabethtown
College**
Elizabethtown, PA
www.etown.edu

Elmhurst College
Elmhurst, IL
www.elmhurst.edu

Elmira College
Elmira, NY
(607) 735-1872
www.elmira.edu

Elms College
Chicopee, MA
(413) 265-2395
www.elms.edu

Elon University
Elon, NC
(336) 278-6800
www.elon.edu

Emerson College
Boston, MA
(617) 824-8690
www.emerson.edu

**Emmanuel College
(Massachusetts)**
Boston, MA
(617) 735-9849
www.emmanuel.edu

**Emory and Henry
College**
Emory, VA
(276) 944-6233
www.ehc.edu

Emory University
Atlanta, GA
(404) 727-6553
www.emory.edu

**Emporia State
University**
Emporia, KS
www.emporia.edu

Endicott College
Beverly, MA
(978) 232-2304
www.endicott.edu

Erskine College
Due West, SC
(864) 379-8859
www.erskine.edu

Eureka College
Eureka, IL
(309) 467-6373
www.eureka.edu

Fairfield University
Fairfield, CT
(203) 254-4216
www.fairfield.edu

**Fairleigh Dickinson
University, Madison**
Madison, NJ
(973) 443-8960
www.fdu.edu

**Fairleigh Dickinson
University, Teaneck**
Teaneck, NJ
(201) 692-2208
www.fdu.edu

**Fairmont State
College**
Fairmont, WV
(304) 367-4220
www.fscwv.edu

**Fayetteville State
University**
Fayetteville, NC
(910) 672-1349
www.uncfsu.edu

Felician College
Lodi, NJ
(201) 559-3507
www.felician.edu

**Ferris State
University**
Big Rapids, MI
(231) 591-2863
www.ferris.edu

Ferrum College
Ferrum, VA
(540) 365-4488
www.ferrum.edu

Finlandia University
Hancock, MI
www.finlandia.edu

Fisk University
Nashville, TN
www.fisk.edu

**Fitchburg State
College**
Fitchburg, MA
(978) 665-3314
www.fsc.edu

**Florida A&M
University**
Tallahassee, FL
(850) 599-3878
www.famu.edu

**Florida Atlantic
University**
Boca Raton, FL
(561) 297-3199
www.fau.edu

**Florida Gulf Coast
University**
Ft. Myers, FL
(239) 590-7012
www.fgcu.edu

**Florida Institute of
Technology**
Melbourne, FL
(321) 674-8032
www.fit.edu

**Florida International
University**
Miami, FL
(305) 348-2756
www.fiu.edu

Florida Southern College
Lakeland, FL
(863) 680-4254
www.flsouthern.edu

Florida State University
Tallahassee, FL
(850) 644-2525
www.fsu.edu

Fontbonne University
St Louis, MO
www.fontbonne.edu

Fordham University
Bronx, NY
(718) 817-4300
www.fordham.edu

Fort Hays State University
Hays, KS
(785) 628-4353
www.fhsu.edu

Fort Lewis College
Durango, CO
www.fortlewis.edu

Fort Valley State University
Fort Valley, GA
(478) 825-6238
www.fvsu.edu

Framingham State College
Framingham, MA
(508) 626-4614
www.framingham.edu

Francis Marion University
Florence, SC
(843) 661-1237
www.fmarion.edu

Franklin & Marshall College
Lancaster, PA
(717) 358-4477
www.fandm.edu

Franklin College
Franklin, IN
(317) 738-8121
www.franklincollege.edu

Franklin Pierce College
Rindge, NH
(630) 899-4087
www.fpc.edu

Frostburg State University
Frostburg, MD
(301) 687-4471
www.frostburg.edu

Furman University
Greenville, SC
(864) 294-2000
www.furman.edu

Gallaudet University
Washington, DC
(202) 651-5603
www.gallaudet.edu

Gannon University
Erie, PA
(814) 871-7664
www.gannon.edu

Gardner-Webb University
Boiling Springs, NC
(704) 406-3926
www.gardner-web.edu

George Fox University
Newberg, OR
(503) 554-2926
www.georgefox.edu

George Mason University
Fairfax, VA
(703) 993-3256
www.gmu.edu

George Washington University
Washington, DC
(703) 993-3256
www.gwu.edu

Georgetown University
Washington, DC
(202) 687-2435
www.georgetown.edu

Georgia College & State University
Milledgeville, GA
(478) 445-6341
www.gcsu.edu

Georgia Institute of Technology
Atlanta, GA
(404) 894-5445
www.gatech.edu

Georgia Southern University
Statesboro, GA
(912) 681-5376
www.georgiasouthern.edu

Georgia State University
Atlanta, GA
(404) 651-3173
www.gsu.edu

Georgian Court College
Lakewood, NJ
(732) 987-2683
www.georgian.edu

Gettysburg College
Gettysburg, PA
(717) 337-6401
www.gettysburg.edu

Glenville State College
Glenville, WV
(304) 462-7361 x7220
www.glenville.wvnet.edu

Goldey-Beacom College
Wilmington, DE
(302) 225-6330
goldey.gbc.edu

Gonzaga University
Spokane, WA
(509) 323-3519
www.gonzaga.edu

Gordon College
Wenham, MA
(978) 867-4136
www.gordon.edu

Goucher College
Towson, MD
(410) 337-6474
www.goucher.edu

Grambling State University
Grambling, LA
(318) 274-2374
www.gram.edu

Grand Canyon University
Phoenix, AZ
(602) 589-2043
www.grand-canyon.edu

Grand Valley State University
Allendale, MI
www.gvsu.edu

Green Mountain College
Poultney, VT
(802) 287-8238
www.greenmtn.edu

Greensboro College
Greensboro, NC
(336) 272-7102 x235
www.gborocollege.edu

Greenville College
Greenville, IL
(618) 664-6622
www.greenville.edu

Grinnell College
Grinnell, IA
(641) 269-3800
www.grinnell.edu

Grove City College
Grove City, PA
(724) 458-2122
www.gcc.edu

Guilford College
Greensboro, NC
(336) 316-2190
www.guilford.edu

Gustavus Adolphus College
St. Peter, MN
(507) 933-7617
www.gustavus.edu

Gwynedd-Mercy College
Gwynedd Valley, PA
(215) 641-5574
www.gmc.edu

Hamilton College
Clinton, NY
(315) 859-4114
www.hamilton.edu

Hamline University
St. Paul, MN
(651) 523-2326
www.hamline.edu

Hampden-Sydney College
Hampden-Sydney, VA
(434) 223-6153
www.hsc.edu

Hampton University
Hampton, VA
(757) 727-5737
www.hamptonu.edu

Hanover College
Hanover, IN
(812) 866-7385
www.hanover.edu

Hardin-Simmons University
Abilene, TX
(325) 670-1273
www.hsutx.edu

Harding University
Searcy, AR
(501) 279-4305
www.harding.edu

Hartwick College
Oneonta, NY
(607) 431-4701
www.hartwick.edu

Harvard University
Boston, MA
(617) 495-2203
www.harvard.edu

Haverford College
Haverford, PA
(610) 896-1120
www.haverford.edu

Hawaii Pacific University
Honolulu, HI
web2.hpu.edu

Heidelberg College
Tiffin, OH
(419) 448-2140
www.heidelberg.edu

Henderson State University
Arkadelphia, AR
(870) 230-5072
www.hsu.edu

Hendrix College
Conway, AR
(501) 450-1391
www.hendrix.edu

High Point University
High Point, NC
(336) 841-9276
www.highpoint.edu

Hilbert College
Hamburg, NY
(716) 649-7900 x233
www.hilbert.edu

Hillsdale College
Hillsdale, MI
(517) 437-7364
www.hillsdale.edu

Hiram College
Hiram, OH
(330) 569-5340
www.hiram.edu

Hobart and William Smith Colleges
Geneva, NY
www.hws.edu

Hofstra University
Hempstead, NY
(516) 463-6750
www.hofstra.edu

Hollins University
Roanoke, VA
(540) 362-6435
www.hollins.edu

Holy Family University
Philadelphia, PA
(215) 637-7700 x3368
www.hfc.edu

Hood College
Frederick, MD
(301) 696-3499
www.hood.edu

Hope College
Holland, MI
(616) 395-7698
www.hope.edu

Howard Payne University
Brownwood, TX
(325) 649-8109
www.hputx.edu

Howard University
Washington, DC
(202) 806-7140
www.howard.edu

Humboldt State University
Arcata, CA
(707) 826-3666
www.humboldt.edu

Hunter College
New York, NY
(212) 772-4783
www.hunter.cuny.edu

Huntingdon College
Montgomery, AL
(334) 833-4497
www.huntingdon.edu

Husson College
Bangor, ME
(207) 941-7026
www.husson.edu

Idaho State University
Pocatello, ID
(208) 282-4064
www.isu.edu

Illinois College
Jacksonville, IL
(217) 245-3400
www.ic.edu

Illinois State University
Normal, IL
(309) 438-3636
www.ilstu.edu

Illinois Wesleyan University
Bloomington, IL
(309) 556-3196
titan.iwu.edu

Immaculata University
Immaculata, PA
(610) 647-4400 x3736
www.immaculata.edu

Indiana State University
Terre Haute, IN
(812) 237-4089
www.indstate.edu

Indiana University of Pennsylvania
Indiana, PA
(724) 357-2782
www.iup.edu

Indiana University, Bloomington
Bloomington, IN
(812) 855-2794
www.iu.edu

Indiana University-Purdue University, Fort Wayne
Fort Wayne, IN
(317) 278-2599
www.iupui.edu

Indiana University-Purdue University, Fort Wayne
Indianapolis, IN
(317) 278-2599
www.iupui.edu

Iona College
New Rochelle, NY
(914) 633-2311
www.iona.edu

Iowa State University
Ames, IA
(515) 294-0123
www.iastate

Ithaca College
Ithaca, NY
(607) 274-3209
www.ithaca.edu

Jackson State University
Jackson, MS
(601) 979-2291
www.jsums.edu

Jacksonville State University
Jacksonville, AL
(256) 782-5368
www.jsu.edu

Jacksonville University
Jacksonville, FL
(904) 256-7406
www.jacksonville.edu

James Madison University
Harrisonburg, VA
(540) 568-6164
www.jmu.edu

John Carroll University
University Hgts., OH
(216) 397-4676
www.jcu.edu

John Jay College of Criminal Justice
New York, NY
(212) 237-8371
www.jjay.cuny.edu

Johns Hopkins University
Baltimore, MD
(410) 516-7490
www.jhu.edu

Johnson and Wales University
Providence, RI
(401) 598-1604
www.jwu.edu

Johnson C. Smith University
Charlotte, NC
(704) 378-1164
www.jcsu.ed

Johnson State College
Johnson, VT
(802) 635-1485
www.jsc.vsc.edu

Juniata College
Huntingdon, PA
(814) 641-3512
www.juniata.edu

Kalamazoo College
Kalamazoo, MI
(269) 337-7082
www.kzoo.edu

Kansas State University
Manhattan, KS
(785) 532-6912
www.ksu.edu

Kean University
Union, NJ
(908) 737-5820
www.kean.edu

Keene State College
Keene, NH
(603) 358-2813
www.keene.edu

Kennesaw State University
Kennesaw, GA
(770) 423-6284
www.kennesaw.edu

Kent State University
Kent, OH
(330) 672-5979
www.kent.edu

Kentucky State University
Frankfort, KY
(502) 597-6019
www.kysu.edu

Kentucky Wesleyan College
Owensboro, KY
(270) 852-3330
www.kwc.edu

Kenyon College
Gambier, OH
(740) 427-5811
www.kenyon.edu

Keuka College
Keuka Park, NY
(315) 279-5682
www.keuka.edu

King's College (Pennsylvania)
Wilkes-Barre, PA
(570) 208-5900 x5855
www.kings.edu

Knox College
Galesburg, IL
(309) 341-7280
www.knox.edu

Kutztown University of Pennsylvania
Kutztown, PA
(610) 683-4094
www.kutztown.edu

La Grange College
La Grange, GA
(706) 880-8262
www.lagrange.edu

La Roche College
Pittsburgh, PA
(412) 536-1011
www.laroche.edu

La Salle University
Philadelphia, PA
(215) 951-1516
www.lasalle.edu

Lafayette College
Easton, PA
(610) 330-5470
www.lafayette.edu

Lake Erie College
Painesville, OH
(440) 375-7475
www.lec.edu

Lake Forest College
Lake Forest, IL
(847) 735-5290
www.lakeforest.edu

Lake Superior State University
Sault Ste. Marie, MI
(906) 635-2878
www.lssu.edu

Lakeland College
Sheboygan, WI
(920) 565-1240
www.lakeland.edu

Lamar University
Beaumont, TX
(409) 880-8323
www.lamar.edu

Lander University
Greenwood, SC
(864) 388-8316
www.lander.edu

Lane College
Jackson, TN
www.lanecollege.edu

Lasell College
Newton, MA
(617) 243-2147
www.lasell.edu

Le Moyne College
Syracuse, NY
(315) 445-4630
www.lemoyne.edu

Lebanon Valley College
Annville, PA
(717) 867-6261
www.lvc.edu

Lees-McRae College
Banner Elk, NC
www.lmc.edu

Lehigh University
Bethlehem, PA
(610) 758-4320
www.lehigh.edu

Lehman College, City University of New York
Bronx, NY
(718) 960-8101
www.lehman.cuny.edu

LeMoyne-Owen College
Memphis, TN
(901) 774-9090 x327
www.lemoyne-owen.edu

Lenoir-Rhyne College
Hickory, NC
(828) 328-7116
www.lrc.edu

Lesley University
Cambridge, MA
(617) 349-8498
www.lesley.edu

LeTourneau University
Longview, TX
(903) 233-3762
www.letu.edu

Lewis and Clark College
Portland, OR
(503) 768-7548
www.lclark.edu

Lewis University
Romeoville, IL
(815) 836-5937
www.lewisu.edu

Liberty University
Lynchburg, VA
(434) 582-2100
www.liberty.edu

Limestone College
Gaffney, SC
(864) 488-8219
www.limestone.edu

Lincoln Memorial University
Harrogate, TN
(423) 869-6285
www.lmunet.edu

Lincoln University (Missouri)
Jefferson City, MO
(573) 681-5336
www.lincolnu.edu

Lincoln University (Pennsylvania)
Lincoln Univ., PA
(610) 932-8300 x3385
www.lincoln.edu

Linfield College
Mc Minnville, OR
(503) 883-2229
www.linfield.edu

Lipscomb University
Nashville, TN
(615) 279-5850
www.lipscomb.edu

Livingstone College
Salisbury, NC
(704) 216-6013
www.livingstone.edu

Lock Haven University of Pennsylvania
Lock Haven, PA
(570) 893-2102
www.lhup.edu

Long Beach State University
Long Beach, CA
(562) 985-4655
www.longbeachstate.edu

Long Island University-Brooklyn Campus
Brooklyn, NY
(718) 488-1292
www.liu.edu

Longwood University
Farmville, VA
(434) 395-2057
www.longwood.edu

Loras College
Dubuque, IA
(563) 588-7112
www.loras.edu

Louisiana State University
Baton Rouge, LA
(225) 578-8001
www.lsu.edu

Louisiana Tech University
Ruston, LA
(318) 257-4111
www.latech.edu

Loyola College (Maryland)
Baltimore, MD
(410) 617-5014
www.loyola.edu

Loyola Marymount University
Los Angeles, CA
(319) 338-5940
www.lmu.edu

Loyola University (Illinois)
Chicago, IL
(773) 508-2560
www.luc.edu

Luther College
Decorah, IA
(563) 387-1583
www.luther.edu

Lycoming College
Williamsport, PA
(570) 321-4260
www.lycoming.edu

Lynchburg College
Lynchburg, VA
(434) 544-8286
www.lynchburg.edu

Lynn University
Boca Raton, FL
(561) 237-7279
www.lynn.edu

Macalester College
St. Paul, MN
www.macalester.edu

MacMurray College
Jacksonville, IL
www.mac.edu

Maine Maritime Academy
Castine, ME
(207) 326-2450
www.mainemaritime.edu

Manchester College
North Manchester, IN
(260) 982-5390
www.manchester.edu

Manhattan College
Riverdale, NY
(718) 862-7228
www.manhattan.edu

Manhattanville College
Purchase, NY
(914) 323-7277
www.manhattanville.edu

Mansfield University of Pennsylvania
Mansfield, PA
(570) 662-4636
www.mnsfld.edu

Maranatha Baptist Bible College
Watertown, WI
www.mbbc.edu

Marian College (Wisconsin)
Fond Du Lac, WI
(920) 923-8156
www.mariancollege.edu

Marietta College
Marietta, OH
(740) 376-4667
www.marietta.edu

Marist College
Poughkeepsie, NY
(845) 575-3699
www.marist.edu

Marquette University
Milwaukee, WI
(414) 288-6303
www.marquette.edu

Mars Hill College
Mars Hill, NC
(828) 689-1215
www.mhc.edu

Marshall University
Huntington, WV
(314) 696-5408
www.marshall.edu

Martin Luther College
New Ulm, MN
(507) 354-8221 x232
www.mlc-wels.edu

Mary Baldwin College
Staunton, VA
(540) 887-7160
www.mbc.edu

Marymount University (Virginia)
Arlington, VA
(703) 284-1619
www.marymount.edu

Maryville College (Tennessee)
Maryville, TN
(865) 981-8287
www.maryvillecollege.edu

Maryville University of Saint Louis
St. Louis, MO
(314) 529-9313
www.maryville.edu

Marywood University
Scranton, PA
(570) 961-4724
www.marywood.edu

Massachusetts College of Liberal Arts
North Adams, MA
(413) 662-5411
www.mcla.mass.edu

Massachusetts Institute of Technology
Cambridge, MA
(617) 253-4497
web.mit.edu

Massachusetts Maritime Academy
Buzzards Bay, MA
www.maritime.edu

McDaniel College
Westminster, MD
(410) 857-2291
www.mcdaniel.edu

McMurry University
Abilene, TX
(325) 793-4631
www.mcm.edu

McNeese State University
Lake Charles, LA
(337) 475-5563
www.mcneese.edu

Medaille College
Buffalo, NY
(716) 884-3411
www.medaille.edu

Medgar Evers College
Brooklyn, NY
(718) 270-6072
www.mec.cuny.edu

Menlo College
Atherton, CA
(650) 543-3770
www.menlo.edu

Mercer University
Macon, GA
(478) 301-2994
www.mercer.edu

Mercy College
Dobbs Ferry, NY
www.mercynet.edu

Mercyhurst College
Erie, PA
(814) 824-2226
www.mercyhurst.edu

Meredith College
Raleigh, NC
(919) 760-8198
www.meredith.edu

Merrimack College
North Andover, MA
(978) 837-5341
www.merrimack.edu

Mesa State College
Grand Junction, CO
(970) 248-1879
www.mesastate.edu

Messiah College
Grantham, PA
(717) 691-6018
www.messiah.edu

Methodist College
Fayetteville, NC
(910) 630-7175
www.methodist.edu

Metropolitan State College of Denver
Denver, CO
(303) 556-8300
www.mscd.edu

Miami University (Ohio)
Oxford, OH
(513) 529-7290
www.muohio.edu

Michigan State University
East Lansing, MI
(517) 432-5510
www.msu.edu

Michigan Technological University
Houghton, MI
(906) 487-3070
www.mtu.edu

Middle Tennessee State University
Murfreesboro, TN
(615) 898-2452
www.mtsu.edu

Middlebury College
Middlebury, VT
(802) 443-5253
www.middlebury.edu

Midwestern State University
Wichita Falls, TX
(940) 397-4044
www.mwsu.edu

Miles College
Birmingham, AL
(205) 929-1617
www.miles.edu

Millersville University of Pennsylvania
Millersville, PA
(717) 872-3100
muweb.millersville.edu

Millikin University
Decatur, IL
www.millikin.edu

Mills College
Oakland, CA
(510) 430-3285
www.mills.edu

Millsaps College
Jackson, MS
(601) 974-1243
www.millsaps.edu

Milwaukee School of Engineering
Milwaukee, WI
(414) 277-7230
www.msoe.edu

Minnesota State University Mankato
Mankato, MN
(507) 389-6111
www.mnsu.edu

Minnesota State University Moorhead
Moorhead, MN
(218) 477-5824
www.mnstate.edu

Mississippi College
Clinton, MS
(601) 925-3819
www.mc.edu

Mississippi State University
Mississippi State, MS
(662) 325-8082
www.msstate.edu

Mississippi Valley State University
Itta Bena, MS
(662) 254-3550
www.mvsu.edu

Missouri Southern State University-Joplin
Joplin, MO
(417) 625-9574
www.mssu.edu

Missouri Western State College
St. Joseph, MO
(816) 271-4257
www.mwsc.edu

Molloy College
Rockville Centre, NY
(516) 256-2207
www.molloy.edu

Monmouth College (Illinois)
Monmouth, IL
(309) 457-2176
www.monm.edu

Monmouth University
West Long Branch, NJ
(732) 263-5189
www.monmouth.edu

Montana State University-Billings
Billings, MT
(406) 247-2282
www.msubillings.edu

Montana State University-Bozeman
Bozeman, MT
(406) 994-4226
www.montana.edu

Montclair State University
Upper Montclair, NJ
(973) 655-5234
www.montclair.edu

Montclair State University
Upper Montclair, NJ
(973) 655-5234
www.montclair.edu

Moravian College
Bethlehem, PA
www.moravian.edu

Morehead State University
Morehead, KY
(606) 783-2088
www.morehead.edu

Morehouse College
Atlanta, GA
(404) 681-2800
www.morehouse.edu

Morgan State University
Baltimore, MD
(443) 885-3050
www.morgan.edu

Mount Holyoke College
South Hadley, MA
(413) 538-2310
www.mtholyoke.edu

Mount Ida College
Newton Centre, MA
(617) 928-7201
www.mountida.edu

Mount Mary College
Milwaukee, WI
(414) 256-1211
www.mtmary.edu

Mount Olive College
Mount Olive, NC
(919) 658-2502
www.mountolivecollege.edu

Mount St. Mary College (New York)
Newburgh, NY
(845) 569-3592
www.msmc.edu

Mount St. Mary's College
Emmitsburg, MD
(845) 569-3591
www.msmc.edu

Mount Union College
Alliance, OH
(330) 829-8224
www.muc.edu

Muhlenberg College
Allentown, PA
(484) 664-3380
www.muhlenberg.edu

Murray State University
Murray, KY
(270) 762-6800
www.murraystate.edu

Muskingum College
New Concord, OH
(740) 826-8320
muskingum.edu

Nazareth College
Rochester, NY
(585) 389-2196
www.naz.edu

Nebraska Wesleyan University
Lincoln, NE
(402) 465-2360
www.nebrwesleyan.edu

Neumann College
Aston, PA
(610) 558-5627
www.neumann.edu

New England College
Henniker, NH
(603) 428-2292
www.nec.edu

New Jersey City University
Jersey City, NJ
(201) 200-3317
www.njcu.edu

New Jersey Institute of Technology
Newark, NJ
(973) 596-3638
www.njit.edu

New Mexico Highlands University
Las Vegas, NM
(505) 454-3351
www.nmhu.edu

New Mexico State University
Las Cruces, NM
(505) 646-1211
www.nmsu.edu

New York City College of Technology
Brooklyn, NY
(718) 260-5102
www.citytech.cuny.edu

New York Institute of Technology
Old Westbury, NY
(516) 686-7888
www.nyit.edu

New York University
New York, NY
(212) 998-2040
www.nyu.edu

Newberry College
Newberry, SC
(803) 321-5166
www.newberry.edu

Newbury College
Brookline, MA
(617) 730-7091
www.newbury.edu

Niagara University
Niagara Univ., NY
(716) 286-8600
www.niagara.edu

Nicholls State University
Thibodaux, LA
(985) 448-4793
www.nicholls.edu

Nichols College
Dudley, MA
(508) 213-2368
www.nichols.edu

Norfolk State University
Norfolk, VA
(757) 823-8152
www.nsu.edu

North Carolina A&T State University
Greensboro, NC
(336) 334-7686
www.ncat.edu

North Carolina Central University
Durham, NC
(919) 530-7057
www.nccu.edu

North Carolina State University
Raleigh, NC
(919) 515-2109
www.ncsu.edu

North Carolina Wesleyan College
Rocky Mount, NC
(252) 985-5218
www.ncwc.edu

North Central College
Naperville, IL
(630) 637-5500
www.noctrl.edu

North Dakota State University
Fargo, ND
(701) 231-8982
www.ndsu.nodak.edu

North Greenville College
Tigerville, SC
(864) 977-7151
sharepoint.ngc.edu

North Park University
Chicago, IL
www.northpark.edu

Northeastern State University
Tahlequah, OK
(918) 456-5511 x3900
www.nsuok.edu

Northeastern University
Boston, MA
(617) 373-7590
www.northeastern.edu

Northern Arizona University
Flagstaff, AZ
(928)-523-5353
www.nau.edu

Northern Illinois University
De Kalb, IL
(815)-753-1894
www.niu.edu

Northern Kentucky University
Highland Heights, KY
(859) 572-5631
www.nku.edu

Northern Michigan University
Marquette, MI
(906) 227-1826
www.nmu.edu

Northern State University
Aberdeen, SD
(605) 626-7732
www.northern.edu

Northland College
Ashland, WI
(715) 682-1243
www.northland.edu

Northwest Missouri State University
Maryville, MO
(660) 562-1306
www.nwmissouri.edu

Northwest Nazarene University
Nampa, ID
(208) 467-8825
www.nnu.edu

Northwestern State University
Natchitoches, LA
(318)-3575251
www.nsula.edu

Northwestern University
Evanston, IL
(847)-4918880
www.northwestern.edu

Northwood University
Midland, MI
(989) 837-4385
www.northwood.edu

Norwich University
Northfield, VT
(802) 485-2230
www.norwich.edu

Nova Southeastern University
Fort Lauderdale, FL
www.nova.edu

Nyack College
Nyack, NY
(845) 358-1710 x181
www.nyackcollege.edu

Oakland City University
Oakland City, IN
(812) 749-1290
www.oak.edu

Oakland University
Rochester, MI
(248) 370-3190
www.oakland.edu

Oberlin College
Oberlin, OH
(440) 775-6401
www.oberlin.edu

Occidental College
Los Angeles, CA
(323) 259-2608
www.oxy.edu

Oglethorpe University
Atlanta, GA
(404) 364-8415
www.oglethorpe.edu

Ohio Northern University
Ada, OH
(419) 772-2450
www.onu.edu

Ohio State University
Columbus, OH
(614) 292-2477
www.osu.edu

Ohio University
Athens, OH
(740) 593-0983
www.ohio.edu

Ohio Valley College
Vienna, WV
(304) 865-6041
www.ovc.edu

Ohio Wesleyan University
Delaware, OH
(740) 368-3738
www.owu.edu

Oklahoma Panhandle State University
Goodwell, OK
www.opsu.edu

Oklahoma State University
Stillwater, OK
(405) 325-8208
www.okstate.edu

Old Dominion University
Norfolk, VA
(757) 683-3369
www.odu.edu

Olivet College
Olivet, MI
(269) 749-7593
www.olivetcollege.edu

Olivet Nazarene U
Kankakee, IL
(815) 939-5001
www.olivet.edu

Oral Roberts University
Tulsa, OK
(918) 495-7150
www.oru.edu

Oregon State University
Corvallis, OR
(541) 737-7478
www.oregonstate.edu

Otterbein College
Westerville, OH
(614) 823-3530
www.otterbein.edu

Ouachita Baptist University
Arkadelphia, AR
(870) 245-5182
www.obu.edu

Pace University
Pleasantville, NY
(914) 773-3481
www.pace.edu

Pacific Lutheran University
Tacoma, WA
(253) 535-7361
www.plu.edu

Pacific University (Oregon)
Forest Grove, OR
(503) 352-2260
www.pacificu.edu

Paine College
Augusta, GA
www.paine.edu

Palm Beach Atlantic University
West Palm Beach, FL
(561) 803-2578
www.pbac.edu

Peace College
Raleigh, NC
(919) 508-2328
www.peace.edu

Penn State Altoona
Altoona, PA
(814) 949-5410
www.aa.psu.edu

Penn State Berks-Lehigh Valley College
Reading, PA
(610) 396-6151
www.bk.psu.edu

Pennsylvania State Univ. Erie, the Behrend College
Erie, PA
(814) 898-6379
www.pserie.psu.edu

Pennsylvania State University
University Park, PA
(814) 865-1086
www.psu.edu

Pepperdine University
Malibu, CA
(310) 506-4242
www.pepperdine.edu

Pfeiffer University
Misenheimer, NC
(704) 463-1360 x2400
www.pfeiffer.edu

Philadelphia Biblical University
Langhorne, PA
(215) 702-4400
www.pbu.edu

Philadelphia University
Philadelphia, PA
(215) 951-2720
www.philau.edu

Piedmont College
Demorest, GA
(706) 778-3000
www.piedmont.edu

Pine Manor College
Chestnut Hill, MA
(617) 731-7056
www.pmc.edu

Pittsburg State University
Pittsburg, KS
(620) 235-4651
www.pittstate.edu

Plattsburgh State University of New York
Plattsburgh, NY
(518) 564-4147
www.plattsburgh.edu

Plymouth State College
Plymouth, NH
(603) 535-2750
www.plymouth.edu

Polytechnic University (New York)
Brooklyn, NY
(718) 260-3453
www.poly.edu

Pomona-Pitzer Colleges
Claremont, CA
(909) 621-8423
www.pomona.edu

Portland State University
Portland, OR
(503) 725-2500
www.pdx.edu

Prairie View A&M University
Prairie View, TX
(936) 857-2127
www.pvamu.edu

Presbyterian College
Clinton, SC
(864) 833-8241
www.presby.edu

Princeton University
Princeton, NJ
(609) 258-3535
www.princeton.edu

Principia College
Elsah, IL
(618) 374-5026
www.prin.edu

Providence College
Providence, RI
(401) 865-2090
www.providence.edu

Purdue University
West Lafayette, IN
(765) 494-3189
www.purdue.edu

Queens College (New York)
Flushing, NY
(718) 997-2795
www.qc.edu

Queens University of Charlotte
Charlotte, NC
(704) 337-2509
www.queens.edu

Quincy University
Quincy, IL
www.quincy.edu

Quinnipiac University
Hamden, CT
(203) 582-8621
www.quinnipiac.edu

Radford University
Radford, VA
(540) 831-5228
www.radford.edu

Ramapo College
Mahwah, NJ
(201) 684-7674
www.ramapo.edu

Randolph-Macon College
Ashland, VA
(804) 752-7223
www.rmc.edu

Randolph-Macon Woman's College
Lynchburg, VA
www.rmwc.edu

Regis College (Massachusetts)
Weston, MA
(781) 768-7147
www.regiscollege.edu

Regis University (Colorado)
Denver, CO
(303) 458-4070
www.regis.edu

Rensselaer Polytechnic Institute
Troy, NY
(518) 276-2556
www.rpi.edu

Rhode Island College
Providence, RI
(401) 456-8007
www.ric.edu

Rhodes College
Memphis, TN
(901) 843-3939
www.rhodes.edu

Rice University
Houston, TX
(713) 348-6920
www.rice.edu

Richard Stockton College of New Jersey
Pomona, NJ
(609) 652-4217
www2.stockton.edu

Rider University
Lawrenceville, NJ
(609) 896-5338
www.rider.edu

Ripon College
Ripon, WI
(920) 748-8133
www.ripon.edu

Rivier College
Nashua, NH
(603) 897-8257
www.rivier.edu

Roanoke College
Salem, VA
(540) 375-2337
www.roanoke.edu

Robert Morris University
Moon Township, PA
(412) 262-8302
www.rmu.edu

Rochester Institute of Technology
Rochester, NY
(585) 475-6154
www.rit.edu

Rockford College
Rockford, IL
(815) 394-5061
www.rockford.edu

Rockhurst University
Kansas City, MO
(816) 501-4141
www.rockhurst.edu

Roger Williams University
Bristol, RI
(401) 254-3129
www.rwu.edu

Rollins College
Winter Park, FL
(407) 646-2198
www.rollins.edu

Rose-Hulman Institute of Technology
Terre Haute, IN
(812) 877-8252
www.rose-hulman.edu

Rosemont College
Rosemont, PA
(610) 527-0200 x4265
www.rosemont.edu

Rowan University
Glassboro, NJ
(856) 256-4686
www.rowan.edu

Russell Sage College
Troy, NY
(518) 244-2283
www.sage.edu/RSC

Rust College
Holly Springs, MS
www.rustcollege.edu

Rutgers, State Univ of New Jersey, New Brunswick
New Brunswick, NJ
(732) 445-8610
www.rutgers.edu

Rutgers, State Univ. of New Jersey, Camden
Camden, NJ
(856) 225-6197
www.camden.rutgers.edu

Sacred Heart University
Fairfield, CT
(203) 365-7649
www.sacredheart.edu

Saginaw Valley State University
University Center, MI
(989) 791-7310
www.svsu.edu

Saint Anselm College
Manchester, NH
(603) 641-7800
www.anselm.edu

Saint Francis University (Pennsylvania)
Loretto, PA
(814) 472-3276
www.francis.edu

Saint Joseph's College (Indiana)
Rensselaer, IN
www.saintjoe.edu

Saint Joseph's College (Maine)
Standish, ME
(207) 893-6672
www.sjcme.edu

Saint Joseph's University
Philadelphia, PA
(610) 660-1707
www.sju.edu

Saint Louis University
St. Louis, MO
(314) 977-3178
www.slu.edu

Saint Mary's College (Indiana)
Notre Dame, IN
(574) 284-5547
www.saintmarys.edu

Saint Mary's University of Minnesota
Winona, MN
(507) 457-1781
www.smumn.edu

Saint Michael's College
Colchester, VT
(802) 654-2200
www.smcvt.edu

Salem International University
Salem, WV
www.salemiu.edu

Salem State College
Salem, MA
(978) 542-7260
www.salemstate.edu

Salisbury University
Salisbury, MD
(410) 548-3503
www.salisbury.edu

Salve Regina University
Newport, RI
(401) 341-2268
www.salve.edu

Sam Houston State University
Huntsville, TX
(936) 294-4205
www.shsu.edu

Samford University
Birmingham, AL
(205) 726-2131
www.samford.edu

San Diego State University
San Diego, CA
(619) 594-6357
www.sdsu.edu

San Francisco State University
San Francisco, CA
(415) 338-2218
www.sfsu.edu

San Jose State University
San Jose, CA
(408) 924-1200
www.sjsu.edu

Santa Clara University
Santa Clara, CA
(408) 551-1669
www.scu.edu

Savannah State University
Savannah, GA
(912) 353-5181
www.savstate.edu

Schreiner University
Kerrville, TX
(830) 792-7309
www.schreiner.edu

Seattle Pacific University
Seattle, WA
(206) 281-2085
www.spu.edu

Seattle University
Seattle, WA
(206) 296-6400
www.seattleu.edu

Seton Hall University
South Orange, NJ
(973) 761-9498
www.shu.edu

Shaw University
Raleigh, NC
(919) 546-8281
www.shawuniversity.edu

Shenandoah University
Winchester, VA
(540) 665-4566
www.su.edu

Shepherd College
Shepherdstown, WV
www.shepherd.edu

Shippensburg University of Pennsylvania
Shippensburg, PA
www.ship.edu

Siena College
Loudonville, NY
(518) 783-2450
www.siena.edu

Simmons College
Boston, MA
(617) 521-1038
www.simmons.edu

Simpson College
Indianola, IA
(515) 961-1495
www.simpson.edu

Skidmore College
Saratoga Springs, NY
(518) 580-5370
www.skidmore.edu

Slippery Rock University of Pennsylvania
Slippery Rock, PA
(724) 738-2767
www.sru.edu

Smith College
Northampton, MA
(413) 585-2701
www.smith.edu

Sonoma State University
Rohnert Park, CA
(707) 664-2639
www.sonoma.edu

South Carolina State University
Orangeburg, SC
(803) 536-8717
www.scsu.edu

South Dakota State University
Brookings, SD
(605) 688-5625
www3.sdstate.edu

Southampton Campus of Long Island University
Southampton, NY
(631) 287-8386
www.southampton.liu.edu

Southeast Missouri State University
Cape Girardeau, MO
(573) 651-2227
www.smsu.edu

Southeastern Louisiana University
Hammond, LA
(985) 549-2420
www.selu.edu

Southeastern Oklahoma State University
Durant, OK
(580) 745-2250
www.sosu.edu

Southern Arkansas University
Magnolia, AR
(870) 235-4132
www.saumag.edu

Southern Connecticut State University
New Haven, CT
(203) 392-6000
www.southernct.edu

Southern Illinois University at Carbondale
Carbondale, IL
(618) 453-5311
www.siu.edu

Southern Illinois University, Edwardsville
Edwardsville, IL
(618) 650-2869
www.siue.edu

Southern Methodist University
Dallas, TX
(214) 768-4301
www.smu.edu

Southern New Hampshire University
Manchester, NH
(603) 645-9604
www.snhu.edu

Southern University, Baton Rouge
Baton Rouge, LA
(225) 771-2712
www.subr.edu

Southern Utah University
Cedar City, UT
(435) 586-5469
www.suu.edu

Southern Vermont College
Bennington, VT
(802) 447-4660
www.svc.edu

Southwest Baptist University
Bolivar, MO
(417) 328-1787
www.sbuniv.edu

Southwest Minnesota State University
Marshall, MN
(507) 828-0638
www.southwest.msus.edu

Southwest Missouri State University
Springfield, MO
(417) 836-5244
www.smsu.edu

Southwestern Oklahoma State University
Weatherford, OK
(580) 774-3182
www.swosu.edu

Southwestern University (Texas)
Georgetown, TX
(512) 863-1381
www.southwestern.edu

Spelman College
Atlanta, GA
(404) 270-5711
www.spelman.edu

Springfield College
Springfield, MA
(413) 748-3333
www.spfldcol.edu

St. Andrews Presbyterian College
Laurinburg, NC
(910) 277-5274
www.sapc.edu

St. Augustine's College
Raleigh, NC
www.st-aug.edu

St. Bonaventure University
St. Bonaventure, NY
(716) 375-2282
www.sbu.edu

St. Cloud State University
St. Cloud, MN
(320) 308-3102
www.stcloudstate.edu

St. Edward's University
Austin, TX
(512) 448-8744
www.stedwards.edu

St. Francis College (New York)
Brooklyn Heights, NY
(718) 489-5486
www.stfranciscollege.edu

St. John Fisher College
Rochester, NY
(585) 385-8310
www.sjfc.edu

St. John's University (Minnesota)
Collegeville, MN
(320) 363-2757
www.csbsju.edu

St. John's University (New York)
Jamaica, NY
(718) 990-1433
www.new.stjohns.edu

St. Joseph College (Connecticut)
West Hartford, CT

St. Joseph's College (Long Island)
Patchogue, NY
(631) 447–3352
www.sjcny.edu/patchogue/

St. Lawrence University
Canton, NY
(315) 229-5784
web.stlawu.edu

St. Martin's College
Lacey, WA
(360) 438-4368
www.stmartin.edu

St. Mary's College of California
Moraga, CA
(925) 631-4399
www.stmarys-ca.edu

St. Mary's College of Maryland
St. Mary's City, MD
(240) 895-4295
www.smcm.edu

St. Mary's University (Texas)
San Antonio, TX
(210) 436-3528
www.stmarytx.edu

St. Norbert College
De Pere, WI
(920) 403-3031
www.snc.edu

St. Olaf College
Northfield, MN
(507) 646-3638
www.stolaf.edu

St. Paul's College
Lawrenceville, VA
(434) 848-1828
www.saintpauls.edu

St. Peter's College
Jersey City, NJ
(201) 915-9100
www.spc.edu

St. Thomas Aquinas College
Sparkill, NY
www.stac.edu

Stanford University
Stanford, CA
(650) 723-4596
www.stanford.edu

**State University
College at Brockport**
Brockport, NY
(585) 395-5328
www.brockport.edu

**State University
College at Cortland**
Cortland, NY
(607) 753-4953
www.cortland.edu

**State University
College at Fredonia**
Fredonia, NY
(716) 673-3101
ww1.fredonia.edu

**State University
College at Geneseo**
Geneseo, NY
(585) 245-5345
www.geneseo.edu

**State University
College at New Paltz**
New Paltz, NY
(845) 257-3908
www.newpaltz.edu

**State University
College at Old
Westbury**
Old Westbury, NY
(516) 876-3241
www.oldwestbury.edu

**State University
College at Oneonta**
Oneonta, NY
(607) 436-3494
www.oneonta.edu

**State University
College at Potsdam**
Potsdam, NY
(315) 267-3135
www.potsdam.edu

**State University of
New York at
Binghamton**
Binghamton, NY
(607) 777-4255
www.binghampton .edu

**State University of
New York at
Farmingdale**
Farmingdale, NY
(631) 420-2482
www.farmingdale.edu

**State University of
New York at Oswego**
Oswego, NY
(315) 312-2378
www.oswego.edu

**State University of
New York Institute of
Technology**
Utica, NY
(315) 792-7520
www.sunyit.edu

**State University of
New York Maritime
College**
Bronx, NY
(718) 409-7331
www.sunymaritime.edu

**State University of
West Georgia**
Carrollton, GA
(770) 836-6533
www.westga.edu

**Stephen F. Austin
State University**
Nacogdoches, TX
(409) 468-4540
www.sfasu.edu

Stephens College
Columbia, MO
(573) 876-7212
www.stephens.edu

Stetson University
De Land, FL
(386) 822-7157
www.stetson.edu

**Stevens Institute of
Technology**
Hoboken, NJ
(201) 216-5688
www.stevens.edu

Stillman College
Tuscaloosa, AL
(205) 366-8987
www.stillman.edu

Stonehill College
Easton, MA
(508) 565-1391
www.stonehill.edu

**Stony Brook
University**
Stony Brook, NY
(631) 632-7131
www.stonybrook.edu

Suffolk University
Boston, MA
(617) 573-8379
www.suffolk.edu

Sul Ross State University
Alpine, TX
(432) 837-8226
www.sulross.edu

Susquehanna University
Selinsgrove, PA
(570) 372-4270
www.susqu.edu

Swarthmore College
Swarthmore, PA
(610) 328-8218
www.swarthmore.edu

Sweet Briar College
Sweet Briar, VA
(434) 381-6305
www.sbc.edu

Syracuse University
Syracuse, NY
(315) 443-2385
www.syracuse.edu

Tarleton State University
Stephenville, TX
(254) 968-9178
www.tarleton.edu

Teikyo Post University
Waterbury, CT
(203) 596-4531
www.teikyopost.edu

Temple University
Philadelphia, PA
(215) 204-2585
www.temple.edu

Tennessee State University
Nashville, TN
(615) 963-1545
www.tnstate.edu

Tennessee Technological University
Cookeville, TN
(931) 372-3939
www.tntech.edu

Texas A&M University, College Station
College Station, TX
(979) 845-5129
www.tamu.edu

Texas A&M University-Commerce
Commerce, TX
(903) 886-5558
www7.tamu-commerce.edu

Texas A&M University-Corpus Christi
Corpus Christi, TX
(361) 825-5541
www.tamucc.edu

Texas A&M University-Kingsville
Kingsville, TX
(361) 593-2411
www.tamuk.edu

Texas Christian University
Fort Worth, TX
(817) 257-7710
www.tcu.edu

Texas Lutheran University
Seguin, TX
(830) 372-6877
www.tlu.edu

Texas Southern University
Houston, TX
(713) 313-4204
www.tsu.edu

Texas State University-San Marcos
San Marcos, TX
(512) 245-2114
www.swt.edu

Texas Tech University
Lubbock, TX
(806) 742-3355
www.texastech.edu

Texas Woman's University
Denton, TX
(940) 898-2378
www.twu.edu

The Citadel
Charleston, SC
(843) 953-5030
www.citadel.edu

The College of New Jersey
Ewing, NJ
(609) 771-2231
www.tcnj.edu

Thiel College
Greenville, PA
(724) 589-2138
www.thiel.edu

Thomas College
Waterville, ME
(207) 859-1404
www.thomas.edu

Thomas More College
Crestview Hills, KY
(859) 344-3536
www.thomasmore.edu

Tiffin University
Tiffin, OH
(419) 448-3288
www.tiffin.edu

Towson University
Towson, MD
(410) 704-2758
www.towson.edu

**Transylvania
University**
Lexington, KY
(859) 233-8284
www.transy.edu

**Trinity College
(Connecticut)**
Hartford, CT
(860) 297-2055
www.trincoll.edu

**Trinity College
(District of Columbia)**
Washington, DC
(202) 884-9606
www.trinitydc.edu

**Trinity University
(Texas)**
San Antonio, TX
(210) 999-8237
www.trinity.ed

Troy State University
Troy, AL
(334)- 670-3482
www.troy.edu

**Truman State
University**
Kirksville, MO
(660) 785-4235
www.truman.edu

Tufts University
Medford, MA
(617) 627-3232
www.tufts.edu

Tulane University
New Orleans, LA
(504) 865-5500
www.tulane.edu

Tusculum College
Greeneville, TN
www.tusculum.edu

Tuskegee University
Tuskegee, AL
(334) 724-4800
www.tuskegee.edu

**U.S. Air Force
Academy**
USAF Academy, CO
(719) 333-4008
www.usafa.edu

**U.S. Coast Guard
Academy**
New London, CT
www.cga.edu

**U.S. Merchant Marine
Academy**
Kings Point, NY
(516) 773-5859
www.usmma.edu

U.S. Military Academy
West Point, NY
(845) 938-3701
www.usma.edu

U.S. Naval Academy
Annapolis, MD
(410) 293-2700
www.usna.edu

**Union College
(New York)**
Schenectady, NY
(518) 388-6284
www.union.edu

University at Albany
Albany, NY
(518) 442-2562
www.albany.edu

**University at Buffalo,
the State University
of New**
Buffalo, NY
(716) 645-3141
www.buffalo.edu

University of Akron
Akron, OH
(330) 972-7080
www.uakron.edu

**University of
Alabama at
Birmingham**
Birmingham, AL
(205) 934-7252
www.uab.edu

**University of
Alabama, Huntsville**
Huntsville, AL
(256) 824-6144
www.uah.edu

**University of
Alabama, Tuscaloosa**
Tuscaloosa, AL
(205) 348-3697
www.ua.edu

University of Alaska Anchorage
Anchorage, AK
(907) 786-1230
www.uaa.alaska.edu

University of Alaska Fairbanks
Fairbanks, AK
(907) 474-7205
www.uaf.edu

University of Arizona
Tucson, AZ
(520) 621-4622
www.arizona.edu

University of Arkansas, Fayetteville
Fayetteville, AR
(479) 575-4959
www.uark.edu

University of Arkansas, Little Rock
Little Rock, AR
(501) 569-3167
www.ualr.edu

University of Arkansas, Monticello
Monticello, AR
www.uamont.edu

University of Arkansas, Pine Bluff
Pine Bluff, AR
(870) 575-8675
www.uapb.edu

University of Bridgeport
Bridgeport, CT
(203) 576-4735
www.bridgeport.edu

University of California, Berkeley
Berkeley, CA
(510) 642-6000
www.berkeley.edu

University of California, Davis
Davis, CA
(530) 752-1111
www.ucdavis.edu

University of California, Irvine
Irvine, CA
(949) 824-6932
www.uci.edu

University of California, Los Angeles
Los Angeles, CA
(310) 825-8699
www.ucla.edu

University of California, Riverside
Riverside, CA
(909) 787-5432
www.ucr.edu

University of California, San Diego
La Jolla, CA
(858) 534-4211
www.ucsd.edu

University of California, Santa Barbara
Santa Barbara, CA
(805) 893-3400
www.ucsb.edu

University of California, Santa Cruz
Santa Cruz, CA
(831) 459-2531
www.ucsc.edu

University of Central Arkansas
Conway, AR
(501) 450-3150
www.uca.edu

University of Central Florida
Orlando, FL
(407) 823-5895
www.ucf.edu

University of Central Oklahoma
Edmond, OK
(405) 974-2502
www.ucok.edu

University of Charleston (West Virginia)
Charleston, WV
(304) 357-4820
www.ucwv.edu

University of Chicago
Chicago, IL
(773) 702-7684
www.uchicago.edu

University of Cincinnati
Cincinnati, OH
(513) 556-5601
www.uc.edu

University of Colorado, Boulder
Boulder, CO
(303) 492-7930
www.colorado.edu

University of Colorado, Colorado Springs
Colorado Springs, CO
www.uccs.edu

University of Connecticut
Storrs, CT
(860) 486-2725
www.uconn.edu

University of Dallas
Irving, TX
(972) 721-5009
www.udallas.edu

University of Dayton
Dayton, OH
(937) 229-4875
www.udayton.edu

University of Delaware
Newark, DE
(302) 831-4006
www.udel.edu

University of Denver
Denver, CO
(303) 871-3399
www.du.edu

University of Detroit Mercy
Detroit, MI
(313) 993-1700
www.udmercy.edu

University of Dubuque
Dubuque, IA
(563) 589-3599
www.dbq.edu

University of Evansville
Evansville, IN
(812) 479-2237
www.evansville.edu

University of Findlay
Findlay, OH
(419) 434-4651
www.findlay.edu

University of Florida
Gainesville, FL
(352) 375-4683
www.ufl.edu

University of Georgia
Athens, GA
(706) 548-0448
www.uga.edu

University of Hartford
West Hartford, CT
(860) 768-4145
www.hartford.edu

University of Hawaii at Hilo
Hilo, HI
(808) 974-7606
www.uhh.hawaii.edu

University of Hawaii, Manoa
Honolulu, HI
(808) 956-7301
www.uhm.hawaii.edu

University of Houston
Houston, TX
(713) 743-9370
www.uh.edu

University of Idaho
Moscow, ID
(208) 885-8929
www.uidaho.edu

University of Illinois at Chicago
Chicago, IL
(312) 996-4639
www.uic.edu

University of Illinois, Champaign
Champaign, IL
(217) 333-3630
www.uiuc.edu

University of Indianapolis
Indianapolis, IN
(317) 788-3412
www.uindy.edu

University of Iowa
Iowa City, IA
(319) 335-9227
www.uiowa.edu

University of Kansas
Lawrence, KS
(785) 864-3143
www.ku.edu

University of Kentucky
Lexington, KY
(859) 257-8000
www.kyu.edu

University of La Verne
La Verne, CA
www.ulv.edu

University of Louisiana at Lafayette
Lafayette, LA
(337) 482-5393
www.louisiana.edu

**University of
Louisiana at Monroe**
Monroe, LA
(318) 342-5360
www.ulm.edu

**University of
Louisville**
Louisville, KY
(502) 852-0863
www.louisville.edu

**University of Maine
at Presque Isle**
Presque Isle, ME
(207) 768-9506
www.umpi.maine.edu

**University of Maine,
Farmington**
Farmington, ME
(207) 778-7264
www.umf.maine.edu

**University of Maine,
Orono**
Orono, ME
(207) 581-1052
www.umaine.edu

**University of Mary
Hardin-Baylor**
Belton, TX
(254) 295-4611
www2.umhb.edu

**University of Mary
Washington**
Fredericksburg, VA
(540) 654-1876
www.umw.edu

**University of Maryland,
Baltimore County**
Baltimore, MD
(410) 706-7529
www.umaryland.edu

**University of Maryland,
College Park**
College Park, MD
(301) 314-7075
www.umd.edu

**University of Maryland,
Eastern Shore**
Princess Anne, MD
(410) 651-6496
www.umes.edu

**University of
Massachusetts at
Lowell**
Lowell, MA
(978) 934-2310
www.uml.edu

**University of
Massachusetts,
Amherst**
Amherst, MA
(413) 545-4086
www.umass.edu

**University of
Massachusetts,
Boston**
Boston, MA
(617) 287-7810
www.umb.edu

**University of
Massachusetts,
Dartmouth**
North Dartmouth, MA
(508) 999-8720
www.umassd.edu

University of Memphis
Memphis, TN
(901) 678-3083
www.memphis.edu

**University of Miami
(Florida)**
Coral Gables, FL
(305) 284-2692
www.miami.edu

**University of
Michigan**
Ann Arbor, MI
(734) 647-BLUE
www.umich.edu

**University of
Minnesota, Duluth**
Duluth, MN
(218) 726-8718
www.d.umn.edu

**University of
Minnesota, Crookston**
Crookston, MN
(218) 281-8422
www.crk.umn.edu

**University of
Minnesota, Morris**
Morris, MN
(320) 589-6421
www.mrs.umn.edu

**University of
Minnesota, Twin Cities**
Minneapolis, MN
(612) 624-4497
www.umn.edu

**University of
Mississippi**
University, MS
(662) 915-1594
www.umiss.edu

**University of
Missouri, Columbia**
Columbia, MO
(573) 884-1440
www.mizzou.edu

**University of
Missouri, Kansas City**
Kansas City, MO
(816) 235-1048
www.umkc.edu

**University of
Missouri, Rolla**
Rolla, MO
(573) 341-4175
www.umr.edu

**University of
Missouri, St. Louis**
St. Louis, MO
(314) 516-5657
www.umsl.edu

University of Montana
Missoula, MT
(406) 243-4420
www.umt.edu

**University of
Montevallo**
Montevallo, AL
(205) 665-6600
www.montevallo.edu

**University of
Nebraska at Kearney**
Kearney, NE
(308) 865-8332
www.unk.edu

**University of
Nebraska at Omaha**
Omaha, NE
(402) 554-3389
www.unomaha.edu

**University of
Nebraska, Lincoln**
Lincoln, NE
(402) 472-3011
www.unl.edu

University of Nevada
Reno, NV
(775) 784-6900
www.unr.edu

**University of Nevada,
Las Vegas**
Las Vegas, NV
(702) 895-1620
www.unlv.edu

**University of New
England**
Biddeford, ME
(207) 283-2376
www.une.edu

**University of New
Hampshire**
Durham, NH
(603) 862-2013
www.unh.edu

**University of New
Haven**
West Haven, CT
(203) 932-7020
www.newhaven.edu

**University of New
Mexico**
Albuquerque, NM
(505) 925-5502
www.unm.edu

**University of New
Orleans**
New Orleans, LA
(504) 280-6102
www.uno.edu

**University of North
Alabama**
Florence, AL
(256) 765-4397
www.una.edu

**University of North
Carolina at
Greensboro**
Greensboro, NC
(336) 334-3000
www.uncg.edu

**University of North
Carolina at Pembroke**
Pembroke, NC
(910) 521-6560
www.uncp.edu

**University of North
Carolina, Asheville**
Asheville, NC
(828) 251-6930
www.unca.edu

**University of North
Carolina, Chapel Hill**
Chapel Hill, NC
(919) 962-6000
www.unc.edu

**University of North
Carolina, Charlotte**
Charlotte, NC
(704) 687-4920
www.uncc.edu

**University of North
Carolina, Wilmington**
Wilmington, NC
(910) 962-7625
www.uncw.edu

**University of North
Dakota**
Grand Forks, ND
(701) 777-2234
www.und.nodak.edu

University of North Florida
Jacksonville, FL
(904) 620-2833
www.unf.edu

University of North Texas
Denton, TX
(940) 565 3646
www.unt.edu

University of Northern Colorado
Greeley, CO
(970) 351-2534
www.unco.edu

University of Northern Iowa
Cedar Falls, IA
(319) 273-2470
www.uni.edu

University of Notre Dame
Notre Dame, IN
(574) 631-7546
www.nd.edu

University of Oklahoma
Norman, OK
(405) 325-8208
www.ou.edu

University of Oregon
Eugene, OR
(541) 346-5464
www.uoregon.edu

University of Pennsylvania
Philadelphia, PA
(215) 898-6121
www.upenn.edu

University of Pittsburgh
Pittsburgh, PA
(412) 648-8230
www.pitt.edu

University of Pittsburgh, Bradford
Bradford, PA
www.upb.pitt.edu

University of Pittsburgh, Greensburg
Greensburg, PA
(724) 836-9949
www.upg.pitt.edu

University of Pittsburgh, Johnstown
Johnstown, PA
(814) 269-2000
www.upj.pitt.edu

University of Portland
Portland, OR
(503) 943-7117
www.up.edu

University of Puerto Rico, Bayamon
Bayamon, PR
(787) 786-2885
www.uprb.edu

University of Puerto Rico, Cayey
Cayey, PR
www.upr.clu.edu

University of Puerto Rico, Mayaguez Campus
Mayaguez, PR
www.uprm.edu

University of Puerto Rico, Rio Piedras
San Juan, PR
www.rrp.upr.edu

University of Puget Sound
Tacoma, WA
(253) 879-3426
www.ups.edu

University of Redlands
Redlands, CA
(909) 335-4004
www.redlands.edu

University of Rhode Island
Kingston, RI
(401) 874-5245
www.uri.edu

University of Richmond
Richmond, VA
(804) 289-8371
www.richmond.edu

University of Rochester
Rochester, NY
(585) 275-4301
www.rochester.edu

University of San Diego
San Diego, CA
(619) 260-4803
www.acusd.edu

University of San Francisco
San Francisco, CA
(415) 422-6891
www.usfca.edu

University of Scranton
Scranton, PA
(570) 941-7440
matrix.scranton.edu

University of South Alabama
Mobile, AL
(251) 460-7121
www.southalabama.edu

University of South Carolina at Aiken
Aiken, SC
(803) 648-6851
www.usca.edu

University of South Carolina, Columbia
Columbia, SC
(803) 777-8881
www.sc.edu

University of South Carolina-Spartanburg
Spartanburg, SC
(864) 503-5144
www.uscs.edu

University of South Dakota
Vermillion, SD
(605) 677-5309
www.usd.edu

University of South Florida
Tampa, FL
(813) 974-3979
www.usf.edu

University of Southern California
Los Angeles, CA
(213) 740-8177
www.usc.edu

University of Southern Indiana
Evansville, IN
(812) 465-7164
www.usi.edu

University of Southern Maine
Gorham, ME
(207) 780-5430
www.usm.maine.edu

University of Southern Mississippi
Hattiesburg, MS
(601) 266-7011
www.usm.edu

University of St. Thomas (Minnesota)
St. Paul, MN
(651) 962-5903
www.stthomas.edu

University of Tampa
Tampa, FL
www.utampa.edu

University of Tennessee at Chattanooga
Chattanooga, TN
(423) 425-2270
www.utc.edu

University of Tennessee at Martin
Martin, TN
(731) 587-7661
www.utm.edu

University of Tennessee, Knoxville
Knoxville, TN
(865) 974-0001
www.utk.edu

University of Texas at Arlington
Arlington, TX
(817) 272-5039
www.uta.edu

University of Texas at Austin
Austin, TX
(512) 471-5757
www.utexas.edu

University of Texas at Dallas
Richardson, TX
(972) 883-2055
www.utdallas.edu

University of Texas at El Paso
El Paso, TX
(915) 747-6822
www.utep.edu

University of Texas at San Antonio
San Antonio, TX
(210)-4584444
www.utsa.edu

University of Texas at Tyler
Tyler, TX
(903) 566-7105
www.uttyler.edu

University of Texas, Pan American
Edinburg, TX
(956) 381-2222
www.panam.edu

University of the District of Columbia
Washington, DC
(202) 274-5024
www.universityofdc.org

University of the Incarnate Word
San Antonio, TX
(210) 829-6053
www.uiw.edu

University of the Ozarks (Arkansas)
Clarksville, AR
(479) 979-1210
www.ozarks.edu

University of the Pacific
Stockton, CA
(209) 946-3945
www.uop.edu

University of the Sciences in Philadelphia
Philadelphia, PA
(215) 596-8916
www.usip.edu

University of the South
Sewanee, TN
(931) 598-1136
www.sewanee.edu

University of Toledo
Toledo, OH
(419) 530-4987
www.toledo.edu

University of Tulsa
Tulsa, OK
(918) 631-2181
www.utulsa.edu

University of Utah
Salt Lake City, UT
(801) 581-5605
www.utah.edu

University of Vermont
Burlington, VT
(802) 656-3075
www.uvm.edu

University of Virginia
Charlottesville, VA
(434) 982-5100
www.virginia.edu

University of Washington
Seattle, WA
(206) 543-2212
www.washington .edu

University of West Alabama
Livingston, AL
(205) 652-3784
www.uwa.edu

University of West Florida
Pensacola, FL
(850) 474-3003
www.uwf.edu

University of Wisconsin, Eau Claire
Eau Claire, WI
(715) 836-5858
www.uwec.edu

University of Wisconsin, Green Bay
Green Bay, WI
(920) 465-2145
www.uwgb.edu

University of Wisconsin, La Crosse
La Crosse, WI
(608) 785-8616
www.uwlax.edu

University of Wisconsin, Madison
Madison, WI
(608) 262-5068
www.wisc.edu

University of Wisconsin, Milwaukee
Milwaukee, WI
(414) 229-4016
www.uwm.edu

University of Wisconsin, Oshkosh
Oshkosh, WI
(920) 424-1034
www.uwosh.edu

University of Wisconsin, Parkside
Kenosha, WI
(262) 595-2308
www.uwp.edu

University of Wisconsin, Platteville
Platteville, WI
(608) 342-1567
www.uwplatt.edu

University of Wisconsin, River Falls
River Falls, WI
(715) 425-3900
www.uwrf.edu

University of Wisconsin, Stevens Point
Stevens Point, WI
(715) 346-3888
www.uwsp.edu

University of Wisconsin, Stout
Menomonie, WI
(715) 232-2161
www.uwstout.edu

University of Wisconsin, Superior
Superior, WI
(715) 395-4693
www.uwsuper.edu

University of Wisconsin, Whitewater
Whitewater, WI
(262) 472-1543
www.uww.edu

University of Wyoming
Laramie, WY
(307) 766-2292
www.wyoming.edu

Upper Iowa University
Fayette, IA
(563) 425-5293
www.uiu.edu

Ursinus College
Collegeville, PA
(610) 409-3606
www.ursinus.edu

Utah State University
Logan, UT
(435) 797-2060
www.usu.edu

Utah Valley State College
Orem, UT
(801) 863-8563
www.uvsc.edu

Utica College
Utica, NY
(315) 792-3051
www.utica.edu

Valdosta State University
Valdosta, GA
(229) 333-5890
www.valdosta.edu

Valparaiso University
Valparaiso, IN
(219) 464-5230
www.valparaiso.edu

Vanderbilt University
Nashville, TN
(615) 322-1813
www.vanderbilt.edu

Vassar College
Poughkeepsie, NY
(845) 437-7450
www.vassar.edu

Villa Julie College
Stevenson, MD
(443) 334-2250
www.vjc.edu

Villanova University
Villanova, PA
(610) 519-4110
www.villanova.edu

Virginia Commonwealth University
Richmond, VA
(804) 828-8110
www.vcu.edu

Virginia Military Institute
Lexington, VA
(540) 464-7251
www.vmi.edu

Virginia Polytechnic Institute & State University
Blacksburg, VA
(540) 231-3977
www.vt.edu

Virginia State University
Petersburg, VA
(804) 524-5650
www.vsu.edu

Virginia Union University
Richmond, VA
(804) 342-1264
www.vuu.edu

Virginia Wesleyan College
Norfolk, VA
(757) 455-3303
www.vwc.edu

Wabash College
Crawfordsville, IN
(765) 361-6233
www.wabash.edu

Wagner College
Staten Island, NY
(718) 390-3433
www.wagner.edu

Wake Forest University
Winston-Salem, NC
(336) 758-5616
www.wfu.edu

Wartburg College
Waverly, IA
(319) 352-8470
www.wartburg.edu

**Washburn University
of Topeka**
Topeka, KS
(785) 231-1010 x1794
www.washburn.edu

**Washington and
Jefferson College**
Washington, PA
(724) 250-3461
www.washjeff.edu

**Washington and Lee
University**
Lexington, VA
(540) 458-8671
www2.wlu.edu

**Washington College
(Maryland)**
Chestertown, MD
(410) 778-7231
www.washcoll.edu

**Washington State
University**
Pullman, WA
(509) 335-0200
www.wsu.edu

**Washington
University in St. Louis**
St. Louis, MO
(314) 935-5220
www.wustl.edu

**Wayne State College
(Nebraska)**
Wayne, NE
(402) 375-7520
www.wsc.edu

**Wayne State
University (Michigan)**
Detroit, MI
(313) 577-4280
www.wayne.edu

Waynesburg College
Waynesburg, PA
(724) 852-3230
www.waynesburg.edu

**Weber State
University**
Ogden, UT
(801) 626-6817
www.weber.edu

Webster University
Webster Groves, MO
(314) 961-2660 x7576
www.webster.edu

Wellesley College
Wellesley, MA
(781) 283-2001
www.wellesley.edu

Wells College
Aurora, NY
(315) 364-3410
www.wells.edu

**Wentworth Institute
of Technology**
Boston, MA
(617) 989-4146
www.wit.edu

Wesley College
Dover, DE
(302) 736-2545
www.wesley.edu

**Wesleyan College
(Georgia)**
Macon, GA
www.wesleyancollege.edu

**Wesleyan University
(Connecticut)**
Middletown, CT
(860) 685-2690
www.wesleyan.edu

**Westchester
University of
Pennsylvania**
Westchester, PA
(610) 436-3555
www.wcupa.edu

**West Liberty State
College**
West Liberty, WV
(304) 336-8046
www.wlsc.edu

**West Texas A&M
University**
Canyon, TX
(806) 651-4400
www.wtamu.edu

**West Virginia State
College**
Institute, WV
(304) 766-3165
www.wvsc.edu

**West Virginia
University**
Morgantown, WV
(304) 293-5621
www.wvu.edu

**West Virginia
University Institute of
Technology**
Montgomery, WV
(304) 442-3181
www.wvutech.edu

**West Virginia
Wesleyan College**
Buckhannon, WV
(304) 473-8098
www.wvwc.edu

**Western Carolina
University**
Cullowhee, NC
(828) 227-7338
www.wcu.edu

**Western Connecticut
State University**
Danbury, CT
(203) 837-9013
www.wcsu.edu

**Western Illinois
University**
Macomb, IL
(309) 298-1106
www.wiu.edu

**Western Kentucky
University**
Bowling Green, KY
(270) 745-5276
www.wku.edu

**Western Michigan
University**
Kalamazoo, MI
(269) 387-3061
www.wmich.edu

**Western New England
College**
Springfield, MA
(413) 782-1202
www.wnec.edu

**Western New Mexico
University**
Silver City, NM
(505) 538-6233
www.wnmu.edu

**Western Oregon
University**
Monmouth, OR
(503) 838-8252
www.wou.edu

**Western State
College of Colorado**
Gunnison, CO
(970) 943-2079
www.western.edu

**Western Washington
University**
Bellingham, WA
(360) 650-3109
www.wwu.edu

**Westfield State
College**
Westfield, MA
(413) 572-5433
www.wsc.mass.edu

**Westminster College
(Missouri)**
Fulton, MO
(573) 592-5200
www.westminster-mo.edu

**Westminster College
(Pennsylvania)**
New Wilmington, PA
(724) 946-7307
www.westminster.edu

**Wheaton College
(Illinois)**
Wheaton, IL
(630) 752-5079
www.wheaton.edu

**Wheaton College
(Massachusetts)**
Norton, MA
(508) 286-3998
www.wheatoncollege.edu

**Wheeling Jesuit
University**
Wheeling, WV
(304) 243-2365
www.wju.edu

Wheelock College
Boston, MA
(617) 879-2238
www.wheelock.edu

Whitman College
Walla Walla, WA
www.whitman.edu

Whittier College
Whittier, CA
(562) 907-4271
www.whittier.edu

Whitworth College
Spokane, WA
(509) 777-4392
www.whitworth.edu

**Wichita State
University**
Wichita, KS
(316) 978-3250
www.wichita.edu

Widener University
Chester, PA
(610) 499-4454
www.widener.edu

Wilkes University
Wilkes-Barre, PA
(570) 408-4777
www.wilkes.edu

Willamette University
Salem, OR
(503) 370-6420
www.willamette.edu

William Paterson University of New Jersey
Wayne, NJ
(973) 720-2754
ww2.wpunj.edu

Williams College
Williamstown, MA
(413) 597-4982
www.williams.edu

Wilmington College (Delaware)
New Castle, DE
(302) 328-9441 x147
www.wilmcoll.edu

Wilmington College (Ohio)
Wilmington, OH
(937) 382-6661 x250
www.wilmington.edu

Wilson College
Chambersburg, PA
(717) 262-2012
www.wilson.edu

Wingate University
Wingate, NC
(704) 233-8194
www.wingate.edu

Winona State University
Winona, MN
(507) 457-5212
www.winona.edu

Winston-Salem State University
Winston-Salem, NC
(336) 750-2143
www.wssu.edu

Winthrop University
Rock Hill, SC
(803) 323-2129
www.winthrop.edu

Wisconsin Lutheran College
Milwaukee, WI
(414) 443-8808
www.wlc.edu

Wittenberg University
Springfield, OH
(937) 327-6450
www.wittenberg.edu

Worcester Polytechnic Institute
Worcester, MA
(508) 831-5243
www.wpi.edu

Worcester State College
Worcester, MA
(508) 929-8034
www.worcester.edu

Wright State University
Dayton, OH
(937) 775-2771
www.wright.edu

Xavier University
Cincinnati, OH
(513) 745-3413
www.xavier.edu

Yale University
New Haven, CT
(203) 432-1414
www.yale.edu

Yeshiva University
New York, NY
(212) 960-5211
www.yu.edu

York College (New York)
Jamaica, NY
(718) 262-5100
www.york.cuny.edu

York College (Pennsylvania)
York, PA
(717) 849-1614
www.ycp.edu

Youngstown State University
Youngstown, OH
(330) 941-1910
www.ysu.edu

Appendix 3

Women's Sports

These lists identify institutions that offer specific sports, as well as in which division the sport competes. Go to their websites for complete information.

ARCHERY
DIVISION I

Columbia University
James Madison University
TX A&M U–College Station

BADMINTON
DIVISION III

Albright College
Bryn Mawr College
Swarthmore College

BASKETBALL
DIVISION I

AL A&M University
Alabama State U
Alcorn State U
American University
Appalachian State U
Arizona State U
Arkansas State U
Auburn University
Austin Peay State U
Ball State U
Baylor University
Belmont University
Bethune-Cookman College
Birmingham-Southern
    College
Boise State U

Boston College
Boston University
Bowling Green State U
Bradley University
Brigham Young University
Brown University
Bucknell University
Butler University
CA Polytechnic State U
CA State U, Fresno
CA State U, Fullerton
CA State U, Northridge
CA State U, Sacramento
Campbell University
Canisius College
Centenary College (LA)
Central CT State U
Central MI University
Charleston Southern U
Chicago State U
Clemson University
Cleveland State U
Coastal Carolina University
Colgate University
College of Charleston (SC)
College of the Holy Cross
College of William & Mary
Colorado State U
Columbia University
Coppin State College
Cornell University
Creighton University
Dartmouth College

Davidson College
Delaware State U
DePaul University
Drake University
Drexel University
Duke University
Duquesne University
East Carolina University
East Tennessee State U
Eastern IL University
Eastern KY University
Eastern MI University
Eastern WA University
Elon University
Fairfield University
Fairleigh Dickinson U,
    Teaneck
FL A&M University
FL Atlantic University
FL International University
Florida State U
Fordham University
Furman University
Gardner-Webb University
George Mason University
George Washington U
Georgetown University
GA Institute of Technology
GA Southern University
Georgia State U
Gonzaga University
Grambling State U
Hampton University

Harvard University
High Point University
Hofstra University
Howard University
Idaho State U
Illinois State U
Indiana State U
IN University, Bloomington
IN U-Purdue, U Fort Wayne
Iona College
Iowa State U
Jackson State U
Jacksonville State U
Jacksonville University
James Madison University
Kansas State U
Kent State U
La Salle University
Lafayette College
Lamar University
Lehigh University
Liberty University
Lipscomb University
Long Beach State U
Long Island U-Brooklyn
   Campus
Louisiana State U
LA Tech University
Loyola College (MD)
Loyola Marymount U
Loyola University (IL)
Manhattan College
Marist College
Marquette University
Marshall University
McNeese State U
Mercer University
Miami University (OH)
Michigan State U
Middle Tennessee State U
Mississippi State U
MS Valley State U
Monmouth University
MT State U-Bozeman
Morehead State U
Morgan State U

Mount St. Mary's College
Murray State U
New Mexico State U
NY Institute of Technology
Nicholls State U
Norfolk State U
NC A&T State U
North Carolina State U
Northeastern University
Northern AZ University
Northern IL University
Northwestern State U
Northwestern University
Oakland University
Ohio State U
Ohio University
Oklahoma State U
Old Dominion University
Oral Roberts University
Oregon State U
Pennsylvania State U
Pepperdine University
Portland State U
Prairie View A&M U
Princeton University
Providence College
Purdue University
Quinnipiac University
Radford University
Rice University
Rider University
Robert Morris University
Rutgers, State U of NJ,
   New Brunswick
Sacred Heart University
Saint Francis University (PA)
Saint Joseph's University
Saint Louis University
Sam Houston State U
Samford University
San Diego State U
San Jose State U
Santa Clara University
Savannah State U
School Name
Seton Hall University

Siena College
South Carolina State U
Southeast MO State U
Southeastern LA University
Southern IL U-Carbondale
Southern Methodist U
Southern U-Baton Rouge
Southern UT University
Southwest MO State U
St. Bonaventure University
St. Francis College (NY)
St. John's University (NY)
St. Mary's College of CA
St. Peter's College
Stanford University
State U of NY-Binghamton
Stephen F. Austin State U
Stetson University
Stony Brook University
Syracuse University
Temple University
Tennessee State U
TN Technological U
TX A&M U-College Station
TX A&M U-Corpus Christi
TX Christian University
TX Southern University
TX State U-San Marcos
TX Tech University
Towson University
Troy State U
Tulane University
U.S. Air Force Academy
U.S. Military Academy
U.S. Naval Academy
University at Albany
U at Buffalo, the State U of
   NY
U of Akron
U of AL-Birmingham
U of AL-Tuscaloosa
U of Arizona
U of AR, Fayetteville
U of AR, Little Rock
U of AR, Pine Bluff
U of CA, Berkeley

U of CA, Irvine
U of CA, Los Angeles
U of CA, Riverside
U of CA, Santa Barbara
U of Central FL
U of Cincinnati
U of CO, Boulder
U of Connecticut
U of Dayton
U of Delaware
U of Denver
U of Detroit Mercy
U of Evansville
U of Florida
U of Georgia
U of Hartford
U of Hawaii–Manoa
U of Houston
U of Idaho
U of IL at Chicago
U of IL, Champaign
U of Iowa
U of Kansas
U of Kentucky
U of LA at Lafayette
U of LA at Monroe
U of Louisville
U of ME, Orono
U of MD, Baltimore Co.
U of MD, College Park
U of MD, Eastern Shore
U of MA, Amherst
U of Memphis
U of Miami (FL)
U of Michigan
U of MN, Twin Cities
U of Mississippi
U of MO, Columbia
U of MO, KS City
U of Montana
U of NE, Lincoln
U of Nevada
U of Nevada, Las Vegas
U of New Hampshire
U of New Mexico
U of New Orleans

U of NC at Greensboro
U of NC, Asheville
U of NC, Chapel Hill
U of NC, Charlotte
U of NC, Wilmington
U of North TX
U of Northern IA
U of Notre Dame
U of Oklahoma
U of Oregon
U of Pennsylvania
U of Pittsburgh
U of Portland
U of Rhode Island
U of Richmond
U of San Diego
U of San Francisco
U of South AL
U of SC, Columbia
U of South Florida
U of Southern CA
U of Southern MS
U of TN at Chattanooga
U of TN at Martin
U of TN, Knoxville
U of TX at ARlington
U of TX at Austin
U of TX at El Paso
U of TX at San Antonio
U of TX, Pan American
U of the Pacific
U of Toledo
U of Tulsa
U of Utah
U of Vermont
U of Virginia
U of Washington
U of WI, Green Bay
U of WI, Madison
U of WI, Milwaukee
U of Wyoming
Utah State U
UT Valley State College
Valparaiso University
Vanderbilt University
Villanova University

VA Commonwealth U
VA Polytechnic Institute &
  State U
Wagner College
Wake Forest University
WA State U
Weber State U
West VA University
Western Carolina U
Western IL University
Western KY University
Western MI University
Wichita State U
Winthrop University
Wofford College
Wright State U
Xavier University
Yale University
Youngstown State U

BASKETBALL
DIVISION II

Abilene Christian U
Adams State College
Adelphi University
Albany State U (GA)
Alderson-Broaddus College
American International
  College
Anderson College (SC)
Angelo State U
AR Tech University
Armstrong Atlantic State U
Ashland University
Assumption College
Augusta State U
Augustana College (SD)
Barry University
Barton College
Bellarmine University
Belmont Abbey College
Bemidji State U
Benedict College
Bentley College
Bloomfield College

Bloomsburg U of PA
Bluefield State College
Bowie State U
Bryant College
C.W. Post Campus/Long
    Island U
Caldwell College
CA State Polytechnic
    U–Pomona
CA State U, Bakersfield
CA State U, Chico
CA State U, Dominguez
    Hills
CA State U, Los Angeles
CA State U–San Bernardino
CA State U–Stanislaus
California U of PA
Cameron University
Carson-Newman College
Catawba College
Central MO State U
Central State U
Central WA University
Chadron State College
Cheyney U of Pennsylvania
Christian Brothers U
Clarion U of Pennsylvania
Clark Atlanta University
Clayton College & State U
Coker College
College of Saint Rose
CO Christian University
CO School of Mines
CO State U-Pueblo
Columbia Union College
Columbus State U
Concord College
Concordia College (NY)
Concordia U, St. Paul
Converse College
Davis and Elkins College
Delta State U
Dominican College (NY)
Dowling College
Drury University
East Central University

East Stroudsburg U of PA
Eastern NM University
Eckerd College
Edinboro U of PA
Elizabeth City State U
Emporia State U
Erskine College
Fairmont State College
Fayetteville State U
Felician College
Ferris State U
FL Gulf Coast University
FL Institute of Technology
FL Southern College
Fort Hays State U
Fort Lewis College
Fort Valley State U
Francis Marion University
Franklin Pierce College
Gannon University
GA College & State U
Georgian Court College
Glenville State College
Goldey-Beacom College
Grand CAnyon University
Grand Valley State U
Green Mountain College
Harding University
Henderson State U
Hillsdale College
Holy Family University
Humboldt State U
Indiana U of PA
Johnson C. Smith U
Kennesaw State U
Kentucky State U
KY Wesleyan College
Kutztown U of PA
Lake Superior State U
Lander University
Lane College
Le Moyne College
Lees-McRae College
LeMoyne-Owen College
Lenoir-Rhyne College
Lewis University

Limestone College
Lincoln Memorial U
Lincoln University (MO)
Livingstone College
Lock Haven U of PA
Longwood University
Lynn University
Mansfield U of PA
Mars Hill College
Mercy College
Mercyhurst College
Merrimack College
Mesa State College
Metropolitan State College
    of Denver
MI Technological U
Midwestern State U
Miles College
Millersville U of PA
MN State U–Mankato
MN State U Moorhead
MO Southern State U-Joplin
MO Western State College
Molloy College
MT State U–Billings
Mount Olive College
NJ Institute of Technology
NM Highlands University
NY Institute of Technology
Newberry College
NC Central University
North Dakota State U
North Greenville College
Northeastern State U
Northern KY University
Northern MI University
Northern State U
Northwest MO State U
Northwest Nazarene U
Northwood University
Nova Southeastern U
Nyack College
Oakland City University
OH Valley College
OK Panhandle State U
Ouachita Baptist University

Pace University
Paine College
Pfeiffer University
Philadelphia University
Pittsburg State U
Presbyterian College
Queens College (NY)
Queens U of Charlotte
Quincy University
Regis University (CO)
Rockhurst University
Rollins College
Saginaw Valley State U
Saint Anselm College
Saint Joseph's College (IN)
Saint Leo University
Saint Michael's College
Salem International U
San Francisco State U
Seattle Pacific University
Seattle University
Shaw University
Shepherd College
Shippensburg U of PA
Slippery Rock U of PA
Sonoma State U
South Dakota State U
Southampton
    Campus–Long Island U
Southeastern OK State U
Southern AR University
Southern CT State U
Southern IL U–Edwardsville
Southern NH University
Southwest Baptist U
Southwest MN State U
Southwestern OK State U
St. Andrews Presbyterian
    College
St. Augustine's College
St. Cloud State U
St. Edward's University
St. Martin's College
St. Mary's University (TX)
St. Paul's College
St. Thomas Aquinas College

State U of West GA
Stonehill College
Tarleton State U
Teikyo Post University
TX A&M U-Commerce
TX A&M Uy–Kingsville
TX Woman's University
Tiffin University
Truman State U
Tusculum College
Tuskegee University
U of Alaska, Huntsville
U of Alaska Anchorage
U of Alaska Fairbanks
U of AR, Monticello
U of Bridgeport
U of CA, Davis
U of CA, San Diego
U of Central AR
U of Central Oklahoma
U of Charleston (West VA)
U of CO, CO Springs
U of Findlay
U of Indianapolis
U of MA at Lowell
U of MN Duluth
U of MN, Crookston
U of MN, Morris
U of MO, Rolla
U of MO, St. Louis
U of Montevallo
U of NE at Kearney
U of NE at Omaha
U of New Haven
U of North AL
U of NC at Pembroke
U of North Dakota
U of North Florida
U of Northern CO
U of Pittsburgh–Johnstown
U of Puerto Rico, Bayamon
U of Puerto Rico, Cayey
U of Puerto Rico, Mayaguez
    Campus
U of Puerto Rico, Rio
    Piedras

U of SC at Aiken
U of SC–Spartanburg
U of South Dakota
U of Southern IN
U of Tampa
U of the DC
U of the Incarnate Word
U of the Sciences in
    Philadelphia
U of West Alabama
U of West Florida
U of WI, Parkside
Valdosta State U
Virginia State U
VA Union University
Washburn U of Topeka
Wayne State College (NE)
Wayne State U (MI)
Westchester U of PA
West Liberty State College
West TX A&M University
West VA State College
West VA U Institute of Tech
West VA Wesleyan College
Western NM University
Western OR University
Western State College (CO)
Western WA University
Wheeling Jesuit University
Wilmington College (DE)
Wingate University
Winona State U
Winston-Salem State U

BASKETBALL
DIVISION III

Adrian College
Agnes Scott College
Albertus Magnus College
Albion College
Albright College
Alfred University
Allegheny College
Alma College
Alvernia College

Alverno College
Amherst College
Anderson University (IN)
Anna Maria College
Arcadia University
Augsburg College
Augustana College (IL)
Aurora University
Austin College
Averett University
Babson College
Baldwin-Wallace College
Baptist Bible College
Bard College
Bates College
Bay Path College
Becker College
Beloit College
Benedictine University (IL)
Bennett College
Bernard M. Baruch College
Bethany College (West VA)
Bethel University
Blackburn College
Bluffton College
Bowdoin College
Brandeis University
Bridgewater College (VA)
Bridgewater State College
Brooklyn College
Bryn Mawr College
Buena Vista University
Buffalo State College
Cabrini College
CA Institute of Technology
CA Lutheran University
CA State U, Hayward
Calvin College
Capital University
Carleton College
Carnegie Mellon University
Carroll College (WI)
Carthage College
Case Western Reserve U
Castleton State College
Catholic University

Cazenovia College
Cedar Crest College
Centenary College (NJ)
Central College (IA)
Centre College
Chapman University
Chatham College
Chestnut Hill College
Chowan College
Christopher Newport U
City College of NY
Claremont McKenna-
   Harvey Mudd-Scripps
   Colleges
Clark University (MA)
Clarke College
Clarkson University
Coe College
Colby College
Colby-Sawyer College
College Misericordia
College of Mt. St. Joseph
College of Mt. St. Vincent
College of New Rochelle
College of Notre Dame
   (MD)
College of Saint Elizabeth
College of St. Benedict
College of St. CAtherine
College of St. Scholastica
College of Staten Island
College of Wooster
Colorado College
Concordia
   College–Moorhead
Concordia University (IL)
Concordia University (WI)
Concordia U–Austin
Connecticut College
Cornell College
Curry College
D'Youville College
Daniel Webster College
Defiance College
DE Valley College
Denison University

DePauw University
DeSales University
Dickinson College
Dominican University (IL)
Drew University
Earlham College
East TX Baptist University
Eastern CT State U
Eastern Mennonite U
Eastern Nazarene College
Eastern University
Edgewood College
Elizabethtown College
Elmhurst College
Elmira College
Emerson College
Emmanuel College (MA)
Emory and Henry College
Emory University
Endicott College
Eureka College
Fairleigh Dickinson U,
   Madison
Ferrum College
Finlandia University
Fisk University
Fitchburg State College
Fontbonne University
Framingham State College
Franklin & Marshall College
Franklin College
Frostburg State U
Gallaudet University
George Fox University
Gettysburg College
Gordon College
Goucher College
Greensboro College
Greenville College
Grinnell College
Grove City College
Guilford College
Gustavus Adolphus College
Gwynedd-Mercy College
Hamilton College
Hamline University

Hanover College
Hardin-Simmons University
Hartwick College
Haverford College
Heidelberg College
Hendrix College
Hilbert College
Hiram College
Hobart and William Smith
  Colleges
Hollins University
Hood College
Hope College
Howard Payne University
Hunter College
Huntingdon College
Husson College
Illinois College
IL Wesleyan University
Immaculata University
Ithaca College
John Carroll University
John Jay College of
  Criminal Justice
Johns Hopkins University
Johnson and Wales U
Johnson State College
Juniata College
Kalamazoo College
Kean University
Keene State College
Kenyon College
Keuka College
King's College (PA)
Knox College
La Grange College
La Roche College
Lake Erie College
Lake Forest College
Lakeland College
Lasell College
Lawrence University
Lebanon Valley College
Lehman College, City U of
  NY
Lesley University

LeTourneau University
Lewis and Clark College
Lincoln University (PA)
Linfield College
Loras College
Louisiana College
Luther College
Lycoming College
Lynchburg College
Macalester College
MacMurray College
ME Maritime Academy
Manchester College
Manhattanville College
Maranatha Baptist Bible
  College
Marian College (WI)
Marietta College
Martin Luther College
Mary Baldwin College
Marymount University (VA)
Maryville College (TN)
Maryville U of Saint Louis
Marywood University
MA College of Liberal Arts
MA Institute of Tech
McDaniel College
McMurry University
Medaille College
Medgar Evers College
Menlo College
Meredith College
Messiah College
Methodist College
Middlebury College
Millikin University
Millsaps College
Milwaukee School of
  Engineering
Mississippi College
Monmouth College (IL)
Montclair State U
Moravian College
Mount Holyoke College
Mount Ida College
Mount Mary College

Mt. St. Mary College (NY)
Mount Union College
Muhlenberg College
Muskingum College
Nazareth College
NE Wesleyan University
Neumann College
New England College
NJ City University
NY City College of Tech
New York University
Newbury College
Nichols College
NC Wesleyan College
North Central College
North Park University
Northland College
Norwich University
Oberlin College
Occidental College
Oglethorpe University
OH Northern University
OH Wesleyan University
Olivet College
Otterbein College
Pacific Lutheran University
Pacific University (OR)
Palm Beach Atlantic U
Peace College
Penn State Altoona
Penn State Berks-Lehigh
  Valley College
PA State Univ. Erie, the
  Behrend College
Philadelphia Biblical U
Piedmont College
Pine Manor College
Plattsburgh State U of NY
Plymouth State College
Polytechnic University (NY)
Pomona-Pitzer Colleges
Principia College
Ramapo College
Randolph-Macon College
Randolph-Macon Woman's
  College

Regis College (MA)
Rensselaer Polytechnic
    Institute
Rhode Island College
Rhodes College
Richard Stockton College
    of NJ
Ripon College
Rivier College
Roanoke College
Rochester Institute of Tech
Rockford College
Roger Williams University
Rose-Hulman Institute of
    Tech
Rosemont College
Rowan University
Russell Sage College
Rust College
Rutgers, The State U of NJ,
    Camden
Rutgers, The State U of NJ,
    Newark
Saint Joseph's College (ME)
Saint Mary's College (IN)
Saint Mary's U of MN
Salem State College
Salisbury University
Salve Regina University
Schreiner University
Shenandoah University
Simmons College
Simpson College
Skidmore College
Smith College
Southern VT College
Southwestern U (TX)
Spelman College
Springfield College
St. John Fisher College
St. John's University (MN)
St. Joseph's College (Long
    Island)
St. Lawrence University
St. Mary's College of MD
St. Norbert College

St. Olaf College
State U College–Brockport
State U College–Cortland
State U College at Fredonia
State U College–Geneseo
State U College–New Paltz
State U College–Geneseo
State U College–Old
    Westbury
State U College–Oneonta
State U College–Potsdam
State U of NY–Farmingdale
State U of NY–Oswego
State U of NY Institute of
    Tech
State U of NY Maritime
    College
Stephens College
Stevens Institute of Tech
Stillman College
Suffolk University
Sul Ross State U
Susquehanna University
Swarthmore College
TX Lutheran University
The College of NJ
Thiel College
Thomas College
Thomas More College
Transylvania University
Trinity College (CT)
Trinity College (D. C.)
Trinity University (TX)
Tufts University
U.S. Coast Guard Academy
U.S. Merchant Marine
    Academy
Union College (NY)
U of CA, Santa Cruz
U of Chicago
U of Dallas
U of Dubuque
U of La Verne
U of ME at Presque Isle
U of ME, Farmington
U of Mary Hardin-Baylor

U of Mary Washington
U of MA, Boston
U of MA, Dartmouth
U of New England
U of Pittsburgh, Bradford
U of Pittsburgh–
    Greensburg
U of Puget Sound
U of Redlands
U of Rochester
U of Scranton
U of Southern ME
U of St. Thomas (MN)
U of TX at Dallas
U of TX at Tyler
U of the Ozarks (AR)
U of the South
U of WI, Eau Claire
U of WI, La Crosse
U of WI, Oshkosh
U of WI, Platteville
U of WI, River Falls
U of WI, Stevens Point
U of WI, Stout
U of WI, Superior
U of WI, Whitewater
Upper IA University
Ursinus College
Utica College
Vassar College
Villa Julie College
VA Wesleyan College
Wartburg College
Washington and Jefferson
    College
Washington and Lee U
Washington College (MD)
Washington U in St. Louis
Waynesburg College
Webster University
Wellesley College
Wentworth Institute of
    Tech
Wesley College
Wesleyan College (GA)
Wesleyan University (CT)

Western CT State U
Western New England
College
Westfield State College
Westminster College (MO)
Westminster College (PA)
Wheaton College (IL)
Wheaton College (MA)
Wheelock College
Whitman College
Whittier College
Whitworth College
Widener University
Wilkes University
Willamette University
William Paterson U of NJ
Williams College
Wilmington College (OH)
Wilson College
WI Lutheran College
Wittenberg University
Worcester Polytechnic
Institute
Worcester State College
York College (NY)
York College (PA)

BOWLING
DIVISION I

AL A&M University
Alabama State U
Alcorn State U
Bethune-Cookman College
Coppin State College
Delaware State U
Fairleigh Dickinson U,
Teaneck
FL A&M University
Grambling State U
Hampton University
Howard University
Jackson State U
MS Valley State U
Morgan State U
Norfolk State U

NC A&T State U
Prairie View A&M U
Sacred Heart University
Savannah State U
South Carolina State U
Southern U–Baton Rouge
St. Peter's College
TX Southern University
U of AR, Pine Bluff
U of MD, Eastern Shore
U of NE, Lincoln

BOWLING
DIVISION II

Bowie State U
Central MO State U
Cheyney U of Pennsylvania
Elizabeth City State U
Fayetteville State U
Johnson C. Smith U
Livingstone College
NC Central University
Shaw University
St. Augustine's College
St. Paul's College
Virginia State U
VA Union University
Winston-Salem State U

BOWLING
DIVISION III

NJ City University
U of WI, Whitewater

CROSS-COUNTRY
DIVISION I

AL A&M University
Alabama State U
Alcorn State U
American University
Appalachian State U

Arizona State U
Arkansas State U
Auburn University
Austin Peay State U
Ball State U
Baylor University
Belmont University
Bethune-Cookman College
Birmingham-Southern
College
Boise State U
Boston College
Boston University
Bowling Green State U
Bradley University
Brigham Young University
Brown University
Bucknell University
Butler University
CA Polytechnic State U
CA State U, Fresno
CA State U, Fullerton
CA State U, Northridge
CA State U, Sacramento
Campbell University
Canisius College
Centenary College (LA)
Central CT State U
Central MI University
Charleston Southern U
Chicago State U
Clemson University
Cleveland State U
Coastal Carolina University
Colgate University
College of Charleston (SC)
College of the Holy Cross
College of William & Mary
Colorado State U
Columbia University
Coppin State College
Cornell University
Creighton University
Dartmouth College
Davidson College
Delaware State U

DePaul University
Drake University
Duke University
Duquesne University
East Carolina University
East Tennessee State U
Eastern IL University
Eastern KY University
Eastern MI University
Eastern WA University
Elon University
Fairfield University
Fairleigh Dickinson U,
   Teaneck
FL A&M University
FL Atlantic University
FL International University
Florida State U
Fordham University
Furman University
Gardner-Webb University
George Mason University
George Washington U
Georgetown University
GA Institute of Technology
GA Southern University
Georgia State U
Gonzaga University
Grambling State U
Hampton University
Harvard University
High Point University
Hofstra University
Howard University
Idaho State U
Illinois State U
Indiana State U
IN University, Bloomington
IN U-Purdue, U Fort Wayne
Iona College
Iowa State U
Jackson State U
Jacksonville State U
Jacksonville University
James Madison University
Kansas State U

Kent State U
La Salle University
Lafayette College
Lamar University
Lehigh University
Liberty University
Lipscomb University
Long Beach State U
Long Island U-Brooklyn
   Campus
Louisiana State U
LA Tech University
Loyola College (MD)
Loyola Marymount U
Loyola University (IL)
Manhattan College
Marist College
Marquette University
Marshall University
McNeese State U
Mercer University
Miami University (OH)
Michigan State U
Middle Tennessee State U
Mississippi State U
MS Valley State U
Monmouth University
MT State U-Bozeman
Morehead State U
Morgan State U
Mount St. Mary's College
Murray State U
New Mexico State U
NY Institute of Technology
Niagara University
Nicholls State U
Norfolk State U
NC A&T State U
North Carolina State U
Northeastern University
Northern AZ University
Northern IL University
Northwestern State U
Northwestern University
Oakland University
Ohio State U

Ohio University
Oklahoma State U
Oral Roberts University
Pennsylvania State U
Pepperdine University
Portland State U
Prairie View A&M U
Princeton University
Providence College
Purdue University
Quinnipiac University
Radford University
Rice University
Rider University
Robert Morris University
Rutgers, State U of NJ,
   New Brunswick
Sacred Heart University
Saint Francis University (PA)
Saint Joseph's University
Saint Louis University
Sam Houston State U
Samford University
San Diego State U
San Jose State U
Santa Clara University
Savannah State U
Seton Hall University
Siena College
South Carolina State U
Southeast MO State U
Southeastern LA University
Southern IL U-Carbondale
Southern Methodist U
Southern U-Baton Rouge
Southern UT University
Southwest MO State U
St. Bonaventure University
St. Francis College (NY)
St. John's University (NY)
St. Mary's College of CA
St. Peter's College
Stanford University
State U of NY-Binghamton
Stephen F. Austin State U
Stetson University

Stony Brook University
Syracuse University
Tennessee State U
TN Technological U
TX A&M U–College Station
TX A&M U-Corpus Christi
TX Christian University
TX Southern University
TX State U–San Marcos
TX Tech University
The Citadel
Towson University
Troy State U
U.S. Air Force Academy
U.S. Military Academy
U.S. Naval Academy
University at Albany
U at Buffalo, the State U of NY
U of Akron
U of AL–Birmingham
U of AL–Tuscaloosa
U of Arizona
U of AR, Fayetteville
U of AR, Little Rock
U of AR, Pine Bluff
U of CA, Berkeley
U of CA, Irvine
U of CA, Los Angeles
U of CA, Riverside
U of CA, Santa Barbara
U of Central FL
U of Cincinnati
U of CO, Boulder
U of Connecticut
U of Dayton
U of Delaware
U of Detroit Mercy
U of Evansville
U of Florida
U of Georgia
U of Hartford
U of Hawaii– Manoa
U of Houston
U of Idaho
U of IL at Chicago

U of IL, Champaign
U of Iowa
U of Kansas
U of Kentucky
U of LA at Lafayette
U of LA at Monroe
U of Louisville
U of ME, Orono
U of MD, Baltimore Co.
U of MD, College Park
U of MD, Eastern Shore
U of MA, Amherst
U of Memphis
U of Miami (FL)
U of Michigan
U of MN, Twin Cities
U of Mississippi
U of MO, Columbia
U of MO, KS City
U of Montana
U of NE, Lincoln
U of Nevada
U of NV, Las Vegas
U of New Hampshire
U of New Mexico
U of New Orleans
U of NC at Greensboro
U of NC, Asheville
U of NC, Chapel Hill
U of NC, Charlotte
U of NC, Wilmington
U of North TX
U of Northern IA
U of Notre Dame
U of Oklahoma
U of Oregon
U of Pennsylvania
U of Pittsburgh
U of Portland
U of Rhode Island
U of Richmond
U of San Diego
U of San Francisco
U of South AL
U of SC, Columbia
U of South Florida

U of Southern CA
U of Southern MS
U of TN at Chattanooga
U of TN at Martin
U of TN, Knoxville
U of TX at Arlington
U of TX at Austin
U of TX at El Paso
U of TX at San Antonio
U of TX, Pan American
U of the Pacific
U of Toledo
U of Tulsa
U of Utah
U of Vermont
U of Virginia
U of Washington
U of WI, Green Bay
U of WI, Madison
U of WI, Milwaukee
U of Wyoming
Utah State U
UT Valley State College
Valparaiso University
Vanderbilt University
Villanova University
VA Commonwealth U
VA Military Institute
VA Polytechnic Institute & State U
Wagner College
Wake Forest University
Washington State U
Weber State U
West VA University
Western Carolina U
Western IL University
Western KY University
Western MI University
Wichita State U
Winthrop University
Wofford College
Wright State U
Xavier University
Yale University
Youngstown State U

CROSS-COUNTRY

DIVISION II

Abilene Christian U
Adams State College
Adelphi University
Albany State U (GA)
Alderson-Broaddus College
Anderson College (SC)
Angelo State U
AR Tech University
Ashland University
Assumption College
Augusta State U
Augustana College (SD)
Barton College
Bellarmine University
Belmont Abbey College
Bemidji State U
Benedict College
Bentley College
Bloomsburg U of PA
Bluefield State College
Bowie State U
Brigham Young U, HI
Bryant College
C.W. Post Campus/Long Island U
Caldwell College
CA State Polytechnic U–Pomona
CA State U, Bakersfield
CA State U, Chico
CA State U, Dominguez Hills
CA State U, Los Angeles
CA State U–San Bernardino
CA State U–Stanislaus
California U of PA
Carson-Newman College
Catawba College
Central MO State U
Central State U
Central WA University
Chaminade University

Cheyney U of Pennsylvania
Christian Brothers U
Clarion U of Pennsylvania
Clark Atlanta University
Clayton College & State U
Coker College
College of Saint Rose
CO Christian University
CO School of Mines
Columbia Union College
Columbus State U
Concord College
Concordia College (NY)
Concordia U–St. Paul
Converse College
Dallas Baptist University
Davis and Elkins College
Delta State U
Dominican College (NY)
Dowling College
Drury University
East Central University
East Stroudsburg U of PA
Eastern NM University
Eckerd College
Edinboro U of PA
Elizabeth City State U
Emporia State U
Erskine College
Fairmont State College
Fayetteville State U
Felician College
Ferris State U
FL Gulf Coast University
FL Institute of Technology
FL Southern College
Fort Hays State U
Fort Lewis College
Fort Valley State U
Francis Marion University
Franklin Pierce College
Gannon University
GA College & State U
Georgian Court College
Glenville State College
Goldey-Beacom College

Grand Valley State U
Green Mountain College
Harding University
HI Pacific University
Henderson State U
Hillsdale College
Holy Family University
Humboldt State U
Indiana U of PA
Johnson C. Smith U
Kennesaw State U
Kentucky State U
Kutztown U of PA
Lake Superior State U
Lander University
Lane College
Le Moyne College
Lees-McRae College
LeMoyne-Owen College
Lenoir-Rhyne College
Lewis University
Limestone College
Lincoln Memorial U
Lincoln University (MO)
Livingstone College
Lock Haven U of PA
Longwood University
Mansfield U of PA
Mars Hill College
Mercy College
Mercyhurst College
Merrimack College
Mesa State College
MI Technological U
Miles College
Millersville U of PA
MN State U–Mankato
MN State U Moorhead
MO Southern State U-Joplin
Molloy College
MT State U–Billings
Mount Olive College
NJ Institute of Technology
NM Highlands University
NY Institute of Technology
Newberry College

NC Central University
North Dakota State U
North Greenville College
Northern KY University
Northern MI University
Northern State U
Northwest MO State U
Northwest Nazarene U
Northwood University
Nova Southeastern U
Nyack College
Oakland City University
OH Valley College
OK Panhandle State U
Ouachita Baptist University
Pace University
Paine College
Pfeiffer University
Pittsburg State U
Presbyterian College
Queens U of Charlotte
Regis University (CO)
Rollins College
Saginaw Valley State U
Saint Anselm College
Saint Joseph's College (IN)
Saint Leo University
Saint Michael's College
Salem International U
San Francisco State U
Seattle Pacific University
Seattle University
Shaw University
Shepherd College
Shippensburg U of PA
Slippery Rock U of PA
Sonoma State U
South Dakota State U
Southeastern OK State U
Southern AR University
Southern CT State U
Southern IL U–Edwardsville
Southern NH University
Southwest Baptist U
Southwestern OK State U
St. Andrews Presbyterian
   College

St. Augustine's College
St. Cloud State U
St. Edward's University
St. Martin's College
St. Mary's University (TX)
St. Paul's College
St. Thomas Aquinas College
State U of West GA
Stonehill College
Tarleton State U
TX A&M U-Commerce
TX A&M Uy–Kingsville
Tiffin University
Truman State U
Tusculum College
Tuskegee University
U of AL, Huntsville
U of ALaska Anchorage
U of ALaska Fairbanks
U of AR, Monticello
U of Bridgeport
U of CA, Davis
U of CA, San Diego
U of Central AR
U of Central Oklahoma
U of Charleston (West VA)
U of CO, CO Springs
U of Findlay
U of Hawaii–Hilo
U of Indianapolis
U of MA at Lowell
U of MN Duluth
U of MN, Morris
U of MO, Rolla
U of NE at Kearney
U of NE at Omaha
U of New Haven
U of North AL
U of NC at Pembroke
U of North Dakota
U of North Florida
U of Northern CO
U of Pittsburgh–Johnstown
U of Puerto Rico, Bayamon
U of Puerto Rico, Cayey
U of Puerto Rico, Mayaguez
   Campus

U of Puerto Rico, Rio
   Piedras
U of SC at Aiken
U of SC–Spartanburg
U of South Dakota
U of Southern IN
U of Tampa
U of the DC
U of the Incarnate Word
U of the Sciences in
   Philadelphia
U of West Alabama
U of West Florida
U of WI, Parkside
Valdosta State U
Virginia State U
VA Union University
Wayne State College (NE)
Wayne State U (MI)
Westchester U of PA
West Liberty State College
West TX A&M University
West VA Wesleyan College
Western OR University
Western State College (CO)
Western WA University
Wheeling Jesuit University
Wilmington College (DE)
Wingate University
Winona State U
Winston-Salem State U

CROSS-COUNTRY
DIVISION III

Adrian College
Agnes Scott College
Albertus Magnus College
Albion College
Albright College
Alfred University
Allegheny College
Alma College
Alvernia College
Alverno College

Amherst College
Anderson University (IN)
Anna Maria College
Arcadia University
Augsburg College
Augustana College (IL)
Aurora University
Averett University
Babson College
Baldwin-Wallace College
Baptist Bible College
Bard College
Bates College
Bay Path College
Becker College
Beloit College
Benedictine University (IL)
Bernard M. Baruch College
Bethany College (West VA)
Bethel University
Blackburn College
Bluffton College
Bowdoin College
Brandeis University
Bridgewater College (VA)
Bridgewater State College
Brooklyn College
Bryn Mawr College
Buena Vista University
Buffalo State College
Cabrini College
CA Institute of Technology
CA Lutheran University
CA State U, Hayward
Calvin College
Capital University
Carleton College
Carnegie Mellon University
Carroll College (WI)
Carthage College
Case Western Reserve U
Castleton State College
Catholic University
Cazenovia College
Cedar Crest College
Central College (IA)

Centre College
Chapman University
Chowan College
Christopher Newport U
Claremont McKenna-
    Harvey Mudd-Scripps
    Colleges
Clark University (MA)
Clarke College
Clarkson University
Coe College
Colby College
College Misericordia
College of Mt. St. Joseph
College of Mt. St. Vincent
College of New Rochelle
College of St. Benedict
College of St. Catherine
College of St. Scholastica
Colorado College
Concordia
    College–Moorhead
Concordia University (IL)
Concordia University (WI)
Concordia U–Austin
Connecticut College
Cornell College
Curry College
D'Youville College
Daniel Webster College
Defiance College
DE Valley College
Denison University
DePauw University
DeSales University
Dickinson College
Dominican University (IL)
Drew University
Earlham College
East TX Baptist University
Eastern CT State U
Eastern Mennonite U
Eastern Nazarene College
Edgewood College
Elizabethtown College
Elmhurst College

Elms College
Emerson College
Emmanuel College (MA)
Emory and Henry College
Emory University
Endicott College
Fairleigh Dickinson U,
    Madison
Ferrum College
Finlandia University
Fisk University
Fitchburg State College
Fontbonne University
Framingham State College
Franklin & Marshall College
Franklin College
Frostburg State U
Gallaudet University
George Fox University
Gettysburg College
Gordon College
Goucher College
Greensboro College
Greenville College
Grinnell College
Grove City College
Gustavus Adolphus College
Gwynedd-Mercy College
Hamilton College
Hamline University
Hanover College
Hartwick College
Haverford College
Heidelberg College
Hendrix College
Hilbert College
Hiram College
Hobart and William Smith
    Colleges
Hollins University
Hood College
Hope College
Hunter College
Husson College
Illinois College
IL Wesleyan University

Immaculata University
Ithaca College
John Carroll University
John Jay College of
    Criminal Justice
Johns Hopkins University
Johnson and Wales U
Johnson State College
Juniata College
Kalamazoo College
Kean University
Keene State College
Kenyon College
Keuka College
King's College (PA)
Knox College
La Grange College
La Roche College
Lake Erie College
Lake Forest College
Lasell College
Lawrence University
Lebanon Valley College
Lehman College, City U of
    NY
Lewis and Clark College
Lincoln University (PA)
Linfield College
Loras College
Louisiana College
Luther College
Lycoming College
Lynchburg College
Macalester College
MacMurray College
ME Maritime Academy
Manchester College
Maranatha Baptist Bible
    College
Marietta College
Martin Luther College
Mary Baldwin College
Maryville College (TN)
Marywood University
MA College of Liberal Arts
MA Institute of Tech

MA Maritime Academy
McDaniel College
McMurry University
Medaille College
Medgar Evers College
Menlo College
Messiah College
Methodist College
Middlebury College
Millikin University
Mills College
Millsaps College
Milwaukee School of
    Engineering
Mississippi College
Monmouth College (IL)
Montclair State U
Moravian College
Mount Holyoke College
Mount Ida College
Mount Union College
Muhlenberg College
Muskingum College
Nazareth College
NE Wesleyan University
New England College
NJ City University
NY City College of Tech
New York University
Newbury College
North Central College
North Park University
Northland College
Norwich University
Oberlin College
Occidental College
Oglethorpe University
OH Northern University
OH Wesleyan University
Olivet College
Otterbein College
Pacific Lutheran University
Pacific University (OR)
Palm Beach Atlantic U
Peace College
Penn State ALtoona

Penn State Berks-Lehigh
    Valley College
PA State U Erie, the
    Behrend College
Piedmont College
Pine Manor College
Plattsburgh State U of NY
Polytechnic University (NY)
Pomona-Pitzer Colleges
Principia College
Ramapo College
Regis College (MA)
Rensselaer Polytechnic Inst.
Rhode Island College
Rhodes College
Richard Stockton College
    (NJ)
Ripon College
Rivier College
Roanoke College
Rochester Institute of Tech
Roger Williams University
Rose-Hulman Institute of
    Tech
Rowan University
Rust College
Rutgers, The State U of NJ,
    Camden
Saint Joseph's College (ME)
Saint Mary's College (IN)
Saint Mary's U of MN
Salem State College
Salisbury University
Salve Regina University
Shenandoah University
Simpson College
Smith College
Southern VT College
Southwestern U (TX)
Spelman College
Springfield College
St. Joseph College (CT)
St. Joseph's College (Long
    Island)
St. Lawrence University
St. Norbert College

St. Olaf College
State U College–Brockport
State U College–Cortland
State U College at Fredonia
State U College–Geneseo
State U College–New Paltz
State U College–Geneseo
State U College–Old
 Westbury
State U College–Oneonta
State U College–Potsdam
State U of NY–Farmingdale
State U of NY–Oswego
State U of NY Inst. of Tech
State U of NY Maritime
 College
Stevens Institute of Tech
Stillman College
Suffolk University
Sul Ross State U
Susquehanna University
Swarthmore College
TX Lutheran University
The College of NJ
Thiel College
Transylvania University
Trinity College (CT)
Trinity University (TX)
Tufts University
U.S. Coast Guard Academy
U.S. Merchant Marine
 Academy
Union College (NY)
U of CA, Santa Cruz
U of Chicago
U of Dallas
U of Dubuque
U of La Verne
U of ME at Presque Isle
U of ME, Farmington
U of Mary Washington
U of MA, Boston
U of MA, Dartmouth
U of New England
U of Pittsburgh, Bradford
U of Pittsburgh–
 Greensburg

U of Puget Sound
U of Redlands
U of Rochester
U of Scranton
U of Southern ME
U of St. Thomas (MN)
U of TX at Dallas
U of TX at Tyler
U of the Ozarks (AR)
U of the South
Upper IA University
Ursinus College
Vassar College
Villa Julie College
VA Wesleyan College
Wartburg College
Washington and Jefferson
 College
Washington and Lee U
Washington U in St. Louis
Waynesburg College
Webster University
Wellesley College
Wesley College
Wesleyan University (CT)
Western New England
 College
Westfield State College
Westminster College (PA)
Wheaton College (IL)

EQUESTRIAN
DIVISION I

Auburn University
Brown University
CA State U, Fresno
College of Charleston (SC)
Cornell University
Dartmouth College
Kansas State U
Oklahoma State U
Sacred Heart University
Southern Methodist U
TX A&M U–College Station
U of Georgia
U of SC, Columbia

EQUESTRIAN
DIVISION II

Molloy College
Pace University
Stonehill College
U of MN, Crookston
West TX A&M University

EQUESTRIAN
DIVISION III

Becker College
Drew University
Elms College
Endicott College
Goucher College
Hartwick College
Hollins University
Lynchburg College
Mount Holyoke College
Mount Ida College
Nazareth College
Skidmore College
Smith College
St. Joseph's College (Long
 Island)
State U College–Potsdam
U of MA, Dartmouth
U of the South
Wilson College

FENCING
DIVISION I

Boston College
Brown University
CA State U, Fullerton
Cleveland State U
Columbia University
Cornell University
Duke University
Fairleigh Dickinson U,
 Teaneck
Harvard University
James Madison University
Northwestern University

Ohio State U
Pennsylvania State U
Princeton University
Rutgers, State U of NJ,
   New Brunswick
Sacred Heart University
St. John's University (NY)
Stanford University
Temple University
U.S. Air Force Academy
U of Detroit Mercy
U of NC, Chapel Hill
U of Notre Dame
U of Pennsylvania
Yale University

FENCING
DIVISION II

NJ Institute of Technology
U of CA, San Diego
Wayne State U (MI)

FENCING
DIVISION III

Brandeis University
CA Institute of Technology
Case Western Reserve U
City College of NY
Drew University
Haverford College
Hunter College
Johns Hopkins University
Lawrence University
MA Institute of Tech
New York University
Stevens Institute of Tech
Tufts University
Vassar College
Wellesley College

FIELD HOCKEY
DIVISION I

American University
Appalachian State U
Ball State U
Boston College
Boston University
Brown University
Bucknell University
Central MI University
Colgate University
College of the Holy Cross
College of William & Mary
Columbia University,
   Barnard College
Cornell University
Dartmouth College
Davidson College
Drexel University
Duke University
Fairfield University
Georgetown University
Harvard University
Hofstra University
IN University, Bloomington
James Madison University
Kent State U
La Salle University
Lafayette College
Lehigh University
Miami University (Ohio)
Michigan State U
Monmouth University
Northeastern University
Northwestern University
Ohio State U
Ohio University
Old Dominion University
Pennsylvania State U
Princeton University
Providence College
Quinnipiac University
Radford University

Rider University
Rutgers, State U of New
   Jersey, New Brunswick
Pennsylvania State U
Sacred Heart University
Saint Francis University (PA)
Saint Joseph's University
Saint Louis University
Siena College
Southwest MO State U
Stanford University
Syracuse University
Temple University
Towson University
University at ALbany
U of CA, Berkeley
U of Connecticut
U of Delaware
U of Iowa
U of Louisville
U of ME, Orono
U of MD, Baltimore Co.
U of MD, College Park
U of MA, Amherst
U of Michigan
U of New Hampshire
U of NC–Chapel Hill
U of Pennsylvania
U of Rhode Island
U of Richmond
U of the Pacific
U of Vermont
U of Virginia
Villanova University
VA Commonwealth
   University
Wake Forest University
Westchester U of
   Pennsylvania
Yale University

FIELD HOCKEY
DIVISION II

American International College
Assumption College
Bellarmine University
Bentley College
Bloomsburg U of PA
Bryant College
C.W. Post Campus/Long Island University
Catawba College
East Stroudsburg U of PA
Franklin Pierce College
Indiana U of PA
Kutztown U of PA
Lock Haven U of PA
Longwood University
Mansfield U of PA
Mercyhurst College
Merrimack College
Millersville U of PA
Philadelphia University
Saint Anselm College
Saint Michael's College
Shippensburg U of PA
Slippery Rock U of PA
Southern CT State U
Stonehill College
U of MA at Lowell

FIELD HOCKEY
DIVISION III

Albright College
Alvernia College
Amherst College
Anna Maria College
Arcadia University
Babson College
Bates College
Becker College

Bowdoin College
Bridgewater College (VA)
Bridgewater State College
Bryn Mawr College
Cabrini College
Castleton State College
Catholic University
Cedar Crest College
Centre College
Christopher Newport U
Clark University (MA)
Colby College
College Misericordia
College of Mt. St. Joseph
College of Notre Dame (MD)
College of Wooster
Connecticut College
DE Valley College
Denison University
DePauw University
Dickinson College
Drew University
Earlham College
Eastern CT State U
Eastern Mennonite U
Eastern University
Elizabethtown College
Elmira College
Elms College
Endicott College
Fairleigh Dickinson U, Madison
Fitchburg State College
Framingham State College
Franklin & Marshall College
Frostburg State U
Gettysburg College
Gordon College
Goucher College
Gwynedd-Mercy College
Hamilton College
Hartwick College
Haverford College
Hobart and William Smith Colleges

Hollins University
Hood College
Husson College
Immaculata University
Ithaca College
Johns Hopkins University
Juniata College
Kean University
Keene State College
Kenyon College
King's College (PA)
Lasell College
Lebanon Valley College
Lynchburg College
Manhattanville College
Mary Baldwin College
Marywood University
MIT
McDaniel College
Messiah College
Middlebury College
Montclair State U
Moravian College
Mount Holyoke College
Muhlenberg College
Nazareth College
Neumann College
New England College
Nichols College
Oberlin College
OH Wesleyan University
Philadelphia Biblical U
Plymouth State College
Ramapo College
Randolph-Macon College
Randolph-Macon Woman's College
Regis College (MA)
Rensselaer Polytechnic Institute
Rhodes College
Richard Stockton College (NJ)
Roanoke College
Rosemont College
Rowan University

Saint Joseph's College (ME)
Salem State College
Salisbury University
Salve Regina University
Shenandoah University
Simmons College
Skidmore College
Smith College
Springfield College
St. Lawrence University
St. Mary's College of MD
State U College–Brockport
State U College–Cortland
State U College–Geneseo
State U College–New Paltz
State U College–Geneseo
State U College–Oneonta
State U of NY at Oswego
Susquehanna University
Swarthmore College
Sweet Briar College
The College of New Jersey
Thomas College
Transylvania University
Trinity College (CT)
Trinity College (DC)
Tufts University
Union College (NY)
U of ME, Farmington
U of Mary WA
U of MA, Dartmouth
U of New England
U of Rochester
U of Scranton
U of Southern ME
U of the South
Ursinus College
Utica College
Vassar College
Villa Julie College
VA Wesleyan College
Washington and Jefferson
   College
Washington and Lee U
WA College (MD)
Webster University

Wells College
Wesley College
Wesleyan University (CT)
Western New England
   College
Westfield State College
Wheaton College (MA)
Wheelock College
Widener University
Wilkes University
William Paterson U of NJ
Williams College
Wilmington College (OH)
Wittenberg University
Worcester Polytechnic
   Institute
Worcester State College
York College (PA)

GOLF
DIVISION I

AL A&M University
Alabama State U
Alcorn State U
Appalachian State U
Arizona State U
Arkansas State U
Auburn University
Augusta State U
Austin Peay State U
Ball State U
Baylor University
Belmont University
Bethune-Cookman College
Birmingham-Southern
   College
Boise State U
Boston College
Boston University
Bowling Green State U
Bradley University
Brigham Young University
Brown University
Bucknell University
Butler University

CA Polytechnic State U
CA State U, Northridge
CA State U, Sacramento
Campbell University
Centenary College (LA)
Central CT State U
Charleston Southern U
Chicago State U
Cleveland State U
Coastal Carolina U
College of Charleston (SC)
College of the Holy Cross
College of William & Mary
Colorado State U
Columbia University
Creighton University
Dartmouth College
Duke University
East Carolina University
East Tennessee State U
Eastern IL University
Eastern KY University
Eastern MI University
Eastern WA University
Elon University
Fairfield University
FL Atlantic University
FL International University
Florida State U
Furman University
Gardner-Webb University
Georgetown University
Georgia State U
Gonzaga University
Grambling State U
Hampton University
Harvard University
High Point University
Hofstra University
Idaho State U
Illinois State U
IN University, Bloomington
IN U-Purdue, U Fort Wayne
Iowa State U
Jackson State U
Jacksonville State U

Jacksonville University
James Madison University
Kansas State U
Kent State U
Lamar University
Lehigh University
Lipscomb University
Long Beach State U
Long Island U-Brooklyn
　Campus
Louisiana State U
Loyola University (IL)
Manhattan College
Marshall University
McNeese State U
Mercer University
Michigan State U
Middle Tennessee State U
Mississippi State U
MS Valley State U
Monmouth University
MT State U-Bozeman
Mount St. Mary's College
Murray State U
New Mexico State U
Nicholls State U
North Carolina State U
Northern AZ University
Northern IL University
Northwestern University
Oakland University
Ohio State U
Ohio University
Oklahoma State U
Old Dominion University
Oral Roberts University
Oregon State U
Pennsylvania State U
Pepperdine University
Portland State U
Prairie View A&M U
Princeton University
Purdue University
Radford University
Robert Morris University
Rutgers, State U of NJ,
　New Brunswick

Sacred Heart University
Saint Francis University (PA)
Sam Houston State U
Samford University
San Diego State U
San Jose State U
Santa Clara University
Savannah State U
Siena College
South Carolina State U
Southern IL U-Carbondale
Southern Methodist U
Southern U-Baton Rouge
Southwest MO State U
St. John's University (NY)
Stanford University
Stetson University
Tennessee State U
TN Technological U
TX A&M U-College Station
TX A&M U-Corpus Christi
TX Christian University
TX Southern University
TX State U-San Marcos
TX Tech University
The Citadel
Troy State U
Tulane University
University at Albany
U of AL-Birmingham
U of AL-Tuscaloosa
U of Arizona
U of AR, Fayetteville
U of AR, Little Rock
U of AR, Pine Bluff
U of CA, Berkeley
U of CA, Irvine
U of CA, Los Angeles
U of CA, Riverside
U of Central FL
U of Cincinnati
U of CO, Boulder
U of Dayton
U of Denver
U of Evansville
U of Florida
U of Georgia

U of Hartford
U of Hawaii- Manoa
U of Idaho
U of IL, Champaign
U of Iowa
U of Kansas
U of Kentucky
U of Louisville
U of MD, College Park
U of Memphis
U of Miami (FL)
U of Michigan
U of MN, Twin Cities
U of Mississippi
U of MO, Columbia
U of MO, KS City
U of Montana
U of NE, Lincoln
U of Nevada
U of NV, Las Vegas
U of New Mexico
U of New Orleans
U of NC at Greensboro
U of NC, Chapel Hill
U of NC, Wilmington
U of North TX
U of Northern IA
U of Notre Dame
U of Oklahoma
U of Oregon
U of Pennsylvania
U of Portland
U of Richmond
U of San Francisco
U of South AL
U of SC, Columbia
U of South Florida
U of Southern CA
U of Southern MS
U of TN, Knoxville
U of TX at Austin
U of TX at El Paso
U of TX, Pan American
U of Toledo
U of Tulsa
U of Virginia
U of Washington

U of WI, Madison
U of Wyoming
Vanderbilt University
Wagner College
Wake Forest University
Washington State U
Weber State U
Western Carolina U
Western IL University
Western KY University
Western MI University
Wichita State U
Winthrop University
Wofford College
Xavier University
Yale University
Youngstown State U

GOLF
DIVISION II

NJ Institute of Technology
U of CA, San Diego
Wayne State U (MI)

GOLF
DIVISION III

Adrian College
Albion College
Alma College
Amherst College
Anderson University (IN)
Augsburg College
Augustana College (IL)
Aurora University
Baldwin-Wallace College
Bates College
Beloit College
Bluffton College
Bowdoin College
Buena Vista University
CA State U, Hayward
Calvin College
Capital University
Carleton College

Carroll College (WI)
Carthage College
Central College (IA)
Centre College
Clarke College
Coe College
College of Mt. St. Joseph
College of St. Benedict
Concordia
  College–Moorhead
Concordia University (WI)
Concordia U–Austin
Cornell College
Defiance College
DePauw University
Dickinson College
Edgewood College
Elmhurst College
Elmira College
Franklin & Marshall College
Franklin College
Gettysburg College
Grinnell College
Grove City College
Gustavus Adolphus College
Hanover College
Hardin-Simmons University
Heidelberg College
Hendrix College
Hiram College
Hollins University
Hood College
Hope College
Illinois College
IL Wesleyan University
John Carroll University
Kalamazoo College
Knox College
Lakeland College
LeTourneau University
Lewis and Clark College
Linfield College
Loras College
Luther College
Macalester College
MacMurray College

Manchester College
Marian College (WI)
McDaniel College
McMurry University
Methodist College
Middlebury College
Millikin University
Millsaps College
Milwaukee School of
  Engineering
Monmouth College (IL)
Mount Holyoke College
Mount Union College
Muhlenberg College
Muskingum College
Nazareth College
NE Wesleyan University
North Central College
North Park University
Oberlin College
Oglethorpe University
OH Northern University
Olivet College
Otterbein College
Pacific Lutheran University
Pacific University (OR)
PA State U Erie, the
  Behrend College
Piedmont College
Plattsburgh State U of NY
Rhodes College
Ripon College
Rose-Hulman Institute of
  Tech
Saint Mary's College (IN)
Saint Mary's U of MN
Simpson College
Southwestern U (TX)
Spelman College
St. Lawrence University
St. Norbert College
St. Olaf College
State U College–Cortland
Susquehanna University
TX Lutheran University
Thiel College

Thomas More College
Transylvania University
Trinity University (TX)
U of CA, Santa Cruz
U of Dubuque
U of Mary Hardin-Baylor
U of Pittsburgh, Bradford
U of Pittsburgh–
    Greensburg
U of Puget Sound
U of St. Thomas (MN)
U of TX at Dallas
U of TX at Tyler
U of the South
U of WI, Eau Claire
U of WI, Oshkosh
U of WI, Platteville
U of WI, River Falls
U of WI, Stevens Point
U of WI, Whitewater
Upper IA University
Ursinus College
Vassar College
Villa Julie College
Wartburg College
Washington and Jefferson
    College
Waynesburg College
Wellesley College
Westminster College (MO)
Westminster College (PA)
Wheaton College (IL)
Whitman College
Whitworth College
Willamette University
Wilmington College (OH)
WI Lutheran College
Wittenberg University

GYMNASTICS
DIVISION I

Arizona State U
Auburn University
Ball State U
Boise State U
Bowling Green State U

Brigham Young University
Brown University
CA State U, Fullerton
CA State U, Sacramento
Centenary College (LA)
Central MI University
College of William & Mary
Cornell University
Eastern MI University
George Washington U
Iowa State U
James Madison University
Kent State U
Louisiana State U
Michigan State U
North Carolina State U
Northern IL University
Ohio State U
Oregon State U
Pennsylvania State U
Rutgers, State U of NJ,
    New Brunswick
San Jose State U
Southeast MO State U
Southern UT University
Stanford University
Temple University
Towson University
U.S. Air Force Academy
U of AL–Tuscaloosa
U of Arizona
U of AR, Fayetteville
U of CA, Berkeley
U of CA, Davis
U of CA, Los Angeles
U of Denver
U of Florida
U of Georgia
U of IL at Chicago
U of IL, Champaign
U of Iowa
U of Kentucky
U of MD, College Park
U of Michigan
U of MN, Twin Cities
U of MO, Columbia
U of NE, Lincoln

U of New Hampshire
U of NC, Chapel Hill
U of Oklahoma
U of Pennsylvania
U of Pittsburgh
U of Rhode Island
U of Utah
U of Washington
Utah State U
West VA University
Western MI University
Yale University

GYMNASTICS
DIVISION II

Seattle Pacific University
Southern CT State U
TX Woman's University
U of Alaska Anchorage
U of Bridgeport
Westchester U of PA
Winona State U

GYMNASTICS
DIVISION III

Gustavus Adolphus College
Hamline University
Ithaca College
MA Institute of Tech
Rhode Island College
Springfield College
State U College–Brockport
State U College–Cortland
U of WI, Eau Claire
U of WI, La Crosse
U of WI, Oshkosh
U of WI, Stout
U of WI, Whitewater
Ursinus College
Wilson College

ICE HOCKEY
DIVISION I

Bemidji State U

Boston College
Brown University
Clarkson University
Colgate University
College of the Holy Cross
Cornell University
Dartmouth College
Harvard University
Mercyhurst College
MN State U Mankato
Niagara University
Northeastern University
Ohio State U
Princeton University
Providence College
Quinnipiac University
Sacred Heart University
St. Cloud State U
St. Lawrence University
U of Connecticut
U of Findlay
U of ME, Orono
U of MN Duluth
U of MN, Twin Cities
U of New Hampshire
U of Vermont
U of WI, Madison
Wayne State U (MI)
Yale University

ICE HOCKEY
DIVISION II

Saint Michael's College
U of North Dakota

ICE HOCKEY
DIVISION III

Amherst College
Augsburg College
Bethel University
Bowdoin College
Buffalo State College
Chatham College
Colby College

College of St. Benedict
College of St. CAtherine
Concordia
  College–Moorhead
Connecticut College
Elmira College
Gustavus Adolphus College
Hamilton College
Hamline University
Lake Forest College
Manhattanville College
MA Institute of Tech
Middlebury College
Neumann College
New England College
Plattsburgh State U of NY
Rensselaer Polytechnic Inst.
Rochester Institute of Tech
Saint Mary's U of MN
Salve Regina University
St. Olaf College
State U College–Cortland
Trinity College (CT)
Union College (NY)
U of MA, Boston
U of Southern ME
U of St. Thomas (MN)
U of WI, Eau Claire
U of WI, River Falls
U of WI, Stevens Point
U of WI, Superior
Utica College
Wesleyan University (CT)
Williams College

LACROSSE
DIVISION I

American University
Boston College
Boston University
Brown University
Bucknell University
Butler University
Canisius College
Central CT State U

Colgate University
College of the Holy Cross
College of William & Mary
Columbia University
Cornell University
Dartmouth College
Davidson College
Drexel University
Duke University
Duquesne University
Fairfield University
George Mason University
George Washington U
Georgetown University
Harvard University
Hofstra University
Howard University
James Madison University
Johns Hopkins University
La Salle University
Lafayette College
Le Moyne College
Lehigh University
Long Island U-Brooklyn
  Campus
Loyola College (MD)
Manhattan College
Marist College
Monmouth University
Mount St. Mary's College
Niagara University
Northwestern University
Ohio State U
Ohio University
Old Dominion University
Pennsylvania State U
Princeton University
Providence College
Quinnipiac University
Rutgers, State U of NJ,
  New Brunswick
Sacred Heart University
Saint Francis University (PA)
Saint Joseph's University
Siena College
St. Bonaventure University

St. Mary's College of CA
Stanford University
State U of NY–Binghamton
Stony Brook University
Syracuse University
Temple University
Towson University
University at Albany
U of CA, Berkeley
U of Connecticut
U of Delaware
U of Denver
U of MD, Baltimore Co.
U of MD, College Park
U of MA, Amherst
U of New Hampshire
U of NC, Chapel Hill
U of Notre Dame
U of Pennsylvania
U of Richmond
U of Vermont
U of Virginia
Vanderbilt University
Villanova University
VA Polytechnic Institute & State U
Wagner College
Yale University

LACROSSE
DIVISION II

Adelphi University
American International College
Assumption College
Bentley College
Bloomsburg U of PA
Bryant College
C.W. Post Campus/Long Island U
East Stroudsburg U of PA
Franklin Pierce College
Gannon University
Indiana U of PA
Lees-McRae College

Limestone College
Lock Haven U of PA
Longwood University
Mercyhurst College
Merrimack College
Millersville U of PA
Pfeiffer University
Philadelphia University
Queens U of Charlotte
Regis University (CO)
Saint Anselm College
Saint Michael's College
Shippensburg U of PA
Southern CT State U
Southern NH University
St. Andrews Presbyterian College
Stonehill College
U of CA, Davis
U of New Haven
Westchester U of PA

LACROSSE
DIVISION III

Alfred University
Allegheny College
Alvernia College
Amherst College
Arcadia University
Averett University
Babson College
Bates College
Bowdoin College
Bridgewater College (VA)
Bridgewater State College
Bryn Mawr College
Buffalo State College
Cabrini College
Castleton State College
Catholic University
Cazenovia College
Cedar Crest College
Centenary College (NJ)
Chestnut Hill College
Christopher Newport U

Claremont McKenna-Harvey Mudd-Scripps Colleges
Clarkson University
Colby College
Colby-Sawyer College
College Misericordia
College of Notre Dame (MD)
College of Wooster
Colorado College
Connecticut College
Curry College
Denison University
Dickinson College
Drew University
Eastern CT State U
Eastern University
Elizabethtown College
Elmira College
Elms College
Emerson College
Endicott College
Fairleigh Dickinson U, Madison
Ferrum College
Franklin & Marshall College
Frostburg State U
Gettysburg College
Gordon College
Goucher College
Greensboro College
Guilford College
Gwynedd-Mercy College
Hamilton College
Hartwick College
Haverford College
Hobart and William Smith Colleges
Hollins University
Hood College
Immaculata University
Ithaca College
Kean University
Keene State College
Kenyon College

King's College (PA)
Lasell College
Linfield College
Lycoming College
Lynchburg College
Manhattanville College
Marymount University (VA)
MA Institute of Tech
McDaniel College
Medaille College
Messiah College
Methodist College
Middlebury College
Montclair State U
Moravian College
Mount Holyoke College
Muhlenberg College
Nazareth College
Neumann College
New England College
Nichols College
Oberlin College
OH Wesleyan University
Plymouth State College
Randolph-Macon College
Rensselaer Polytechnic
  Institute
Rhode Island College
Roanoke College
Rochester Institute of Tech
Roger Williams University
Rosemont College
Rowan University
Salisbury University
Salve Regina University
Shenandoah University
Skidmore College
Smith College
Springfield College
St. John Fisher College
St. Lawrence University
St. Mary's College of MD
State U College–Brockport
State U College–Cortland
State U College at Fredonia
State U College–Geneseo

State U College–Oneonta
State U College–Potsdam
State U of NY–Oswego
Stevens Institute of Tech
Susquehanna University
Swarthmore College
Sweet Briar College
The College of NJ
Trinity College (CT)
Trinity College (DC)
Tufts University
Union College (NY)
U of Dallas
U of Mary Washington
U of MA, Dartmouth
U of New England
U of Puget Sound
U of Redlands
U of Rochester
U of Scranton
U of Southern ME
Ursinus College
Utica College
Vassar College
Villa Julie College
VA Wesleyan College
Washington and Lee U
WA College (MD)
Wellesley College
Wells College
Wesley College
Wesleyan University (CT)
Western CT State U
Western New England
  College
Wheaton College (MA)
Whittier College
Whitworth College
Wilkes University
Williams College
Wittenberg University
Worcester State College

RIFLE
DIVISION I

Austin Peay State U
Birmingham-Southern
  College
Morehead State U
Texas Christian U
The Citadel
U of AL–Birmingham
U of Mississippi
U of NE, Lincoln
U of San Francisco
U of TN at Martin
U of TX at El Paso

RIFLE
DIVISION III

Rose-Hulman Institute of
  Tech
Wentworth Institute of
  Tech

ROWING
DIVISION I

Boston College
Boston University
Brown University
Bucknell University
CA State U, Sacramento
Clemson University
Colgate University
College of the Holy Cross
Columbia University
Cornell University
Creighton University
Dartmouth College
Drake University
Drexel University
Duke University
Duquesne University
Eastern MI University
Fairfield University
Fordham University

George Mason University
George Washington U
Georgetown University
Gonzaga University
Harvard University
IN University, Bloomington
Iona College
Jacksonville University
Kansas State U
La Salle University
Lehigh University
Loyola College (MD)
Loyola Marymount U
Marist College
Michigan State U
Murray State U
Northeastern University
Ohio State U
Oregon State U
Princeton University
Robert Morris University
Rutgers, State U of NJ,
    New Brunswick
Sacred Heart University
Saint Joseph's University
San Diego State U
Santa Clara University
Southern Methodist U
St. Mary's College of CA
Stanford University
Stetson University
Syracuse University
Temple University
U.S. Naval Academy
U at Buffalo, the State U of
    NY
U of CA, Berkeley
U of CA, Irvine
U of CA, Los Angeles
U of Central FL
U of Cincinnati
U of Connecticut
U of Dayton
U of Delaware
U of Iowa
U of Kansas

U of Louisville
U of MA, Amherst
U of Miami (FL)
U of Michigan
U of MN, Twin Cities
U of New Hampshire
U of NC, Chapel Hill
U of Notre Dame
U of Pennsylvania
U of Rhode Island
U of San Diego
U of Southern CA
U of TN, Knoxville
U of TX at Austin
U of Tulsa
U of Virginia
U of Washington
U of WI, Madison
Villanova University
Washington State U
West VA University
Yale University

ROWING
DIVISION II

Assumption College
Barry University
Dowling College
FL Institute of Technology
Franklin Pierce College
Humboldt State U
Lynn University
Mercyhurst College
Nova Southeastern U
Rollins College
Seattle Pacific University
U of CA, Davis
U of CA, San Diego
U of Charleston (West VA)
U of Tampa
Western WA University

ROWING
DIVISION III

Bates College
Bryn Mawr College
Cazenovia College
Chapman University
Clark University (MA)
Colby College
Connecticut College
Hamilton College
Hobart and William Smith
    Colleges
Ithaca College
Johns Hopkins University
Lesley University
Lewis and Clark College
Marietta College
MA Institute of Tech
MA Maritime Academy
Mills College
Mount Holyoke College
North Park University
Pacific Lutheran University
Richard Stockton College
    of NJ
Rochester Institute of Tech
Simmons College
Skidmore College
Smith College
St. Lawrence University
State U of NY Maritime
    College
Trinity College (CT)
Trinity College (DC)
Tufts University
U.S. Coast Guard Academy
U.S. Merchant Marine
    Academy
Union College (NY)
U of Mary Washington
U of Puget Sound
Vassar College
WA College (MD)
Wellesley College
Wesleyan University (CT)

Willamette University
Williams College
Worcester Polytechnic
Institute

RUGBY
DIVISION I

Eastern IL University

RUGBY
DIVISION III

Vassar College

SKIING
DIVISION I

Boise State U
Boston College
Brown University
Dartmouth College
Harvard University
MT State U-Bozeman
U of CO, Boulder
U of Denver
U of MA, Amherst
U of Nevada
U of New Hampshire
U of New Mexico
U of Utah
U of Vermont
U of WI, Green Bay

SKIING
DIVISION II

Green Mountain College
MI Technological U
Northern MI University
Saint Anselm College
Saint Michael's College
St. Cloud State U
U of Alaska Anchorage
U of Alaska Fairbanks
Western State College (CO)

SKIING
DIVISION III

Babson College
Bates College
Bowdoin College
Clarkson University
Colby College
Colby-Sawyer College
College of St. Benedict
Finlandia University
Gustavus Adolphus College
Macalester College
MA Institute of Tech
Middlebury College
Plymouth State College
Smith College
St. Lawrence University
St. Olaf College
U of Puget Sound
Whitman College
Williams College

SOCCER
DIVISION I

AL A&M University
American University
Appalachian State U
Arizona State U
Arkansas State U
Auburn University
Austin Peay State U
Ball State U
Baylor University
Belmont University
Birmingham-Southern
College
Boise State U
Boston College
Boston University
Bowling Green State U
Brigham Young University
Brown University
Bucknell University
Butler University

CA Polytechnic State U
CA State U, Fresno
CA State U, Fullerton
CA State U, Northridge
CA State U, Sacramento
Campbell University
Canisius College
Centenary College (LA)
Central CT State U
Central MI University
Charleston Southern U
Clemson University
Coastal Carolina University
Colgate University
College of Charleston (SC)
College of the Holy Cross
College of William & Mary
Colorado College
Columbia University
Cornell University
Creighton University
Dartmouth College
Davidson College
Delaware State U
DePaul University
Drake University
Drexel University
Drury University
Duke University
Duquesne University
East Carolina University
East Tennessee State U
Eastern IL University
Eastern MI University
Eastern WA University
Elon University
Fairfield University
Fairleigh Dickinson U,
Teaneck
FL Atlantic University
FL International University
Florida State U
Fordham University
Furman University
Gardner-Webb University
George Mason University

George Washington U
Georgetown University
GA Southern University
Georgia State U
Gonzaga University
Grambling State U
Harvard University
High Point University
Hofstra University
Howard University
Idaho State U
Illinois State U
Indiana State U
IN University, Bloomington
IN U-Purdue, U Fort Wayne
Iona College
Iowa State U
Jackson State U
Jacksonville State U
Jacksonville University
James Madison University
Kent State U
La Salle University
Lafayette College
Lehigh University
Liberty University
Lipscomb University
Long Beach State U
Long Island U-Brooklyn
   Campus
Louisiana State U
Loyola College (MD)
Loyola Marymount U
Loyola University (IL)
Manhattan College
Marist College
Marquette University
Marshall University
McNeese State U
Mercer University
Miami University (OH)
Michigan State U
Middle Tennessee State U
Mississippi State U
MS Valley State U
Monmouth University

Morehead State U
Mount St. Mary's College
Murray State U
Niagara University
Nicholls State U
North Carolina State U
Northeastern University
Northern AZ University
Northern IL University
Northwestern State U
Northwestern University
Oakland University
Ohio State U
Ohio University
Oklahoma State U
Old Dominion University
Oral Roberts University
Oregon State U
Pennsylvania State U
Pepperdine University
Portland State U
Prairie View A&M U
Princeton University
Providence College
Purdue University
Quinnipiac University
Radford University
Rice University
Rider University
Robert Morris University
Rutgers, State U of NJ,
   New Brunswick
Sacred Heart University
Saint Francis University (PA)
Saint Joseph's University
Saint Louis University
Sam Houston State U
Samford University
San Diego State U
San Jose State U
Santa Clara University
Seton Hall University
Siena College
South Carolina State U
Southeast MO State U
Southeastern LA University

Southern Methodist U
Southern U–Baton Rouge
Southern UT University
Southwest MO State U
St. Bonaventure University
St. John's University (NY)
St. Mary's College of CA
St. Peter's College
Stanford University
State U of NY–Binghamton
Stephen F. Austin State U
Stetson University
Stony Brook University
Syracuse University
Temple University
TN Technological U
TX A&M U–College Station
TX Christian University
TX State U–San Marcos
TX Tech University
The Citadel
Towson University
Troy State U
Tulane University
U.S. Air Force Academy
U.S. Military Academy
U.S. Naval Academy
University at Albany
U at Buffalo, the State U of
   NY
U of Akron
U of AL–Birmingham
U of AL–Tuscaloosa
U of Arizona
U of AR, Fayetteville
U of AR, Little Rock
U of AR, Pine Bluff
U of CA, Berkeley
U of CA, Irvine
U of CA, Los Angeles
U of CA, Riverside
U of CA, Santa Barbara
U of Central FL
U of Cincinnati
U of CO, Boulder
U of Connecticut

U of Dayton
U of Delaware
U of Denver
U of Detroit Mercy
U of Evansville
U of Florida
U of Georgia
U of Hartford
U of Hawaii– Manoa
U of Houston
U of Idaho
U of IL, Champaign
U of Iowa
U of Kansas
U of Kentucky
U of LA at Lafayette
U of LA at Monroe
U of Louisville
U of ME, Orono
U of MD, Baltimore Co.
U of MD, College Park
U of MA, Amherst
U of Memphis
U of Miami (FL)
U of Michigan
U of MN, Twin Cities
U of Mississippi
U of MO, Columbia
U of Montana
U of NE, Lincoln
U of Nevada
U of NV, Las Vegas
U of New Hampshire
U of New Mexico
U of NC at Greensboro
U of NC, Asheville
U of NC, Chapel Hill
U of NC, Charlotte
U of NC, Wilmington
U of North Texas
U of Northern IA
U of Notre Dame
U of Oklahoma
U of Oregon
U of Pennsylvania
U of Pittsburgh

U of Portland
U of Rhode Island
U of Richmond
U of San Diego
U of San Francisco
U of South AL
U of SC, Columbia
U of South Florida
U of Southern CA
U of Southern MS
U of TN at Chattanooga
U of TN at Martin
U of TN, Knoxville
U of TX at Austin
U of TX at El Paso
U of the Pacific
U of Toledo
U of Tulsa
U of Utah
U of Vermont
U of Virginia
U of Washington
U of WI, Green Bay
U of WI, Madison
U of WI, Milwaukee
U of Wyoming
Utah State U
UT Valley State College
Valparaiso University
Vanderbilt University
Villanova University
VA Commonwealth U
VA Military Institute
VA Polytechnic Institute &
   State U
Wagner College
Wake Forest University
Washington State U
Weber State U
West VA University
Western Carolina U
Western IL University
Western KY University
Western MI University
Winthrop University
Wofford College

Wright State U
Xavier University
Yale University
Youngstown State U

SOCCER
DIVISION II

Adams State College
Adelphi University
American International
   College
Anderson College (SC)
Angelo State U
Ashland University
Assumption College
Augustana College (SD)
Barry University
Barton College
Bellarmine University
Belmont Abbey College
Bemidji State U
Bentley College
Bloomfield College
Bloomsburg U of PA
Bryant College
C.W. Post Campus/Long
   Island U
Caldwell College
CA State Polytechnic
   U–Pomona
CA State U, Bakersfield
CA State U, Chico
CA State U, Dominguez
   Hills
CA State U, Los Angeles
CA State U–San Bernardino
CA State U–Stanislaus
California U of
   Pennsylvania
Carson-Newman College
Catawba College
Central MO State U
Central WA University
Christian Brothers U
Clarion U of Pennsylvania

Clayton College & State U
Coker College
College of Saint Rose
CO Christian University
CO State U-Pueblo
Columbia Union College
Concord College
Concordia College (NY)
Concordia U–St. Paul
Converse College
Dallas Baptist University
Davis and Elkins College
Delta State U
Dominican College (NY)
East Central University
East Stroudsburg U of PA
Eastern NM University
Eckerd College
Edinboro U of PA
Emporia State U
Erskine College
Felician College
Ferris State U
FL Institute of Technology
FL Southern College
Fort Lewis College
Francis Marion University
Franklin Pierce College
Gannon University
GA College & State U
Goldey-Beacom College
Grand Canyon University
Grand Valley State U
Green Mountain College
Harding University
Holy Family University
Humboldt State U
Indiana U of PA
Kennesaw State U
KY Wesleyan College
Kutztown U of PA
Lander University
Le Moyne College
Lees-McRae College
Lenoir-Rhyne College
Lewis University

Limestone College
Lincoln Memorial U
Lock Haven U of PA
Longwood University
Lynn University
Mansfield U of PA
Mars Hill College
Mercy College
Mercyhurst College
Merrimack College
Mesa State College
Metropolitan State College
    of Denver
Midwestern State U
Millersville U of PA
MN State U–Mankato
MN State U Moorhead
MO Southern State U-Joplin
Molloy College
MT State U–Billings
Mount Olive College
NJ Institute of Technology
NM Highlands University
NY Institute of Technology
Newberry College
North Dakota State U
North Greenville College
Northeastern State U
Northern KY University
Northern MI University
Northern State U
Northwest MO State U
Northwest Nazarene U
Northwood University
Nova Southeastern U
Nyack College
Oakland City University
OH Valley College
Ouachita Baptist University
Pace University
Pfeiffer University
Philadelphia University
Presbyterian College
Queens College (NY)
Queens U of Charlotte
Quincy University

Regis University (CO)
Rockhurst University
Rollins College
Saginaw Valley State U
Saint Anselm College
Saint Joseph's College (IN)
Saint Leo University
Saint Michael's College
Salem International U
San Francisco State U
Seattle Pacific University
Seattle University
Shepherd College
Shippensburg U of PA
Slippery Rock U of PA
Sonoma State U
South Dakota State U
Southampton
    Campus–Long Island U
Southern CT State U
Southern IL U–Edwardsville
Southern NH University
Southwest Baptist U
Southwest MN State U
Southwestern OK State U
St. Andrews Presbyterian
    College
St. Cloud State U
St. Edward's University
St. Mary's University (TX)
St. Thomas Aquinas College
Stonehill College
Teikyo Post University
TX A&M U-Commerce
TX A&M Uy–Kingsville
Tiffin University
Truman State U
Tusculum College
U of AL, Huntsville
U of Bridgeport
U of CA, Davis
U of CA, San Diego
U of Central AR
U of Central Oklahoma
U of Charleston (West VA)
U of Findlay

U of Indianapolis
U of MA at Lowell
U of MN Duluth
U of MN, Crookston
U of MN, Morris
U of MO, Rolla
U of MO, St. Louis
U of Montevallo
U of NE at Omaha
U of New Haven
U of North AL
U of NC at Pembroke
U of North Dakota
U of North Florida
U of Northern CO
U of SC at Aiken
U of SC–Spartanburg
U of South Dakota
U of Southern IN
U of Tampa
U of the Incarnate Word
U of West Florida
U of WI, Parkside
Washburn U of Topeka
Wayne State College (NE)
Westchester U of PA
West TX A&M University
West VA U Institute of Tech
West VA Wesleyan College
Western OR University
Western WA University
Wheeling Jesuit University
Wilmington College (DE)
Wingate University
Winona State U

SOCCER
DIVISION III

Adrian College
Agnes Scott College
Albion College
Albright College
Alfred University
Allegheny College
Alma College

Alvernia College
Alverno College
Amherst College
Anderson University (IN)
Anna Maria College
Arcadia University
Augsburg College
Augustana College (IL)
Aurora University
Austin College
Averett University
Babson College
Baldwin-Wallace College
Baptist Bible College
Bard College
Bates College
Bay Path College
Becker College
Beloit College
Benedictine University (IL)
Bethany College (West VA)
Bethel University
Blackburn College
Bluffton College
Bowdoin College
Brandeis University
Bridgewater College (VA)
Bridgewater State College
Bryn Mawr College
Buena Vista University
Buffalo State College
Cabrini College
CA Lutheran University
CA State U, Hayward
Calvin College
Capital University
Carleton College
Carnegie Mellon University
Carroll College (WI)
Carthage College
Case Western Reserve U
Castleton State College
Catholic University
Cazenovia College
Cedar Crest College
Centenary College (NJ)

Central College (IA)
Centre College
Chapman University
Chatham College
Chestnut Hill College
Chowan College
Christopher Newport U
City College of NY
Claremont McKenna-
   Harvey Mudd-Scripps
   Colleges
Clark University (MA)
Clarke College
Clarkson University
Coe College
Colby College
Colby-Sawyer College
College Misericordia
College of Mt. St. Joseph
College of Mt. St. Vincent
College of Notre Dame
   (MD)
College of Saint Elizabeth
College of St. Benedict
College of St. CAtherine
College of St. Scholastica
College of Wooster
Concordia
   College–Moorhead
Concordia University (IL)
Concordia University (WI)
Connecticut College
Cornell College
Curry College
D'Youville College
Defiance College
DE Valley College
Denison University
DePauw University
DeSales University
Dickinson College
Dominican University (IL)
Drew University
Earlham College
East TX Baptist University
Eastern CT State U

Eastern Mennonite U
Eastern Nazarene College
Eastern University
Edgewood College
Elizabethtown College
Elmhurst College
Elmira College
Elms College
Emerson College
Emmanuel College (MA)
Emory and Henry College
Emory University
Endicott College
Fairleigh Dickinson U,
    Madison
Ferrum College
Finlandia University
Fisk University
Fitchburg State College
Fontbonne University
Framingham State College
Franklin & Marshall College
Franklin College
Frostburg State U
Gallaudet University
George Fox University
Gettysburg College
Gordon College
Goucher College
Greensboro College
Greenville College
Grinnell College
Grove City College
Guilford College
Gustavus Adolphus College
Gwynedd-Mercy College
Hamilton College
Hamline University
Hanover College
Hardin-Simmons University
Hartwick College
Haverford College
Heidelberg College
Hendrix College
Hilbert College
Hiram College

Hobart and William Smith
    Colleges
Hollins University
Hood College
Hope College
Huntingdon College
Husson College
Illinois College
IL Wesleyan University
Immaculata University
Ithaca College
John Carroll University
Johns Hopkins University
Johnson and Wales U
Johnson State College
Juniata College
Kalamazoo College
Kean University
Keene State College
Kenyon College
Keuka College
King's College (PA)
Knox College
La Grange College
La Roche College
Lake Erie College
Lake Forest College
Lakeland College
Lasell College
Lawrence University
Lebanon Valley College
Lesley University
LeTourneau University
Lincoln University (PA)
Linfield College
Loras College
Louisiana College
Luther College
Lycoming College
Lynchburg College
Macalester College
MacMurray College
ME Maritime Academy
Manchester College
Manhattanville College
Maranatha Baptist Bible
    College

Marian College (WI)
Marietta College
Martin Luther College
Mary Baldwin College
Marymount University (VA)
Maryville College (TN)
Maryville U of Saint Louis
Marywood University
MA College of Liberal Arts
MA Institute of Tech
McDaniel College
McMurry University
Medaille College
Medgar Evers College
Menlo College
Meredith College
Messiah College
Methodist College
Middlebury College
Millikin University
Mills College
Millsaps College
Milwaukee School of
    Engineering
Mississippi College
Monmouth College (IL)
Montclair State U
Moravian College
Mount Holyoke College
Mount Ida College
Mount Mary College
Mt. St. Mary College (NY)
Mount Union College
Muhlenberg College
Muskingum College
Nazareth College
NE Wesleyan University
Neumann College
New England College
NJ City University
New York University
Nichols College
NC Wesleyan College
North Central College
North Park University
Northland College
Norwich University

Oberlin College
Occidental College
Oglethorpe University
OH Northern University
OH Wesleyan University
Olivet College
Otterbein College
Pacific Lutheran University
Pacific University (OR)
Palm Beach Atlantic U
Peace College
Penn State ALtoona
Penn State Berks-Lehigh
  Valley College
PA State U Erie, the
  Behrend College
Philadelphia Biblical U
Piedmont College
Pine Manor College
Plattsburgh State U of NY
Plymouth State College
Polytechnic University (NY)
Pomona-Pitzer Colleges
Principia College
Ramapo College
Randolph-Macon College
Randolph-Macon Woman's
  College
Regis College (MA)
Rensselaer Polytechnic
  Institute
Rhode Island College
Rhodes College
Richard Stockton College
  of NJ
Ripon College
Rivier College
Roanoke College
Rochester Institute of Tech
Rockford College
Roger Williams University
Rose-Hulman Institute of
  Tech
Rowan University
Russell Sage College
Rutgers, The State U of NJ,
  Camden

Rutgers, The State U of NJ,
  Newark
Saint Joseph's College (ME)
Saint Mary's College (IN)
Saint Mary's U of MN
Salem State College
Salisbury University
Salve Regina University
Schreiner University
Shenandoah University
Simmons College
Simpson College
Skidmore College
Smith College
Southern VT College
Southwestern U (TX)
Spelman College
Springfield College
St. John Fisher College
St. John's University (MN)
St. Joseph's College (Long
  Island)
St. Lawrence University
St. Mary's College of MD
St. Norbert College
St. Olaf College
State U College–Brockport
State U College–Cortland
State U College at Fredonia
State U College–Geneseo
State U College–New Paltz
State U College–Geneseo
State U College–Oneonta
State U College–Potsdam
State U of NY–Farmingdale
State U of NY–Oswego
State U of NY Institute of
  Tech
Stephens College
Stevens Institute of Tech
Susquehanna University
Swarthmore College
Sweet Briar College
TX Lutheran University
The College of NJ
Thiel College
Thomas College

Thomas More College
Transylvania University
Trinity College (CT)
Trinity College (DC)
Trinity University (TX)
Tufts University
U.S. Coast Guard Academy
Union College (NY)
U of CA, Santa Cruz
U of Chicago
U of Dallas
U of Dubuque
U of La Verne
U of ME at Presque Isle
U of ME, Farmington
U of Mary Hardin-Baylor
U of Mary Washington
U of MA, Boston
U of MA, Dartmouth
U of New England
U of Pittsburgh, Bradford
U of Pittsburgh–
  Greensburg
U of Puget Sound
U of Redlands
U of Rochester
U of Scranton
U of Southern ME
U of St. Thomas (MN)
U of TX at Dallas
U of TX at Tyler
U of the Ozarks (AR)
U of the South
U of WI, Eau Claire
U of WI, La Crosse
U of WI, Oshkosh
U of WI, Platteville
U of WI, River Falls
U of WI, Stevens Point
U of WI, Stout
U of WI, Superior
U of WI, Whitewater
Upper IA University
Ursinus College
Utica College
Vassar College
Villa Julie College

VA Wesleyan College
Wartburg College
Washington and Jefferson
  College
Washington and Lee U
WA College (MD)
Washington U in St. Louis
Waynesburg College
Webster University
Wellesley College
Wells College
Wentworth Inst. of Tech
Wesley College
Wesleyan College (GA)
Wesleyan University (CT)
Western CT State U
Western New England
  College
Westfield State College
Westminster College (MO)
Westminster College (PA)
Wheaton College (IL)
Wheaton College (MA)
Wheelock College
Whitman College
Whittier College
Whitworth College
Widener University
Wilkes University
Willamette University
William Paterson U of NJ
Williams College
Wilmington College (OH)
Wilson College
WI Lutheran College
Wittenberg University
Worcester Polytechnic
  Institute
Worcester State College
York College (PA)

SOFTBALL
DIVISION I

AL A&M University
Alabama State U

Alcorn State U
Appalachian State U
Arizona State U
Auburn University
Austin Peay State U
Ball State U
Baylor University
Belmont University
Bethune-Cookman College
Birmingham-Southern
  College
Boston College
Boston University
Bowling Green State U
Bradley University
Brigham Young University
Brown University
Bucknell University
Butler University
CA Polytechnic State U
CA State U, Fresno
CA State U, Fullerton
CA State U, Northridge
CA State U, Sacramento
Campbell University
Canisius College
Centenary College (LA)
Central CT State U
Central MI University
Charleston Southern U
Cleveland State U
Coastal Carolina U
Colgate University
College of Charleston (SC)
College of the Holy Cross
Colorado State U
Columbia University
Coppin State College
Cornell University
Creighton University
Dartmouth College
Delaware State U
DePaul University
Drake University
Drexel University
East Carolina University

East TN State U
Eastern IL University
Eastern KY University
Eastern MI University
Elon University
Fairfield University
Fairleigh Dickinson U,
  Teaneck
FL A&M University
FL Atlantic University
FL International University
Florida State U
Fordham University
Furman University
Gardner-Webb University
George Mason University
George Washington U
GA Institute of Technology
GA Southern University
Georgia State U
Grambling State U
Hampton University
Harvard University
Hofstra University
Howard University
Illinois State U
Indiana State U
IN University, Bloomington
IN U-Purdue, U Fort Wayne
Iona College
Iowa State U
Jackson State U
Jacksonville State U
Jacksonville University
James Madison University
Kent State U
La Salle University
Lafayette College
Lehigh University
Liberty University
Lipscomb University
Long Beach State U
Long Island U-Brooklyn
  Campus
Louisiana State U
LA Tech University

Loyola Marymount U
Loyola University (IL)
Manhattan College
Marist College
Marshall University
McNeese State U
Mercer University
Miami University (OH)
Michigan State U
Middle TN State U
Mississippi State U
MS Valley State U
Monmouth University
Morehead State U
Morgan State U
Mount St. Mary's College
New Mexico State U
Niagara University
Nicholls State U
Norfolk State U
NC A&T State U
North Carolina State U
Northern IL University
Northwestern State U
Northwestern University
Oakland University
Ohio State U
Ohio University
Oklahoma State U
Oregon State U
Pennsylvania State U
Portland State U
Prairie View A&M U
Princeton University
Providence College
Purdue University
Quinnipiac University
Radford University
Rider University
Robert Morris University
Rutgers, State U of NJ,
  New Brunswick
Sacred Heart University
Saint Francis University (PA)
Saint Joseph's University
Saint Louis University

Sam Houston State U
Samford University
San Diego State U
San Jose State U
Santa Clara University
Savannah State U
Seton Hall University
Siena College
South Carolina State U
Southeast MO State U
Southeastern LA University
Southern IL U–Carbondale
Southern U–Baton Rouge
Southern UT University
Southwest MO State U
St. Bonaventure University
St. Francis College (NY)
St. John's University (NY)
St. Mary's College of CA
St. Peter's College
Stanford University
State U of NY–Binghamton
Stephen F. Austin State U
Stetson University
Stony Brook University
Syracuse University
Temple University
Tennessee State U
TN Technological U
TX A&M U–College Station
TX A&M U–Corpus Christi
TX Southern University
TX State U–San Marcos
TX Tech University
Towson University
Troy State U
U.S. Military Academy
University at ALbany
U at Buffalo, the State U of
  NY
U of Akron
U of AL–Birmingham
U of AL, Tuscaloosa
U of Arizona
U of AR, Fayetteville
U of AR, Pine Bluff

U of CA, Berkeley
U of CA, Los Angeles
U of CA, Riverside
U of CA, Santa Barbara
U of Central FL
U of Connecticut
U of Dayton
U of Delaware
U of Detroit Mercy
U of Evansville
U of Florida
U of Georgia
U of Hartford
U of Hawaii–Manoa
U of Houston
U of IL at Chicago
U of IL, Champaign
U of Iowa
U of Kansas
U of Kentucky
U of LA at Lafayette
U of LA at Monroe
U of Louisville
U of ME, Orono
U of MD, Baltimore Co.
U of MD, College Park
U of MD, Eastern Shore
U of MA, Amherst
U of Michigan
U of MN, Twin Cities
U of Mississippi
U of MO, Columbia
U of MO, KS City
U of NE, Lincoln
U of Nevada
U of Nevada, Las Vegas
U of New Mexico
U of NC at Greensboro
U of NC, Chapel Hill
U of NC, Charlotte
U of NC, Wilmington
U of North TX
U of Northern IA
U of Notre Dame
U of Oklahoma
U of Oregon

U of Pennsylvania
U of Pittsburgh
U of Rhode Island
U of San Diego
U of SC–Columbia
U of South FL
U of Southern MS
U of TN at Chattanooga
U of TN at Martin
U of TN, Knoxville
U of TX at ARlington
U of TX at Austin
U of TX at El Paso
U of TX at San Antonio
U of the Pacific
U of Toledo
U of Tulsa
U of Utah
U of Vermont
U of Virginia
U of Washington
U of WI, Green Bay
U of WI, Madison
Utah State U
UT Valley State College
Valparaiso University
Villanova University
VA Polytechnic Institute &
    State U
Wagner College
Western IL University
Western KY University
Western MI University
Wichita State U
Winthrop University
Wright State U
Yale University
Youngstown State U

SOFTBALL
DIVISION II

Abilene Christian U
Adams State College
Adelphi University
Albany State U (GA)

Alderson-Broaddus College
American International
    College
Anderson College (SC)
Angelo State U
AR Tech University
Armstrong Atlantic State U
Ashland University
Assumption College
Augusta State U
Augustana College (SD)
Barry University
Barton College
Bellarmine University
Belmont Abbey College
Bemidji State U
Benedict College
Bentley College
Bloomfield College
Bloomsburg U of PA
Bluefield State College
Bowie State U
Brigham Young U, HI
Bryant College
C.W. Post Campus/Long
    Island U
Caldwell College
CA State U, Bakersfield
CA State U, Chico
CA State U, Dominguez
    Hills
CA State U–San Bernardino
CA State U–Stanislaus
California U of PA
Cameron University
Carson-Newman College
Catawba College
Central MO State U
Central WA University
Chaminade University
Christian Brothers U
Clarion U of Pennsylvania
Clark Atlanta University
Coker College
College of Saint Rose
CO School of Mines

CO State U-Pueblo
Columbia Union College
Columbus State U
Concord College
Concordia College (NY)
Concordia U–St. Paul
Davis and Elkins College
Delta State U
Dominican College (NY)
Dowling College
East Central University
East Stroudsburg U of PA
Eastern NM University
Eckerd College
Edinboro U of PA
Elizabeth City State U
Emporia State U
Erskine College
Fairmont State College
Fayetteville State U
Felician College
Ferris State U
FL Gulf Coast University
FL Institute of Technology
FL Southern College
Fort Hays State U
Fort Lewis College
Fort Valley State U
Francis Marion University
Franklin Pierce College
Gannon University
GA College & State U
Georgian Court College
Glenville State College
Goldey-Beacom College
Grand Canyon University
Grand Valley State U
Green Mountain College
HI Pacific University
Henderson State U
Hillsdale College
Holy Family University
Humboldt State U
Indiana U of PA
Johnson C. Smith U
Kennesaw State U

Kentucky State U
KY Wesleyan College
Kutztown U of PA
Lake Superior State U
Lander University
Lane College
Le Moyne College
Lees-McRae College
LeMoyne-Owen College
Lenoir-Rhyne College
Lewis University
Limestone College
Lincoln Memorial U
Lincoln University (MO)
Livingstone College
Lock Haven U of PA
Longwood University
Lynn University
Mansfield U of PA
Mars Hill College
Mercy College
Mercyhurst College
Merrimack College
Mesa State College
Midwestern State U
Miles College
Millersville U of PA
MN State U–Mankato
MN State U Moorhead
MO Southern State U Joplin
MO Western State College
Molloy College
MT State U–Billings
Mount Olive College
NM Highlands University
NY Institute of Technology
Newberry College
NC Central University
North Dakota State U
North Greenville College
Northeastern State U
Northern KY University
Northern State U
Northwest MO State U
Northwest Nazarene U
Northwood University

Nova Southeastern U
Nyack College
Oakland City University
OH Valley College
OK Panhandle State U
Ouachita Baptist University
Pace University
Paine College
Pfeiffer University
Philadelphia University
Pittsburg State U
Presbyterian College
Queens College (NY)
Queens U of Charlotte
Quincy University
Regis University (CO)
Rollins College
Saginaw Valley State U
Saint Anselm College
Saint Joseph's College (IN)
Saint Leo University
Saint Michael's College
Salem International U
San Francisco State U
Seattle University
Shaw University
Shepherd College
Shippensburg U of PA
Slippery Rock U of PA
Sonoma State U
South Dakota State U
Southampton
    Campus–Long Island U
Southeastern OK State U
Southern AR University
Southern CT State U
Southern IL U–Edwardsville
Southern NH University
Southwest Baptist U
Southwest MN State U
Southwestern OK State U
St. Andrews Presbyterian
    College
St. Augustine's College
St. Cloud State U
St. Edward's University

St. Martin's College
St. Mary's University (TX)
St. Paul's College
St. Thomas Aquinas College
State U of West GA
Stonehill College
Tarleton State U
Teikyo Post University
TX A&M Uy–Kingsville
TX Woman's University
Tiffin University
Truman State U
Tusculum College
Tuskegee University
U of AL, Huntsville
U of AR, Monticello
U of Bridgeport
U of CA, Davis
U of CA, San Diego
U of Central AR
U of Central Oklahoma
U of Charleston (West VA)
U of CO, CO Springs
U of Findlay
U of Hawaii–Hilo
U of Indianapolis
U of MA at Lowell
U of MN Duluth
U of MN, Crookston
U of MN, Morris
U of MO, Rolla
U of MO, St. Louis
U of NE at Kearney
U of NE at Omaha
U of New Haven
U of North AL
U of NC at Pembroke
U of North Dakota
U of North Florida
U of Northern CO
U of Puerto Rico, Cayey
U of Puerto Rico, Mayaguez
    Campus
U of SC at Aiken
U of SC–Spartanburg
U of South Dakota

U of Southern IN
U of Tampa
U of the Incarnate Word
U of the Sciences in
　Philadelphia
U of West Alabama
U of West Florida
U of WI, Parkside
Valdosta State U
Virginia State U
VA Union University
Washburn U of Topeka
Wayne State College (NE)
Wayne State U (MI)
Westchester U of PA
West Liberty State College
West VA State College
West VA U Institute of Tech
West VA Wesleyan College
Western NM University
Western OR University
Western WA University
Wheeling Jesuit University
Wilmington College (DE)
Wingate University
Winona State U
Winston-Salem State U

SOFTBALL
DIVISION III

Adrian College
Agnes Scott College
Albertus Magnus College
Albion College
Albright College
Alfred University
Allegheny College
Alma College
Alvernia College
Alverno College
Amherst College
Anderson University (IN)
Anna Maria College
Arcadia University
Augsburg College

Augustana College (IL)
Aurora University
Averett University
Babson College
Baldwin-Wallace College
Baptist Bible College
Bates College
Bay Path College
Becker College
Beloit College
Benedictine University (IL)
Bernard M. Baruch College
Bethany College (West VA)
Bethel University
Blackburn College
Bluffton College
Bowdoin College
Brandeis University
Bridgewater College (VA)
Bridgewater State College
Brooklyn College
Buena Vista University
Buffalo State College
Cabrini College
CA Lutheran University
CA State U, Hayward
Calvin College
Capital University
Carleton College
Carroll College (WI)
Carthage College
Case Western Reserve U
Castleton State College
Catholic University
Cazenovia College
Cedar Crest College
Centenary College (NJ)
Central College (IA)
Centre College
Chapman University
Chatham College
Chestnut Hill College
Chowan College
Christopher Newport U
Claremont McKenna-
　Harvey Mudd-Scripps

Colleges
Clark University (MA)
Clarke College
Coe College
Colby College
College Misericordia
College of Mt. St. Joseph
College of Mt. St. Vincent
College of New Rochelle
College of Saint Elizabeth
College of St. Benedict
College of St. CAtherine
College of St. Scholastica
College of Staten Island
College of Wooster
Colorado College
Concordia
　College–Moorhead
Concordia University (IL)
Concordia University (WI)
Concordia U–Austin
Cornell College
Curry College
D'Youville College
Daniel Webster College
Defiance College
DE Valley College
Denison University
DePauw University
DeSales University
Dickinson College
Dominican University (IL)
Drew University
East TX Baptist University
Eastern CT State U
Eastern Mennonite U
Eastern Nazarene College
Eastern University
Edgewood College
Elizabethtown College
Elmhurst College
Elmira College
Elms College
Emerson College
Emmanuel College (MA)
Emory and Henry College

Emory University
Endicott College
Eureka College
Fairleigh Dickinson U,
   Madison
Ferrum College
Finlandia University
Fisk University
Fitchburg State College
Fontbonne University
Framingham State College
Franklin & Marshall College
Franklin College
Frostburg State U
Gallaudet University
George Fox University
Gettysburg College
Gordon College
Greensboro College
Greenville College
Grinnell College
Grove City College
Guilford College
Gustavus Adolphus College
Gwynedd-Mercy College
Hamilton College
Hamline University
Hanover College
Hardin-Simmons University
Hartwick College
Haverford College
Heidelberg College
Hendrix College
Hilbert College
Hiram College
Hood College
Hope College
Howard Payne University
Hunter College
Huntingdon College
Husson College
Illinois College
IL Wesleyan University
Immaculata University
Ithaca College
John Carroll University

John Jay College of
   Criminal Justice
Johnson and Wales U
Johnson State College
Juniata College
Kalamazoo College
Kean University
Keene State College
Kenyon College
Keuka College
King's College (PA)
Knox College
La Grange College
La Roche College
Lake Erie College
Lake Forest College
Lakeland College
Lasell College
Lawrence University
Lebanon Valley College
Lehman College, City U of
   NY
Lesley University
LeTourneau University
Lewis and Clark College
Linfield College
Loras College
Louisiana College
Luther College
Lycoming College
Lynchburg College
Macalester College
MacMurray College
ME Maritime Academy
Manchester College
Manhattanville College
Maranatha Baptist Bible
   College
Marian College (WI)
Marietta College
Martin Luther College
Mary Baldwin College
Maryville College (TN)
Maryville U of Saint Louis
Marywood University
MA College of Liberal Arts

MA Institute of Tech
MA Maritime Academy
McDaniel College
Medaille College
Medgar Evers College
Menlo College
Meredith College
Messiah College
Methodist College
Middlebury College
Millikin University
Millsaps College
Milwaukee School of
   Engineering
Mississippi College
Monmouth College (IL)
Montclair State U
Moravian College
Mount Holyoke College
Mount Ida College
Mount Mary College
Mt. St. Mary College (NY)
Mount Union College
Muhlenberg College
Muskingum College
NE Wesleyan University
Neumann College
New England College
NJ City University
NY City College of Tech
Newbury College
Nichols College
NC Wesleyan College
North Central College
North Park University
Northland College
Norwich University
Oberlin College
Occidental College
OH Northern University
OH Wesleyan University
Olivet College
Otterbein College
Pacific Lutheran University
Pacific University (OR)
Palm Beach Atlantic U

Peace College
Penn State ALtoona
PA State U at Erie, the
    Behrend College
Philadelphia Biblical U
Piedmont College
Pine Manor College
Plattsburgh State U of NY
Plymouth State College
Polytechnic University (NY)
Pomona-Pitzer Colleges
Ramapo College
Randolph-Macon College
Randolph-Macon Woman's
    College
Regis College (MA)
Rensselaer Polytechnic
    Institute
Rhode Island College
Rhodes College
Richard Stockton College
    of NJ
Ripon College
Rivier College
Roanoke College
Rochester Institute of Tech
Rockford College
Roger Williams University
Rose-Hulman Institute of
    Tech
Rosemont College
Rowan University
Russell Sage College
Rust College
Rutgers, the State U of NJ,
    Camden
Rutgers, the State U of NJ,
    Newark
Saint Joseph's College (ME)
Saint Mary's College (IN)
Saint Mary's U of MN
Salem State College
Salisbury University
Salve Regina University
Schreiner University
Shenandoah University
Simmons College

Simpson College
Skidmore College
Smith College
Southern VT College
Springfield College
St. John Fisher College
St. John's University (MN)
St. Joseph's College (Long
    Island)
St. Lawrence University
St. Norbert College
St. Olaf College
State U College–Brockport
State U College–Cortland
State U College at Fredonia
State U College–Geneseo
State U College–New Paltz
State U College–Geneseo
State U College–Old
    Westbury
State U College–Oneonta
State U College–Potsdam
State U of NY–Farmingdale
State U of NY–Oswego
State U of NY Institute of
    Technology
State U of NY Maritime
    College
Stillman College
Suffolk University
Sul Ross State U
Susquehanna University
Swarthmore College
TX Lutheran University
The College of NJ
Thiel College
Thomas College
Thomas More College
Transylvania University
Trinity College (CT)
Trinity College (DC)
Trinity University (TX)
Tufts University
U.S. Coast Guard Academy
U.S. Merchant Marine
    Academy
Union College (NY)

U of Chicago
U of Dallas
U of Dubuque
U of La Verne
U of ME at Presque Isle
U of ME, Farmington
U of Mary Hardin-Baylor
U of Mary Washington
U of MA, Boston
U of MA, Dartmouth
U of New England
U of Pittsburgh, Bradford
U of Pittsburgh–
    Greensburg
U of Puget Sound
U of Redlands
U of Rochester
U of Scranton
U of Southern ME
U of St. Thomas (MN)
U of TX at Dallas
U of the Ozarks (AR)
U of the South
U of WI, Eau Claire
U of WI, La Crosse
U of WI, Oshkosh
U of WI, Platteville
U of WI, River Falls
U of WI, Stevens Point
U of WI, Stout
U of WI, Superior
U of WI, Whitewater
Upper IA University
Ursinus College
Utica College
Villa Julie College
VA Wesleyan College
Wartburg College
Washington and Jefferson
    College
WA College (MD)
WA University in St. Louis
Waynesburg College
Webster University
Wells College
Wentworth Institute of
    Tech

Wesley College
Wesleyan College (GA)
Wesleyan University (CT)
Western CT State U
Western New England
  College
Westfield State College
Westminster College (MO)
Westminster College (PA)
Wheaton College (IL)
Wheaton College (MA)
Wheelock College
Whittier College
Whitworth College
Widener University
Wilkes University
Willamette University
William Paterson U of NJ
Williams College
Wilmington College (OH)
Wilson College
WI Lutheran College
Wittenberg University
Worcester Polytechnic
  Institute
Worcester State College
York College (NY)
York College (PA)

SQUASH
DIVISION I

Brown University
Cornell University
Dartmouth College
George Washington U
Harvard University
Princeton University
U of Pennsylvania
Yale University

SQUASH
DIVISION III

Amherst College
Bates College

Bowdoin College
Colby College
Connecticut College
Franklin & Marshall College
Hamilton College
Haverford College
Hobart and William Smith
  Colleges
Middlebury College
Mount Holyoke College
Smith College
St. Lawrence University
Trinity College (CT)
Tufts University
Vassar College
Wellesley College
Wesleyan University (CT)
Williams College

SWIMMING
DIVISION I

American University
Arizona State U
Auburn University
Ball State U
Boston College
Boston University
Bowling Green State U
Brigham Young University
Brown University
Bucknell University
Butler University
CA Polytechnic State U
CA State U, Fresno
CA State U, Northridge
Canisius College
Centenary College (LA)
Central CT State U
Clemson University
Cleveland State U
Colgate University
College of Charleston (SC)
College of the Holy Cross
College of William & Mary
Colorado State U

Columbia University
Cornell University
Dartmouth College
Davidson College
Drexel University
Duke University
Duquesne University
East Carolina University
Eastern IL University
Eastern MI University
Fairfield University
FL A&M University
FL Atlantic University
FL International University
Florida State U
Fordham University
Gardner-Webb University
George Mason University
George Washington U
Georgetown University
GA Institute of Technology
GA Southern University
Harvard University
Howard University
Illinois State U
IN University, Bloomington
IN U-Purdue, U Fort Wayne
Iona College
Iowa State U
James Madison University
La Salle University
Lafayette College
Lehigh University
Louisiana State U
Loyola College (MD)
Loyola Marymount U
Manhattan College
Marist College
Marshall University
Miami University (OH)
Michigan State U
New Mexico State U
Niagara University
NC A&T State U
North Carolina State U
Northeastern University

Northern AZ University
Northwestern University
Oakland University
Ohio State U
Ohio University
Old Dominion University
Oregon State U
Pennsylvania State U
Pepperdine University
Princeton University
Providence College
Purdue University
Radford University
Rice University
Rider University
Rutgers, State U of NJ,
    New Brunswick
Sacred Heart University
Saint Francis University (PA)
Saint Louis University
San Diego State U
San Jose State U
Seton Hall University
Siena College
Southern IL U–Carbondale
Southern Methodist U
Southwest MO State U
St. Bonaventure University
St. Francis College (NY)
St. John's University (NY)
St. Peter's College
Stanford University
State U of NY–Binghamton
Stony Brook University
Syracuse University
TX A&M U–College Station
TX Christian University
Towson University
Tulane University
U.S. Air Force Academy
U.S. Military Academy
U.S. Naval Academy
U at Buffalo, the State U of
    NY
U of Akron
U of AL–Tuscaloosa

U of Arizona
U of AR, Fayetteville
U of AR, Little Rock
U of CA, Berkeley
U of CA, Irvine
U of CA, Los Angeles
U of CA, Santa Barbara
U of Cincinnati
U of Connecticut
U of Delaware
U of Denver
U of Evansville
U of Florida
U of Georgia
U of Hawaii– Manoa
U of Houston
U of IL at Chicago
U of IL, Champaign
U of Iowa
U of Kansas
U of Kentucky
U of LA at Monroe
U of Louisville
U of ME, Orono
U of MD, Baltimore Co.
U of MD, College Park
U of MA, Amherst
U of Miami (FL)
U of Michigan
U of MN, Twin Cities
U of MO, Columbia
U of NE, Lincoln
U of Nevada
U of NV, Las Vegas
U of New Hampshire
U of New Mexico
U of NC, Chapel Hill
U of NC, Wilmington
U of North Florida
U of North TX
U of Northern IA
U of Notre Dame
U of Pennsylvania
U of Pittsburgh
U of Rhode Island
U of Richmond

U of San Diego
U of SC, Columbia
U of Southern CA
U of TN, Knoxville
U of TX at Austin
U of the Pacific
U of Toledo
U of Utah
U of Vermont
U of Virginia
U of Washington
U of WI, Green Bay
U of WI, Green Bay
U of WI, Madison
U of WI, Milwaukee
U of Wyoming
Valparaiso University
Villanova University
VA Polytechnic Institute &
    State U
Wagner College
Washington State U
West VA University
Western IL University
Western KY University
Wright State U
Xavier University
Yale University
Youngstown State U

SWIMMING
DIVISION II

Ashland University
Bentley College
Bloomsburg U of PA
C.W. Post Campus/Long
    Island U
CA State U, Bakersfield
California U of PA
Catawba College
Central WA University
Clarion U of Pennsylvania
College of Saint Rose
CO School of Mines
Delta State U

Drury University
East Stroudsburg U of PA
Edinboro U of PA
Fairmont State College
FL Southern College
Gannon University
Grand Valley State U
Henderson State U
Hillsdale College
Indiana U of PA
Kutztown U of PA
Le Moyne College
Lewis University
Limestone College
Lock Haven U of PA
Mansfield U of PA
Metropolitan State College
 of Denver
Millersville U of PA
MN State U–Mankato
MN State U Moorhead
NJ Institute of Technology
Northern MI University
Ouachita Baptist University
Pace University
Pfeiffer University
Queens College (NY)
Rollins College
Saint Michael's College
Salem International U
San Francisco State U
Seattle University
Shippensburg U of PA
Slippery Rock U of PA
South Dakota State U
Southern CT State U
St. Cloud State U
Truman State U
U of CA, Davis
U of CA, San Diego
U of Charleston (West VA)
U of Findlay
U of Indianapolis
U of NE at Kearney
U of NE at Omaha
U of North Dakota

U of Northern CO
U of Puerto Rico, Bayamon
U of Puerto Rico, Mayaguez
 Campus
U of South Dakota
U of Tampa
U of the Incarnate Word
Wayne State U (MI)
Westchester U of PA
West VA Wesleyan College
Wheeling Jesuit University
Wingate University

SWIMMING
DIVISION III

Agnes Scott College
Albion College
Albright College
Alfred University
Allegheny College
Alma College
Amherst College
Arcadia University
Augsburg College
Augustana College (IL)
Austin College
Babson College
Baldwin-Wallace College
Bates College
Beloit College
Benedictine University (IL)
Bernard M. Baruch College
Bethany College (West VA)
Bowdoin College
Brandeis University
Bridgewater State College
Brooklyn College
Bryn Mawr College
Buena Vista University
Buffalo State College
Cabrini College
CA Institute of Technology
CA Lutheran University
CA State U, Hayward
Calvin College

Carleton College
Carnegie Mellon University
Carroll College (WI)
Carthage College
Case Western Reserve U
Catholic University
Centre College
Chapman University
Chatham College
Claremont McKenna-
 Harvey Mudd-Scripps
 Colleges
Clark University (MA)
Clarkson University
Coe College
Colby College
Colby-Sawyer College
College Misericordia
College of Mt. St. Vincent
College of New Rochelle
College of Notre Dame
 (MD)
College of Saint Elizabeth
College of St. Benedict
College of St. CAtherine
College of Staten Island
College of Wooster
Colorado College
Concordia
 College–Moorhead
Connecticut College
Denison University
DePauw University
Dickinson College
Drew University
Eastern CT State U
Elizabethtown College
Elms College
Emory University
Eureka College
Fairleigh Dickinson U,
 Madison
Franklin & Marshall College
Frostburg State U
Gallaudet University
Gettysburg College

Gordon College
Goucher College
Greensboro College
Grinnell College
Grove City College
Gustavus Adolphus College
Hamilton College
Hamline University
Hartwick College
Hendrix College
Hiram College
Hobart and William Smith
  Colleges
Hollins University
Hood College
Hope College
Hunter College
IL Wesleyan University
Ithaca College
John Carroll University
John Jay College of
  Criminal Justice
Johns Hopkins University
Juniata College
Kalamazoo College
Keene State College
Kenyon College
King's College (PA)
Knox College
La Grange College
Lake Forest College
Lawrence University
Lebanon Valley College
Lehman College, City U of
  NY
Lewis and Clark College
Linfield College
Loras College
Luther College
Lycoming College
Macalester College
Mary Baldwin College
Marymount University (VA)
MA Institute of Tech
McDaniel College
McMurry University

Middlebury College
Millikin University
Mills College
Montclair State U
Mount Holyoke College
Mt. St. Mary College (NY)
Mount Union College
Nazareth College
New York University
North Central College
Norwich University
Oberlin College
Occidental College
OH Northern University
OH Wesleyan University
Olivet College
Pacific Lutheran University
Pacific University (OR)
Penn State ALtoona
PA State U Erie, the
  Behrend College
Plymouth State College
Pomona-Pitzer Colleges
Principia College
Randolph-Macon College
Randolph-Macon Woman's
  College
Regis College (MA)
Rensselaer Polytechnic
  Institute
Rhodes College
Ripon College
Rochester Institute of Tech
Rose-Hulman Institute of
  Tech
Rowan University
Saint Mary's College (IN)
Saint Mary's U of MN
Salisbury University
Simmons College
Simpson College
Skidmore College
Smith College
Southwestern U (TX)
Springfield College
St. John's University (MN)

St. Joseph's College (Long
  Island)
St. Lawrence University
St. Mary's College of MD
St. Norbert College
St. Olaf College
State U College–Brockport
State U College–Cortland
State U College at Fredonia
State U College–Geneseo
State U College–New Paltz
State U College–Geneseo
State U College–Old
  Westbury
State U College–Oneonta
State U College–Potsdam
State U of NY–Oswego
State U of NY Maritime
  College
Stephens College
Stevens Institute of Tech
Susquehanna University
Swarthmore College
Sweet Briar College
The College of NJ
Transylvania University
Trinity College (CT)
Trinity College (DC)
Trinity University (TX)
Tufts University
U.S. Coast Guard Academy
U.S. Merchant Marine
  Academy
Union College (NY)
U of CA, Santa Cruz
U of Chicago
U of La Verne
U of Mary Washington
U of MA, Dartmouth
U of Puget Sound
U of Redlands
U of Rochester
U of Scranton
U of St. Thomas (MN)
U of the South
U of WI, Eau Claire

U of WI, La Crosse
U of WI, Oshkosh
U of WI, River Falls
U of WI, Stevens Point
U of WI, Whitewater
Ursinus College
Utica College
Vassar College
Washington and Jefferson
 College
Washington and Lee U
WA College (MD)
Washington U in St. Louis
Webster University
Wellesley College
Wells College
Wesleyan University (CT)
Western CT State U
Western New England
 College
Westfield State College
Westminster College (PA)
Wheaton College (IL)
Wheaton College (MA)
Wheelock College
Whitman College
Whittier College
Whitworth College
Widener University
Willamette University
William Paterson U of NJ
Williams College
Wilmington College (OH)
Wittenberg University
Worcester Polytechnic
 Institute
York College (NY)
York College (PA)

SYNCHRONIZED SWIMMING
DIVISION I

U of AL–Birmingham
Canisius College
Ohio State U

SYNCHRONIZED SWIMMING
DIVISION II

U of the Incarnate Word

SYNCHRONIZED SWIMMING
DIVISION III

Carleton College
Keuka College
Wheaton College (MA)

TENNIS
DIVISION I

AL A&M University
Alabama State U
Alcorn State U
American University
Appalachian State U
Arizona State U
Arkansas State U
Auburn University
Austin Peay State U
Ball State U
Baylor University
Belmont University
Bethune-Cookman College
Birmingham-Southern
 College
Boise State U
Boston College
Boston University
Bowling Green State U
Bradley University
Brigham Young University
Brown University
Bucknell University
Butler University
CA Polytechnic State U
CA State U, Fresno
CA State U, Fullerton
CA State U, Northridge
CA State U, Sacramento

Campbell University
Centenary College (LA)
Charleston Southern U
Chicago State U
Clemson University
Cleveland State U
Coastal Carolina U
Colgate University
College of Charleston (SC)
College of the Holy Cross
College of William & Mary
Colorado State U
Columbia University
Coppin State College
Cornell University
Creighton University
Dartmouth College
Davidson College
Delaware State U
DePaul University
Drake University
Drexel University
Duke University
Duquesne University
East Carolina University
East Tennessee State U
Eastern IL University
Eastern KY University
Eastern MI University
Eastern WA University
Elon University
Fairfield University
Fairleigh Dickinson U,
 Teaneck
FL A&M University
FL Atlantic University
FL International University
Florida State U
Fordham University
Furman University
Gardner-Webb University
George Mason University
George Washington U
Georgetown University
GA Institute of Technology
GA Southern University
Georgia State U

Gonzaga University
Grambling State U
Hampton University
Harvard University
High Point University
Hofstra University
Howard University
Idaho State U
Illinois State U
Indiana State U
IN University, Bloomington
IN U-Purdue, U Fort Wayne
Iowa State U
Jackson State U
Jacksonville State U
Jacksonville University
James Madison University
Kansas State U
La Salle University
Lafayette College
Lamar University
Lehigh University
Liberty University
Lipscomb University
Long Beach State U
Long Island U-Brooklyn
   Campus
Louisiana State U
LA Tech University
Loyola College (MD)
Loyola Marymount U
Manhattan College
Marist College
Marquette University
Marshall University
McNeese State U
Mercer University
Miami University (OH)
Michigan State U
Middle Tennessee State U
Mississippi State U
MS Valley State U
Monmouth University
MT State U-Bozeman
Morehead State U
Morgan State U

Mount St. Mary's College
Murray State U
New Mexico State U
Niagara University
Nicholls State U
Norfolk State U
NC A&T State U
North Carolina State U
Northern AZ University
Northern IL University
Northwestern State U
Northwestern University
Oakland University
Ohio State U
Oklahoma State U
Old Dominion University
Oral Roberts University
Pennsylvania State U
Pepperdine University
Prairie View A&M U
Princeton University
Providence College
Purdue University
Quinnipiac University
Radford University
Rice University
Rider University
Robert Morris University
Rutgers, State U of NJ,
   New Brunswick
Sacred Heart University
Saint Francis University (PA)
Saint Joseph's University
Saint Louis University
Sam Houston State U
Samford University
San Diego State U
San Jose State U
Santa Clara University
Savannah State U
Seton Hall University
Siena College
South Carolina State U
Southeast MO State U
Southeastern LA University
Southern IL U-Carbondale

Southern Methodist U
Southern U-Baton Rouge
Southern UT University
Southwest MO State U
St. Bonaventure University
St. Francis College (NY)
St. John's University (NY)
St. Mary's College of CA
St. Peter's College
Stanford University
State U of NY-Binghamton
Stephen F. Austin State U
Stetson University
Stony Brook University
Syracuse University
Temple University
Tennessee State U
TN Technological U
TX A&M U-College Station
TX A&M U-Corpus Christi
TX Christian University
TX Southern University
TX State U-San Marcos
TX Tech University
Towson University
Troy State U
Tulane University
U.S. Air Force Academy
U.S. Military Academy
University at Albany
U at Buffalo, the State U of
   NY
U of Akron
U of AL-Birmingham
U of AL-Tuscaloosa
U of Arizona
U of AR, Fayetteville
U of AR, Little Rock
U of AR, Pine Bluff
U of CA, Berkeley
U of CA, Irvine
U of CA, Los Angeles
U of CA, Riverside
U of CA, Santa Barbara
U of Central FL
U of Cincinnati

U of CO, Boulder
U of Connecticut
U of Dayton
U of Delaware
U of Denver
U of Detroit Mercy
U of Evansville
U of Florida
U of Georgia
U of Hartford
U of Hawaii– Manoa
U of Houston
U of Idaho
U of IL at Chicago
U of IL, Champaign
U of Iowa
U of Kansas
U of Kentucky
U of LA at Lafayette
U of LA at Monroe
U of Louisville
U of ME, Orono
U of MD, Baltimore Co.
U of MD, College Park
U of MD, Eastern Shore
U of MA, Amherst
U of Memphis
U of Miami (FL)
U of Michigan
U of MN, Twin Cities
U of Mississippi
U of MO, Columbia
U of MO, KS City
U of Montana
U of NE, Lincoln
U of Nevada
U of NV, Las Vegas
U of New Hampshire
U of New Mexico
U of New Orleans
U of NC at Greensboro
U of NC, Asheville
U of NC, Chapel Hill
U of NC, Charlotte
U of NC, Wilmington
U of North TX

U of Northern IA
U of Notre Dame
U of Oklahoma
U of Oregon
U of Pennsylvania
U of Pittsburgh
U of Portland
U of Rhode Island
U of Richmond
U of San Diego
U of San Francisco
U of South AL
U of SC, Columbia
U of South Florida
U of Southern CA
U of Southern MS
U of TN at Chattanooga
U of TN at Martin
U of TN, Knoxville
U of TX at ARlington
U of TX at Austin
U of TX at El Paso
U of TX at San Antonio
U of TX, Pan American
U of the Pacific
U of Toledo
U of Tulsa
U of Utah
U of Vermont
U of Virginia
U of Washington
U of WI, Green Bay
U of WI, Madison
U of WI, Milwaukee
U of Wyoming
Utah State U
UT Valley State College
Valparaiso University
Vanderbilt University
Villanova University
VA Commonwealth U
VA Polytechnic Institute &
   State U
Wagner College
Wake Forest University
Washington State U

Weber State U
West VA University
Western Carolina U
Western IL University
Western KY University
Western MI University
Wichita State U
Winthrop University
Wofford College
Wright State U
Xavier University
Yale University
Youngstown State U

TENNIS
DIVISION II

Abilene Christian U
Adelphi University
Albany State U (GA)
American International
   College
Anderson College (SC)
AR Tech University
Armstrong Atlantic State U
Ashland University
Assumption College
Augusta State U
Augustana College (SD)
Barry University
Barton College
Bellarmine University
Belmont Abbey College
Bemidji State U
Benedict College
Bentley College
Bloomsburg U of PA
Bluefield State College
Bowie State U
Brigham Young U, HI
Bryant College
C.W. Post Campus/Long
   Island U
Caldwell College
CA State Polytechnic
   U–Pomona

CA State U, Bakersfield
CA State U, Los Angeles
CA State U–San Bernardino
California U of PA
Cameron University
Carson-Newman College
Catawba College
Central State U
Chadron State College
Christian Brothers U
Clarion U of Pennsylvania
Clark Atlanta University
Clayton College & State U
Coker College
CO Christian University
CO State U-Pueblo
Columbus State U
Concord College
Concordia College (NY)
Converse College
Dallas Baptist University
Davis and Elkins College
Delta State U
Dowling College
Drury University
East Central University
East Stroudsburg U of PA
Eastern NM University
Eckerd College
Elizabeth City State U
Emporia State U
Erskine College
Fairmont State College
Fayetteville State U
Ferris State U
FL Gulf Coast University
FL Institute of Technology
FL Southern College
Fort Hays State U
Fort Valley State U
Francis Marion University
Franklin Pierce College
GA College & State U
Georgian Court College
Grand CAnyon University
Grand Valley State U

Green Mountain College
Harding University
HI Pacific University
Henderson State U
Hillsdale College
Indiana U of PA
Johnson C. Smith U
Kennesaw State U
Kentucky State U
KY Wesleyan College
Kutztown U of PA
Lake Superior State U
Lane College
Le Moyne College
Lees-McRae College
LeMoyne-Owen College
Lewis University
Limestone College
Lincoln Memorial U
Lincoln University (MO)
Livingstone College
Longwood University
Lynn University
Mars Hill College
Mercyhurst College
Merrimack College
Mesa State College
Metropolitan State College
   of Denver
MI Technological U
Midwestern State U
Millersville U of PA
MN State U–Mankato
MN State U Moorhead
MO Southern State U-Joplin
MO Western State College
Molloy College
MT State U–Billings
Mount Olive College
NJ Institute of Technology
Newberry College
NC Central University
North Greenville College
Northeastern State U
Northern KY University
Northwest MO State U

Northwood University
Nova Southeastern U
Oakland City University
Ouachita Baptist University
Pace University
Pfeiffer University
Philadelphia University
Presbyterian College
Queens College (NY)
Queens U of Charlotte
Quincy University
Rockhurst University
Rollins College
Saginaw Valley State U
Saint Anselm College
Saint Joseph's College (IN)
Saint Leo University
Saint Michael's College
San Francisco State U
Shaw University
Shepherd College
Shippensburg U of PA
Slippery Rock U of PA
Sonoma State U
South Dakota State U
Southampton
   Campus–Long Island U
Southeastern OK State U
Southern AR University
Southern IL U–Edwardsville
Southern NH University
Southwest Baptist U
Southwest MN State U
St. Andrews Presbyterian
   College
St. Augustine's College
St. Cloud State U
St. Edward's University
St. Mary's University (TX)
St. Paul's College
St. Thomas Aquinas College
Stonehill College
Tarleton State U
Tiffin University
Truman State U
Tusculum College

Tuskegee University
U of AL, Huntsville
U of AR, Monticello
U of CA, Davis
U of CA, San Diego
U of Central AR
U of Central Oklahoma
U of Charleston (West VA)
U of CO, CO Springs
U of Findlay
U of Hawaii–Hilo
U of Indianapolis
U of MN Duluth
U of MN, Morris
U of MO, St. Louis
U of Montevallo
U of NE at Kearney
U of NE at Omaha
U of New Haven
U of North AL
U of NC at Pembroke
U of North Dakota
U of North Florida
U of Northern CO
U of Puerto Rico, CAyey
U of Puerto Rico, Mayaguez
   Campus
U of SC at Aiken
U of SC–Spartanburg
U of South Dakota
U of Southern IN
U of Tampa
U of the DC
U of the Incarnate Word
U of the Sciences in
   Philadelphia
U of West Florida
Valdosta State U
Virginia State U
VA Union University
Washburn U of Topeka
Wayne State U (MI)
Westchester U of PA
West Liberty State College
West VA State College
West VA U Institute of Tech
West VA Wesleyan College

Western NM University
Wingate University
Winona State U
Winston-Salem State U

TENNIS
DIVISION III

Adrian College
Agnes Scott College
Albertus Magnus College
Albion College
Albright College
Alfred University
Allegheny College
Alma College
Alvernia College
Amherst College
Anderson University (IN)
Arcadia University
Augustana College (IL)
Aurora University
Austin College
Averett University
Babson College
Baldwin-Wallace College
Bard College
Bates College
Becker College
Beloit College
Benedictine University (IL)
Bernard M. Baruch College
Bethany College (West VA)
Bethel University
Blackburn College
Bluffton College
Bowdoin College
Brandeis University
Bridgewater College (VA)
Bridgewater State College
Brooklyn College
Bryn Mawr College
Buena Vista University
Cabrini College
CA Institute of Technology
CA Lutheran University
Calvin College

Capital University
Carleton College
Carnegie Mellon University
Carroll College (WI)
Carthage College
Case Western Reserve U
Castleton State College
Catholic University
Cedar Crest College
Central College (IA)
Centre College
Chapman University
Chatham College
Chestnut Hill College
Christopher Newport U
City College of NY
Claremont McKenna-
   Harvey Mudd-Scripps
   Colleges
Clark University (MA)
Clarke College
Clarkson University
Coe College
Colby College
Colby-Sawyer College
College of Mt. St. Joseph
College of Mt. St. Vincent
College of New Rochelle
College of Notre Dame
   (MD)
College of Saint Elizabeth
College of St. Benedict
College of St. Catherine
College of St. Scholastica
College of Staten Island
College of Wooster
Colorado College
Concordia
   College–Moorhead
Concordia University (IL)
Concordia University (WI)
Concordia U–Austin
Connecticut College
Cornell College
Curry College
Defiance College
Denison University

DePauw University
DeSales University
Dickinson College
Dominican University (IL)
Drew University
Earlham College
Eastern Mennonite U
Eastern Nazarene College
Eastern University
Edgewood College
Elizabethtown College
Elmhurst College
Elmira College
Emerson College
Emmanuel College (MA)
Emory and Henry College
Emory University
Endicott College
Eureka College
Fairleigh Dickinson U,
  Madison
Ferrum College
Fisk University
Fontbonne University
Franklin & Marshall College
Franklin College
Frostburg State U
Gallaudet University
George Fox University
Gettysburg College
Gordon College
Goucher College
Greensboro College
Greenville College
Grinnell College
Grove City College
Guilford College
Gustavus Adolphus College
Gwynedd-Mercy College
Hamilton College
Hamline University
Hanover College
Hardin-Simmons University
Hartwick College
Haverford College
Heidelberg College

Hendrix College
Hiram College
Hobart and William Smith
  Colleges
Hollins University
Hood College
Hope College
Howard Payne University
Hunter College
Huntingdon College
Illinois College
IL Wesleyan University
Immaculata University
Ithaca College
John Carroll University
John Jay College of
  Criminal Justice
Johns Hopkins University
Johnson and Wales U
Johnson State College
Juniata College
Kalamazoo College
Kean University
Kenyon College
King's College (PA)
Knox College
La Grange College
Lake Forest College
Lakeland College
Lawrence University
Lebanon Valley College
Lehman College, City U of
  NY
LeTourneau University
Lewis and Clark College
Lincoln University (PA)
Linfield College
Loras College
Louisiana College
Luther College
Lycoming College
Lynchburg College
Macalester College
MacMurray College
Manchester College
Manhattanville College

Marian College (WI)
Marietta College
Martin Luther College
Mary Baldwin College
Maryville College (TN)
Maryville U of Saint Louis
Marywood University
MA College of Liberal Arts
MA Institute of Tech
McDaniel College
McMurry University
Meredith College
Messiah College
Methodist College
Middlebury College
Millikin University
Mills College
Millsaps College
Milwaukee School of
  Engineering
Mississippi College
Monmouth College (IL)
Montclair State U
Moravian College
Mount Holyoke College
Mount Mary College
Mt. St. Mary College (NY)
Mount Union College
Muhlenberg College
Muskingum College
Nazareth College
NE Wesleyan University
Neumann College
NY City College of Tech
New York University
Newbury College
Nichols College
NC Wesleyan College
North Central College
Oberlin College
Occidental College
Oglethorpe University
OH Northern University
OH Wesleyan University
Olivet College
Otterbein College

Pacific Lutheran University
Pacific University (OR)
Palm Beach Atlantic U
Peace College
Penn State ALtoona
PA State U Erie, the
   Behrend College
Philadelphia Biblical U
Piedmont College
Pine Manor College
Plattsburgh State U of NY
Plymouth State College
Polytechnic University (NY)
Pomona-Pitzer Colleges
Principia College
Ramapo College
Randolph-Macon College
Randolph-Macon Woman's
   College
Regis College (MA)
Rhode Island College
Rhodes College
Richard Stockton College
   of NJ
Ripon College
Roanoke College
Rochester Institute of Tech
Rockford College
Roger Williams University
Rose-Hulman Institute of
   Tech
Rosemont College
Russell Sage College
Rust College
Rutgers, The State U of NJ,
   Newark
Saint Mary's College (IN)
Saint Mary's U of MN
Salem State College
Salisbury University
Salve Regina University
Schreiner University
Shenandoah University
Simmons College
Simpson College
Skidmore College

Smith College
Southwestern U (TX)
Spelman College
Springfield College
St. John Fisher College
St. John's University (MN)
St. Joseph's College (Long
   Island)
St. Lawrence University
St. Mary's College of MD
St. Norbert College
St. Olaf College
State U College–Brockport
State U College–Cortland
State U College at Fredonia
State U College–Geneseo
State U College–New Paltz
State U College–Geneseo
State U College–Oneonta
State U College–Potsdam
State U of NY–Oswego
Stephens College
Stevens Institute of Tech
Stillman College
Suffolk University
Sul Ross State U
Susquehanna University
Swarthmore College
Sweet Briar College
TX Lutheran University
The College of NJ
Thiel College
Thomas More College
Transylvania University
Trinity College (CT)
Trinity College (DC)
Trinity University (TX)
Tufts University
Union College (NY)
U of CA, Santa Cruz
U of Chicago
U of Dallas
U of Dubuque
U of La Verne
U of Mary Hardin-Baylor
U of Mary Washington

U of MA, Boston
U of MA, Dartmouth
U of Puget Sound
U of Redlands
U of Rochester
U of Scranton
U of Southern ME
U of St. Thomas (MN)
U of TX at Dallas
U of TX at Tyler
U of the Ozarks (AR)
U of the South
U of WI, Eau Claire
U of WI, La Crosse
U of WI, Oshkosh
U of WI, River Falls
U of WI, Stevens Point
U of WI, Stout
U of WI, Whitewater
Upper IA University
Ursinus College
Utica College
Vassar College
Villa Julie College
VA Wesleyan College
Wartburg College
Washington and Jefferson
   College
Washington and Lee U
WA College (MD)
Washington U in St. Louis
Waynesburg College
Webster University
Wellesley College
Wells College
Wentworth Institute of
   Tech
Wesley College
Wesleyan College (GA)
Wesleyan University (CT)
Western CT State U
Western New England
   College
Westminster College (MO)
Westminster College (PA)
Wheaton College (IL)

Wheaton College (MA)
Whitman College
Whittier College
Whitworth College
Widener University
Wilkes University
Willamette University
Williams College
Wilmington College (OH)
Wilson College
WI Lutheran College
Wittenberg University
Worcester Polytechnic
  Institute
York College (PA)

TRACK
INDOOR
DIVISION I

AL A&M University
Alabama State U
Alcorn State U
American University
Appalachian State U
Arizona State U
Arkansas State U
Auburn University
Austin Peay State U
Ball State U
Baylor University
Belmont University
Bethune-Cookman College
Boise State U
Boston College
Boston University
Bowling Green State U
Bradley University
Brigham Young University
Brown University
Bucknell University
Butler University
CA Polytechnic State U
CA State U, Fresno
CA State U, Fullerton

CA State U, Northridge
CA State U, Sacramento
Campbell University
Central CT State U
Central MI University
Charleston Southern U
Chicago State U
Clemson University
Coastal Carolina U
Colgate University
College of Charleston (SC)
College of the Holy Cross
College of William & Mary
Colorado State U
Columbia University
Coppin State College
Cornell University
Dartmouth College
Davidson College
Delaware State U
DePaul University
Drake University
Duke University
Duquesne University
East Carolina University
East Tennessee State U
Eastern IL University
Eastern KY University
Eastern MI University
Eastern WA University
Elon University
Fairleigh Dickinson U,
  Teaneck
FL A&M University
FL International University
Florida State U
Fordham University
Furman University
Gardner-Webb University
George Mason University
Georgetown University
GA Institute of Technology
GA Southern University
Georgia State U
Grambling State U
Hampton University

Harvard University
High Point University
Howard University
Idaho State U
Illinois State U
Indiana State U
IN University, Bloomington
IN U-Purdue, U Fort Wayne
Iona College
Iowa State U
Jackson State U
Jacksonville State U
Jacksonville University
James Madison University
Kansas State U
Kent State U
La Salle University
Lafayette College
Lamar University
Lehigh University
Liberty University
Lipscomb University
Long Beach State U
Long Island U-Brooklyn
  Campus
Louisiana State U
LA Tech University
Loyola University (IL)
Manhattan College
Marist College
Marquette University
Marshall University
McNeese State U
Miami University (OH)
Michigan State U
Middle Tennessee State U
Mississippi State U
MS Valley State U
Monmouth University
MT State U-Bozeman
Morehead State U
Morgan State U
Mount St. Mary's College
Murray State U
New Mexico State U
Nicholls State U

Norfolk State U
NC A&T State U
North Carolina State U
Northeastern University
Northern AZ University
Northern IL University
Northwestern State U
Ohio State U
Ohio University
Oklahoma State U
Oral Roberts University
Pennsylvania State U
Portland State U
Prairie View A&M U
Princeton University
Providence College
Purdue University
Quinnipiac University
Radford University
Rice University
Rider University
Robert Morris University
Rutgers, State U of NJ,
    New Brunswick
Sacred Heart University
Saint Francis University (PA)
Saint Joseph's University
Sam Houston State U
Samford University
San Diego State U
Savannah State U
Seton Hall University
South Carolina State U
Southeast MO State U
Southeastern LA University
Southern IL U–Carbondale
Southern Methodist U
Southern U–Baton Rouge
Southern UT University
Southwest MO State U
St. Francis College (NY)
St. John's University (NY)
St. Peter's College
Stanford University
State U of NY–Binghamton
Stephen F. Austin State U

Stony Brook University
Syracuse University
Temple University
Tennessee State U
TN Technological U
TX A&M U–College Station
TX A&M U-Corpus Christi
TX Christian University
TX Southern University
TX State U–San Marcos
TX Tech University
The Citadel
Towson University
Troy State U
Tulane University
U.S. Air Force Academy
U.S. Military Academy
U.S. Naval Academy
University at Albany
U at Buffalo, the State U of
    NY
U of Akron
U of AL–Birmingham
U of AL–Tuscaloosa
U of Arizona
U of AR, Fayetteville
U of AR, Little Rock
U of AR, Pine Bluff
U of CA, Berkeley
U of CA, Irvine
U of CA, Los Angeles
U of CA, Riverside
U of Central FL
U of Cincinnati
U of CO, Boulder
U of Connecticut
U of Dayton
U of Delaware
U of Detroit Mercy
U of Florida
U of Georgia
U of Hartford
U of Hawaii– Manoa
U of Houston
U of Idaho
U of IL at Chicago

U of IL, Champaign
U of Iowa
U of Kansas
U of Kentucky
U of LA at Lafayette
U of LA at Monroe
U of Louisville
U of ME, Orono
U of MD, Baltimore Co.
U of MD, College Park
U of MD, Eastern Shore
U of MA, Amherst
U of Memphis
U of Miami (FL)
U of Michigan
U of MN, Twin Cities
U of Mississippi
U of MO, Columbia
U of MO, KS City
U of Montana
U of NE, Lincoln
U of Nevada
U of NV, Las Vegas
U of New Hampshire
U of New Mexico
U of New Orleans
U of NC, Asheville
U of NC, Chapel Hill
U of NC, Charlotte
U of NC, Wilmington
U of North TX
U of Northern IA
U of Notre Dame
U of Oklahoma
U of Oregon
U of Pennsylvania
U of Pittsburgh
U of Portland
U of Rhode Island
U of Richmond
U of South AL
U of SC, Columbia
U of South Florida
U of Southern CA
U of Southern MS
U of TN at Chattanooga

U of TN, Knoxville
U of TX at Arlington
U of TX at Austin
U of TX at El Paso
U of TX at San Antonio
U of TX, Pan American
U of Toledo
U of Tulsa
U of Utah
U of Vermont
U of Virginia
U of Washington
U of WI, Madison
U of WI, Milwaukee
U of Wyoming
Utah State U
UT Valley State College
Valparaiso University
Vanderbilt University
Villanova University
VA Commonwealth U
VA Military Institute
VA Polytechnic Institute &
  State U
Wagner College
Wake Forest University
Washington State U
Weber State U
West VA University
Western Carolina U
Western IL University
Western KY University
Western MI University
Wichita State U
Winthrop University
Wofford College
Wright State U
Yale University
Youngstown State U

TRACK
INDOOR
DIVISION II

Abilene Christian U
Adams State College

U of Alabama, Huntsville
U of Alaska Anchorage
Alderson-Broaddus College
Anderson College (SC)
Ashland University
Assumption College
Augustana College (SD)
Bellarmine University
Bemidji State University
Bentley College
Bloomsburg U of PA
Bowie State University
Bryant University
C.W. Post Campus/Long
  Island U
CA State U, Bakersfield
CA State U, Dominguez
  Hills
CA State U, Los Angeles
CA State U, Stanislaus
California U of PA
U of California, Davis
Central Missouri State U
Central State University
Central Washington U
Chadron State College
Claflin University
Clarion U of PA
Clayton College & State U
Colorado School of Mines
U of CO, Colorado Springs
Concord University
Concordia U, St. Paul
Dallas Baptist University
East Stroudsburg U of PA
Edinboro U of PA
Emporia State University
Fayetteville State U
Ferris State University
University of Findlay
Florida Southern College
Fort Hays State University
Grand Valley State U
Harding University
Hillsdale College
Indiana U of PA
University of Indianapolis

Kutztown U of PA
Lake Superior State U
Lees-McRae College
Lewis University
Lincoln University (MO)
Lock Haven U of PA
Mansfield University of
  Pennsylvania
U of MA at Lowell
Mercy College
Millersville U of PA
MN State U Mankato
MN State U Moorhead
U of Minnesota Duluth
U of Minnesota, Morris
MO Southern State U-
  Joplin
U of Missouri, Rolla
U of Nebraska at Kearney
U of Nebraska at Omaha
University of New Haven
NY, Institute of Tech
North Carolina Central U
University of North Dakota
North Dakota State U
University of North Florida
Northern Kentucky U
Northern Michigan U
Northern State University
Northwest Missouri State U
Northwest Nazarene U
Northwood University
Pfeiffer University
Pittsburg State University
Saginaw Valley State U
San Francisco State U
Seattle Pacific University
Seattle University
Shaw University
Shippensburg U of PA
Slippery Rock U of PA
University of South Dakota
South Dakota State U
Southern CT State U
Southern IL U, Edwardsville
Uy of Southern Indiana
Southwest Baptist U

St. Augustine's College
St. Cloud State University
St. Joseph's College (IN)
St. Martin's College
St. Paul's College
St. Thomas Aquinas College
Stonehill College
Texas A&M U-Commerce
Texas A&M U-Kingsville
Tiffin University
Truman State University
Virginia State University
Wayne State College (NE)
West Chester U of PA
University of West Georgia
West Virginia State U
West Virginia Wesleyan
  College
Western Oregon U
Western State College of
  CO
Western Washington U
Wheeling Jesuit University
Winona State University
U of Wisconsin, Parkside

TRACK
INDOOR
DIVISION III

Adrian College
Albion College
Albright College
Alfred University
Allegheny College
Amherst College
Anderson University (IN)
Augsburg College
Augustana College (IL)
Baldwin-Wallace College
Bates College
Beloit College
Benedictine University (IL)
Bethany College (West VA)
Bethel University

Bluffton College
Bowdoin College
Brandeis University
Bridgewater College (VA)
Bridgewater State College
Bryn Mawr College
Buena Vista University
Buffalo State College
Cabrini College
Calvin College
Capital University
Carleton College
Carnegie Mellon University
Carroll College (WI)
Carthage College
Case Western Reserve U
Catholic University
Central College (IA)
Christopher Newport U
City College of NY
Coe College
Colby College
College Misericordia
College of Mt. St. Joseph
College of St. Benedict
College of St. Catherine
College of St. Scholastica
Colorado College
Concordia
  College–Moorhead
Concordia University (IL)
Concordia University (WI)
Connecticut College
Cornell College
Defiance College
DE Valley College
Denison University
DePauw University
DeSales University
Dickinson College
Earlham College
Eastern CT State U
Eastern Mennonite U
Elizabethtown College
Elmhurst College
Emmanuel College (MA)

Emory University
Fisk University
Fitchburg State College
Franklin & Marshall College
Frostburg State U
Gallaudet University
Gettysburg College
Goucher College
Greenville College
Grinnell College
Gustavus Adolphus College
Gwynedd-Mercy College
Hamilton College
Hamline University
Hanover College
Hartwick College
Haverford College
Heidelberg College
Hiram College
Hunter College
Illinois College
IL Wesleyan University
Ithaca College
John Carroll University
Johns Hopkins University
Juniata College
Kean University
Keene State College
Kenyon College
Knox College
Lawrence University
Lebanon Valley College
Lehman College, City U of
  NY
Lincoln University (PA)
Linfield College
Loras College
Luther College
Lynchburg College
Macalester College
Manchester College
Marietta College
MA Institute of Tech
McDaniel College
McMurry University
Medgar Evers College

Messiah College
Methodist College
Middlebury College
Millikin University
Milwaukee School of
Engineering
Mississippi College
Monmouth College (IL)
Montclair State U
Moravian College
Mount Holyoke College
Mount Union College
Muhlenberg College
Muskingum College
Nazareth College
NE Wesleyan University
NJ City University
NY City College of Tech
New York University
North Central College
North Park University
Oberlin College
Occidental College
Oglethorpe University
OH Northern University
OH Wesleyan University
Olivet College
Otterbein College
Pacific Lutheran University
Pacific University (OR)
PA State U Erie, the
Behrend College
Plattsburgh State U of NY
Polytechnic University (NY)
Principia College
Ramapo College
Regis College (MA)
Rensselaer Polytechnic
Institute
Rhode Island College
Rhodes College
Richard Stockton College
of NJ
Ripon College
Roanoke College
Rochester Institute of Tech

Rose-Hulman Institute of
Tech
Rowan University
Saint Mary's U of MN
Salem State College
Salisbury University
Simpson College
Smith College
Springfield College
St. Lawrence University
St. Norbert College
St. Olaf College
State U College–Brockport
State U College–Cortland
State U College at Fredonia
State U College–Geneseo
State U College–New Paltz
State U College–Geneseo
State U College–Oneonta
State U of NY–Farmingdale
State U of NY–Oswego
Susquehanna University
Swarthmore College
TX Lutheran University
The College of NJ
Thiel College
Trinity College (CT)
Trinity College (DC)
Tufts University
U.S. Coast Guard Academy
U.S. Merchant Marine
Academy
Union College (NY)
U of Chicago
U of Dubuque
U of La Verne
U of Mary Washington
U of MA, Dartmouth
U of Puget Sound
U of Rochester
U of Southern ME
U of St. Thomas (MN)
U of the South
U of WI, Eau Claire
U of WI, La Crosse
U of WI, Oshkosh

U of WI, Platteville
U of WI, River Falls
U of WI, Stevens Point
U of WI, Stout
U of WI, Superior
U of WI, Whitewater
Upper IA University
Ursinus College
Villa Julie College
Wartburg College
Washington and Lee U
Washington U in St. Louis
Wellesley College
Wesleyan University (CT)
Westfield State College
Westminster College (PA)
Wheaton College (IL)
Wheaton College (MA)
Whitworth College
Widener University
William Paterson U of NJ
Williams College
Wilmington College (OH)
WI Lutheran College
Wittenberg University

TRACK OUTDOOR
DIVISION I

AL A&M University
Alabama State U
Alcorn State U
American University
Appalachian State U
Arizona State U
Arkansas State U
Auburn University
Austin Peay State U
Ball State U
Baylor University
Belmont University
Bethune-Cookman College
Boise State U
Boston College

Boston University
Bowling Green State U
Bradley University
Brigham Young University
Brown University
Bucknell University
Butler University
CA Polytechnic State U
CA State U, Fresno
CA State U, Fullerton
CA State U, Northridge
CA State U, Sacramento
Campbell University
Central CT State U
Central MI University
Charleston Southern U
Chicago State U
Clemson University
Coastal Carolina U
Colgate University
College of Charleston (SC)
College of the Holy Cross
College of William & Mary
Colorado State U
Columbia University
Coppin State College
Cornell University
Dartmouth College
Davidson College
Delaware State U
DePaul University
Drake University
Duke University
Duquesne University
East Carolina University
East Tennessee State U
Eastern IL University
Eastern KY University
Eastern MI University
Eastern WA University
Elon University
Fairleigh Dickinson U,
    Teaneck
FL A&M University
FL Atlantic University
FL International University

Florida State U
Fordham University
Furman University
Gardner-Webb University
George Mason University
Georgetown University
GA Institute of Technology
GA Southern University
Georgia State U
Grambling State U
Hampton University
Harvard University
High Point University
Howard University
Idaho State U
Illinois State U
Indiana State U
IN University, Bloomington
IN U-Purdue, U Fort Wayne
Iona College
Iowa State U
Jackson State U
Jacksonville State U
Jacksonville University
James Madison University
Kansas State U
Kent State U
La Salle University
Lafayette College
Lamar University
Lehigh University
Liberty University
Lipscomb University
Long Beach State U
Long Island U-Brooklyn
    Campus
Louisiana State U
LA Tech University
Loyola College (MD)
Loyola University (IL)
Manhattan College
Marist College
Marquette University
Marshall University
McNeese State U
Miami University (OH)

Michigan State U
Middle Tennessee State U
Mississippi State U
MS Valley State U
Monmouth University
MT State U-Bozeman
Morehead State U
Morgan State U
Mount St. Mary's College
Murray State U
New Mexico State U
Nicholls State U
Norfolk State U
NC A&T State U
North Carolina State U
Northeastern University
Northern AZ University
Northern IL University
Northwestern State U
Ohio State U
Ohio University
Oklahoma State U
Oral Roberts University
Pennsylvania State U
Portland State U
Prairie View A&M U
Princeton University
Providence College
Purdue University
Quinnipiac University
Radford University
Rice University
Rider University
Robert Morris University
Rutgers, State U of NJ,
    New Brunswick
Sacred Heart University
Saint Francis University (PA)
Saint Joseph's University
Sam Houston State U
Samford University
San Diego State U
Savannah State U
Seton Hall University
South Carolina State U
Southeast MO State U

Southeastern LA University
Southern IL U–Carbondale
Southern Methodist U
Southern U–Baton Rouge
Southern UT University
Southwest MO State U
St. Francis College (NY)
St. John's University (NY)
St. Peter's College
Stanford University
State U of NY–Binghamton
Stephen F. Austin State U
Stony Brook University
Syracuse University
Temple University
Tennessee State U
TN Technological U
TX A&M U–College Station
TX A&M U-Corpus Christi
TX Christian University
TX Southern University
TX State U–San Marcos
TX Tech University
The Citadel
Towson University
Troy State U
Tulane University
U.S. Air Force Academy
U.S. Military Academy
U.S. Naval Academy
University at Albany
U at Buffalo, the State U of
   NY
U of Akron
U of AL–Birmingham
U of AL–Tuscaloosa
U of Arizona
U of AR, Fayetteville
U of AR, Little Rock
U of AR, Pine Bluff
U of CA, Berkeley
U of CA, Irvine
U of CA, Los Angeles
U of CA, Riverside
U of CA, Santa Barbara
U of Central FL

U of Cincinnati
U of CO, Boulder
U of Connecticut
U of Dayton
U of Delaware
U of Detroit Mercy
U of Florida
U of Georgia
U of Hartford
U of Hawaii– Manoa
U of Houston
U of Idaho
U of IL at Chicago
U of IL, Champaign
U of Iowa
U of Kansas
U of Kentucky
U of LA at Lafayette
U of LA at Monroe
U of Louisville
U of ME, Orono
U of MD, Baltimore Co.
U of MD, College Park
U of MD, Eastern Shore
U of MA, Amherst
U of Memphis
U of Miami (FL)
U of Michigan
U of MN, Twin Cities
U of Mississippi
U of MO, Columbia
U of MO, KS City
U of Montana
U of NE, Lincoln
U of Nevada
U of NV, Las Vegas
U of New Hampshire
U of New Mexico
U of New Orleans
U of NC at Greensboro
U of NC, Asheville
U of NC, Chapel Hill
U of NC, Charlotte
U of NC, Wilmington
U of North TX
U of Northern IA

U of Notre Dame
U of Oklahoma
U of Oregon
U of Pennsylvania
U of Pittsburgh
U of Portland
U of Rhode Island
U of Richmond
U of South AL
U of SC, Columbia
U of South Florida
U of Southern CA
U of Southern MS
U of TN at Chattanooga
U of TN, Knoxville
U of TX at Arlington
U of TX at Austin
U of TX at El Paso
U of TX at San Antonio
U of TX, Pan American
U of Toledo
U of Tulsa
U of Utah
U of Vermont
U of Virginia
U of Washington
U of WI, Madison
U of WI, Milwaukee
U of Wyoming
Utah State U
UT Valley State College
Valparaiso University
Vanderbilt University
Villanova University
VA Commonwealth U
VA Military Institute
VA Polytechnic Institute &
   State U
Wagner College
Wake Forest University
Washington State U
Weber State U
West VA University
Western Carolina U
Western IL University
Western KY University

Western MI University
Wichita State U
Winthrop University
Wofford College
Wright State U
Yale University
Youngstown State U

TRACK
OUTDOOR
DIVISION II

Abilene Christian U
Adams State College
Albany State U (GA)
Alderson-Broaddus College
Anderson College (SC)
Angelo State U
Ashland University
Assumption College
Augustana College (SD)
Bellarmine University
Bemidji State U
Benedict College
Bentley College
Bloomsburg U of PA
Bowie State U
Bryant College
C.W. Post Campus/Long
    Island U
CA State Polytechnic
    U–Pomona
CA State U, Bakersfield
CA State U, Chico
CA State U, Dominguez
    Hills
CA State U, Los Angeles
CA State U–Stanislaus
California U of PA
Carson-Newman College
Central MO State U
Central State U
Central WA University
Chadron State College
Cheyney U of Pennsylvania

Clarion U of Pennsylvania
Clark Atlanta University
Clayton College & State U
CO School of Mines
Columbia Union College
Concord College
Concordia U–St. Paul
Dallas Baptist University
East Stroudsburg U of PA
Eastern NM University
Edinboro U of PA
Emporia State U
Fayetteville State U
Ferris State U
Fort Hays State U
Fort Valley State U
Francis Marion University
Glenville State College
Grand Valley State U
Harding University
Hillsdale College
Humboldt State U
Indiana U of PA
Johnson C. Smith U
Kennesaw State U
Kentucky State U
Kutztown U of PA
Lake Superior State U
Lane College
Lees-McRae College
Lewis University
Lincoln University (MO)
Livingstone College
Lock Haven U of PA
Mansfield U of PA
Mars Hill College
Mercy College
MI Technological U
Miles College
Millersville U of PA
MN State U–Mankato
MN State U Moorhead
MO Southern State U-Joplin
NY Institute of Technology
NC Central University
North Dakota State U

Northern KY University
Northern MI University
Northern State U
Northwest MO State U
Northwest Nazarene U
Northwood University
Pace University
Paine College
Pittsburg State U
Queens U of Charlotte
Saginaw Valley State U
Saint Joseph's College (IN)
San Francisco State U
Seattle Pacific University
Seattle University
Shaw University
Shippensburg U of PA
Slippery Rock U of PA
Sonoma State U
South Dakota State U
Southern AR University
Southern CT State U
Southern IL U–Edwardsville
Southwest Baptist U
St. Andrews Presbyterian
    College
St. Augustine's College
St. Cloud State U
St. Martin's College
St. Paul's College
St. Thomas Aquinas College
State U of West GA
Stonehill College
Tarleton State U
TX A&M U-Commerce
TX A&M Uy–Kingsville
Tiffin University
Truman State U
Tuskegee University
U of AL, Huntsville
U of ALaska Anchorage
U of CA, Davis
U of CA, San Diego
U of Charleston (West VA)
U of CO, Colorado Springs
U of Findlay

U of Indianapolis
U of MA at Lowell
U of MN Duluth
U of MN, Morris
U of MO, Rolla
U of NE at Kearney
U of NE at Omaha
U of New Haven
U of NC at Pembroke
U of North Dakota
U of North Florida
U of Northern CO
U of Pittsburgh–Johnstown
U of Puerto Rico, Bayamon
U of Puerto Rico, CAyey
U of Puerto Rico, Mayaguez
    Campus
U of Puerto Rico, Rio
    Piedras
U of South Dakota
U of Southern IN
U of Tampa
U of the Incarnate Word
U of West Florida
U of WI, Parkside
Virginia State U
VA Union University
Wayne State College (NE)
Westchester U of PA
West Liberty State College
West VA State College
West VA Wesleyan College
Western OR University
Western State College (CO)
Western WA University
Wheeling Jesuit University
Winona State U

TRACK
OUTDOOR
DIVISION III

Adrian College
Albion College
Albright College

Alfred University
Allegheny College
Alma College
Amherst College
Anderson University (IN)
Augsburg College
Augustana College (IL)
Aurora University
Babson College
Baldwin-Wallace College
Bates College
Beloit College
Benedictine University (IL)
Bethany College (West VA)
Bethel University
Bluffton College
Bowdoin College
Brandeis University
Bridgewater College (VA)
Bridgewater State College
Bryn Mawr College
Buena Vista University
Buffalo State College
Cabrini College
CA Institute of Technology
CA Lutheran University
CA State U, Hayward
Calvin College
Capital University
Carleton College
Carnegie Mellon University
Carroll College (WI)
Carthage College
Case Western Reserve U
Catholic University
Central College (IA)
Centre College
Chapman University
Christopher Newport U
City College of NY
Claremont McKenna-
    Harvey Mudd-Scripps
    Colleges
Coe College
Colby College
Colby-Sawyer College

College Misericordia
College of Mt. St. Joseph
College of St. CAtherine
College of St. Scholastica
College of Wooster
Colorado College
Concordia
    College–Moorhead
Concordia University (IL)
Concordia University (WI)
Connecticut College
Cornell College
Defiance College
DE Valley College
Denison University
DePauw University
DeSales University
Dickinson College
Earlham College
Eastern CT State U
Eastern Mennonite U
Elizabethtown College
Elmhurst College
Emmanuel College (MA)
Emory University
Fisk University
Fitchburg State College
Fontbonne University
Franklin & Marshall College
Franklin College
Frostburg State U
Gallaudet University
George Fox University
Gettysburg College
Goucher College
Greenville College
Grinnell College
Grove City College
Gustavus Adolphus College
Gwynedd-Mercy College
Hamilton College
Hamline University
Hanover College
Hartwick College
Haverford College
Heidelberg College

Hendrix College
Hiram College
Hope College
Howard Payne University
Hunter College
Illinois College
IL Wesleyan University
Ithaca College
John Carroll University
Johns Hopkins University
Juniata College
Kean University
Keene State College
Kenyon College
Knox College
Lawrence University
Lebanon Valley College
Lehman College, City U of
    NY
Lewis and Clark College
Lincoln University (PA)
Linfield College
Loras College
Luther College
Lynchburg College
Macalester College
Manchester College
Marietta College
Martin Luther College
MA Institute of Tech
McDaniel College
McMurry University
Medgar Evers College
Messiah College
Methodist College
Middlebury College
Millikin University
Milwaukee School of
    Engineering
Mississippi College
Monmouth College (IL)
Montclair State U
Moravian College
Mount Holyoke College
Mount Union College
Muhlenberg College

Muskingum College
Nazareth College
NE Wesleyan University
NJ City University
NY City College of Tech
New York University
North Central College
North Park University
Oberlin College
Occidental College
Oglethorpe University
OH Northern University
OH Wesleyan University
Olivet College
Otterbein College
Pacific Lutheran University
Pacific University (OR)
PA State U Erie, the
    Behrend College
Plattsburgh State U of NY
Polytechnic University (NY)
Pomona-Pitzer Colleges
Principia College
Ramapo College
Regis College (MA)
Rensselaer Polytechnic
    Institute
Rhode Island College
Rhodes College
Richard Stockton College
    of NJ
Ripon College
Roanoke College
Rochester Institute of Tech
Rose-Hulman Institute of
    Tech
Rowan University
Rust College
Rutgers, The State U of NJ,
    Camden
Saint Mary's U of MN
Salem State College
Salisbury University
Salve Regina University
Simpson College
Smith College

Southern VT College
Southwestern U (TX)
Springfield College
St. Lawrence University
St. Norbert College
St. Olaf College
State U College–Brockport
State U College–Cortland
State U College at Fredonia
State U College–Geneseo
State U College–New Paltz
State U College–Geneseo
State U College–Oneonta
State U of NY–Farmingdale
State U of NY–Oswego
Stevens Institute of Tech
Stillman College
Susquehanna University
Swarthmore College
TX Lutheran University
The College of NJ
Thiel College
Trinity College (CT)
Trinity College (DC)
Trinity University (TX)
Tufts University
U.S. Coast Guard Academy
U.S. Merchant Marine
    Academy
Union College (NY)
U of Chicago
U of Dallas
U of Dubuque
U of La Verne
U of Mary Washington
U of MA, Dartmouth
U of Puget Sound
U of Redlands
U of Rochester
U of Southern ME
U of St. Thomas (MN)
U of the South
U of WI, Eau Claire
U of WI, La Crosse
U of WI, Oshkosh
U of WI, Platteville

U of WI, River Falls
U of WI, Stevens Point
U of WI, Stout
U of WI, Superior
U of WI, Whitewater
Upper IA University
Ursinus College
Wartburg College
Washington and Jefferson
   College
Washington and Lee U
Washington U in St. Louis
Wellesley College
Wesleyan University (CT)
Westfield State College
Westminster College (PA)
Wheaton College (IL)
Wheaton College (MA)
Whittier College
Whitworth College
Widener University
Willamette University
William Paterson U of NJ
Williams College
Wilmington College (OH)
WI Lutheran College
Wittenberg University
Worcester Polytechnic
   Institute
Worcester State College
York College (NY)
York College (PA)

VOLLEYBALL
DIVISION I

AL A&M University
Alabama State U
Alcorn State U
American University
Appalachian State U
Arizona State U
Arkansas State U
Auburn University
Austin Peay State U
Ball State U

Baylor University
Belmont University
Bethune-Cookman College
Birmingham-Southern
   College
Boise State U
Boston College
Bowling Green State U
Bradley University
Brigham Young University
Brown University
Bucknell University
Butler University
CA Polytechnic State U
CA State U, Fresno
CA State U, Fullerton
CA State U, Northridge
CA State U, Sacramento
Campbell University
Canisius College
Centenary College (LA)
Central CT State U
Central MI University
Charleston Southern U
Chicago State U
Clemson University
Cleveland State U
Coastal Carolina University
Colgate University
College of Charleston (SC)
College of the Holy Cross
College of William & Mary
Colorado State U
Columbia University
Coppin State College
Cornell University
Creighton University
Dartmouth College
Davidson College
Delaware State U
DePaul University
Drake University
Duke University
Duquesne University
East Carolina University
East Tennessee State U

Eastern IL University
Eastern KY University
Eastern MI University
Eastern WA University
Elon University
Fairfield University
Fairleigh Dickinson U,
   Teaneck
FL A&M University
FL Atlantic University
FL International University
Florida State U
Fordham University
Furman University
Gardner-Webb University
George Mason University
George Washington U
Georgetown University
GA Institute of Technology
GA Southern University
Georgia State U
Gonzaga University
Grambling State U
Hampton University
Harvard University
High Point University
Hofstra University
Howard University
Idaho State U
Illinois State U
Indiana State U
IN University, Bloomington
IN U-Purdue, U Fort Wayne
Iona College
Iowa State U
Jackson State U
Jacksonville State U
Jacksonville University
James Madison University
Kansas State U
Kent State U
La Salle University
Lafayette College
Lamar University
Lehigh University
Liberty University

Lipscomb University
Long Beach State U
Long Island U-Brooklyn
    Campus
Louisiana State U
LA Tech University
Loyola College (MD)
Loyola Marymount U
Loyola University (IL)
Manhattan College
Marist College
Marquette University
Marshall University
McNeese State U
Mercer University
Miami University (OH)
Michigan State U
Middle Tennessee State U
Mississippi State U
MS Valley State U
MT State U-Bozeman
Morehead State U
Morgan State U
Murray State U
New Mexico State U
Niagara University
Nicholls State U
Norfolk State U
NC A&T State U
North Carolina State U
Northeastern University
Northern AZ University
Northern IL University
Northwestern State U
Northwestern University
Oakland University
Ohio State U
Ohio University
Oral Roberts University
Oregon State U
Pennsylvania State U
Pepperdine University
Portland State U
Prairie View A&M U
Princeton University
Providence College

Purdue University
Quinnipiac University
Radford University
Rice University
Rider University
Robert Morris University
Rutgers, State U of NJ,
    New Brunswick
Sacred Heart University
Saint Francis University (PA)
Saint Louis University
Sam Houston State U
Samford University
San Diego State U
San Jose State U
Santa Clara University
Savannah State U
Seton Hall University
Siena College
South Carolina State U
Southeast MO State U
Southeastern LA University
Southern IL U–Carbondale
Southern Methodist U
Southern U–Baton Rouge
Southwest MO State U
St. Francis College (NY)
St. John's University (NY)
St. Mary's College of CA
St. Peter's College
Stanford University
State U of NY–Binghamton
Stephen F. Austin State U
Stetson University
Stony Brook University
Syracuse University
Temple University
Tennessee State U
TN Technological U
TX A&M U–College Station
TX A&M U-Corpus Christi
TX Christian University
TX Southern University
TX State U–San Marcos
TX Tech University
The Citadel

Towson University
Troy State U
Tulane University
U.S. Air Force Academy
U.S. Military Academy
U.S. Naval Academy
University at Albany
U at Buffalo, the State U of
    NY
U of Akron
U of AL–Birmingham
U of AL–Tuscaloosa
U of Arizona
U of AR, Fayetteville
U of AR, Little Rock
U of AR, Pine Bluff
U of CA, Berkeley
U of CA, Irvine
U of CA, Los Angeles
U of CA, Riverside
U of CA, Santa Barbara
U of Central FL
U of Cincinnati
U of CO, Boulder
U of Connecticut
U of Dayton
U of Delaware
U of Denver
U of Detroit Mercy
U of Evansville
U of Florida
U of Georgia
U of Hartford
U of Hawaii– Manoa
U of Houston
U of Idaho
U of IL at Chicago
U of IL, Champaign
U of Iowa
U of Kansas
U of Kentucky
U of LA at Lafayette
U of LA at Monroe
U of Louisville
U of ME, Orono
U of MD, Baltimore Co.

U of MD, College Park
U of MD, Eastern Shore
U of Memphis
U of Miami (FL)
U of Michigan
U of MN, Twin Cities
U of Mississippi
U of MO, Columbia
U of MO, KS City
U of Montana
U of NE, Lincoln
U of Nevada
U of NV, Las Vegas
U of New Hampshire
U of New Mexico
U of New Orleans
U of NC at Greensboro
U of NC, Asheville
U of NC, Chapel Hill
U of NC, Charlotte
U of NC, Wilmington
U of North TX
U of Northern IA
U of Notre Dame
U of Oklahoma
U of Oregon
U of Pennsylvania
U of Pittsburgh
U of Portland
U of Rhode Island
U of San Diego
U of San Francisco
U of South AL
U of SC, Columbia
U of South Florida
U of Southern CA
U of Southern MS
U of TN at Chattanooga
U of TN at Martin
U of TN, Knoxville
U of TX at Arlington
U of TX at Austin
U of TX at El Paso
U of TX at San Antonio
U of TX, Pan American
U of the Pacific

U of Toledo
U of Tulsa
U of Utah
U of Vermont
U of Virginia
U of Washington
U of WI, Green Bay
U of WI, Madison
U of WI, Milwaukee
U of Wyoming
Utah State U
UT Valley State College
Valparaiso University
Villanova University
VA Commonwealth U
VA Polytechnic Institute &
   State U
Wagner College
Wake Forest University
Washington State U
Weber State U
West VA University
Western Carolina U
Western IL University
Western KY University
Western MI University
Wichita State U
Winthrop University
Wofford College
Wright State U
Xavier University
Yale University
Youngstown State U

VOLLEYBALL
DIVISION II

Abilene Christian U
Adams State College
Adelphi University
Albany State U (GA)
Alderson-Broaddus College
American International
   College
Anderson College (SC)
Angelo State U

AR Tech University
Armstrong Atlantic State U
Ashland University
Assumption College
Augusta State U
Augustana College (SD)
Barry University
Barton College
Bellarmine University
Belmont Abbey College
Bemidji State U
Benedict College
Bentley College
Bloomfield College
Bowie State U
Brigham Young U, HI
Bryant College
C.W. Post Campus/Long
   Island U
CA State Polytechnic
   U–Pomona
CA State U, Bakersfield
CA State U, Chico
CA State U, Dominguez
   Hills
CA State U, Los Angeles
CA State U–San Bernardino
CA State U–Stanislaus
California U of PA
Cameron University
Carson-Newman College
Catawba College
Central MO State U
Central State U
Central WA University
Chadron State College
Chaminade University
Cheyney U of Pennsylvania
Christian Brothers U
Clarion U of Pennsylvania
Clark Atlanta University
Coker College
College of Saint Rose
CO Christian University
CO School of Mines
CO State U-Pueblo

Concord College
Concordia College (NY)
Concordia U–St. Paul
Converse College
Dallas Baptist University
Davis and Elkins College
Dominican College (NY)
Dowling College
Drury University
East Stroudsburg U of PA
Eastern NM University
Eckerd College
Edinboro U of PA
Elizabeth City State U
Emporia State U
Fairmont State College
Fayetteville State U
Ferris State U
FL Institute of Technology
FL Southern College
Fort Hays State U
Fort Lewis College
Fort Valley State U
Francis Marion University
Franklin Pierce College
Gannon University
Georgian Court College
Glenville State College
Goldey-Beacom College
Grand Canyon University
Grand Valley State U
Green Mountain College
Harding University
HI Pacific University
Henderson State U
Hillsdale College
Holy Family University
Humboldt State U
Indiana U of PA
Johnson C. Smith U
Kentucky State U
KY Wesleyan College
Kutztown U of PA
Lake Superior State U
Lander University
Lane College

Le Moyne College
Lees-McRae College
LeMoyne-Owen College
Lenoir-Rhyne College
Lewis University
Limestone College
Lincoln Memorial U
Livingstone College
Lock Haven U of PA
Lynn University
Mars Hill College
Mercy College
Mercyhurst College
Merrimack College
Mesa State College
Metropolitan State College
    of Denver
MI Technological U
Midwestern State U
Miles College
Millersville U of PA
MN State U–Mankato
MN State U Moorhead
MO Southern State U-Joplin
MO Western State College
Molloy College
MT State U–Billings
Mount Olive College
NJ Institute of Technology
NM Highlands University
NY Institute of Technology
Newberry College
NC Central University
North Dakota State U
North Greenville College
Northern KY University
Northern MI University
Northern State U
Northwest MO State U
Northwest Nazarene U
Northwood University
Nova Southeastern U
Nyack College
Oakland City University
OH Valley College
OK Panhandle State U

Ouachita Baptist University
Pace University
Paine College
Pfeiffer University
Philadelphia University
Pittsburg State U
Presbyterian College
Queens College (NY)
Queens U of Charlotte
Quincy University
Regis University (CO)
Rockhurst University
Rollins College
Saginaw Valley State U
Saint Anselm College
Saint Joseph's College (IN)
Saint Leo University
Saint Michael's College
Salem International U
San Francisco State U
Seattle Pacific University
Seattle University
Shaw University
Shepherd College
Shippensburg U of PA
Slippery Rock U of PA
Sonoma State U
South Dakota State U
Southampton
    Campus–Long Island U
Southeastern OK State U
Southern AR University
Southern CT State U
Southern IL U–Edwardsville
Southern NH University
Southwest Baptist U
Southwest MN State U
St. Andrews Presbyterian
    College
St. Augustine's College
St. Cloud State U
St. Edward's University
St. Martin's College
St. Mary's University (TX)
St. Paul's College
State U of West GA

Stonehill College
Tarleton State U
Teikyo Post University
TX A&M U-Commerce
TX A&M Uy–Kingsville
TX Woman's University
Tiffin University
Truman State U
Tusculum College
Tuskegee University
U of AL, Huntsville
U of ALaska Anchorage
U of ALaska Fairbanks
U of Bridgeport
U of CA, Davis
U of CA, San Diego
U of Central AR
U of Central Oklahoma
U of Charleston (West VA)
U of CO, CO Springs
U of Findlay
U of Hawaii–Hilo
U of Indianapolis
U of MA at Lowell
U of MN Duluth
U of MN, Crookston
U of MN, Morris
U of MO, St. Louis
U of Montevallo
U of NE at Kearney
U of NE at Omaha
U of New Haven
U of North AL
U of NC at Pembroke
U of North Dakota
U of North Florida
U of Northern CO
U of Pittsburgh–Johnstown
U of Puerto Rico, Bayamon
U of Puerto Rico, Cayey
U of Puerto Rico, Mayaguez
   Campus
U of Puerto Rico, Rio
   Piedras
U of SC at Aiken
U of SC–Spartanburg

U of South Dakota
U of Southern IN
U of Tampa
U of the DC
U of the Incarnate Word
U of the Sciences in
   Philadelphia
U of West Alabama
U of West Florida
U of WI, Parkside
Valdosta State U
Virginia State U
VA Union University
Washburn U of Topeka
Wayne State College (NE)
Wayne State U (MI)
Westchester U of PA
West Liberty State College
West TX A&M University
West VA State College
West VA U Institute of Tech
West VA Wesleyan College
Western NM University
Western OR University
Western State College (CO)
Western WA University
Wheeling Jesuit University
Wilmington College (DE)
Wingate University
Winona State U
Winston-Salem State U

VOLLEYBALL
DIVISION III

Adrian College
Agnes Scott College
Albertus Magnus College
Albion College
Albright College
Alfred University
Allegheny College
Alma College
Alvernia College
Alverno College
Amherst College

Anderson University (IN)
Anna Maria College
Arcadia University
Augsburg College
Augustana College (IL)
Aurora University
Austin College
Averett University
Babson College
Baldwin-Wallace College
Baptist Bible College
Bard College
Bates College
Bay Path College
Becker College
Beloit College
Benedictine University (IL)
Bernard M. Baruch College
Bethany College (West VA)
Bethel University
Blackburn College
Bluffton College
Bowdoin College
Brandeis University
Bridgewater College (VA)
Bridgewater State College
Brooklyn College
Bryn Mawr College
Buena Vista University
Buffalo State College
Cabrini College
CA Institute of Technology
CA Lutheran University
CA State U, Hayward
Calvin College
Capital University
Carleton College
Carnegie Mellon University
Carroll College (WI)
Carthage College
Case Western Reserve U
Catholic University
Cazenovia College
Cedar Crest College
Centenary College (NJ)
Central College (IA)

Centre College
Chapman University
Chatham College
Chestnut Hill College
Chowan College
Christopher Newport U
City College of NY
Claremont McKenna-
Harvey Mudd-Scripps
Colleges
Clark University (MA)
Clarke College
Clarkson University
Coe College
Colby College
Colby-Sawyer College
College Misericordia
College of Mt. St. Joseph
College of Mt. St. Vincent
College of New Rochelle
College of Notre Dame
(MD)
College of Saint Elizabeth
College of St. Benedict
College of St. CAtherine
College of St. Scholastica
College of Staten Island
College of Wooster
Colorado College
Concordia
College–Moorhead
Concordia University (IL)
Concordia University (WI)
Concordia U–Austin
Connecticut College
Cornell College
D'Youville College
Daniel Webster College
Defiance College
DE Valley College
Denison University
DePauw University
DeSales University
Dickinson College
Dominican University (IL)
Earlham College

East TX Baptist University
Eastern CT State U
Eastern Mennonite U
Eastern Nazarene College
Eastern University
Edgewood College
Elizabethtown College
Elmhurst College
Elmira College
Elms College
Emerson College
Emmanuel College (MA)
Emory and Henry College
Emory University
Endicott College
Eureka College
Fairleigh Dickinson U,
Madison
Ferrum College
Finlandia University
Fisk University
Fontbonne University
Framingham State College
Franklin & Marshall College
Franklin College
Frostburg State U
Gallaudet University
George Fox University
Gettysburg College
Gordon College
Goucher College
Greensboro College
Greenville College
Grinnell College
Grove City College
Guilford College
Gustavus Adolphus College
Gwynedd-Mercy College
Hamilton College
Hamline University
Hanover College
Hardin-Simmons University
Hartwick College
Haverford College
Heidelberg College
Hendrix College

Hilbert College
Hiram College
Hollins University
Hood College
Hope College
Howard Payne University
Hunter College
Huntingdon College
Husson College
Illinois College
IL Wesleyan University
Immaculata University
Ithaca College
John Carroll University
John Jay College of
Criminal Justice
Johns Hopkins University
Johnson and Wales U
Juniata College
Kalamazoo College
Kean University
Keene State College
Kenyon College
Keuka College
King's College (PA)
Knox College
La Grange College
La Roche College
Lake Erie College
Lake Forest College
Lakeland College
Lasell College
Lawrence University
Lebanon Valley College
Lehman College, City U of
NY
Lesley University
LeTourneau University
Lewis and Clark College
Lincoln University (PA)
Linfield College
Loras College
Luther College
Lycoming College
Lynchburg College
Macalester College

MacMurray College
ME Maritime Academy
Manchester College
Maranatha Baptist Bible
　College
Marian College (WI)
Marietta College
Martin Luther College
Mary Baldwin College
Marymount University (VA)
Maryville College (TN)
Maryville U of Saint Louis
Marywood University
MA College of Liberal Arts
MA Institute of Tech
MA Maritime Academy
McDaniel College
McMurry University
Medaille College
Medgar Evers College
Menlo College
Meredith College
Messiah College
Methodist College
Middlebury College
Millikin University
Mills College
Millsaps College
Milwaukee School of
　Engineering
Mississippi College
Monmouth College (IL)
Montclair State U
Moravian College
Mount Holyoke College
Mount Ida College
Mount Mary College
Mt. St. Mary College (NY)
Mount Union College
Muhlenberg College
Muskingum College
Nazareth College
NE Wesleyan University
Neumann College
NJ City University
NY City College of Tech

New York University
Newbury College
NC Wesleyan College
North Central College
North Park University
Northland College
Oberlin College
Occidental College
Oglethorpe University
OH Northern University
OH Wesleyan University
Olivet College
Otterbein College
Pacific Lutheran University
Pacific University (OR)
Palm Beach Atlantic U
Peace College
Penn State ALtoona
Penn State Berks-Lehigh
　Valley College
PA State U Erie, the
　Behrend College
Philadelphia Biblical U
Piedmont College
Pine Manor College
Plattsburgh State U of NY
Plymouth State College
Polytechnic University (NY)
Pomona-Pitzer Colleges
Principia College
Ramapo College
Randolph-Macon College
Randolph-Macon Woman's
　College
Regis College (MA)
Rhode Island College
Rhodes College
Richard Stockton College
　of NJ
Ripon College
Rivier College
Roanoke College
Rochester Institute of Tech
Rockford College
Roger Williams University
Rose-Hulman Institute of

Tech
Rosemont College
Rowan University
Russell Sage College
Rust College
Rutgers, The State U of NJ,
　Camden
Rutgers, The State U of NJ,
　Newark
Saint Joseph's College (ME)
Saint Mary's College (IN)
Saint Mary's U of MN
Salem State College
Salisbury University
Salve Regina University
Schreiner University
Shenandoah University
Simmons College
Simpson College
Skidmore College
Smith College
Southern VT College
Southwestern U (TX)
Spelman College
Springfield College
St. John Fisher College
St. John's University (MN)
St. Joseph's College (Long
　Island)
St. Lawrence University
St. Mary's College of MD
St. Norbert College
St. Olaf College
State U College–Brockport
State U College–Cortland
State U College at Fredonia
State U College–Geneseo
State U College–New Paltz
State U College–Geneseo
State U College–Old
　Westbury
State U College–Oneonta
State U College–Potsdam
State U of NY–Farmingdale
State U of NY–Oswego
State U of NY Institute of

Tech

State U of NY Maritime
College

Stephens College

Stevens Institute of Tech

Stillman College

Suffolk University

Sul Ross State U

Susquehanna University

Swarthmore College

Sweet Briar College

TX Lutheran University

Thiel College

Thomas College

Thomas More College

Transylvania University

Trinity College (CT)

Trinity College (DC)

Trinity University (TX)

Tufts University

U.S. Coast Guard Academy

U.S. Merchant Marine
Academy

Union College (NY)

U of CA, Santa Cruz

U of Chicago

U of Dallas

U of Dubuque

U of La Verne

U of ME at Presque Isle

U of ME, Farmington

U of Mary Hardin-Baylor

U of Mary Washington

U of MA, Boston

U of MA, Dartmouth

U of New England

U of Pittsburgh, Bradford

U of Pittsburgh–
Greensburg

U of Puget Sound

U of Redlands

U of Rochester

U of Scranton

U of Southern ME

U of St. Thomas (MN)

U of TX at Tyler

U of the South

U of WI, Eau Claire

U of WI, La Crosse

U of WI, Oshkosh

U of WI, Platteville

U of WI, River Falls

U of WI, Stevens Point

U of WI, Stout

U of WI, Superior

U of WI, Whitewater

Upper IA University

Ursinus College

Utica College

Vassar College

Villa Julie College

VA Wesleyan College

Wartburg College

Washington and Jefferson
College

Washington and Lee U

WA College (MD)

Washington U in St. Louis

Waynesburg College

Webster University

Wellesley College

Wentworth Institute of
Tech

Wesleyan College (GA)

Wesleyan University (CT)

Western CT State U

Western New England
College

Westfield State College

Westminster College (MO)

Westminster College (PA)

Wheaton College (IL)

Wheaton College (MA)

Whitman College

Whittier College

Whitworth College

Widener University

Wilkes University

Willamette University

William Paterson U of NJ

Williams College

Wilmington College (OH)

Wilson College

WI Lutheran College

Wittenberg University

Worcester Polytechnic
Institute

Worcester State College

York College (NY)

York College (PA)

WATER POLO
DIVISION I

Arizona State U

Brown University

Bucknell University

CA State U, Northridge

George Washington U

Hartwick College

Harvard University

IN University, Bloomington

Iona College

Long Beach State U

Loyola Marymount U

Marist College

Princeton University

San Diego State U

San Jose State U

Santa Clara University

Siena College

St. Francis College (NY)

Stanford University

U of CA, Berkeley

U of CA, Irvine

U of CA, Los Angeles

U of CA, Santa Barbara

U of Hawaii–Manoa

U of MD, College Park

U of Michigan

U of Southern CA

U of the Pacific

Villanova University

Wagner College

WATER POLO
DIVISION II

CA State U, Bakersfield
CA State U–San Bernardino
Gannon University
Mercyhurst College
Queens College (NY)
Salem International U
Slippery Rock U of PA
Sonoma State U
U of CA, Davis
U of CA, San Diego

WATER POLO
DIVISION III

CA Institute of Technology
CA Lutheran University
CA , Hayward
Chapman University
Claremont McKenna-
    Harvey Mudd-Scripps
    Colleges
Connecticut College
Grove City College
Macalester College
Occidental College
PA State U Erie, the
    Behrend College
Pomona-Pitzer Colleges
U of CA, Santa Cruz
U of La Verne
U of Redlands
Utica College
Washington and Jefferson
    College
Wheaton College (IL)
Whittier College

Appendix 4

Men's Sports

These lists identify institutions that offer specific sports, as well as in which division the sport competes. Go to their websites for complete information.

BASEBALL
DIVISION I

Alabama A&M University
Alabama State U
Alcorn State U
Appalachian State U
Arizona State U
Arkansas State U
Auburn University
Austin Peay State U
Ball State University
Baylor University
Belmont University
Bethune-Cookman College
Birmingham-Southern
  College
Boston College
Bowling Green State U
Bradley University
Brigham Young University
Brown University
Bucknell University
Butler University
CA Polytechnic State U
CA State U, Fresno
CA State U, Fullerton
CA State U, Northridge
CA State U, Sacramento
Campbell University
Canisius College
Centenary College (LA)
Central CT State U

Central MI University
Charleston Southern U
Chicago State U
Clemson University
Cleveland State U
Coastal Carolina University
College of Charleston (SC)
College of the Holy Cross
College of William & Mary
Columbia University
Coppin State College
Cornell University
Creighton University
Dartmouth College
Davidson College
Delaware State U
Duke University
Duquesne University
East Carolina University
East TN State U
Eastern IL University
Eastern KY University
Eastern MI University
Elon University
Fairfield University
Fairleigh Dickinson U,
  Teaneck
FL A&M University
FL Atlantic University
FL International University
Florida State U
Fordham University
Furman University

Gardner-Webb University
George Mason University
George WA University
Georgetown University
GA Institute of Technology
GA Southern University
Georgia State U
Gonzaga University
Grambling State U
Harvard University
High Point University
Hofstra University
Illinois State U
Indiana State U
IN University, Bloomington
IN U-Purdue U, Fort Wayne
Iona College
Jackson State U
Jacksonville State U
Jacksonville University
James Madison University
Kansas State U
Kent State U
La Salle University
Lafayette College
Lamar University
Le Moyne College
Lehigh University
Liberty University
Lipscomb University
Long Beach State U
Long Island U-Brooklyn
  Campus

Louisiana State U
LA Tech University
Loyola Marymount U
Manhattan College
Marist College
Marshall University
McNeese State U
Mercer University
Miami University (Ohio)
Michigan State U
Middle TN State U
Mississippi State U
MS Valley State U
Monmouth University
Morehead State U
Mount St. Mary's College
Murray State U
New Mexico State U
NY Institute of Technology
Niagara University
Nicholls State U
Norfolk State U
NC A&T State U
North Carolina State U
Northeastern University
Northern IL University
Northwestern State U
Northwestern University
Oakland University
Ohio State U
Ohio University
Oklahoma State U
Old Dominion University
Oral Roberts University
Oregon State U
Pace University
Pennsylvania State U
Pepperdine University
Prairie View A&M U
Princeton University
Purdue University
Quinnipiac University
Radford University
Rice University
Rider University

Rutgers, State U of NJ,
    New Brunswick
Sacred Heart University
Saint Joseph's University
Saint Louis University
Sam Houston State U
Samford University
San Diego State U
San Jose State U
Santa Clara University
Savannah State U
Seton Hall University
Siena College
Southeast MO State U
Southeastern LA University
Southern IL U at
    Carbondale
Southern U, Baton Rouge
Southern UT University
Southwest MO State U
St. Bonaventure University
St. Francis College (NY)
St. John's University (NY)
St. Mary's College of CA
St. Peter's College
Stanford University
State U of NY at
    Binghamton
Stetson University
Stony Brook University
Temple University
TN Technological
    University
TX A&M U, College Station
TX A&M U-Corpus Christi
TX Christian University
TX Southern University
TX State U-San Marcos
TX Tech University
The Citadel
Towson University
Troy State U
Tulane University
U.S. Air Force Academy
U.S. Military Academy
U.S. Naval Academy

University at Albany
U at Buffalo, the State U
    of NY
U of Akron
U of AL at Birmingham
U of AL, Tuscaloosa
U of Arizona
U of AR, Fayetteville
U of AR, Little Rock
U of AR, Pine Bluff
U of CA, Berkeley
U of CA, Irvine
U of CA, Los Angeles
U of CA, Riverside
U of CA, Santa Barbara
U of Central Florida
U of Cincinnati
U of Connecticut
U of Dayton
U of Delaware
U of Detroit Mercy
U of Evansville
U of Florida
U of Georgia
U of Hartford
U of HI at Hilo
U of Hawaii–Manoa
U of Houston
U of IL at Chicago
U of IL, Champaign
U of Iowa
U of Kansas
U of Kentucky
U of LA at Lafayette
U of LA at Monroe
U of Louisville
U of ME, Orono
U of MD, Baltimore Co.
U of MD, College Park
U of MD, Eastern Shore
U of MA, Amherst
U of Memphis
U of Miami (FL)
U of Michigan
U of MN, Twin Cities
U of Mississippi

U of MO, Columbia
U of NE, Lincoln
U of Nevada
U of NV, Las Vegas
U of New Mexico
U of New Orleans
U of NC at Greensboro
U of NC, Asheville
U of NC, Chapel Hill
U of NC, Charlotte
U of NC, Wilmington
U of Northern IA
U of Notre Dame
U of Oklahoma
U of Pennsylvania
U of Pittsburgh
U of Portland
U of Rhode Island
U of Richmond
U of San Diego
U of San Francisco
U of South AL
U of SC, Columbia
U of South Florida
U of Southern CA
U of Southern MS
U of TN at Martin
U of TN, Knoxville
U of TX at Arlington
U of TX at Austin
U of TX at San Antonio
U of TX, Pan American
U of the Pacific
U of Toledo
U of Utah
U of Vermont
U of Virginia
U of Washington
U of WI, Milwaukee
UT Valley State College
Valparaiso University
Vanderbilt University
Villanova University
VA Commonwealth U
VA Military Institute

VA Polytechnic Institute &
    State University
Wagner College
Wake Forest University
WA State University
WVA University
Western Carolina U
Western IL University
Western KY University
Western MI University
Wichita State U
Winthrop University
Wofford College
Wright State U
Xavier University
Yale University
Youngstown State U

BASEBALL
DIVISION II

Abilene Christian U
Adelphi University
Albany State U (GA)
Alderson-Broaddus College
American International
    College
Anderson College (SC)
AR Tech University
Armstrong Atlantic State U
Ashland University
Assumption College
Augusta State U
Augustana College (SD)
Barry University
Barton College
Bellarmine University
Belmont Abbey College
Bemidji State U
Benedict College
Bentley College
Bloomfield College
Bloomsburg U of PA
Bluefield State College
Bryant College

C.W. Post Campus/Long
    Island University
Caldwell College
CA State Polytechnic
    U–Pomona
CA State U, Chico
CA State U, Dominguez
    Hills
CA State U, Los Angeles
CA State U, San Bernardino
CA State U, Stanislaus
California U of PA
Cameron University
Carson-Newman College
Catawba College
Central MO State U
Central WA University
Christian Brothers U
Clarion U of PA
Clark Atlanta University
Coker College
College of Saint Rose
CO School of Mines
CO State U-Pueblo
Columbia Union College
Columbus State U
Concord College
Concordia College (NY)
Concordia U, St. Paul
Dallas Baptist University
Davis and Elkins College
Delta State U
Dominican College (NY)
Dowling College
East Central University
East Stroudsburg U of PA
Eastern NM University
Eckerd College
Elizabeth City State U
Emporia State U
Erskine College
Fairmont State College
Felician College
FL Gulf Coast University
FL Institute of Technology
FL Southern College

Fort Hays State U
Francis Marion University
Franklin Pierce College
Gannon University
GA College & State U
Grand Canyon University
Grand Valley State U
Harding University
Hawaii Pacific University
Henderson State U
Hillsdale College
IN U of PA
Kennesaw State U
Kentucky State U
KY Wesleyan College
Kutztown U of PA
Lander University
Lane College
LeMoyne-Owen College
Lenoir-Rhyne College
Lewis University
Limestone College
Lincoln Memorial U
Lincoln University (MO)
Lock Haven U of PA
Longwood University
Lynn University
Mansfield U of PA
Mars Hill College
Mercy College
Mercyhurst College
Merrimack College
Mesa State College
Metropolitan State College
  of Denver
Miles College
Millersville U of PA
MN State U Mankato
MO Southern State U-
  Joplin
MO Western State College
Molloy College
Morehouse College
Mount Olive College
NJ Institute of Technology
NM Highlands University

Newberry College
North Dakota State U
North Greenville College
Northeastern State U
Northern KY University
Northern State U
Northwest MO State U
Northwest Nazarene U
Northwood University
Nova Southeastern U
Nyack College
Oakland City University
Ohio Valley College
OK Panhandle State U
Ouachita Baptist University
Paine College
Pfeiffer University
Philadelphia University
Pittsburg State U
Presbyterian College
Queens College (NY)
Quincy University
Regis University (CO)
Rockhurst University
Rollins College
Saginaw Valley State U
Saint Anselm College
Saint Joseph's College (IN)
Saint Leo University
Saint Michael's College
Salem International U
San Francisco State U
Shaw University
Shepherd College
Shippensburg U of PA
Slippery Rock U of PA
Sonoma State U
South Dakota State U
Southeastern OK State U
Southern AR University
Southern CT State U
Southern IL U, Edwardsville
Southern New Hampshire U
Southwest Baptist U
Southwest MN State U
Southwestern OK State U

St. Andrews Presbyterian
  College
St. Augustine's College
St. Cloud State U
St. Edward's University
St. Martin's College
St. Mary's University (TX)
St. Paul's College
St. Thomas Aquinas College
State U of West GA
Stonehill College
Tarleton State U
Teikyo Post University
TX A&M U-Kingsville
Tiffin University
Truman State U
Tusculum College
Tuskegee University
U of AL, Huntsville
U of AR, Monticello
U of Bridgeport
U of CA, Davis
U of CA, San Diego
U of Central AR
U of Central OK
U of Charleston (WVA)
U of Findlay
U of Indianapolis
U of MA at Lowell
U of MN Duluth
U of MN, Crookston
U of MN, Morris
U of MO, Rolla
U of MO, St. Louis
U of Montevallo
U of NE at Kearney
U of NE at Omaha
U of New Haven
U of North AL
U of NC at Pembroke
U of North Dakota
U of North Florida
U of Northern CO
U of Pittsburgh,
  Johnstown
U of Puerto Rico, Bayamon

U of Puerto Rico, Cayey
U of Puerto Rico, Mayaguez
U of SC at Aiken
U of SC-Spartanburg
U of South Dakota
U of Southern IN
U of Tampa
U of the Incarnate Word
U of the Sciences in
   Philadelphia
U of West AL
U of West Florida
U of WI, Parkside
Valdosta State U
VA State University
Washburn U of Topeka
Wayne State College (NE)
Wayne State U (MI)
Westchester U of PA
West Liberty State College
West TX A&M University
WVA State College
WVA U Institute of Tech
WVA Wesleyan College
Western OR University
Wilmington College (DE)
Wingate University
Winona State U

BASEBALL
DIVISION III

Adrian College
Albertus Magnus College
Albion College
Albright College
Allegheny College
Alma College
Alvernia College
Amherst College
Anderson University (IN)
Anna Maria College
Arcadia University
Augsburg College
Augustana College (IL)
Aurora University

Austin College
Averett University
Babson College
Baldwin-Wallace College
Bates College
Becker College
Beloit College
Benedictine University (IL)
Bernard M. Baruch College
Bethany College (WVA)
Bethel University
Blackburn College
Bluffton College
Bowdoin College
Brandeis University
Bridgewater College (VA)
Bridgewater State College
Buena Vista University
CA Institute of Technology
CA Lutheran University
CA State U, Hayward
Calvin College
Capital University
Carleton College
Carroll College (WI)
Carthage College
Case Western Reserve U
Castleton State College
Catholic University
Cazenovia College
Centenary College (NJ)
Central College (IA)
Centre College
Chapman University
Chowan College
Christopher Newport U
Claremont McKenna-
   Harvey Mudd-Scripps
   Colleges
Clark University (MA)
Clarke College
Clarkson University
Coe College
Colby College
Colby-Sawyer College
College Misericordia

College of Mt. St. Joseph
College of St. Scholastica
College of Staten Island
College of Wooster
Concordia
   College–Moorhead
Concordia University (IL)
Concordia University (WI)
Concordia U at Austin
Cornell College
Curry College
D'Youville College
Daniel Webster College
Defiance College
DE Valley College
Denison University
DePauw University
DeSales University
Dickinson College
Dominican University (IL)
Drew University
Earlham College
East TX Baptist University
Eastern CT State U
Eastern Mennonite U
Eastern Nazarene College
Eastern University
Edgewood College
Elizabethtown College
Elmhurst College
Emerson College
Emory and Henry College
Emory University
Endicott College
Eureka College
Fairleigh Dickinson
   U–Madison
Ferrum College
Finlandia University
Fisk University
Fitchburg State College
Fontbonne University
Framingham State College
Franklin & Marshall College
Franklin College
Frostburg State U

Gallaudet University
George Fox University
Gettysburg College
Gordon College
Greensboro College
Greenville College
Grinnell College
Grove City College
Guilford College
Gustavus Adolphus College
Gwynedd-Mercy College
Hamilton College
Hamline University
Hampden-Sydney College
Hanover College
Hardin-Simmons University
Hartwick College
Haverford College
Heidelberg College
Hendrix College
Hilbert College
Hiram College
Hope College
Howard Payne University
Huntingdon College
Husson College
IL College
IL Wesleyan University
Ithaca College
John Carroll University
John Jay College of
    Criminal Justice
Johns Hopkins University
Johnson and Wales U
Juniata College
Kalamazoo College
Kean University
Keene State College
Kenyon College
Keuka College
King's College (PA)
Knox College
La Grange College
La Roche College
Lake Erie College
Lakeland College

Lawrence University
Lebanon Valley College
Lehman College, City U of
    NY
LeTourneau University
Lewis and Clark College
Lincoln University (PA)
Linfield College
Loras College
Louisiana College
Luther College
Lynchburg College
Macalester College
MacMurray College
Manchester College
Manhattanville College
Maranatha Baptist Bible
    College
Marian College (WI)
Marietta College
Martin Luther College
Maryville College (TN)
Maryville U of Saint Louis
Marywood University
MA College of Liberal Arts
MA Institute of Tech
MA Maritime Academy
McDaniel College
McMurry University
Medaille College
Menlo College
Messiah College
Methodist College
Middlebury College
Millikin University
Millsaps College
Milwaukee School of
    Engineering
MS College
Monmouth College (IL)
Montclair State U
Moravian College
Mt. St. Mary College (NY)
Mount Union College
Muhlenberg College
Muskingum College

NE Wesleyan University
Neumann College
New England College
NJ City University
Nichols College
NC Wesleyan College
North Central College
North Park University
Northland College
Norwich University
Oberlin College
Occidental College
Oglethorpe University
Ohio Northern University
Ohio Wesleyan University
Olivet College
Otterbein College
Pacific Lutheran University
Pacific University (OR)
Palm Beach Atlantic U
PA State Altoona
PA State Berks-Lehigh
    Valley College
PA State U Erie, the
    Behrend College
Philadelphia Biblical U
Piedmont College
Plattsburgh State U of NY
Plymouth State College
Polytechnic University (NY)
Pomona-Pitzer Colleges
Principia College
Ramapo College
Randolph-Macon College
Rensselaer Polytechnic
    Institute
Rhode Island College
Rhodes College
Richard Stockton College
    (NJ)
Ripon College
Rivier College
Roanoke College
Rochester Institute of Tech
Rockford College
Roger Williams University

Rose-Hulman Institute of Tech
Rowan University
Rust College
Rutgers, The State U. of NJ, Camden
Rutgers, The State U. of NJ, Newark
Saint Joseph's College (ME)
Saint Mary's U of MN
Salem State College
Salisbury University
Salve Regina University
Schreiner University
Shenandoah University
Simpson College
Skidmore College
Southern Vermont College
Southwestern U (TX)
Springfield College
St. John Fisher College
St. John's University (MN)
St. Joseph's College (Long Island)
St. Lawrence University
St. Mary's College of MD
St. Norbert College
St. Olaf College
State U College–Brockport
State U College– Cortland
State U College– Fredonia
State U College–New Paltz
State U College–Old Westbury
State U College– Oneonta
State U of NY–Farmingdale
State U of NY at Oswego
State U of NY Institute of Tech
State U of NY Maritime College
Stevens Institute of Tech
Stillman College
Suffolk University
Sul Ross State U
Susquehanna University

Swarthmore College
TX Lutheran University
The College of NJ
Thiel College
Thomas College
Thomas More College
Transylvania University
Trinity College (CT)
Trinity University (TX)
Tufts University
U.S. Coast Guard Academy
U.S. Merchant Marine Academy
Union College (NY)
U of Chicago
U of Dallas
U of Dubuque
U of La Verne
U of ME at Presque Isle
U of ME, Farmington
U of Mary Hardin-Baylor
U of Mary Washington
U of MA, Boston
U of MA, Dartmouth
U of Pittsburgh, Bradford
U of Pittsburgh–Greensburg
U of Puget Sound
U of Redlands
U of Rochester
U of Scranton
U of Southern ME
U of St. Thomas (MN)
U of TX at Dallas
U of TX at Tyler
U of the Ozarks (AR)
U of the South
U of WI, La Crosse
U of WI, Oshkosh
U of WI, Platteville
U of WI, Stevens Point
U of WI, Stout
U of WI, Superior
U of WI, Whitewater
Upper IA University
Ursinus College

Utica College
Vassar College
Villa Julie College
VA Wesleyan College
Wabash College
Wartburg College
Washington and Jefferson College
Washington and Lee U
WA College (MD)
Washington U–St. Louis
Waynesburg College
Webster University
Wentworth Institute of Tech
Wesley College
Wesleyan University (CT)
Western CT State U
Western New England College
Westfield State College
Westminster College (MO)
Westminster College (PA)
Wheaton College (IL)
Wheaton College (MA)
Whitman College
Whittier College
Whitworth College
Widener University
Wilkes University
Willamette University
William Paterson U of NJ
Williams College
Wilmington College (Ohio)
WI Lutheran College
Wittenberg University
Worcester Polytechnic Institute
Worcester State College
York College (PA)

BASKETBALL
DIVISION I

AL A&M University
Alabama State U

Alcorn State U
American University
Appalachian State U
Arizona State U
Arkansas State U
Auburn University
Austin Peay State U
Ball State University
Baylor University
Belmont University
Bethune-Cookman College
Birmingham-Southern
    College
Boise State University
Boston College
Boston University
Bowling Green State U
Bradley University
Brigham Young University
Brown University
Bucknell University
Butler University
CA Polytechnic State U
CA State U, Fresno
CA State U, Fullerton
CA State U, Northridge
CA State U, Sacramento
Campbell University
Canisius College
Centenary College (LA)
Central CT State U
Central MI University
Charleston Southern U
Chicago State U
Clemson University
Cleveland State U
Coastal Carolina University
Colgate University
College of Charleston (SC)
College of the Holy Cross
College of William & Mary
Colorado State U
Columbia University
Coppin State College
Cornell University
Creighton University

Dartmouth College
Davidson College
Delaware State U
DePaul University
Drake University
Drexel University
Duke University
Duquesne University
East Carolina University
East TN State U
Eastern IL University
Eastern KY University
Eastern MI University
Eastern WA University
Elon University
Fairfield University
Fairleigh Dickinson
    U–Teaneck
FL A&M University
FL Atlantic University
FL International University
Florida State U
Fordham University
Furman University
Gardner-Webb University
George Mason University
George WA University
Georgetown University
GA Institute of Technology
GA Southern University
Georgia State U
Gonzaga University
Grambling State U
Hampton University
Harvard University
High Point University
Hofstra University
Howard University
Idaho State U
Illinois State University
Indiana State University
IN University, Bloomington
IN U-Purdue U, Fort Wayne
Iona College
Iowa State U
Jackson State U

Jacksonville State U
Jacksonville University
James Madison University
Kansas State U
Kent State U
La Salle University
Lafayette College
Lamar University
Lehigh University
Liberty University
Lipscomb University
Long Beach State U
Long Island U-Brooklyn
    Campus
Louisiana State U
LA Tech University
Loyola College (MD)
Loyola Marymount U
Loyola University (IL)
Manhattan College
Marist College
Marquette University
Marshall University
McNeese State U
Mercer University
Miami University (Ohio)
Michigan State U
Middle TN State U
Mississippi State U
MS Valley State U
Monmouth University
MT State U-Bozeman
Morehead State U
Morgan State U
Mount St. Mary's College
Murray State U
New Mexico State U
NY Institute of Technology
Niagara University
Nicholls State U
Norfolk State U
NC A&T State U
North Carolina State U
Northeastern University
Northern AZ University
Northern IL University

Northwestern State U
Northwestern University
Oakland University
Ohio State U
Ohio University
Oklahoma State U
Old Dominion University
Oral Roberts University
Oregon State U
Pace University
Pennsylvania State U
Pepperdine University
Portland State U
Prairie View A&M U
Princeton University
Providence College
Purdue University
Quinnipiac University
Radford University
Rice University
Rider University
Robert Morris University
Rutgers, State U of NJ,
  New Brunswick
Sacred Heart University
Saint Francis U (PA)
Saint Joseph's University
Saint Louis University
Sam Houston State U
Samford University
San Diego State U
San Jose State U
Santa Clara University
Savannah State U
Seton Hall University
Siena College
South Carolina State U
Southeast MO State U
Southeastern LA University
Southern IL U–Carbondale
Southern Methodist U
Southern U–Baton Rouge
Southern UT University
Southwest MO State U
St. Bonaventure University
St. Francis College (NY)

St. John's University (NY)
St. Mary's College of CA
St. Peter's College
Stanford University
State U of NY–Binghamton
Stephen F. Austin State U
Stetson University
Stony Brook University
Syracuse University
Temple University
TN State U
TN Technological U
TX A&M U–College Station
TX A&M U-Corpus Christi
TX Christian University
TX Southern University
TX State U-San Marcos
TX Tech University
The Citadel
Towson University
Troy State U
Tulane University
U.S. Air Force Academy
U.S. Military Academy
U.S. Naval Academy
University at Albany
U at Buffalo, the State U
  of NY
U of Akron
U of AL at Birmingham
U of AL, Tuscaloosa
U of Arizona
U of AR, Fayetteville
U of AR, Little Rock
U of AR, Pine Bluff
U of CA, Berkeley
U of CA, Irvine
U of CA, Los Angeles
U of CA, Riverside
U of CA, Santa Barbara
U of Central Florida
U of Cincinnati
U of CO, Boulder
U of Connecticut
U of Dayton
U of Delaware

U of Denver
U of Detroit Mercy
U of Evansville
U of Florida
U of Georgia
U of Hartford
U of Hawaii–Manoa
U of Houston
U of Idaho
U of IL at Chicago
U of IL, Champaign
U of Iowa
U of Kansas
U of Kentucky
U of LA at Lafayette
U of LA at Monroe
U of Louisville
U of ME, Orono
U of MD, Baltimore Co.
U of MD, College Park
U of MD, Eastern Shore
U of MA, Amherst
U of Memphis
U of Miami (FL)
U of Michigan
U of MN, Twin Cities
U of Mississippi
U of MO, Columbia
U of MO, Kansas City
U of Montana
U of NE, Lincoln
U of Nevada
U of Nevada, Las Vegas
U of New Hampshire
U of New Mexico
U of New Orleans
U of NC at Greensboro
U of NC, Asheville
U of NC, Chapel Hill
U of NC, Charlotte
U of NC, Wilmington
U of North TX
U of Northern IA
U of Notre Dame
U of Oklahoma
U of Oregon

U of Pennsylvania
U of Pittsburgh
U of Portland
U of Rhode Island
U of Richmond
U of San Diego
U of San Francisco
U of South AL
U of SC, Columbia
U of South Florida
U of Southern CA
U of Southern MS
U of TN at Chattanooga
U of TN at Martin
U of TN, Knoxville
U of TX at Arlington
U of TX at Austin
U of TX at El Paso
U of TX at San Antonio
U of TX, Pan American
U of the Pacific
U of Toledo
U of Tulsa
U of Utah
U of Vermont
U of Virginia
U of Washington
U of WI, Green Bay
U of WI, Madison
U of WI, Milwaukee
U of Wyoming
UT State U
UT Valley State College
Valparaiso University
Vanderbilt University
Villanova University
VA Commonwealth U
VA Military Institute
VA Polytechnic Institute &
   State U
Wagner College
Wake Forest University
Washington State U
Weber State U
WVA University
Western Carolina U

Western IL University
Western KY University
Western MI University
Wichita State U
Winthrop University
Wofford College
Wright State U
Xavier University
Yale University
Youngstown State U

BASKETBALL
DIVISION II

Abilene Christian
   University
Adams State College
Adelphi University
Albany State U (GA)
Alderson-Broaddus College
American International
   College
Anderson College (SC)
Angelo State U
AR Tech University
Armstrong Atlantic State U
Ashland University
Assumption College
Augusta State U
Augustana College (SD)
Barry University
Barton College
Bellarmine University
Belmont Abbey College
Bemidji State U
Benedict College
Bentley College
Bloomfield College
Bloomsburg U of PA
Bluefield State College
Bowie State U
Brigham Young U, HI
Bryant College
C.W. Post Campus/Long
   Island University
Caldwell College

CA State Polytechnic
   U–Pomona
CA State U, Bakersfield
CA State U, Chico
CA State U, Dominguez
   Hills
CA State U, Los Angeles
CA State U, San Bernardino
CA State U, Stanislaus
California U of PA
Cameron University
Carson-Newman College
Catawba College
Central MO State U
Central State U
Central WA University
Chadron State College
Chaminade University
Cheyney U of Pennsylvania
Christian Brothers U
Clarion U of Pennsylvania
Clark Atlanta University
Clayton College & State U
Coker College
College of Saint Rose
CO Christian University
CO School of Mines
Colorado State U-Pueblo
Columbia Union College
Columbus State U
Concord College
Concordia College (NY)
Concordia U, St. Paul
Dallas Baptist University
Davis and Elkins College
Delta State U
Dominican College (NY)
Dowling College
Drury University
East Central University
East Stroudsburg U of PA
Eastern NM University
Eckerd College
Edinboro U of PA
Elizabeth City State U
Emporia State U

Erskine College
Fairmont State College
Fayetteville State U
Felician College
Ferris State U
FL Gulf Coast University
FL Institute of
    Technology
FL Southern College
Fort Hays State U
Fort Lewis College
Fort Valley State U
Francis Marion University
Franklin Pierce College
Gannon University
GA College & State U
Glenville State College
Goldey-Beacom College
Grand Canyon University
Grand Valley State U
Green Mountain College
Harding University
Hawaii Pacific University
Henderson State U
Hillsdale College
Holy Family University
Humboldt State U
IN U of PA
Johnson C. Smith U
Kennesaw State U
Kentucky State U
KY Wesleyan College
Kutztown U of PA
Lake Superior State U
Lander University
Lane College
Le Moyne College
Lees-McRae College
LeMoyne-Owen College
Lenoir-Rhyne College
Lewis University
Limestone College
Lincoln Memorial U
Lincoln University (MO)
Livingstone College
Lock Haven U of PA

Longwood University
Lynn University
Mansfield U of PA
Mars Hill College
Mercy College
Mercyhurst College
Merrimack College
Mesa State College
Metropolitan State College
    of Denver
MI Tech University
Midwestern State U
Miles College
Millersville U of PA
MN State U Mankato
MN State U Moorhead
MO Southern State U-Joplin
MO Western State College
Molloy College
MT State U-Billings
Morehouse College
Mount Olive College
NJ Institute of Technology
NM Highlands University
NY Institute of Technology
Newberry College
NC Central University
North Dakota State U
North Greenville College
Northeastern State U
Northern KY University
Northern MI University
Northern State U
Northwest MO State U
Northwest Nazarene U
Northwood University
Nova Southeastern U
Nyack College
Oakland City University
Ohio Valley College
OK Panhandle State U
Ouachita Baptist University
Pace University
Paine College
Pfeiffer University
Philadelphia University

Pittsburg State U
Presbyterian College
Queens College (NY)
Queens U of Charlotte
Quincy University
Regis University (CO)
Rockhurst University
Rollins College
Saginaw Valley State U
Saint Anselm College
Saint Joseph's College (IN)
Saint Leo University
Saint Michael's College
Salem International U
San Francisco State U
Seattle Pacific University
Seattle University
Shaw University
Shepherd College
Shippensburg U of PA
Slippery Rock U of PA
Sonoma State U
South Dakota State U
Southampton Campus of
    Long Island U
Southeastern OK State U
Southern AR University
Southern CT State U
Southern IL U–Edwardsville
Southern NH University
Southwest Baptist U
Southwest MN State U
Southwestern OK State U
St. Andrews Presbyterian
    College
St. Augustine's College
St. Cloud State U
St. Edward's University
St. Martin's College
St. Mary's University (TX)
St. Paul's College
St. Thomas Aquinas College
State U of West GA
Stonehill College
Tarleton State U
Teikyo Post University

TX A&M U-Commerce
TX A&M U-Kingsville
Tiffin University
Truman State U
Tusculum College
Tuskegee University
U of AL, Huntsville
U of Alaska Anchorage
U of Alaska Fairbanks
U of AR, Monticello
U of Bridgeport
U of CA, Davis
U of CA, San Diego
U of Central AR
U of Central OK
U of Charleston (WVA)
U of CO, Colorado Springs
U of Findlay
U of HI at Hilo
U of Indianapolis
U of MA at Lowell
U of MN Duluth
U of MN, Crookston
U of MN, Morris
U of MO, Rolla
U of MO, St. Louis
U of Montevallo
U of NE at Kearney
U of NE at Omaha
U of New Haven
U of North AL
U of NC at Pembroke
U of North Dakota
U of North Florida
U of Northern CO
U of Pittsburgh, Johnstown
U of Puerto Rico, Bayamon
U of Puerto Rico, Cayey
U of Puerto Rico, Mayaguez
U of Puerto Rico, Rio
   Piedras
U of SC at Aiken
U of SC-Spartanburg
U of South Dakota
U of Southern IN
U of Tampa

U of the DC
U of the Incarnate Word
U of the Sciences in
   Philadelphia
U of West AL
U of West Florida
U of WI, Parkside
Valdosta State U
Virginia State U
VA Union University
Washburn U of Topeka
Wayne State College (NE)
Wayne State U (MI)
Westchester U of PA
West Liberty State College
West TX A&M University
WVA State College
WVA U Institute of Tech
WVA Wesleyan College
Western NM University
Western OR University
Western State College (CO)
Western WA University
Wheeling Jesuit University
Wilmington College (DE)
Wingate University
Winona State U
Winston-Salem State U

BASKETBALL
DIVISION III

Adrian College
Albertus Magnus College
Albion College
Albright College
Alfred University
Allegheny College
Alma College
Alvernia College
Amherst College
Anderson University (IN)
Anna Maria College
Arcadia University
Augsburg College
Augustana College (IL)

Aurora University
Austin College
Averett University
Babson College
Baldwin-Wallace College
Baptist Bible College
Bard College
Bates College
Becker College
Beloit College
Benedictine University (IL)
Bernard M. Baruch College
Bethany College (WVA)
Bethel University
Blackburn College
Bluffton College
Bowdoin College
Brandeis University
Bridgewater College (VA)
Bridgewater State College
Brooklyn College
Buena Vista University
Buffalo State College
Cabrini College
CA Institute of Technology
CA Lutheran University
CA State U, Hayward
Calvin College
Capital University
Carleton College
Carnegie Mellon University
Carroll College (WI)
Carthage College
Case Western Reserve U
Castleton State College
Catholic University
Cazenovia College
Centenary College (NJ)
Central College (IA)
Centre College
Chapman University
Chestnut Hill College
Chowan College
Christopher Newport U
City College of NY
Claremont McKenna-

Harvey Mudd-Scripps
Colleges
Clark University (MA)
Clarke College
Clarkson University
Coe College
Colby College
Colby-Sawyer College
College Misericordia
College of Mt. St. Joseph
College of Mt. St. Vincent
College of St. Scholastica
College of Staten Island
College of Wooster
Colorado College
Concordia
College–Moorhead
Concordia University (IL)
Concordia University (WI)
Concordia U at Austin
Connecticut College
Cornell College
Curry College
D'Youville College
Daniel Webster College
Defiance College
DE Valley College
Denison University
DePauw University
DeSales University
Dickinson College
Dominican University (IL)
Drew University
Earlham College
East TX Baptist University
Eastern CT State U
Eastern Mennonite U
Eastern Nazarene College
Eastern University
Edgewood College
Elizabethtown College
Elmhurst College
Elmira College
Elms College
Emerson College
Emmanuel College (MA)

Emory and Henry College
Emory University
Endicott College
Eureka College
Fairleigh Dickinson
U–Madison
Ferrum College
Finlandia University
Fisk University
Fitchburg State College
Fontbonne University
Framingham State College
Franklin & Marshall College
Franklin College
Frostburg State U
Gallaudet University
George Fox University
Gettysburg College
Gordon College
Goucher College
Greensboro College
Greenville College
Grinnell College
Grove City College
Guilford College
Gustavus Adolphus College
Gwynedd-Mercy College
Hamilton College
Hamline University
Hampden-Sydney College
Hanover College
Hardin-Simmons University
Hartwick College
Haverford College
Heidelberg College
Hendrix College
Hilbert College
Hiram College
Hobart and William Smith
Colleges
Hood College
Hope College
Howard Payne University
Hunter College
Huntingdon College
Husson College

Illinois College
IL Wesleyan University
Ithaca College
John Carroll University
John Jay College of
Criminal Justice
Johns Hopkins University
Johnson and Wales U
Johnson State College
Juniata College
Kalamazoo College
Kean University
Keene State College
Kenyon College
Keuka College
King's College (PA)
Knox College
La Grange College
La Roche College
Lake Erie College
Lake Forest College
Lakeland College
Lasell College
Lawrence University
Lebanon Valley College
Lehman College, City U of
NY
LeTourneau University
Lewis and Clark College
Lincoln University (PA)
Linfield College
Loras College
Louisiana College
Luther College
Louisiana College
Lycoming College
Lynchburg College
Macalester College
MacMurray College
ME Maritime Academy
Manchester College
Manhattanville College
Maranatha Baptist Bible
College
Marian College (WI)
Marietta College

Martin Luther College
Mary Baldwin College
Maryville College (TN)
Maryville U of Saint Louis
Marywood University
MA College of Liberal Arts
MA Institute of Tech
McDaniel College
McMurry University
Medaille College
Medgar Evers College
Menlo College
Messiah College
Methodist College
Middlebury College
Millikin University
Millsaps College
Milwaukee School of
   Engineering
Mississippi College
Monmouth College (IL)
Montclair State U
Moravian College
Mount Ida College
Mt. St. Mary College (NY)
Mount Union College
Muhlenberg College
Muskingum College
Nazareth College
NE Wesleyan University
Neumann College
New England College
NJ City University
NY City College of Tech
New York University
Newbury College
Nichols College
NC Wesleyan College
North Central College
North Park University
Northland College
Norwich University
Oberlin College
Occidental College
Oglethorpe University
Ohio Northern University

Ohio Wesleyan University
Olivet College
Otterbein College
Pacific Lutheran University
Pacific University (OR)
Palm Beach Atlantic U
PA State Altoona
PA State Berks-Lehigh
   Valley College
PA State U Erie, the
   Behrend College
Philadelphia Biblical U
Piedmont College
Plattsburgh State U of NY
Plymouth State College
Polytechnic University (NY)
Pomona-Pitzer Colleges
Principia College
Ramapo College
Randolph-Macon College
Rensselaer Polytechnic
   Institute
Rhode Island College
Rhodes College
Richard Stockton College
   (NJ)
Ripon College
Rivier College
Roanoke College
Rochester Institute of Tech
Rockford College
Roger Williams University
Rose-Hulman Institute of
   Tech
Rowan University
Rust College
Rutgers, The State U of NJ,
   Camden
Rutgers, The State U of NJ,
   Newark
Saint Joseph's College (ME)
Saint Mary's U of MN
Salem State College
Salisbury University
Salve Regina University
Schreiner University

Shenandoah University
Simpson College
Skidmore College
Southern Vermont College
Southwestern U (TX)
Springfield College
St. John Fisher College
St. John's University (MN)
St. Joseph's College (Long
   Island)
St. Lawrence University
St. Mary's College of MD
St. Norbert College
St. Olaf College
State U College–Brockport
State U College–Cortland
State U College–Fredonia
State U College at Geneseo
State U College–New Paltz
State U College–Brockport
State U College–Old
   Westbury
State U College–Oneonta
State U College–Potsdam
State U of NY–Farmingdale
State U of NY–Oswego
State U of NY Institute of
   Tech
State U of NY Maritime
   College
Stevens Institute of Tech
Stillman College
Suffolk University
Sul Ross State U
Susquehanna University
Swarthmore College
TX Lutheran University
The College of NJ
Thiel College
Thomas College
Thomas More College
Transylvania University
Trinity College (CT)
Trinity University (TX)
Tufts University
U.S. Coast Guard Academy

U.S. Merchant Marine
Academy
Union College (NY)
U of CA, Santa Cruz
U of Chicago
U of Dallas
U of Dubuque
U of La Verne
U of ME at Presque Isle
U of ME, Farmington
U of Mary Hardin-Baylor
U of Mary Washington
U of MA, Boston
U of MA, Dartmouth
U of New England
U of Pittsburgh, Bradford
U of Pittsburgh–Greensburg
U of Puget Sound
U of Redlands
U of Rochester
U of Scranton
U of Southern ME
U of St. Thomas (MN)
U of TX at Dallas
U of TX at Tyler
U of the Ozarks (AR)
U of the South
U of WI, Eau Claire
U of WI, La Crosse
U of WI, Oshkosh
U of WI, Platteville
U of WI, River Falls
U of WI, Stevens Point
U of WI, Stout
U of WI, Superior
U of WI, Whitewater
Upper IA University
Ursinus College
Utica College
Vassar College
Villa Julie College
VA Wesleyan College
Wabash College
Wartburg College
Washington & Jefferson
College

Washington and Lee U
WA College (MD)
Washington U–St. Louis
Waynesburg College
Webster University
Wentworth Institute of
Tech
Wesley College
Wesleyan University (CT)
Western CT State U
Western New England
College
Westfield State College
Westminster College (MO)
Westminster College (PA)
Wheaton College (IL)
Wheaton College (MA)
Whitman College
Whittier College
Whitworth College
Widener University
Wilkes University
Willamette University
William Paterson U of NJ
Williams College
Wilmington College (Ohio)
WI Lutheran College
Wittenberg University
Worcester Polytechnic
Institute
Worcester State College
Yeshiva University
York College (NY)
York College (PA)

CROSS-COUNTRY
DIVISION I

AL A&M University
Alabama State U
Alcorn State U
American University
Appalachian State U
Arizona State U

Arkansas State U
Auburn University
Austin Peay State U
Ball State University
Baylor University
Belmont University
Bethune-Cookman College
Birmingham-Southern
College
Boise State University
Boston College
Boston University
Bowling Green State U
Bradley University
Brigham Young University
Brown University
Bucknell University
Butler University
CA Polytechnic State U
CA State U, Fullerton
CA State U, Northridge
CA State U, Sacramento
Campbell University
Canisius College
Centenary College (LA)
Central CT State U
Central MI University
Charleston Southern U
Chicago State U
Clemson University
Coastal Carolina University
Colgate University
College of Charleston (SC)
College of the Holy Cross
College of William & Mary
Colorado State U
Columbia University
Coppin State College
Cornell University
Creighton University
Dartmouth College
Davidson College
Delaware State U
DePaul University
Drake University
Duke University

Duquesne University
East Carolina University
East TN State U
Eastern IL University
Eastern KY University
Eastern MI University
Eastern WA University
Elon University
Fairfield University
Fairleigh Dickinson
   U–Teaneck
FL A&M University
FL Atlantic University
FL International University
Florida State U
Fordham University
Furman University
Gardner-Webb University
George Mason University
George WA University
Georgetown University
GA Institute of Technology
Georgia State U
Gonzaga University
Grambling State U
Hampton University
Harvard University
High Point University
Hofstra University
Howard University
Idaho State U
Illinois State University
Indiana State University
IN University, Bloomington
IN U-Purdue U, Fort Wayne
Iona College
Iowa State U
Jackson State U
Jacksonville State U
Jacksonville University
James Madison University
Kansas State U
Kent State U
La Salle University
Lafayette College
Lamar University

Lehigh University
Liberty University
Lipscomb University
Long Beach State U
Long Island U-Brooklyn
   Campus
Louisiana State U
LA Tech University
Loyola College (MD)
Loyola Marymount U
Loyola University (IL)
Manhattan College
Marist College
Marquette University
Marshall University
McNeese State U
Mercer University
Miami University (Ohio)
Michigan State U
Middle TN State U
Mississippi State U
MS Valley State U
Monmouth University
MT State U-Bozeman
Morehead State U
Morgan State U
Mount St. Mary's College
Murray State U
New Mexico State U
Niagara University
Nicholls State U
Norfolk State U
NC A&T State U
North Carolina State U
Northeastern University
Northern AZ University
Northern IL University
Northwestern State U
Northwestern University
Oakland University
Ohio State U
Ohio University
Oklahoma State U
Old Dominion University
Oral Roberts University
Oregon State U

Pace University
Pennsylvania State U
Pepperdine University
Portland State U
Prairie View A&M U
Princeton University
Providence College
Purdue University
Quinnipiac University
Radford University
Rice University
Rider University
Robert Morris University
Rutgers, State U of NJ,
   New Brunswick
Sacred Heart University
Saint Francis U (PA)
Saint Joseph's University
Saint Louis University
Sam Houston State U
Samford University
San Jose State U
Santa Clara University
Savannah State U
Seton Hall University
Siena College
South Carolina State U
Southeast MO State U
Southeastern LA University
Southern IL U–Carbondale
Southern Methodist U
Southern U–Baton Rouge
Southern UT University
Southwest MO State U
St. Bonaventure University
St. Francis College (NY)
St. Mary's College of CA
St. Peter's College
Stanford University
State U of NY–Binghamton
Stephen F. Austin State U
Stetson University
Stony Brook University
Syracuse University
TN State U
TN Technological University

TX A&M U–College Station
TX A&M U-Corpus Christi
TX Christian University
TX Southern University
TX State U-San Marcos
TX Tech University
The Citadel
Towson University
Troy State U
Tulane University
U.S. Air Force Academy
U.S. Military Academy
U.S. Naval Academy
University at Albany
U at Buffalo, the State U
  of NY
U of Akron
U of AL, Tuscaloosa
U of Arizona
U of AR, Fayetteville
U of AR, Little Rock
U of AR, Pine Bluff
U of CA, Berkeley
U of CA, Irvine
U of CA, Los Angeles
U of CA, Riverside
U of CA, Santa Barbara
U of Central Florida
U of Cincinnati
U of CO, Boulder
U of Connecticut
U of Dayton
U of Delaware
U of Detroit Mercy
U of Evansville
U of Florida
U of Georgia
U of Hartford
U of Houston
U of Idaho
U of IL at Chicago
U of IL, Champaign
U of Iowa
U of Kansas
U of Kentucky
U of LA at Lafayette

U of LA at Monroe
U of Louisville
U of ME, Orono
U of MD, Baltimore Co.
U of MD, College Park
U of MD, Eastern Shore
U of MA, Amherst
U of Memphis
U of Miami (FL)
U of Michigan
U of MN, Twin Cities
U of Mississippi
U of MO, Columbia
U of MO, Kansas City
U of Montana
U of NE, Lincoln
U of New Hampshire
U of New Mexico
U of New Orleans
U of NC at Greensboro
U of NC, Asheville
U of NC, Chapel Hill
U of NC, Chapel Hill
U of NC, Charlotte
U of NC, Charlotte
U of NC, Wilmington
U of North TX
U of Northern IA
U of Notre Dame
U of Oklahoma
U of Oregon
U of Pennsylvania
U of Pittsburgh
U of Portland
U of Rhode Island
U of Richmond
U of San Diego
U of San Francisco
U of South AL
U of SC, Columbia
U of South Florida
U of TN at Chattanooga
U of TN at Martin
U of TN, Knoxville
U of TX at Arlington
U of TX at Austin

U of TX at El Paso
U of TX at San Antonio
U of TX, Pan American
U of Toledo
U of Tulsa
U of Utah
U of Vermont
U of Virginia
U of Washington
U of WI, Green Bay
U of WI, Madison
U of WI, Milwaukee
U of Wyoming
Utah State U
UT Valley State College
Valparaiso University
Vanderbilt University
Villanova University
VA Commonwealth U
VA Military Institute
VA Polytechnic Institute &
  State University
Wagner College
Wake Forest University
Washington State U
Weber State U
Western Carolina U
Western IL University
Western KY University
Western MI University
Wichita State U
Winthrop University
Wofford College
Wright State U
Xavier University
Yale University
Youngstown State U

CROSS-COUNTRY
DIVISION II

Abilene Christian
  University
Adams State College

Adelphi University
Albany State U (GA)
Alderson-Broaddus College
Anderson College (SC)
Angelo State U
Ashland University
Assumption College
Augustana College (SD)
Barton College
Bellarmine University
Belmont Abbey College
Benedict College
Bentley College
Bloomfield College
Bloomsburg U of
    Pennsylvania
Bluefield State College
Bowie State U
Brigham Young U, HI
Bryant College
C.W. Post Campus/Long
    Island University
CA State Polytechnic
    U–Pomona
CA State U, Chico
CA State U, Stanislaus
California U of PA
Carson-Newman College
Catawba College
Central MO State U
Central State U
Central WA University
Chaminade University
Cheyney U of Pennsylvania
Christian Brothers U
Clarion U of Pennsylvania
Clark Atlanta University
Clayton College & State U
Coker College
College of Saint Rose
CO Christian University
CO School of Mines
Columbia Union College
Columbus State U
Concord College
Concordia College (NY)

Concordia U, St. Paul
Dallas Baptist University
Davis and Elkins College
Dominican College (NY)
Drury University
East Central University
East Stroudsburg U of PA
Eastern NM University
Eckerd College
Edinboro U of PA
Elizabeth City State U
Emporia State U
Erskine College
Fairmont State College
Fayetteville State U
Felician College
Ferris State U
FL Gulf Coast University
FL Institute of Technology
FL Southern College
Fort Hays State U
Fort Lewis College
Fort Valley State U
Francis Marion University
Franklin Pierce College
Gannon University
GA College & State U
Glenville State College
Goldey-Beacom College
Grand Valley State U
Green Mountain College
Harding University
Hawaii Pacific University
Hillsdale College
Holy Family University
Humboldt State U
IN U of PA
Johnson C. Smith U
Kennesaw State U
Kentucky State U
Kutztown U of PA
Lake Superior State U
Lane College
Le Moyne College
Lees-McRae College
LeMoyne-Owen College

Lenoir-Rhyne College
Lewis University
Limestone College
Lincoln Memorial U
Livingstone College
Lock Haven U of PA
Longwood University
Mansfield U of PA
Mars Hill College
Mercy College
Mercyhurst College
Merrimack College
MI Tech University
Miles College
Millersville U of PA
MN State U Mankato
MN State U Moorhead
MO Southern State U-Joplin
Molloy College
MT State U-Billings
Morehouse College
Mount Olive College
NJ Institute of Technology
NM Highlands University
NY Institute of Technology
Newberry College
NC Central University
North Dakota State U
North Greenville College
Northern KY University
Northern State U
Northwest MO State U
Northwest Nazarene U
Northwood University
Nova Southeastern U
Nyack College
Oakland City University
Ohio Valley College
OK Panhandle State U
Pace University
Paine College
Pfeiffer University
Pittsburg State U
Presbyterian College
Queens U of Charlotte
Regis University (CO)

Rollins College
Saginaw Valley State U
Saint Anselm College
Saint Joseph's College (IN)
Saint Leo University
Saint Michael's College
Salem International U
San Francisco State U
Seattle Pacific University
Seattle University
Shaw University
Shepherd College
Shippensburg U of PA
Slippery Rock U of PA
South Dakota State U
Southern AR University
Southern CT State U
Southern IL U–Edwardsville
Southern NH University
Southwest Baptist U
St. Andrews Presbyterian
   College
St. Augustine's College
St. Cloud State U
St. Edward's University
St. Martin's College
St. Paul's College
St. Thomas Aquinas College
State U of West GA
Stonehill College
Tarleton State U
Teikyo Post University
TX A&M U-Commerce
TX A&M U-Kingsville
Tiffin University
Truman State U
Tusculum College
Tuskegee University
U of AL, Huntsville
U of Alaska Anchorage
U of Alaska Fairbanks
U of Bridgeport
U of CA, Davis
U of CA, San Diego
U of Charleston (WVA)
U of CO, Colorado Springs

U of Findlay
U of HI at Hilo
U of Indianapolis
U of MA at Lowell
U of MN Duluth
U of MO, Rolla
U of NE at Kearney
U of New Haven
U of North Alabama
U of NC at Pembroke
U of North Dakota
U of North Florida
U of Puerto Rico, Bayamon
U of Puerto Rico, Cayey
U of Puerto Rico, Mayaguez
U of Puerto Rico, Rio
   Piedras
U of SC-Spartanburg
U of South Dakota
U of Southern IN
U of Tampa
U of the DC
U of the Incarnate Word
U of the Sciences in
   Philadelphia
U of West AL
U of West Florida
U of WI, Parkside
Valdosta State U
Virginia State U
VA Union University
Wayne State College (NE)
Wayne State U (MI)
Westchester U of PA
West Liberty State College
West TX A&M University
WVA Wesleyan College
Western OR University
Western State College (CO)
Western WA University
Wheeling Jesuit University
Wilmington College (DE)
Wingate University
Winona State U
Winston-Salem State U

CROSS-COUNTRY
DIVISION III

Adrian College
Albertus Magnus College
Albion College
Albright College
Alfred University
Allegheny College
Alma College
Alvernia College
Amherst College
Anderson University (IN)
Anna Maria College
Arcadia University
Augsburg College
Augustana College (IL)
Aurora University
Averett University
Babson College
Baldwin-Wallace College
Baptist Bible College
Bard College
Bates College
Becker College
Beloit College
Benedictine University (IL)
Bethany College (WVA)
Bethel University
Blackburn College
Bluffton College
Bowdoin College
Brandeis University
Bridgewater College (VA)
Bridgewater State College
Brooklyn College
Buena Vista University
Buffalo State College
Cabrini College
CA Institute of Technology
CA Lutheran University
CA State U, Hayward
Calvin College
Capital University
Carleton College

Carnegie Mellon University
Carroll College (WI)
Carthage College
Case Western Reserve U
Castleton State College
Catholic University
Cazenovia College
Central College (IA)
Centre College
Chapman University
Chowan College
Christopher Newport U
Claremont McKenna-
   Harvey Mudd-Scripps
   Colleges
Clark University (MA)
Clarke College
Clarkson University
Coe College
Colby College
College Misericordia
College of Mt. St. Joseph
College of Mt. St. Vincent
College of St. Scholastica
College of Wooster
Colorado College
Concordia
   College–Moorhead
Concordia University (IL)
Concordia University (WI)
Concordia U at Austin
Connecticut College
Cornell College
Daniel Webster College
Defiance College
DE Valley College
Denison University
DePauw University
DeSales University
Dickinson College
Dominican University (IL)
Drew University
Earlham College
East TX Baptist University
Eastern CT State U
Eastern Mennonite U

Eastern Nazarene College
Edgewood College
Elizabethtown College
Elmhurst College
Elms College
Emerson College
Emmanuel College (MA)
Emory and Henry College
Emory University
Endicott College
Fairleigh Dickinson
   U–Madison
Ferrum College
Finlandia University
Fisk University
Fitchburg State College
Framingham State College
Franklin & Marshall College
Franklin College
Frostburg State U
Gallaudet University
George Fox University
Gettysburg College
Gordon College
Goucher College
Greensboro College
Greenville College
Grinnell College
Grove City College
Gustavus Adolphus College
Gwynedd-Mercy College
Hamilton College
Hamline University
Hampden-Sydney College
Hanover College
Hartwick College
Haverford College
Heidelberg College
Hendrix College
Hilbert College
Hiram College
Hobart and William Smith
   Colleges
Hope College
Hunter College
Huntingdon College

Husson College
Illinois College
IL Wesleyan University
Ithaca College
John Carroll University
John Jay College of
   Criminal Justice
Johns Hopkins University
Johnson and Wales U
Johnson State College
Juniata College
Kalamazoo College
Kean University
Keene State College
Kenyon College
Keuka College
King's College (PA)
Knox College
La Grange College
La Roche College
Lake Erie College
Lake Forest College
Lasell College
Lawrence University
Lebanon Valley College
Lehman College, City U of
   NY
LeTourneau University
Lewis and Clark College
Lincoln University (PA)
Linfield College
Loras College
Luther College
Lycoming College
Lynchburg College
Macalester College
MacMurray College
ME Maritime Academy
Manchester College
Maranatha Baptist Bible
   College
Marietta College
Martin Luther College
Maryville College (TN)
Maryville U of Saint Louis
Marywood University

MA College of Liberal Arts
MA Institute of Tech
MA Maritime Academy
McDaniel College
McMurry University
Medgar Evers College
Menlo College
Messiah College
Methodist College
Middlebury College
Millikin University
Millsaps College
Milwaukee School of
  Engineering
Mississippi College
Monmouth College (IL)
Montclair State U
Moravian College
Mount Union College
Muhlenberg College
Muskingum College
Nazareth College
NE Wesleyan University
New England College
NJ City University
NY City College of Tech
New York University
Newbury College
North Central College
North Park University
Northland College
Norwich University
Oberlin College
Occidental College
Oglethorpe University
Ohio Northern University
Ohio Wesleyan University
Olivet College
Otterbein College
Pacific Lutheran University
Pacific University (OR)
Palm Beach Atlantic U
PA State Altoona
PA State Berks-Lehigh
  Valley College
PA State U Erie, the
  Behrend College

Piedmont College
Plattsburgh State U of NY
Polytechnic University (NY)
Pomona-Pitzer Colleges
Principia College
Ramapo College
Rensselaer Polytechnic
  Institute
Rhode Island College
Rhodes College
Richard Stockton College
  (NJ)
Ripon College
Rivier College
Roanoke College
Rochester Institute of Tech
Roger Williams University
Rose-Hulman Institute of
  Tech
Rowan University
Rust College
Rutgers, The State U of NJ,
  Camden
Saint Joseph's College (ME)
Saint Mary's U of MN
Salem State College
Salisbury University
Shenandoah University
Simpson College
Southern Vermont College
Southwestern U (TX)
Springfield College
St. John's University (MN)
St. Joseph's College (Long
  Island)
St. Lawrence University
St. Norbert College
St. Olaf College
State U College–Brockport
State U College–Cortland
State U College–Fredonia
State U College at Geneseo
State U College–New Paltz
State U College–Brockport
State U College–Old
  Westbury
State U College–Oneonta

State U College–Potsdam
State U of NY–Farmingdale
State U of NY–Oswego
State U of NY Institute of
  Tech
State U of NY Maritime
  College
Stevens Institute of Tech
Stillman College
Suffolk University
Susquehanna University
Swarthmore College
The College of NJ
Thiel College
Transylvania University
Trinity College (CT)
Trinity University (TX)
Tufts University
U.S. Coast Guard Academy
U.S. Merchant Marine
  Academy
Union College (NY)
U of Chicago
U of Dallas
U of Dubuque
U of La Verne
U of ME at Presque Isle
U of ME, Farmington
U of Mary Washington
U of MA, Boston
U of MA, Dartmouth
U of New England
U of Pittsburgh, Bradford
U of Pittsburgh–Greensburg
U of Puget Sound
U of Redlands
U of Rochester
U of Scranton
U of Southern ME
U of St. Thomas (MN)
U of TX at Dallas
U of TX at Tyler
U of the Ozarks (AR)
U of the South
U of WI, Eau Claire
U of WI, La Crosse
U of WI, Oshkosh

U of WI, Platteville
U of WI, River Falls
U of WI, Stevens Point
U of WI, Stout
U of WI, Superior
U of WI, Whitewater
Upper IA University
Ursinus College
Vassar College
Villa Julie College
VA Wesleyan College
Wabash College
Wartburg College
Washington & Jefferson
    College
Washington and Lee U
Washington U–St. Louis
Waynesburg College
Wesley College
Wesleyan University (CT)
Western New England
    College
Westfield State College
Westminster College (PA)
Wheaton College (IL)
Wheaton College (MA)
Whitman College
Whittier College
Whitworth College
Widener University
Willamette University
William Paterson U of NJ
Williams College
Wilmington College (Ohio)
WI Lutheran College
Wittenberg University
Worcester Polytechnic
    Institute
Worcester State College
Yeshiva University
York College (NY)
York College (PA)

FENCING
DIVISION I

Boston College
Brown University
CA State U, Fullerton
Cleveland State U
Columbia University
Duke University
Harvard University
Ohio State U
Pennsylvania State U
Princeton University
Rutgers, State U of NJ, New
    Brunswick
Sacred Heart University
St. John's University (NY)
Stanford University
U.S. Air Force Academy
U of Detroit Mercy
U of NC, Chapel Hill
U of Notre Dame
U of Pennsylvania
Yale University

FENCING
DIVISION III

Brandeis University
CA Institute of Technology
Case Western Reserve U
Drew University
Haverford College
Hunter College
Johns Hopkins University
Lawrence University
MA Institute of Tech
New York University
Stevens Institute of Tech
Vassar College
Yeshiva University

FOOTBALL
DIVISION IA

Arizona State U

Arkansas State U
Auburn University
Ball State University
Baylor University
Boise State University
Boston College
Bowling Green State U
Brigham Young University
CA State U, Fresno
Central MI University
Clemson University
Colorado State U
Duke University
East Carolina University
Eastern MI University
Florida State U
GA Institute of Technology
IN University, Bloomington
IN U-Purdue U, Fort Wayne
Iowa State U
Kansas State U
Kent State U
Louisiana State U
LA Tech University
Marshall University
Miami University (Ohio)
Michigan State U
Middle TN State U
Mississippi State U
New Mexico State U
North Carolina State U
Northern IL University
Northwestern University
Ohio State U
Ohio University
Oklahoma State U
Oregon State U
Pennsylvania State U
Purdue University
Rice University
Rutgers, State U of NJ,
    New Brunswick
San Diego State U
San Jose State U
Southern Methodist U
Stanford University

Syracuse University
Temple University
TX A&M U–College Station
TX Christian University
TX Tech University
Troy State U
Tulane University
U.S. Air Force Academy
U.S. Military Academy
U.S. Naval Academy
U at Buffalo, the State U
 of NY
U of Akron
U of AL at Birmingham
U of AL, Tuscaloosa
U of Arizona
U of AR, Fayetteville
U of CA, Berkeley
U of CA, Los Angeles
U of Central Florida
U of Cincinnati
U of CO, Boulder
U of Connecticut
U of Florida
U of Georgia
U of Hawaii–Manoa
U of Houston
U of Idaho
U of IL, Champaign
U of Iowa
U of Kansas
U of Kentucky
U of LA at Lafayette
U of LA at Monroe
U of Louisville
U of MD, College Park
U of Memphis
U of Miami (FL)
U of Michigan
U of MN, Twin Cities
U of Mississippi
U of MO, Columbia
U of NE, Lincoln
U of Nevada
U of Nevada, Las Vegas
U of New Mexico

U of NC, Chapel Hill
U of North TX
U of Notre Dame
U of Oklahoma
U of Oregon
U of Pittsburgh
U of SC, Columbia
U of South FL
U of Southern CA
U of Southern MS
U of TN, Knoxville
U of TX at Austin
U of TX at El Paso
U of Toledo
U of Tulsa
U of Utah
U of Virginia
U of Washington
U of WI, Madison
U of Wyoming
UT State U
Vanderbilt University
VA Polytechnic Institute &
 State University
Wake Forest University
WA State U
WVA University
Western MI University

FOOTBALL
DIVISION IAA

AL A&M University
AL State U
Alcorn State U
Appalachian State U
Austin Peay State U
Bethune-Cookman College
Brown University
Bucknell University
Butler University
CA Polytechnic State U
CA State U, Sacramento
Central CT State U
Charleston Southern U
Coastal Carolina University

Colgate University
College of the Holy Cross
College of William & Mary
Columbia University
Cornell University
Dartmouth College
Davidson College
DE State U
Duke University
Duquesne University
East TN State U
Eastern IL University
Eastern KY University
Eastern MI University
Elon University
FL A&M University
FL Atlantic University
FL International University
Fordham University
Furman University
Gardner-Webb University
Georgetown University
GA Southern University
Grambling State U
Hampton University
Harvard University
Hofstra University
Howard University
Idaho State U
Illinois State U
Indiana State U
Iona College
Jackson State U
Jacksonville State U
Jacksonville University
James Madison University
La Salle University
Lafayette College
Lehigh University
Liberty University
Marist College
McNeese State U
MS Valley State U
Monmouth University
MT State U-Bozeman
Morehead State U

Murray State U
Nicholls State U
Norfolk State U
NC A&T State U
Northeastern University
Northern AZ University
Northwestern State U
Portland State U
Prairie View A&M U
Princeton University
Robert Morris University
Sacred Heart University
Saint Francis U (PA)
Sam Houston State U
Samford University
Savannah State U
Siena College
South Carolina State U
Southeast MO State U
Southeastern LA University
Southern IL U–Carbondale
Southern U–Baton Rouge
Southern UT University
Southwest MO State U
St. Mary's College of CA
St. Peter's College
Stephen F. Austin State U
Stony Brook University
Temple University
TN State U
TN Technological
   University
TX Southern University
TX State U-San Marcos
The Citadel
Towson University
University at Albany
U of AR, Pine Bluff
U of Dayton
U of Delaware
U of ME, Orono
U of MA, Amherst
U of Montana
U of New Hampshire
U of Northern IA
U of Pennsylvania

U of Rhode Island
U of Richmond
U of San Diego
U of TN at Chattanooga
U of TN at Martin
Valparaiso University
Villanova University
VA Military Institute
Wagner College
Weber State U
Western Carolina U
Western IL University
Western KY University
Wofford College
Yale University
Youngstown State U

FOOTBALL
DIVISION II

Abilene Christian U
Adams State College
Albany State U (GA)
American International
   College
Anderson College (SC)
Angelo State U
AR Tech University
Ashland University
Assumption College
Augustana College (SD)
Bemidji State U
Benedict College
Bentley College
Bloomsburg U of PA
Bowie State U
Bryant College
C.W. Post Campus/Long
   Island University
California U of PA
Carson-Newman College
Catawba College
Central MO State U
Central WA University
Chadron State College
Cheyney U of Pennsylvania

Clarion U of Pennsylvania
Clark Atlanta University
CO School of Mines
Concord College
Concordia U, St. Paul
Delta State U
East Central University
East Stroudsburg U of PA
Eastern NM University
Edinboro U of PAa
Elizabeth City State U
Emporia State U
Fairmont State College
Fayetteville State U
Ferris State U
Fort Hays State U
Fort Lewis College
Fort Valley State U
Gannon University
Glenville State College
Grand Valley State U
Harding University
Henderson State U
Hillsdale College
Humboldt State U
IN U of Pennsylvania
Johnson C. Smith U
Kentucky State U
KY Wesleyan College
Kutztown U of PA
Lane College
Lenoir-Rhyne College
Lincoln University (MO)
Livingstone College
Lock Haven U of PA
Mansfield U of PA
Mars Hill College
Mercyhurst College
Merrimack College
Mesa State College
MI Tech University
Midwestern State U
Miles College
Millersville U of PA
MN State U Mankato
MN State U Moorhead

MO Southern State U Joplin
MO Western State College
Morehouse College
NM Highlands University
Newberry College
NC Central University
North Dakota State U
North Greenville College
Northeastern State U
Northern MI University
Northern State U
Northwest MO State U
Northwood University
OK Panhandle State U
Ouachita Baptist University
Pace University
Pittsburg State U
Presbyterian College
Quincy University
Saginaw Valley State U
Saint Anselm College
Saint Joseph's College (IN)
Shaw University
Shepherd College
Shippensburg U of PA
Slippery Rock U of PA
South Dakota State U
Southeastern OK State U
Southern AR University
Southern CT State U
Southwest Baptist U
Southwest MN State U
Southwestern OK State U
St. Augustine's College
St. Cloud State U
State U of West GA
Stonehill College
Tarleton State U
Teikyo Post University
TX A&M U-Commerce
TX A&M U-Kingsville
Tiffin University
Truman State U
Tusculum College
Tuskegee University
U of AR, Monticello

U of CA, Davis
U of Central AR
U of Central OK
U of Charleston (WVA)
U of Findlay
U of Indianapolis
U of MN Duluth
U of MN, Crookston
U of MN, Morris
U of MO, Rolla
U of NE at Kearney
U of NE at Omaha
U of New Haven
U of North AL
U of North Dakota
U of Northern CO
U of South Dakota
U of West AL
Valdosta State U
Virginia State U
VA Union University
Washburn U of Topeka
Wayne State College (NE)
Wayne State U (MI)
Westchester U of
  Pennsylvania
West Liberty State College
West TX A&M University
WVA State College
WVA U Institute of Tech
WVA Wesleyan College
Western NM University
Western OR University
Western State College of
  CO
Western WA University
Wingate University
Winona State U
Winston-Salem State U

FOOTBALL
DIVISION III

Adrian College
Albion College
Albright College

Alfred University
Allegheny College
Alma College
Amherst College
Anderson University (IN)
Augsburg College
Augustana College (IL)
Aurora University
Austin College
Averett University
Baldwin-Wallace College
Bates College
Beloit College
Benedictine University (IL)
Bethany College (WV)
Bethel University (MN)
Blackburn College
Bluffton University
Bowdoin College
Bridgewater College (VA)
Bridgewater State College
Buena Vista University
Buffalo State College
California Lutheran U
Capital University
Carleton College
Carnegie Mellon University
Carroll College (Wisconsin)
Carthage College
Case Western Reserve U
Catholic University
Central College (Iowa)
Centre College
Chapman University
Chowan College
Christopher Newport U
Claremont McKenna-Harvey
  Mudd-Scripps Colleges
Coe College
Colby College
College of Mt. St. Joseph
College of Wooster
Colorado College
Concordia College,
  Moorhead
Concordia University (IL)

Concordia University (WI)
Cornell College
Crown College (MN)
Curry College
Defiance College
Delaware Valley College
Denison University
DePauw University
Dickinson College
University of Dubuque
Earlham College
East Texas Baptist U
Elmhurst College
Emory and Henry College
Endicott College
Eureka College
Fairleigh Dickinson U, Madison
Ferrum College
Fitchburg State College
Framingham State College
Franklin & Marshall College
Franklin College
Frostburg State University
Gettysburg College
Greensboro College
Greenville College
Grinnell College
Grove City College
Guilford College
Gustavus Adolphus College
Hamilton College
Hamline University
Hampden-Sydney College
Hanover College
Hardin-Simmons University
Hartwick College
Heidelberg College
Hiram College
Hobart College
Hope College
Howard Payne University
Huntingdon College
Husson College
Illinois College
Illinois Wesleyan University

Ithaca College
John Carroll University
Johns Hopkins University
Juniata College
Kalamazoo College
Kean University
Kenyon College
King's College (PA)
Knox College
University of La Verne
Lake Forest College
Lakeland College
Lawrence University
Lebanon Valley College
Lewis & Clark College
Linfield College
Loras College
Louisiana College
Luther College
Lycoming College
Macalester College
MacMurray College
Maine Maritime Academy
Manchester College
Maranatha Baptist Bible College
Marietta College
Martin Luther College
Maryville College (TN)
MA Institute of Tech
MA Maritime Academy
McDaniel College
McMurry University
Menlo College
Methodist College
Middlebury College
Millikin University
Millsaps College
Mississippi College
Monmouth College (IL)
Montclair State University
Moravian College
Mount Ida College
Mount Union College
Muhlenberg College
Muskingum College

Nebraska Wesleyan U
Nichols College
NC Wesleyan College
North Central College
North Park University
Oberlin College
Occidental College
Ohio Northern University
Ohio Wesleyan University
Olivet College
Otterbein College
Pacific Lutheran University
Plymouth State College
Pomona-Pitzer Colleges
Principia College
Randolph-Macon College
Rensselaer Polytechnic Institute
Rhodes College
Ripon College
Rockford College
Rose-Hulman Institute of Technology
Rowan University
Salisbury University
Salve Regina University
Shenandoah University
Simpson College
State U College at Brockport
State U College at Cortland
St. John Fisher College
St. John's University (MN)
St. Lawrence University
St. Norbert College
St. Olaf College
Stillman College
Sul Ross State University
Susquehanna University
Texas Lutheran University
The College of New Jersey
Thiel College
Thomas More College
Tri-State University
Trinity College (CT)
Trinity University (TX)

Tufts University
U.S. Merchant Marine
  Academy
Union College (New York)
University of Chicago
U of Mary Hardin-Baylor
U of MA, Dartmouth
University of Puget Sound
University of Redlands
University of Rochester
University of the South
U of St. Thomas (MN)
U of Wisconsin, Eau Claire
U of Wisconsin, La Crosse
U of Wisconsin, Oshkosh
U of Wisconsin, Platteville
U of Wisconsin, River Falls
U of WI, Stevens Point
U of Wisconsin, Stout
U of Wisconsin, Whitewater
Upper Iowa University
Ursinus College
Utica College
Wabash College
Wartburg College
Washington & Jefferson
  College
Washington & Lee U
Washington U (MO)
Waynesburg College
Wesley College
Wesleyan University (CT)
Western CT State U
Western New England
  College
Westfield State College
Westminster College (MO)
Westminster College (PA)
Wheaton College (IL)
Whittier College
Whitworth College
Widener University
Wilkes University
Willamette University
William Paterson U of NJ
Williams College

Wilmington College (Ohio)
WI Lutheran College
Wittenberg University
Worcester Polytechnic
  Institute
Worcester State College

GOLF
DIVISION I

AL A&M University
Alabama State U
Alcorn State U
American University
Appalachian State U
Arizona State U
Arkansas State U
Auburn University
Augusta State U
Austin Peay State U
Ball State University
Baylor University
Belmont University
Bethune-Cookman College
Birmingham-Southern
  College
Boise State University
Boston College
Boston University
Bowling Green State U
Bradley University
Brigham Young University
Brown University
Bucknell University
Butler University
CA Polytechnic State U
CA State U, Fresno
CA State U, Northridge
CA State U, Sacramento
Campbell University
Canisius College
Centenary College (LA)
Central CT State U
Charleston Southern U
Chicago State U
Clemson University

Cleveland State U
Coastal Carolina University
Colgate University
College of Charleston (SC)
College of the Holy Cross
College of William & Mary
Colorado State U
Columbia University
Cornell University
Creighton University
Dartmouth College
Davidson College
DePaul University
Drake University
Drexel University
Duke University
Duquesne University
East Carolina University
East TN State U
Eastern IL University
Eastern KY University
Eastern MI University
Elon University
Fairfield University
Fairleigh Dickinson
  U–Teaneck
FL A&M University
FL Atlantic University
Florida State U
Fordham University
Furman University
Gardner-Webb University
George Mason University
George WA University
Georgetown University
GA Institute of Technology
GA Southern University
Georgia State U
Gonzaga University
Grambling State U
Hampton University
Harvard University
High Point University
Hofstra University
Idaho State U
Illinois State University

IN University, Bloomington	Ohio University	TN State U
IN U-Purdue U, Fort Wayne	Oklahoma State U	TN Technological University
Iona College	Old Dominion University	TX A&M U–College Station
Iowa State U	Oral Roberts University	TX Christian University
Jackson State U	Oregon State U	TX Southern University
Jacksonville State U	Pennsylvania State U	TX State U-San Marcos
Jacksonville University	Pepperdine University	TX Tech University
James Madison University	Prairie View A&M U	The Citadel
Kansas State U	Princeton University	Towson University
Kent State U	Purdue University	Troy State U
La Salle University	Quinnipiac University	Tulane University
Lafayette College	Radford University	U.S. Air Force Academy
Lamar University	Rice University	U.S. Military Academy
Lehigh University	Rider University	U.S. Naval Academy
Liberty University	Robert Morris University	U of Akron
Lipscomb University	Rutgers, State U of NJ,	U of AL at Birmingham
Long Beach State U	New Brunswick	U of AL, Tuscaloosa
Long Island U-Brooklyn	Sacred Heart University	U of Arizona
Campus	Saint Francis U (PA)	U of AR, Fayetteville
Louisiana State U	Saint Joseph's University	U of AR, Little Rock
LA Tech University	Saint Louis University	U of AR, Pine Bluff
Loyola College (MD)	Sam Houston State U	U of CA, Berkeley
Loyola Marymount U	Samford University	U of CA, Irvine
Loyola University (IL)	San Diego State U	U of CA, Los Angeles
Manhattan College	San Jose State U	U of CA, Riverside
Marquette University	Santa Clara University	U of CA, Santa Barbara
Marshall University	Savannah State U	U of Central Florida
McNeese State U	Seton Hall University	U of Cincinnati
Mercer University	Siena College	U of CO, Boulder
Miami University (Ohio)	South Carolina State U	U of Connecticut
Michigan State U	Southeast MO State U	U of Dayton
Middle TN State U	Southeastern LA University	U of Delaware
Mississippi State U	Southern IL U–Carbondale	U of Denver
MS Valley State U	Southern Methodist U	U of Detroit Mercy
Monmouth University	Southern U–Baton Rouge	U of Evansville
Morehead State U	Southern UT University	U of Florida
Mount St. Mary's College	Southwest MO State U	U of Georgia
Murray State U	St. Bonaventure University	U of Hartford
New Mexico State U	St. John's University (NY)	U of Hawaii–Manoa
Niagara University	St. Mary's College of CA	U of Houston
Nicholls State U	St. Peter's College	U of Idaho
North Carolina State U	Stanford University	U of IL, Champaign
Northern IL University	State U of NY, Binghamton	U of Iowa
Northwestern University	Stephen F. Austin State U	U of Kansas
Oakland University	Stetson University	U of Kentucky
Ohio State U	Temple University	U of LA at Lafayette

U of LA at Monroe
U of Louisville
U of MD, College Park
U of Memphis
U of Michigan
U of MN, Twin Cities
U of Mississippi
U of MO, Columbia
U of MO, Kansas City
U of NE, Lincoln
U of Nevada
U of Nevada, Las Vegas
U of New Mexico
U of New Orleans
U of NC at Greensboro
U of NC, Chapel Hill
U of NC, Charlotte
U of NC, Wilmington
U of North Florida
U of North TX
U of Northern IA
U of Notre Dame
U of Oklahoma
U of Oregon
U of Pennsylvania
U of Portland
U of Rhode Island
U of Richmond
U of San Diego
U of San Francisco
U of South AL
U of SC, Columbia
U of South Florida
U of Southern CA
U of Southern MS
U of TN at Chattanooga
U of TN at Martin
U of TN, Knoxville
U of TX at Arlington
U of TX at Austin
U of TX at El Paso
U of TX at San Antonio
U of TX, Pan American
U of the Pacific
U of Toledo
U of Tulsa

U of Utah
U of Vermont
U of Virginia
U of Washington
U of WI, Green Bay
U of WI, Madison
U of Wyoming
Utah State U
UT Valley State College
Vanderbilt University
Villanova University
VA Commonwealth U
VA Polytechnic Institute &
   State U
Wagner College
Wake Forest University
Washington State U
Weber State U
Western Carolina U
Western IL University
Western KY University
Wichita State U
Winthrop University
Wofford College
Wright State U
Xavier University
Yale University
Youngstown State U

GOLF
DIVISION II

Abilene Christian U
Adams State College
Adelphi University
American International
   College
Anderson College (SC)
AR Tech University
Armstrong Atlantic State U
Ashland University
Assumption College
Augustana College (SD)
Barry University
Barton College
Bellarmine University

Belmont Abbey College
Bemidji State U
Benedict College
Bentley College
Bluefield State College
Bryant College
Caldwell College
CA State U, Bakersfield
CA State U, Chico
CA State U, Dominguez
   Hills
CA State U, San Bernardino
CA State U, Stanislaus
Cameron University
Carson-Newman College
Catawba College
Central MO State U
Central State U
Christian Brothers U
Clarion U of Pennsylvania
Clayton College & State U
Coker College
College of Saint Rose
CO Christian University
CO School of Mines
Colorado State U-Pueblo
Columbus State U
Concord College
Dallas Baptist University
Davis and Elkins College
Delta State U
Dominican College (NY)
Dowling College
Drury University
East Central University
Eckerd College
Elizabeth City State U
Fairmont State College
Fayetteville State U
Ferris State U
FL Gulf Coast University
FL Institute of Technology
FL Southern College
Fort Hays State U
Fort Lewis College
Francis Marion University

Franklin Pierce College
Gannon University
GA College & State U
Glenville State College
Goldey-Beacom College
Grand Canyon University
Grand Valley State U
Green Mountain College
Harding University
Henderson State U
Hillsdale College
Holy Family University
IN U of PA
Johnson C. Smith U
Kennesaw State U
Kentucky State U
KY Wesleyan College
Lake Superior State U
Le Moyne College
Lees-McRae College
Lenoir-Rhyne College
Lewis University
Limestone College
Lincoln Memorial U
Lincoln University (MO)
Longwood University
Lynn University
Mars Hill College
Mercy College
Mercyhurst College
Millersville U of PA
MN State U Mankato
MO Southern State U-Joplin
MO Western State College
MT State U-Billings
Morehouse College
Mount Olive College
Newberry College
NC Central University
North Dakota State U
North Greenville College
Northeastern State U
Northern KY University
Northern MI University
Northern State U
Northwest Nazarene U

Northwood University
Nova Southeastern U
Nyack College
Oakland City University
Ohio Valley College
OK Panhandle State U
Ouachita Baptist University
Pace University
Pfeiffer University
Philadelphia University
Pittsburg State U
Presbyterian College
Queens College (NY)
Queens U of Charlotte
Quincy University
Regis University (CO)
Rockhurst University
Rollins College
Saginaw Valley State U
Saint Anselm College
Saint Joseph's College (IN)
Saint Leo University
Saint Michael's College
Salem International U
Shepherd College
Slippery Rock U of PA
Sonoma State U
South Dakota State U
Southern AR University
Southern NH University
Southwest Baptist U
Southwestern OK State U
St. Andrews Presbyterian
   College
St. Augustine's College
St. Cloud State U
St. Edward's University
St. Martin's College
St. Mary's University (TX)
St. Paul's College
St. Thomas Aquinas College
Teikyo Post University
TX A&M U-Commerce
Tiffin University
Truman State U
Tusculum College

U of AR, Monticello
U of CA, Davis
U of CA, San Diego
U of Central AR
U of Central OK
U of Charleston (WVA)
U of CO, Colorado Springs
U of Findlay
U of Hawaii–Hilo
U of Indianapolis
U of MN, Crookston
U of MN, Morris
U of MO, St. Louis
U of Montevallo
U of NE at Kearney
U of New Haven
U of North Alabama
U of NC at Pembroke
U of North Dakota
U of Northern CO
U of SC at Aiken
U of SC-Spartanburg
U of South Dakota
U of Southern IN
U of Tampa
U of the Incarnate Word
U of West Florida
U of WI, Parkside
Valdosta State U
VA Union University
Washburn U of Topeka
Wayne State College (NE)
Wayne State U (MI)
Westchester U of PA
West Liberty State College
West TX A&M University
WVA U Institute of Tech
WVA Wesleyan College
Western NM University
Western WA University
Wheeling Jesuit University
Wingate University
Winona State U
Winston-Salem State U

GOLF
DIVISION III

Adrian College
Albion College
Albright College
Allegheny College
Alma College
Alvernia College
Amherst College
Anderson University (IN)
Anna Maria College
Arcadia University
Augsburg College
Augustana College (IL)
Aurora University
Austin College
Averett University
Babson College
Baldwin-Wallace College
Bates College
Becker College
Beloit College
Benedictine University (IL)
Bethel University
Blackburn College
Bluffton College
Bowdoin College
Brandeis University
Bridgewater College (VA)
Buena Vista University
Cabrini College
CA Institute of Technology
CA Lutheran University
CA State U, Hayward
Calvin College
Capital University
Carleton College
Carnegie Mellon University
Carroll College (WI)
Carthage College
Case Western Reserve U
Cazenovia College
Centenary College (NJ)
Central College (IA)
Centre College

Chapman University
Chowan College
Christopher Newport U
Clarke College
Clarkson University
Coe College
College Misericordia
College of Mt. St. Joseph
College of Wooster
Concordia
    College–Moorhead
Concordia University (WI)
Concordia U at Austin
Cornell College
Defiance College
DE Valley College
Denison University
DePauw University
DeSales University
Dickinson College
Eastern University
Edgewood College
Elizabethtown College
Elmhurst College
Elmira College
Elms College
Emory and Henry College
Emory University
Eureka College
Fairleigh Dickinson
    U–Madison
Ferrum College
Fisk University
Fontbonne University
Franklin & Marshall College
Franklin College
Gettysburg College
Greensboro College
Grinnell College
Grove City College
Guilford College
Gustavus Adolphus College
Gwynedd-Mercy College
Hamilton College
Hampden-Sydney College
Hanover College

Hardin-Simmons University
Hartwick College
Heidelberg College
Hendrix College
Hiram College
Hobart and William Smith
    Colleges
Hood College
Hope College
Huntingdon College
Husson College
Illinois College
IL Wesleyan University
John Carroll University
Kalamazoo College
Kenyon College
King's College (PA)
Knox College
La Grange College
La Roche College
Lake Erie College
Lakeland College
Lawrence University
Lebanon Valley College
LeTourneau University
Lewis and Clark College
Linfield College
Loras College
Louisiana College
Luther College
Lycoming College
Lynchburg College
Macalester College
MacMurray College
ME Maritime Academy
Manchester College
Manhattanville College
Marian College (WI)
Martin Luther College
Mary Baldwin College
Maryville U of Saint Louis
MA College of Liberal Arts
MA Institute of Tech
McDaniel College
McMurry University
Menlo College

Messiah College
Methodist College
Middlebury College
Millikin University
Millsaps College
Milwaukee School of
  Engineering
Monmouth College (IL)
Moravian College
Mount Union College
Muhlenberg College
Muskingum College
Nazareth College
NE Wesleyan University
Neumann College
New York University
Newbury College
Nichols College
NC Wesleyan College
North Central College
North Park University
Oberlin College
Occidental College
Oglethorpe University
Ohio Northern University
Ohio Wesleyan University
Olivet College
Otterbein College
Pacific Lutheran University
Pacific University (OR)
PA State Altoona
PA State Berks-Lehigh
  Valley College
PA State U Erie, the
  Behrend College
Philadelphia Biblical U
Piedmont College
Plattsburgh State U of NY
Pomona-Pitzer Colleges
Principia College
Randolph-Macon College
Rensselaer Polytechnic
  Institute
Rhode Island College
Rhodes College
Ripon College

Roanoke College
Rockford College
Roger Williams University
Rose-Hulman Institute of
  Tech
Rutgers, The State U of NJ,
  Camden
Saint Joseph's College (ME)
Saint Mary's U of MN
Salem State College
Schreiner University
Shenandoah University
Simpson College
Skidmore College
Southwestern U (TX)
Springfield College
St. John Fisher College
St. John's University (MN)
St. Joseph's College (Long
  Island)
St. Lawrence University
St. Norbert College
St. Olaf College
State U College–Potsdam
State U of NY–Farmingdale
State U of NY–Oswego
State U of NY Inst. of Tech
Suffolk University
Susquehanna University
Swarthmore College
TX Lutheran University
The College of NJ
Thiel College
Thomas College
Thomas More College
Transylvania University
Trinity College (CT)
Trinity University (TX)
Tufts University
U.S. Merchant Marine
  Academy
U of Dallas
U of Dubuque
U of La Verne
U of ME at Presque Isle
U of ME, Farmington

U of Mary Hardin-Baylor
U of MA, Dartmouth
U of New England
U of Pittsburgh, Bradford
U of Pittsburgh–Greensburg
U of Puget Sound
U of Redlands
U of Rochester
U of Scranton
U of St. Thomas (MN)
U of TX at Dallas
U of TX at Tyler
U of the Ozarks (AR)
U of the South
U of WI, Eau Claire
Upper IA University
Ursinus College
Utica College
Villa Julie College
VA Wesleyan College
Wabash College
Wartburg College
Washington and Jefferson
  College
Washington and Lee U
Waynesburg College
Webster University
Wentworth Institute of
  Tech
Wesley College
Wesleyan University (CT)
Western New England
  College
Westminster College (MO)
Westminster College (PA)
Wheaton College (IL)
Whitman College
Whittier College
Whitworth College
Widener University
Wilkes University
Willamette University
Williams College
Wilmington College (Ohio)
WI Lutheran College
Wittenberg University

Worcester Polytechnic
Institute
Worcester State College
Yeshiva University
York College (PA)

GYMNASTICS
DIVISION I

College of William & Mary
James Madison University
Ohio State U
Pennsylvania State U
Stanford University
Temple University
U.S. Air Force Academy
U.S. Military Academy
U.S. Naval Academy
U of CA, Berkeley
U of IL at Chicago
U of IL, Champaign
U of Iowa
U of Michigan
U of MN, Twin Cities
U of NE, Lincoln
U of Oklahoma

GYMNASTICS
DIVISION II

Southern CT State U

GYMNASTICS
DIVISION III

MA Institute of Tech
Springfield College

ICE HOCKEY
DIVISION I

American International
College
Bemidji State U
Bentley College
Boston College

Boston University
Bowling Green State U
Brown University
Canisius College
Clarkson University
Colgate University
College of the Holy Cross
Colorado College
Cornell University
Dartmouth College
Ferris State U
Harvard University
Lake Superior State U
Mercyhurst College
Merrimack College
Miami University (Ohio)
Michigan State U
MI Tech University
MN State U Mankato
Niagara University
Northeastern University
Northern MI University
Ohio State U
Princeton University
Providence College
Quinnipiac University
Rensselaer Polytechnic
Institute
Sacred Heart University
St. Cloud State U
St. Lawrence University
U.S. Air Force Academy
U.S. Military Academy
Union College (NY)
U of AL, Huntsville
U of Alaska Anchorage
U of Alaska Fairbanks
U of Connecticut
U of Denver
U of Findlay
U of ME, Orono
U of MA at Lowell
U of MA, Amherst
U of Michigan
U of MN Duluth
U of MN, Twin Cities

U of NE at Omaha
U of New Hampshire
U of North Dakota
U of Notre Dame
U of Vermont
U of WI, Madison
Wayne State U (MI)
Western MI University
Yale University

ICE HOCKEY
DIVISION II

Assumption College
Franklin Pierce College
U of MN, Crookston
Saint Anselm College
Southern NH University
Saint Michael's College
Stonehill College

ICE HOCKEY
DIVISION III

Amherst College
Augsburg College
Babson College
Bethel University
Bowdoin College
Buffalo State College
Castleton State College
Colby College
College of St. Scholastica
Concordia
College–Moorhead
Connecticut College
Curry College
Elmira College
Finlandia University
Fitchburg State College
Framingham State College
Gustavus Adolphus College
Hamilton College
Hamline University
Hobart and William Smith
Colleges

Johnson and Wales U
Lake Forest College
Lawrence University
Lebanon Valley College
Manhattanville College
Marian College (WI)
MA Institute of Tech
Middlebury College
Milwaukee School of
   Engineering
Neumann College
New England College
Nichols College
Northland College
Norwich University
Plattsburgh State U of NY
Plymouth State College
Rochester Institute of Tech
Saint Mary's U of MN
Salem State College
Salve Regina University
Skidmore College
St. John's University (MN)
St. Norbert College
St. Olaf College
State U College–Brockport
State U College–Cortland
State U College–Fredonia
State U College at Geneseo
State U College–Potsdam
State U of NY–Oswego
Suffolk University
Trinity College (CT)
Tufts U of MA, Boston
U of MA, Dartmouth
U of Scranton
U of Southern ME
U of St. Thomas (MN)
U of WI, Eau Claire
U of WI, River Falls
U of WI, Stevens Point
U of WI, Stout
U of WI, Superior
Utica College
Wentworth Institute of
   Tech

Wesleyan University (CT)
Western New England
   College
Williams College
Worcester State College

LACROSSE
DIVISION I

Adelphi University
American International
   College
Assumption College
Bentley College
Bryant College
C.W. Post Campus/Long
   Island University
Catawba College
Dominican College (NY)
Dowling College
Franklin Pierce College
Green Mountain College
Le Moyne College
Lees-McRae College
Limestone College
Mars Hill College
Mercyhurst College
Merrimack College
Molloy College
NY Institute of Technology
Pace University
Pfeiffer University
Queens U of Charlotte
Saint Anselm College
Saint Michael's College
Southampton Campus of
   Long Island University
Southern NH University
St. Andrews Presbyterian
   College
Wheeling Jesuit University
Wingate University

LACROSSE
DIVISION II

Adelphi University
American International
   College
Assumption College
Bentley College
Bryant College
C.W. Post Campus/Long
   Island University
Catawba College
Dominican College (NY)
Dowling College
Franklin Pierce College
Green Mountain College
Le Moyne College
Lees-McRae College
Limestone College
Mars Hill College
Mercyhurst College
Merrimack College
Molloy College
NY Institute of Technology
Pace University
Pfeiffer University
Queens U of Charlotte
Saint Anselm College
Saint Michael's College
Southampton Campus of
   Long Island University
Southern NH University
St. Andrews Presbyterian
   College
Wheeling Jesuit University
Wingate University

LACROSSE
DIVISION III

Alfred University
Alvernia College
Amherst College
Babson College
Bates College
Bowdoin College

Cabrini College
Castleton State College
Catholic University
Cazenovia College
Centenary College (NJ)
Clark University (MA)
Clarkson University
Colby College
College Misericordia
College of Wooster
Colorado College
Connecticut College
Curry College
Daniel Webster College
Denison University
DeSales University
Dickinson College
Drew University
Eastern CT State U
Elizabethtown College
Elmira College
Emerson College
Endicott College
Fairleigh Dickinson
    U–Madison
Franklin & Marshall College
Gettysburg College
Gordon College
Goucher College
Greensboro College
Guilford College
Hamilton College
Hampden-Sydney College
Hartwick College
Haverford College
Ithaca College
Johnson State College
Kean University
Keene State College
Kenyon College
Keuka College
King's College (PA)
Lasell College
Lycoming College
Lynchburg College
ME Maritime Academy

Manhattanville College
Mary Baldwin College
MA Institute of Tech
MA Maritime Academy
McDaniel College
Medaille College
Messiah College
Middlebury College
Montclair State U
Moravian College
Mount Ida College
Muhlenberg College
Nazareth College
Neumann College
New England College
Nichols College
Norwich University
Oberlin College
Ohio Wesleyan University
Plattsburgh State U of NY
Plymouth State College
Randolph-Macon College
Rensselaer Polytechnic
    Institute
Richard Stockton College
    (NJ)
Roanoke College
Rochester Institute of Tech
Roger Williams University
Salisbury University
Salve Regina University
Shenandoah University
Skidmore College
Springfield College
St. John Fisher College
St. Lawrence University
St. Mary's College of MD
State U College–Brockport
State U College–Cortland
State U College at Geneseo
State U College–Oneonta
State U College–Potsdam
State U of NY–Farmingdale
State U of NY–Oswego
State U of NY Institute of
    Tech

State U of NY Maritime
    College
Stevens Institute of Tech
Susquehanna University
Swarthmore College
Trinity College (CT)
Tufts University
U.S. Merchant Marine
    Academy
Union College (NY)
U of Mary Washington
U of MA, Boston
U of MA, Dartmouth
U of New England
U of Scranton
U of Southern ME
Ursinus College
Utica College
Vassar College
Villa Julie College
VA Wesleyan College
Washington and Jefferson
    College
Washington and Lee U
WA College (MD)
Wentworth Institute of
    Tech
Wesley College
Wesleyan University (CT)
Western CT State U
Western New England
    College
Wheaton College (MA)
Whittier College
Widener University
Williams College
Wittenberg University
York College (PA)

RIFLE
DIVISION I

The Citadel
Jacksonville State U
U of San Francisco
VA Military Institute

RIFLE
DIVISION III

Norwich University
Rose-Hulman Institute of
    Tech
State U of NY Maritime
    College
U.S. Coast Guard Academy

SKIING
DIVISION I

Boston College
Dartmouth College
Harvard University
MT State U-Bozeman
U of CO, Boulder
U of Denver
U of MA, Amherst
U of Nevada
U of New Hampshire
U of New Mexico
U of Utah
U of Vermont
U of WI, Green Bay

SKIING
DIVISION II

Green Mountain College
MI Tech University
Northern MI University
Saint Anselm College
Saint Michael's College
U of Alaska Anchorage
U of Alaska Fairbanks
Western State College (CO)

SKIING
DIVISION III

Babson College
Bates College
Bowdoin College
Clarkson University

Colby College
Colby-Sawyer College
Finlandia University
Gustavus Adolphus College
Macalester College
MA Institute of Tech
Middlebury College
Plymouth State College
St. John's University (MN)
St. Lawrence University
St. Olaf College
U of Puget Sound
Whitman College
Williams College

SOCCER
DIVISION I

AL A&M University
American University
Appalachian State U
Belmont University
Birmingham-Southern
    College
Boston College
Boston University
Bowling Green State U
Bradley University
Brown University
Bucknell University
Butler University
CA Polytechnic State U
CA State U, Fresno
CA State U, Fullerton
CA State U, Northridge
CA State U, Sacramento
Campbell University
Canisius College
Centenary College (LA)
Central CT State U
Clemson University
Cleveland State U
Coastal Carolina University
Colgate University
College of Charleston (SC)
College of the Holy Cross

College of William & Mary
Columbia University
Cornell University
Creighton University
Dartmouth College
Davidson College
DePaul University
Drake University
Drexel University
Drury University
Duke University
Duquesne University
East Carolina University
Eastern IL University
Elon University
Fairfield University
Fairleigh Dickinson
    U–Teaneck
FL Atlantic University
FL International University
Fordham University
Furman University
Gardner-Webb University
George Mason University
George WA University
Georgetown University
GA Southern University
Georgia State U
Gonzaga University
Harvard University
High Point University
Hofstra University
Howard University
IN University, Bloomington
IN U-Purdue U, Fort Wayne
Iona College
Jacksonville University
James Madison University
La Salle University
Lafayette College
Lehigh University
Liberty University
Lipscomb University
Long Island U-Brooklyn
    Campus
Loyola College (MD)

Loyola Marymount U
Loyola University (IL)
Manhattan College
Marist College
Marquette University
Marshall University
Mercer University
Michigan State U
Monmouth University
Mount St. Mary's College
Niagara University
North Carolina State U
Northeastern University
Northern IL University
Northwestern University
Oakland University
Ohio State U
Old Dominion University
Oral Roberts University
Oregon State U
Pennsylvania State U
Philadelphia University
Princeton University
Providence College
Quinnipiac University
Radford University
Rider University
Robert Morris University
Rutgers, State U of NJ,
 New Brunswick
Sacred Heart University
Saint Francis U (PA)
Saint Joseph's University
Saint Louis University
San Diego State U
San Jose State U
Santa Clara University
Seton Hall University
Siena College
Southern Methodist U
Southwest MO State U
St. Bonaventure University
St. Francis College (NY)
St. John's University (NY)
St. Mary's College of CA
St. Peter's College

Stanford University
State U College–Oneonta
State U of NY–Binghamton
Stetson University
Stony Brook University
Syracuse University
Temple University
Towson University
U.S. Air Force Academy
U.S. Military Academy
U.S. Naval Academy
University at Albany
U at Buffalo, the State U
 of NY
U of Akron
U of AL at Birmingham
U of CA, Berkeley
U of CA, Irvine
U of CA, Los Angeles
U of CA, Riverside
U of CA, Santa Barbara
U of Central Florida
U of Cincinnati
U of Connecticut
U of Dayton
U of Delaware
U of Denver
U of Detroit Mercy
U of Evansville
U of Hartford
U of IL at Chicago
U of Kentucky
U of Louisville
U of ME, Orono
U of MD, Baltimore Co.
U of MD, College Park
U of MA, Amherst
U of Memphis
U of Michigan
U of MO, Kansas City
U of Nevada, Las Vegas
U of New Hampshire
U of New Mexico
U of NC at Greensboro
U of NC, Asheville
U of NC, Chapel Hill

U of NC, Charlotte
U of NC, Wilmington
U of Notre Dame
U of Pennsylvania
U of Pittsburgh
U of Portland
U of Rhode Island
U of Richmond
U of San Diego
U of San Francisco
U of SC, Columbia
U of South Florida
U of Tulsa
U of Vermont
U of Virginia
U of Washington
U of WI, Green Bay
U of WI, Madison
U of WI, Milwaukee
Valparaiso University
Vanderbilt University
Villanova University
VA Commonwealth U
VA Military Institute
VA Polytechnic Institute &
 State University
Wake Forest University
WVA University
Western IL University
Western KY University
Western MI University
Winthrop University
Wofford College
Wright State U
Xavier University
Yale University

SOCCER
DIVISION II

Alderson-Broaddus College
American International
 College
Anderson College (SC)
Ashland University
Assumption College

Barry University
Barton College
Bellarmine University
Belmont Abbey College
Bentley College
Bloomfield College
Bloomsburg U of PA
Bryant College
C.W. Post Campus/Long
   Island University
Caldwell College
CA State Polytechnic
   U–Pomona
CA State U, Bakersfield
CA State U, Chico
CA State U, Dominguez
   Hills
CA State U, Los Angeles
CA State U, San Bernardino
CA State U, Stanislaus
California U of PA
Carson-Newman College
Catawba College
Christian Brothers U
Clayton College & State U
Coker College
College of Saint Rose
CO Christian University
CO School of Mines
Colorado State U-Pueblo
Columbia Union College
Concordia College (NY)
Dallas Baptist University
Davis and Elkins College
Delta State U
Dominican College (NY)
Dowling College
East Stroudsburg U of PA
Eckerd College
Erskine College
Felician College
FL Institute of Technology
FL Southern College
Fort Lewis College
Francis Marion University
Franklin Pierce College

Gannon University
Goldey-Beacom College
Grand Canyon University
Green Mountain College
Harding University
Holy Family University
Humboldt State U
KY Wesleyan College
Kutztown U of PA
Lander University
Le Moyne College
Lees-McRae College
Lenoir-Rhyne College
Lewis University
Limestone College
Lincoln Memorial U
Lock Haven U of PA
Longwood University
Lynn University
Mars Hill College
Mercy College
Mercyhurst College
Merrimack College
Metropolitan State College
   of Denver
Midwestern State U
Millersville U of PA
MO Southern State U-Joplin
Molloy College
MT State U-Billings
Mount Olive College
NJ Institute of Technology
NY Institute of Technology
Newberry College
North Greenville College
Northeastern State U
Northern KY University
Northwood University
Nova Southeastern U
Nyack College
Oakland City University
Ohio Valley College
Ouachita Baptist University
Pfeiffer University
Presbyterian College
Queens U of Charlotte

Quincy University
Regis University (CO)
Rockhurst University
Rollins College
Saginaw Valley State U
Saint Anselm College
Saint Joseph's College (IN)
Saint Leo University
Saint Michael's College
Salem International U
San Francisco State U
Seattle Pacific University
Seattle University
Shepherd College
Shippensburg U of PA
Slippery Rock U of PA
Sonoma State U
Southampton Campus of
   Long Island University
Southern CT State U
Southern IL U–Edwardsville
Southern NH University
Southwestern OK State U
St. Andrews Presbyterian
   College
St. Edward's University
St. Mary's University (TX)
St. Thomas Aquinas College
Stonehill College
Teikyo Post University
Tiffin University
Truman State U
Tusculum College
U of AL, Huntsville
U of Bridgeport
U of CA, Davis
U of CA, San Diego
U of Central AR
U of Charleston (WVA)
U of CO, Colorado Springs
U of Findlay
U of Indianapolis
U of MA at Lowell
U of MO, Rolla
U of MO, St. Louis
U of Montevallo

U of New Haven
U of NC at Pembroke
U of North Florida
U of Pittsburgh, Johnstown
U of Puerto Rico,
   Mayaguez
U of SC at Aiken
U of SC-Spartanburg
U of Southern IN
U of Tampa
U of the DC
U of the Incarnate Word
U of West Florida
U of WI, Parkside
Westchester U of PA
West TX A&M University
WVA Wesleyan College
Western WA University
Wheeling Jesuit University
Wilmington College (DE)
Wingate University

SOCCER
DIVISION III

Adrian College
Albertus Magnus College
Albion College
Albright College
Alfred University
Allegheny College
Alma College
Alvernia College
Amherst College
Anderson University (IN)
Anna Maria College
Arcadia University
Augsburg College
Augustana College (IL)
Aurora University
Austin College
Averett University
Babson College
Baldwin-Wallace College
Baptist Bible College
Bard College

Bates College
Becker College
Beloit College
Benedictine University (IL)
Bernard M. Baruch College
Bethany College (WVA)
Bethel University
Blackburn College
Bluffton College
Bowdoin College
Brandeis University
Bridgewater College (VA)
Bridgewater State College
Brooklyn College
Buena Vista University
Buffalo State College
Cabrini College
CA Institute of Technology
CA Lutheran University
CA State U, Hayward
Calvin College
Capital University
Carleton College
Carnegie Mellon University
Carroll College (WI)
Carthage College
Case Western Reserve U
Castleton State College
Catholic University
Cazenovia College
Centenary College (NJ)
Central College (IA)
Centre College
Chapman University
Chowan College
Christopher Newport U
City College of NY
Claremont McKenna-
   Harvey Mudd-Scripps
   Colleges
Clark University (MA)
Clarke College
Clarkson University
Coe College
Colby College
Colby-Sawyer College

College Misericordia
College of Mt. St. Vincent
College of St. Scholastica
College of Staten Island
College of Wooster
Colorado College
Concordia
   College–Moorhead
Concordia University (IL)
Concordia University (WI)
Concordia U at Austin
Connecticut College
Cornell College
Curry College
D'Youville College
Daniel Webster College
Defiance College
DE Valley College
Denison University
DePauw University
DeSales University
Dickinson College
Dominican University (IL)
Drew University
Earlham College
East TX Baptist University
Eastern CT State U
Eastern Mennonite U
Eastern Nazarene College
Eastern University
Edgewood College
Elizabethtown College
Elmira College
Elms College
Emerson College
Emmanuel College (MA)
Emory and Henry College
Emory University
Endicott College
Fairleigh Dickinson
   U–Madison
Ferrum College
Finlandia University
Fisk University
Fitchburg State College
Fontbonne University

Framingham State College
Franklin & Marshall College
Franklin College
Frostburg State U
Gallaudet University
George Fox University
Gettysburg College
Gordon College
Goucher College
Greensboro College
Greenville College
Grinnell College
Grove City College
Guilford College
Gustavus Adolphus College
Gwynedd-Mercy College
Hamilton College
Hamline University
Hampden-Sydney College
Hanover College
Hardin-Simmons University
Haverford College
Heidelberg College
Hendrix College
Hilbert College
Hiram College
Hobart and William Smith
    Colleges
Hope College
Hunter College
Huntingdon College
Husson College
Illinois College
IL Wesleyan University
Ithaca College
John Carroll University
John Jay College of
    Criminal Justice
Johns Hopkins University
Johnson and Wales U
Johnson State College
Juniata College
Kalamazoo College
Kean University
Keene State College
Kenyon College

Keuka College
King's College (PA)
Knox College
La Grange College
La Roche College
Lake Erie College
Lake Forest College
Lakeland College
Lasell College
Lawrence University
Lebanon Valley College
LeTourneau University
Lincoln University (PA)
Linfield College
Loras College
Louisiana College
Luther College
Louisiana College
Lycoming College
Lynchburg College
Macalester College
MacMurray College
ME Maritime Academy
Manchester College
Manhattanville College
Maranatha Baptist Bible
    College
Marian College (WI)
Marietta College
Martin Luther College
Mary Baldwin College
Maryville College (TN)
Maryville U of Saint Louis
Marywood University
MA College of Liberal Arts
MA Institute of Tech
MA Maritime Academy
McDaniel College
McMurry University
Medaille College
Medgar Evers College
Menlo College
Messiah College
Methodist College
Middlebury College
Millikin University

Millsaps College
Milwaukee School of
    Engineering
Mississippi College
Monmouth College (IL)
Montclair State U
Moravian College
Mount Ida College
Mt. St. Mary College (NY)
Mount Union College
Muhlenberg College
Muskingum College
Nazareth College
NE Wesleyan University
Neumann College
New England College
NJ City University
NY City College of Tech
New York University
Newbury College
Nichols College
NC Wesleyan College
North Central College
North Park University
Northland College
Norwich University
Oberlin College
Occidental College
Oglethorpe University
Ohio Northern University
Ohio Wesleyan University
Olivet College
Otterbein College
Pacific Lutheran University
Pacific University (OR)
Palm Beach Atlantic U
PA State Altoona
PA State Berks-Lehigh
    Valley College
PA State U Erie, the
    Behrend College
Philadelphia Biblical U
Piedmont College
Plattsburgh State U of NY
Plymouth State College
Polytechnic University (NY)

Pomona-Pitzer Colleges
Principia College
Ramapo College
Randolph-Macon College
Rensselaer Polytechnic
    Institute
Rhode Island College
Rhodes College
Richard Stockton College
    (NJ)
Ripon College
Rivier College
Roanoke College
Rochester Institute of Tech
Rockford College
Roger Williams University
Rose-Hulman Institute of
    Tech
Rowan University
Rust College
Rutgers, The State U of NJ,
    Camden
Rutgers, The State U of NJ,
    Newark
Saint Joseph's College (ME)
Saint Mary's U of MN
Salem State College
Salisbury University
Salve Regina University
Schreiner University
Shenandoah University
Simpson College
Skidmore College
Southern Vermont College
Southwestern U (TX)
Springfield College
St. John Fisher College
St. John's University (MN)
St. Joseph's College (Long
    Island)
St. Lawrence University
St. Mary's College of MD
St. Norbert College
St. Olaf College
State U College–Brockport
State U College–Cortland

State U College–Fredonia
State U College at Geneseo
State U College–New Paltz
State U College–Brockport
State U College–Old
    Westbury
State U College–Potsdam
State U of NY–Farmingdale
State U of NY–Oswego
State U of NY Institute of
    Tech
State U of NY Maritime
    College
Stevens Institute of Tech
Suffolk University
Susquehanna University
Swarthmore College
TX Lutheran University
The College of NJ
Thiel College
Thomas College
Thomas More College
Transylvania University
Trinity College (CT)
Trinity University (TX)
Tufts University
U.S. Coast Guard Academy
U.S. Merchant Marine
    Academy
Union College (NY)
U of CA, Santa Cruz
U of Chicago
U of Dallas
U of Dubuque
U of La Verne
U of ME at Presque Isle
U of ME, Farmington
U of Mary Hardin-Baylor
U of Mary Washington
U of MA, Boston
U of MA, Dartmouth
U of New England
U of Pittsburgh, Bradford
U of Pittsburgh–Greensburg
U of Puget Sound
U of Redlands

U of Rochester
U of Scranton
U of Southern ME
U of St. Thomas (MN)
U of TX at Dallas
U of TX at Tyler
U of the Ozarks (AR)
U of the South
U of WI, Oshkosh
U of WI, Platteville
U of WI, Superior
U of WI, Whitewater
Upper IA University
Ursinus College
Utica College
Vassar College
Villa Julie College
VA Wesleyan College
Wabash College
Wartburg College
Washington and Jefferson
    College
Washington and Lee U
WA College (MD)
Washington U–St. Louis
Waynesburg College
Webster University
Wentworth Institute of
    Tech
Wesley College
Wesleyan University (CT)
Western CT State U
Western New England
    College
Westfield State College
Westminster College (MO)
Westminster College (PA)
Wheaton College (IL)
Wheaton College (MA)
Whitman College
Whittier College
Whitworth College
Widener University
Wilkes University
Willamette University
William Paterson U of NJ

Williams College
Wilmington College (Ohio)
WI Lutheran College
Wittenberg University
Worcester Polytechnic
  Institute
Worcester State College
Yeshiva University
York College (NY)
York College (PA)

SWIMMING
DIVISION I

American University
Arizona State U
Auburn University
Ball State University
Boston College
Boston University
Brigham Young University
Brown University
Bucknell University
Butler University
CA Polytechnic State U
CA State U, Northridge
Canisius College
Centenary College (LA)
Clemson University
Cleveland State U
Colgate University
College of Charleston (SC)
College of the Holy Cross
College of William & Mary
Columbia University
Cornell University
Dartmouth College
Davidson College
Drexel University
Duke University
Duquesne University
East Carolina University
Eastern IL University
Eastern MI University
Fairfield University
FL A&M University

FL Atlantic University
Florida State U
Fordham University
George Mason University
George WA University
Georgetown University
GA Institute of Technology
Harvard University
Howard University
IN University, Bloomington
IN U-Purdue U, Fort Wayne
Iona College
James Madison University
La Salle University
Lafayette College
Lehigh University
Louisiana State U
Loyola College (MD)
Marist College
Miami University (Ohio)
Michigan State U
Niagara University
North Carolina State U
Northwestern University
Oakland University
Ohio State U
Ohio University
Old Dominion University
Pennsylvania State U
Princeton University
Providence College
Purdue University
Rider University
Rutgers, State U of NJ,
  New Brunswick
Saint Louis University
Seton Hall University
Southern IL U–Carbondale
Southern Methodist U
Southwest MO State U
St. Bonaventure University
St. Francis College (NY)
St. John's University (NY)
St. Peter's College
Stanford University
State U of NY–Binghamton

Stony Brook University
Syracuse University
TX A&M U–College Station
TX Christian University
Towson University
U.S. Air Force Academy
U.S. Military Academy
U.S. Naval Academy
U at Buffalo, the State U
  of NY
U of AL, Tuscaloosa
U of Arizona
U of CA, Berkeley
U of CA, Irvine
U of CA, Santa Barbara
U of Cincinnati
U of Connecticut
U of Delaware
U of Denver
U of Evansville
U of Florida
U of Georgia
U of Hawaii–Manoa
U of IL at Chicago
U of Iowa
U of Kentucky
U of LA at Monroe
U of Louisville
U of ME, Orono
U of MD, Baltimore Co.
U of MD, College Park
U of MA, Amherst
U of Miami (FL)
U of Michigan
U of MN, Twin Cities
U of MO, Columbia
U of Nevada, Las Vegas
U of New Hampshire
U of NC, Chapel Hill
U of NC, Wilmington
U of Notre Dame
U of Pennsylvania
U of Pittsburgh
U of Rhode Island
U of SC, Columbia
U of Southern CA

U of TN, Knoxville
U of TX at Austin
U of the Pacific
U of Utah
U of Vermont
U of Virginia
U of Washington
U of WI, Green Bay
U of WI, Madison
U of WI, Milwaukee
U of Wyoming
Valparaiso University
Villanova University
VA Military Institute
VA Polytechnic Institute & State University
WVA University
Western IL University
Western KY University
Wright State U
Xavier University
Yale University

SWIMMING
DIVISION II

Ashland University
Bentley College
Bloomsburg U of PA
CA State U, Bakersfield
Central WA University
Clarion U of Pennsylvania
College of Saint Rose
CO School of Mines
Delta State U
Drury University
Edinboro U of PA
Fairmont State College
FL Southern College
Gannon University
Grand Valley State U
Henderson State U
IN U of PA
Kutztown U of PA
Le Moyne College
Lewis University

Metropolitan State College of Denver
MN State U Mankato
NJ Institute of Technology
Ouachita Baptist University
Pace University
Queens College (NY)
Rollins College
Saint Michael's College
Salem International U
San Francisco State U
Seattle University
Shippensburg U of PA
Slippery Rock U of PA
South Dakota State U
Southern CT State U
St. Cloud State U
Truman State U
U of CA, Davis
U of CA, San Diego
U of Charleston (WVA)
U of Findlay
U of Indianapolis
U of MO, Rolla
U of North Dakota
U of Puerto Rico, Bayamon
U of Puerto Rico, Mayaguez
U of South Dakota
U of Tampa
Wayne State U (MI)
Westchester U of PA
WVA Wesleyan College
Wheeling Jesuit University

SWIMMING
DIVISION III

Albion College
Albright College
Alfred University
Allegheny College
Alma College
Amherst College
Arcadia University
Augustana College (IL)
Austin College

Babson College
Baldwin-Wallace College
Bates College
Beloit College
Benedictine University (IL)
Bernard M. Baruch College
Bethany College (WVA)
Bowdoin College
Brandeis University
Bridgewater State College
Brooklyn College
Buena Vista University
Buffalo State College
CA Institute of Technology
CA Lutheran University
Calvin College
Carleton College
Carnegie Mellon University
Carroll College (WI)
Carthage College
Case Western Reserve U
Catholic University
Centre College
Claremont McKenna-Harvey Mudd-Scripps Colleges
Clark University (MA)
Clarkson University
Coe College
Colby College
Colby-Sawyer College
College Misericordia
College of Staten Island
College of Wooster
Colorado College
Connecticut College
Denison University
DePauw University
Dickinson College
Drew University
Elizabethtown College
Elms College
Emory University
Eureka College
Fairleigh Dickinson U–Madison
Franklin & Marshall College

Frostburg State U
Gallaudet University
Gettysburg College
Gordon College
Goucher College
Grinnell College
Grove City College
Gustavus Adolphus College
Hamilton College
Hamline University
Hartwick College
Hendrix College
Hiram College
Hood College
Hope College
IL Wesleyan University
Ithaca College
John Carroll University
Johns Hopkins University
Kalamazoo College
Keene State College
Kenyon College
King's College (PA)
Knox College
La Grange College
Lake Forest College
Lawrence University
Lebanon Valley College
Lehman College, City U of
    NY
Lewis and Clark College
Linfield College
Loras College
Luther College
Lycoming College
Macalester College
Marymount University (VA)
MA Institute of Tech
McDaniel College
McMurry University
Middlebury College
Millikin University
Montclair State U
Mt. St. Mary College (NY)
Mount Union College
Nazareth College

New York University
North Central College
Norwich University
Oberlin College
Occidental College
Ohio Northern University
Ohio Wesleyan University
Olivet College
Pacific Lutheran University
Pacific University (OR)
PA State Altoona
PA State U Erie, the
    Behrend College
Pomona-Pitzer Colleges
Principia College
Randolph-Macon College
Rensselaer Polytechnic
    Institute
Rhodes College
Ripon College
Rochester Institute of Tech
Rose-Hulman Institute of
    Tech
Rowan University
Saint Mary's U of MN
Salisbury University
Skidmore College
Southwestern U (TX)
Springfield College
St. John's University (MN)
St. Lawrence University
St. Mary's College of MD
St. Olaf College
State U College–Brockport
State U College–Cortland
State U College–Fredonia
State U College at Geneseo
State U College–New Paltz
State U College–Brockport
State U College–Old
    Westbury
State U College–Oneonta
State U College–Potsdam
State U of NY–Oswego
State U of NY Maritime
    College

Stevens Institute of Tech
Susquehanna University
Swarthmore College
The College of NJ
Transylvania University
Trinity College (CT)
Trinity University (TX)
Tufts University
U.S. Coast Guard Academy
U.S. Merchant Marine
    Academy
Union College (NY)
U of CA, Santa Cruz
U of Chicago
U of La Verne
U of Mary Washington
U of MA, Dartmouth
U of Puget Sound
U of Redlands
U of Rochester
U of Scranton
U of St. Thomas (MN)
U of the South
U of WI, Eau Claire
U of WI, La Crosse
U of WI, Oshkosh
U of WI, River Falls
U of WI, Stevens Point
U of WI, Whitewater
Ursinus College
Utica College
Vassar College
Wabash College
Washington & Jefferson
    College
Washington and Lee U
WA College (MD)
Washington U–St. Louis
Webster University
Wesleyan University (CT)
Westminster College (PA)
Wheaton College (IL)
Wheaton College (MA)
Whitman College
Whittier College
Whitworth College

Widener University
Willamette University
William Paterson U of NJ
Williams College
Wilmington College (Ohio)
Wittenberg University
Worcester Polytechnic
  Institute
York College (NY)
York College (PA)

TENNIS
DIVISION I

AL A&M University
Alabama State U
Alcorn State U
American University
Appalachian State U
Arizona State U
Auburn University
Austin Peay State U
Ball State University
Baylor University
Belmont University
Bethune-Cookman College
Birmingham-Southern
  College
Boise State University
Boston College
Boston University
Bradley University
Brigham Young University
Brown University
Bucknell University
Butler University
CA Polytechnic State U
CA State U, Fresno
CA State U, Sacramento
Campbell University
Centenary College (LA)
Charleston Southern U
Chicago State U
Clemson University
Cleveland State U
Coastal Carolina University

Colgate University
College of Charleston (SC)
College of the Holy Cross
College of William & Mary
Columbia University
Coppin State College
Cornell University
Creighton University
Dartmouth College
Davidson College
Delaware State U
DePaul University
Drake University
Drexel University
Duke University
Duquesne University
East Carolina University
East TN State U
Eastern IL University
Eastern KY University
Eastern WA University
Elon University
Fairfield University
Fairleigh Dickinson
  U–Teaneck
FL A&M University
FL Atlantic University
Florida State U
Fordham University
Furman University
Gardner-Webb University
George Mason University
George WA University
Georgetown University
GA Institute of Technology
GA Southern University
Georgia State U
Gonzaga University
Grambling State U
Hampton University
Harvard University
High Point University
Hofstra University
Howard University
Idaho State U
Illinois State University

Indiana State University
IN University, Bloomington
IN U-Purdue U, Fort Wayne
Jackson State U
Jacksonville State U
Jacksonville University
James Madison University
La Salle University
Lafayette College
Lamar University
Lehigh University
Liberty University
Lipscomb University
Louisiana State U
Loyola College (MD)
Loyola Marymount U
Manhattan College
Marist College
Marquette University
Mercer University
Michigan State U
Middle TN State U
Mississippi State U
MS Valley State U
Monmouth University
MT State U-Bozeman
Morehead State U
Morgan State U
Mount St. Mary's College
Murray State U
New Mexico State U
Niagara University
Norfolk State U
NC A&T State U
North Carolina State U
Northern AZ University
Northern IL University
Northwestern University
Ohio State U
Oklahoma State U
Old Dominion University
Oral Roberts University
Pennsylvania State U
Pepperdine University
Prairie View A&M U
Princeton University

Purdue University	U.S. Naval Academy	U of New Hampshire
Quinnipiac University	U at Buffalo, the State U	U of New Mexico
Radford University	of NY	U of New Orleans
Rice University	U of AL at Birmingham	U of NC at Greensboro
Rider University	U of AL, Tuscaloosa	U of NC, Asheville
Robert Morris University	U of Arizona	U of NC, Chapel Hill
Rutgers, State U of NJ,	U of AR, Fayetteville	U of NC, Charlotte
New Brunswick	U of AR, Little Rock	U of NC, Wilmington
Sacred Heart University	U of AR, Pine Bluff	U of Notre Dame
Saint Francis U (PA)	U of CA, Berkeley	U of Oklahoma
Saint Joseph's University	U of CA, Irvine	U of Oregon
Saint Louis University	U of CA, Los Angeles	U of Pennsylvania
Samford University	U of CA, Riverside	U of Portland
San Diego State U	U of CA, Santa Barbara	U of Rhode Island
Santa Clara University	U of Central Florida	U of Richmond
Savannah State U	U of Cincinnati	U of San Diego
Siena College	U of CO, Boulder	U of San Francisco
South Carolina State U	U of Connecticut	U of South AL
Southeastern LA University	U of Dayton	U of SC, Columbia
Southern IL U–Carbondale	U of Delaware	U of South Florida
Southern Methodist U	U of Denver	U of Southern CA
Southern U–Baton Rouge	U of Evansville	U of Southern MS
Southwest MO State U	U of Florida	U of TN at Chattanooga
St. Bonaventure University	U of Georgia	U of TN at Martin
St. Francis College (NY)	U of Hartford	U of TN, Knoxville
St. John's University (NY)	U of Hawaii–Manoa	U of TX at Arlington
St. Mary's College of CA	U of Idaho	U of TX at Austin
St. Peter's College	U of IL at Chicago	U of TX at San Antonio
Stanford University	U of IL, Champaign	U of TX, Pan American
State U of NY–Binghamton	U of Iowa	U of the Pacific
Stetson University	U of Kentucky	U of Toledo
Stony Brook University	U of LA at Lafayette	U of Tulsa
Temple University	U of Louisville	U of Utah
TN State U	U of MD, Baltimore Co.	U of Vermont
TN Technological University	U of MD, College Park	U of Virginia
TX A&M U–College Station	U of MD, Eastern Shore	U of Washington
TX A&M U-Corpus Christi	U of Memphis	U of WI, Green Bay
TX Christian University	U of Miami (FL)	U of WI, Madison
TX Southern University	U of Michigan	Utah State U
TX Tech University	U of MN, Twin Cities	Valparaiso University
The Citadel	U of Mississippi	Vanderbilt University
Towson University	U of MO, Kansas City	Villanova University
Troy State U	U of Montana	VA Commonwealth U
Tulane University	U of NE, Lincoln	VA Polytechnic Institute &
U.S. Air Force Academy	U of Nevada	State University
U.S. Military Academy	U of Nevada, Las Vegas	Wagner College

Wake Forest University
Weber State U
Western IL University
Western KY University
Western MI University
Wichita State U
Winthrop University
Wofford College
Wright State U
Xavier University
Yale University
Youngstown State U

TENNIS
DIVISION II

Abilene Christian U
Adelphi University
American International
    College
Anderson College (SC)
Armstrong Atlantic State U
Assumption College
Augusta State U
Augustana College (SD)
Barry University
Barton College
Bellarmine University
Belmont Abbey College
Benedict College
Bentley College
Bloomsburg U of
    Pennsylvania
Bluefield State College
Brigham Young U, HI
Bryant College
Caldwell College
CA State Polytechnic
    U–Pomona
Cameron University
Carson-Newman College
Catawba College
Central State U
Chaminade University
Christian Brothers U
Coker College

CO Christian University
CO School of Mines
Colorado State U-Pueblo
Columbus State U
Concord College
Concordia College (NY)
Dallas Baptist University
Davis and Elkins College
Delta State U
Dowling College
Drury University
East Central University
East Stroudsburg U of PA
Eckerd College
Emporia State U
Erskine College
Fairmont State College
Ferris State U
FL Gulf Coast University
FL Institute of Technology
FL Southern College
Fort Valley State U
Francis Marion University
Franklin Pierce College
GA College & State U
Grand Valley State U
Green Mountain College
Harding University
Hawaii Pacific University
Johnson C. Smith U
Kentucky State U
Kutztown U of PA
Lake Superior State U
Lander University
Lane College
Le Moyne College
Lees-McRae College
LeMoyne-Owen College
Lewis University
Limestone College
Lincoln Memorial U
Longwood University
Lynn University
Mars Hill College
Mercy College
Mercyhurst College

Merrimack College
Mesa State College
Metropolitan State College
    of Denver
MI Tech University
Midwestern State U
Millersville U of PA
MN State U Mankato
MT State U-Billings
Morehouse College
Mount Olive College
NJ Institute of Technology
Newberry College
NC Central University
North Greenville College
Northern KY University
Northwest MO State U
Northwood University
Oakland City University
Ouachita Baptist University
Pace University
Pfeiffer University
Philadelphia University
Presbyterian College
Queens College (NY)
Queens U of Charlotte
Quincy University
Rockhurst University
Rollins College
Saint Anselm College
Saint Joseph's College (IN)
Saint Leo University
Saint Michael's College
Salem International U
Shaw University
Shepherd College
Slippery Rock U of PA
Sonoma State U
South Dakota State U
Southampton Campus of
    Long Island University
Southeastern OK State U
Southern IL U–Edwardsville
Southern NH University
Southwest Baptist U
St. Andrews Presbyterian

College
St. Augustine's College
St. Cloud State U
St. Edward's University
St. Mary's University (TX)
St. Paul's College
St. Thomas Aquinas College
Stonehill College
Tiffin University
Truman State U
Tusculum College
Tuskegee University
U of AL, Huntsville
U of CA, Davis
U of CA, San Diego
U of Central OK
U of Charleston (WVA)
U of CO, Colorado Springs
U of Findlay
U of Hawaii–Hilo
U of Indianapolis
U of MN, Morris
U of MO, St. Louis
U of NE at Kearney
U of North Alabama
U of North Florida
U of Northern CO
U of Puerto Rico, Cayey
U of Puerto Rico, Mayaguez
U of Puerto Rico, Rio
   Piedras
U of SC at Aiken
U of SC-Spartanburg
U of Southern IN
U of the DC
U of the Incarnate Word
U of the Sciences in
   Philadelphia
U of West Florida
Valdosta State U
Virginia State U
VA Union University
Washburn U of Topeka
Wayne State U (MI)
Westchester U of PA
West Liberty State College

WVA State College
WVA U Institute of Tech
WVA Wesleyan College
Western NM University
Wingate University
Winona State U
Winston-Salem State U

TENNIS
DIVISION III

Adrian College
Albertus Magnus College
Albion College
Albright College
Alfred University
Allegheny College
Alma College
Alvernia College
Amherst College
Anderson University (IN)
Arcadia University
Augustana College (IL)
Aurora University
Austin College
Averett University
Babson College
Baldwin-Wallace College
Bard College
Bates College
Becker College
Beloit College
Bernard M. Baruch College
Bethany College (WVA)
Bethel University
Bluffton College
Bowdoin College
Brandeis University
Bridgewater College (VA)
Bridgewater State College
Brooklyn College
Buena Vista University
Cabrini College
CA Institute of Technology
CA Lutheran University
Calvin College

Capital University
Carleton College
Carnegie Mellon University
Carroll College (WI)
Carthage College
Case Western Reserve U
Castleton State College
Catholic University
Central College (IA)
Centre College
Chapman University
Christopher Newport U
City College of NY
Claremont McKenna-Harvey
   Mudd-Scripps Colleges
Clark University (MA)
Clarke College
Clarkson University
Coe College
Colby College
Colby-Sawyer College
College of Mt. St. Joseph
College of Mt. St. Vincent
College of St. Scholastica
College of Staten Island
College of Wooster
Colorado College
Concordia
   College–Moorhead
Concordia University (IL)
Concordia University (WI)
Concordia U at Austin
Connecticut College
Cornell College
Curry College
Defiance College
Denison University
DePauw University
DeSales University
Dickinson College
Dominican University (IL)
Drew University
Earlham College
Eastern Mennonite U
Eastern Nazarene College
Eastern University

Elizabethtown College
Elmhurst College
Elmira College
Emerson College
Emory and Henry College
Emory University
Endicott College
Eureka College
Fairleigh Dickinson
U–Madison
Ferrum College
Fisk University
Fontbonne University
Franklin & Marshall College
Franklin College
Frostburg State U
Gallaudet University
George Fox University
Gettysburg College
Gordon College
Goucher College
Greensboro College
Greenville College
Grinnell College
Grove City College
Gustavus Adolphus College
Gwynedd-Mercy College
Hamilton College
Hamline University
Hampden-Sydney College
Hanover College
Hardin-Simmons University
Hartwick College
Haverford College
Heidelberg College
Hendrix College
Hiram College
Hobart and William Smith
Colleges
Hood College
Hope College
Howard Payne University
Hunter College
Illinois College
IL Wesleyan University
Ithaca College
John Carroll University

John Jay College of
Criminal Justice
Johns Hopkins University
Johnson and Wales U
Juniata College
Kalamazoo College
Kenyon College
King's College (PA)
Knox College
La Grange College
Lake Forest College
Lakeland College
Lawrence University
Lebanon Valley College
Lehman College, City U of
NY
LeTourneau University
Lewis and Clark College
Lincoln University (PA)
Linfield College
Luther College
Lycoming College
Lynchburg College
Macalester College
MacMurray College
Manchester College
Manhattanville College
Marian College (WI)
Marietta College
Martin Luther College
Maryville College (TN)
Maryville U of Saint Louis
Marywood University
MA Institute of Tech
McDaniel College
McMurry University
Messiah College
Methodist College
Middlebury College
Millsaps College
Milwaukee School of
Engineering
Mississippi College
Monmouth College (IL)
Moravian College
Mt. St. Mary College (NY)
Mount Union College

Muhlenberg College
Muskingum College
Nazareth College
NE Wesleyan University
Neumann College
NY City College of Tech
New York University
Newbury College
Nichols College
NC Wesleyan College
North Central College
Norwich University
Oberlin College
Occidental College
Oglethorpe University
Ohio Northern University
Ohio Wesleyan University
Otterbein College
Pacific Lutheran University
Pacific University (OR)
Palm Beach Atlantic U
PA State Altoona
PA State U Erie, the
Behrend College
Philadelphia Biblical U
Piedmont College
Polytechnic University (NY)
Pomona-Pitzer Colleges
Principia College
Ramapo College
Randolph-Macon College
Rensselaer Polytechnic
Institute
Rhode Island College
Rhodes College
Ripon College
Roanoke College
Rochester Institute of Tech
Rockford College
Roger Williams University
Rose-Hulman Institute of
Tech
Rust College
Rutgers, The State U of NJ,
Newark
Saint Mary's U of MN
Salem State College

Salisbury University
Salve Regina University
Schreiner University
Shenandoah University
Simpson College
Skidmore College
Southwestern University(TX)
Springfield College
St. John Fisher College
St. John's University (MN)
St. Lawrence University
St. Mary's College of MD
St. Norbert College
St. Olaf College
State U College–Fredonia
State U College–New Paltz
State U College–Brockport
State U College–Oneonta
State U of NY–Oswego
Stevens Institute of Tech
Stillman College
Suffolk University
Sul Ross State U
Susquehanna University
Swarthmore College
TX Lutheran University
The College of NJ
Thiel College
Thomas College
Thomas More College
Transylvania University
Trinity College (CT)
Trinity University (TX)
Tufts University
U.S. Coast Guard Academy
U.S. Merchant Marine
   Academy
Union College (NY)
U of CA, Santa Cruz
U of Chicago
U of Dallas
U of Dubuque
U of La Verne
U of Mary Hardin-Baylor
U of Mary Washington
U of MA, Boston

U of MA, Dartmouth
U of Pittsburgh–Greensburg
U of Puget Sound
U of Redlands
U of Rochester
U of Scranton
U of Southern ME
U of St. Thomas (MN)
U of TX at Dallas
U of TX at Tyler
U of the Ozarks (AR)
U of the South
U of WI, Eau Claire
U of WI, La Crosse
U of WI, Oshkosh
U of WI, Whitewater
Upper IA University
Ursinus College
Utica College
Vassar College
Villa Julie College
VA Wesleyan College
Wabash College
Wartburg College
Washington and Jefferson
   College
Washington and Lee U
WA College (MD)
Washington U–St. Louis
Waynesburg College
Webster University
Wentworth Institute of
   Tech
Wesley College
Wesleyan University (CT)
Western CT State U
Western New England
   College
Westminster College (MO)
Westminster College (PA)
Wheaton College (IL)
Wheaton College (MA)
Whitman College
Whittier College
Whitworth College
Widener University

Wilkes University
Willamette University
Williams College
Wilmington College (Ohio)
Wittenberg University
Worcester Polytechnic
   Institute
Yeshiva University
York College (NY)
York College (PA)

TRACK INDOOR
DIVISION I

AL A&M University
Alabama State U
Alcorn State U
American University
Appalachian State U
Arizona State U
Arkansas State U
Auburn University
Ball State University
Baylor University
Belmont University
Bethune-Cookman College
Boise State University
Boston College
Boston University
Brigham Young University
Brown University
Bucknell University
Butler University
CA State U, Northridge
CA State U, Sacramento
Campbell University
Central CT State U
Central MI University
Charleston Southern U
Chicago State U
Clemson University
Colgate University
College of the Holy Cross
College of William & Mary

Colorado State U
Columbia University
Coppin State College
Cornell University
Dartmouth College
Davidson College
Delaware State U
DePaul University
Drake University
Duke University
East Carolina University
East TN State U
Eastern IL University
Eastern KY University
Eastern MI University
Eastern WA University
Fairleigh Dickinson
   U–Teaneck
FL A&M University
FL International University
Florida State U
Fordham University
Gardner-Webb University
George Mason University
Georgetown University
GA Institute of Technology
Georgia State U
Grambling State U
Hampton University
Harvard University
High Point University
Howard University
Idaho State U
Illinois State University
Indiana State University
IN University, Bloomington
Iona College
Iowa State U
Jackson State U
James Madison University
Kansas State U
Kent State U
La Salle University
Lafayette College
Lamar University
Lehigh University

Liberty University
Long Beach State U
Long Island U-Brooklyn
   Campus
Louisiana State U
LA Tech University
Loyola University (IL)
Manhattan College
Marist College
Marquette University
McNeese State U
Michigan State U
Middle TN State U
MS Valley State U
Monmouth University
MT State U-Bozeman
Morehead State U
Morgan State U
Mount St. Mary's College
Murray State U
Norfolk State U
NC A&T State U
North Carolina State U
Northeastern University
Northern AZ University
Northwestern State U
Northwestern University
Ohio State U
Ohio University
Oklahoma State U
Oral Roberts University
Pennsylvania State U
Portland State U
Prairie View A&M U
Princeton University
Providence College
Purdue University
Quinnipiac University
Radford University
Rice University
Rider University
Robert Morris University
Rutgers, State U of NJ,
   New Brunswick
Sacred Heart University
Saint Francis U (PA)

Saint Joseph's University
Sam Houston State U
Samford University
Savannah State U
Seton Hall University
South Carolina State U
Southeast MO State U
Southeastern LA University
Southern IL U–Carbondale
Southern Methodist U
Southern U–Baton Rouge
Southern UT University
Southwest MO State U
St. Francis College (NY)
St. Peter's College
Stanford University
State U of NY–Binghamton
Stephen F. Austin State U
Stony Brook University
Syracuse University
Temple University
TN State U
TX A&M U–College Station
TX A&M U-Corpus Christi
TX Christian University
TX Southern University
TX State U-San Marcos
TX Tech University
The Citadel
Towson University
U.S. Air Force Academy
U.S. Military Academy
U.S. Naval Academy
University at Albany
U at Buffalo, the State U
   of NY
U of Akron
U of AL, Tuscaloosa
U of Arizona
U of AR, Fayetteville
U of AR, Little Rock
U of AR, Pine Bluff
U of CA, Berkeley
U of CA, Los Angeles
U of CA, Riverside
U of CO, Boulder

U of Connecticut
U of Delaware
U of Detroit Mercy
U of Florida
U of Georgia
U of Hartford
U of Houston
U of Idaho
U of IL at Chicago
U of IL, Champaign
U of Iowa
U of Kansas
U of Kentucky
U of LA at Lafayette
U of LA at Monroe
U of ME, Orono
U of MD, Baltimore Co.
U of MD, College Park
U of MD, Eastern Shore
U of MA, Amherst
U of Memphis
U of Miami (FL)
U of Michigan
U of MN, Twin Cities
U of Mississippi
U of MO, Columbia
U of MO, Kansas City
U of Montana
U of NE, Lincoln
U of New Hampshire
U of New Mexico
U of New Orleans
U of NC, Asheville
U of NC, Chapel Hill
U of NC, Charlotte
U of NC, Wilmington
U of North TX
U of Northern IA
U of Notre Dame
U of Oklahoma
U of Oregon
U of Pennsylvania
U of Pittsburgh
U of Portland
U of Rhode Island
U of Richmond

U of South AL
U of SC, Columbia
U of Southern CA
U of Southern MS
U of TN at Chattanooga
U of TN, Knoxville
U of TX at Arlington
U of TX at Austin
U of TX at El Paso
U of TX at San Antonio
U of TX, Pan American
U of Tulsa
U of Utah
U of Virginia
U of Washington
U of WI, Madison
U of WI, Milwaukee
U of Wyoming
Utah State U
UT Valley State College
Valparaiso University
Villanova University
VA Commonwealth U
VA Military Institute
VA Polytechnic Institute &
   State University
Wagner College
Wake Forest University
Washington State U
Weber State U
Western Carolina U
Western IL University
Western KY University
Western MI University
Wichita State U
Winthrop University
Wofford College
Yale University
Youngstown State U

TRACK
INDOOR
DIVISION II

Abilene Christian U

Adams State College
Anderson College (SC)
Ashland University
Assumption College
Augustana College (SD)
Bellarmine University
Bemidji State U
Bentley College
Bloomsburg U of PA
Bowie State U
Bryant College
C.W. Post Campus/Long
   Island University
Cabrini College
CA State Polytechnic
   U–Pomona
CA State U, Bakersfield
CA State U, Stanislaus
California U of PA
Carson-Newman College
Central MO State U
Central State U
Central WA University
Chadron State College
Clarion U of Pennsylvania
CO School of Mines
Concord College
Concordia U, St. Paul
Dallas Baptist University
East Stroudsburg U of PA
Emporia State U
Fayetteville State U
Ferris State U
Fort Hays State U
Grand Valley State U
Harding University
Hillsdale College
IN U of PA
Kentucky State U
Kutztown U of PA
Lake Superior State U
Lees-McRae College
Lewis University
Lincoln University (MO)
Livingstone College
Lock Haven U of PA

Mansfield U of PA
Mercy College
Millersville U of PA
MN State U Mankato
MN State U Moorhead
MO Southern State U-Joplin
Morehouse College
NY Institute of Technology
NC Central University
North Dakota State U
Northern KY University
Northern State U
Northwest MO State U
Northwest Nazarene U
Northwood University
Pittsburg State U
Saginaw Valley State U
Saint Joseph's College (IN)
Seattle Pacific University
Seattle University
Shaw University
Shippensburg U of PA
Slippery Rock U of PA
South Dakota State U
Southern CT State U
Southern IL U–Edwardsville
Southwest Baptist U
St. Augustine's College
St. Cloud State U
St. Paul's College
St. Thomas Aquinas College
State U of West GA
Stonehill College
TX A&M U-Commerce
TX A&M U-Kingsville
Tiffin University
Truman State U
U of AL, Huntsville
U of CA, Davis
U of CO, Colorado Springs
U of Findlay
U of Indianapolis
U of MA at Lowell
U of MN Duluth
U of MN, Morris
U of MO, Rolla

U of NE at Kearney
U of New Haven
U of North Dakota
U of North Florida
U of South Dakota
U of Southern IN
U of WI, Parkside
Virginia State U
Wayne State College (NE)
Westchester U of PA
WVA Wesleyan College
Western OR University
Western State College (CO)
Western WA University
Wheeling Jesuit University

TRACK
INDOOR
DIVISION III

Adrian College
Albion College
Albright College
Alfred University
Allegheny College
Amherst College
Anderson University (IN)
Augsburg College
Augustana College (IL)
Baldwin-Wallace College
Bates College
Beloit College
Benedictine University (IL)
Bethany College (WVA)
Bethel University
Bluffton College
Bowdoin College
Brandeis University
Bridgewater College (VA)
Bridgewater State College
Buena Vista University
Buffalo State College
Calvin College
Capital University
Carleton College

Carnegie Mellon University
Carroll College (WI)
Carthage College
Case Western Reserve U
Catholic University
Central College (IA)
Christopher Newport U
City College of NY
Coe College
Colby College
College Misericordia
College of Mt. St. Joseph
College of Wooster
Concordia
    College–Moorhead
Concordia University (IL)
Concordia University (WI)
Connecticut College
Cornell College
Defiance College
DE Valley College
Denison University
DePauw University
DeSales University
Dickinson College
Earlham College
Eastern CT State U
Eastern Mennonite U
Elizabethtown College
Elmhurst College
Emmanuel College (MA)
Emory University
Fisk University
Fitchburg State College
Franklin & Marshall College
Frostburg State U
Gallaudet University
Gettysburg College
Goucher College
Greenville College
Grinnell College
Gustavus Adolphus College
Gwynedd-Mercy College
Hamilton College
Hamline University
Hanover College

Hartwick College
Haverford College
Heidelberg College
Hiram College
Hunter College
Illinois College
IL Wesleyan University
Ithaca College
John Carroll University
Johns Hopkins University
Juniata College
Kean University
Keene State College
Kenyon College
Knox College
Lawrence University
Lebanon Valley College
Lehman College, City U of
   NY
Lincoln University (PA)
Linfield College
Loras College
Luther College
Lynchburg College
Macalester College
Manchester College
Marietta College
MA Institute of Tech
McDaniel College
McMurry University
Medgar Evers College
Messiah College
Methodist College
Middlebury College
Millikin University
Milwaukee School of
   Engineering
Mississippi College
Monmouth College (IL)
Montclair State U
Moravian College
Mount Union College
Muhlenberg College
Muskingum College
Nazareth College
NE Wesleyan University

NJ City University
NY City College of Tech
New York University
North Central College
North Park University
Oberlin College
Occidental College
Oglethorpe University
Ohio Northern University
Ohio Wesleyan University
Olivet College
Otterbein College
Pacific Lutheran University
Pacific University (OR)
PA State U Erie, the
   Behrend College
Plattsburgh State U of NY
Polytechnic University (NY)
Principia College
Ramapo College
Rensselaer Polytechnic
   Institute
Rhode Island College
Rhodes College
Richard Stockton College
   (NJ)
Ripon College
Roanoke College
Rochester Institute of Tech
Rose-Hulman Institute of
   Tech
Rowan University
Saint Mary's U of MN
Salem State College
Salisbury University
Simpson College
Springfield College
St. John's University (MN)
St. Lawrence University
St. Norbert College
St. Olaf College
State U College–Brockport
State U College–Cortland
State U College–Fredonia
State U College at Geneseo
State U College–New Paltz

State U College–Brockport
State U College–Oneonta
State U of NY–Farmingdale
State U of NY–Oswego
Susquehanna University
Swarthmore College
The College of NJ
Thiel College
Trinity College (CT)
Tufts University
U.S. Coast Guard Academy
U.S. Merchant Marine
   Academy
Union College (NY)
U of Chicago
U of Dubuque
U of La Verne
U of Mary Washington
U of MA, Dartmouth
U of Puget Sound
U of Rochester
U of Southern ME
U of St. Thomas (MN)
U of the South
U of WI, Eau Claire
U of WI, La Crosse
U of WI, Oshkosh
U of WI, Platteville
U of WI, River Falls
U of WI, Stevens Point
U of WI, Stout
U of WI, Superior
U of WI, Whitewater
Upper IA University
Ursinus College
Villa Julie College
Wartburg College
Washington and Lee U
Washington U–St. Louis
Wesleyan University (CT)
Westfield State College
Westminster College (PA)
Wheaton College (IL)
Wheaton College (MA)
Whitworth College
Widener University

William Paterson U of NJ
Williams College
Wilmington College (Ohio)
WI Lutheran College
Wittenberg University
Worcester Polytechnic
  Institute
Worcester State College
York College (NY)

TRACK
OUTDOOR
DIVISION I

AL A&M University
Alabama State U
Alcorn State U
American University
Appalachian State U
Arizona State U
Arkansas State U
Auburn University
Ball State University
Baylor University
Belmont University
Bethune-Cookman College
Boise State University
Boston College
Boston University
Brigham Young University
Brown University
Bucknell University
Butler University
CA Polytechnic State U
CA State U, Fresno
CA State U, Fullerton
CA State U, Northridge
CA State U, Sacramento
Campbell University
Central CT State U
Central MI University
Charleston Southern U
Chicago State U
Clemson University
Coastal Carolina University

Colgate University
College of the Holy Cross
College of the Holy Cross
College of William & Mary
Colorado State U
Columbia University
Coppin State College
Cornell University
Dartmouth College
Davidson College
Delaware State U
DePaul University
Drake University
Duke University
Duquesne University
East Carolina University
East TN State U
Eastern IL University
Eastern KY University
Eastern MI University
Eastern WA University
Fairleigh Dickinson
  U–Teaneck
FL A&M University
FL International University
Florida State U
Fordham University
Furman University
Gardner-Webb University
George Mason University
Georgetown University
GA Institute of Technology
Georgia State U
Gonzaga University
Grambling State U
Hampton University
Harvard University
High Point University
Howard University
Idaho State U
Illinois State University
Indiana State University
IN University, Bloomington
Iona College
Iowa State U
Jackson State U

James Madison University
Kansas State U
Kent State U
La Salle University
Lafayette College
Lamar University
Lehigh University
Liberty University
Long Beach State U
Long Island U-Brooklyn
  Campus
Louisiana State U
LA Tech University
Loyola University (IL)
Manhattan College
Marist College
Marquette University
McNeese State U
Miami University (Ohio)
Michigan State U
Middle TN State U
Mississippi State U
MS Valley State U
Monmouth University
MT State U-Bozeman
Morehead State U
Morgan State U
Mount St. Mary's College
Murray State U
Nicholls State U
Norfolk State U
NC A&T State U
North Carolina State U
Northeastern University
Northern AZ University
Northwestern State U
Ohio State U
Ohio University
Oklahoma State U
Oral Roberts University
Pennsylvania State U
Portland State U
Prairie View A&M U
Princeton University
Providence College
Purdue University

Quinnipiac University
Radford University
Rice University
Rider University
Robert Morris University
Rutgers, State U of NJ,
  New Brunswick
Sacred Heart University
Saint Francis U (PA)
Saint Joseph's University
Sam Houston State U
Samford University
Savannah State U
Seton Hall University
South Carolina State U
Southeast MO State U
Southeastern LA University
Southern IL U–Carbondale
Southern Methodist U
Southern U–Baton Rouge
Southern UT University
Southwest MO State U
St. Francis College (NY)
St. Peter's College
Stanford University
State U of NY–Binghamton
Stephen F. Austin State U
Stony Brook University
Syracuse University
Temple University
TN State U
TX A&M U–College Station
TX A&M U-Corpus Christi
TX Christian University
TX Southern University
TX State U-San Marcos
TX Tech University
The Citadel
Towson University
Troy State U
U.S. Air Force Academy
U.S. Military Academy
U.S. Naval Academy
University at Albany
U at Buffalo, the State U
  of NY

U of Akron
U of AL, Tuscaloosa
U of Arizona
U of AR, Fayetteville
U of AR, Little Rock
U of AR, Pine Bluff
U of CA, Berkeley
U of CA, Irvine
U of CA, Los Angeles
U of CA, Riverside
U of CA, Santa Barbara
U of Cincinnati
U of CO, Boulder
U of Connecticut
U of Delaware
U of Detroit Mercy
U of Florida
U of Georgia
U of Hartford
U of Houston
U of Idaho
U of IL at Chicago
U of IL, Champaign
U of Iowa
U of Kansas
U of Kentucky
U of LA at Lafayette
U of LA at Monroe
U of Louisville
U of ME, Orono
U of MD, Baltimore Co.
U of MD, College Park
U of MD, Eastern Shore
U of MA, Amherst
U of Memphis
U of Miami (FL)
U of Michigan
U of MN, Twin Cities
U of Mississippi
U of MO, Columbia
U of MO, Kansas City
U of Montana
U of NE, Lincoln
U of New Hampshire
U of New Mexico
U of New Orleans

U of NC at Greensboro
U of NC, Asheville
U of NC, Chapel Hill
U of NC, Charlotte
U of NC, Wilmington
U of North TX
U of Northern IA
U of Notre Dame
U of Oklahoma
U of Oregon
U of Pennsylvania
U of Pittsburgh
U of Portland
U of Rhode Island
U of Richmond
U of South AL
U of SC, Columbia
U of South Florida
U of Southern CA
U of Southern MS
U of TN at Chattanooga
U of TN, Knoxville
U of TX at Arlington
U of TX at Austin
U of TX at El Paso
U of TX at San Antonio
U of TX, Pan American
U of Tulsa
U of Utah
U of Virginia
U of Washington
U of WI, Madison
U of WI, Milwaukee
U of Wyoming
Utah State U
UT Valley State College
Valparaiso University
Villanova University
VA Commonwealth U
VA Military Institute
VA Polytechnic Institute &
  State University
Wagner College
Wake Forest University
Washington State U
Weber State U

Western Carolina U
Western IL University
Western KY University
Western MI University
Wichita State U
Winthrop University
Wofford College
Yale University
Youngstown State U

TRACK
OUTDOOR
DIVISION II

Abilene Christian U
Adams State College
Albany State U (GA)
Alderson-Broaddus College
Anderson College (SC)
Angelo State U
Ashland University
Assumption College
Augustana College (SD)
Bellarmine University
Bemidji State U
Benedict College
Bentley College
Bloomsburg U of PA
Bowie State U
Bryant College
C.W. Post Campus/Long
    Island University
CA State Polytechnic
    U–Pomona
CA State U, Bakersfield
CA State U, Chico
CA State U, Los Angeles
CA State U, Stanislaus
California U of PA
Carson-Newman College
Central MO State U
Central State U
Central WA University
Chadron State College
Cheyney U of Pennsylvania

Clarion U of Pennsylvania
Clark Atlanta University
Clayton College & State U
CO School of Mines
Columbia Union College
Concord College
Concordia U, St. Paul
Dallas Baptist University
East Stroudsburg U of PA
Eastern NM University
Edinboro U of PA
Emporia State U
Fayetteville State U
Ferris State U
Fort Hays State U
Fort Valley State U
Francis Marion University
Glenville State College
Grand Valley State U
Harding University
Hillsdale College
Humboldt State U
Indiana U of PA
Johnson C. Smith U
Kennesaw State U
Kentucky State U
Kutztown U of PA
Lake Superior State U
Lane College
Lees-McRae College
Lewis University
Lincoln University (MO)
Livingstone College
Lock Haven U of PA
Mansfield U of PA
Mars Hill College
Mercy College
MI Tech University
Miles College
Millersville U of PA
MN State U Mankato
MN State U Moorhead
MO Southern State U-Joplin
Morehouse College
NY Institute of Technology
NC Central University

North Dakota State U
Northern KY University
Northern State U
Northwest MO State U
Northwest Nazarene U
Northwood University
Pace University
Paine College
Pittsburg State U
Queens U of Charlotte
Saginaw Valley State U
Saint Joseph's College (IN)
San Francisco State U
Seattle Pacific University
Seattle University
Shaw University
Shippensburg U of PA
Slippery Rock U of PA
South Dakota State U
Southern AR University
Southern CT State U
Southern IL U–Edwardsville
Southwest Baptist U
St. Andrews Presbyterian
    College
St. Augustine's College
St. Cloud State U
St. Martin's College
St. Paul's College
St. Thomas Aquinas College
State U of West GA
Stonehill College
Tarleton State U
TX A&M U-Commerce
TX A&M U-Kingsville
Tiffin University
Truman State U
Tuskegee University
U of AL, Huntsville
U of Alaska Anchorage
U of CA, Davis
U of CA, San Diego
U of Charleston (WVA)
U of CO, Colorado Springs
U of Findlay
U of Indianapolis

U of MA at Lowell
U of MN Duluth
U of MN, Morris
U of MO, Rolla
U of NE at Kearney
U of New Haven
U of NC at Pembroke
U of North Dakota
U of North Florida
U of Northern CO
U of Puerto Rico, Bayamon
U of Puerto Rico, Cayey
U of Puerto Rico, Mayaguez
U of Puerto Rico, Rio
    Piedras
U of South Dakota
U of Southern IN
U of Tampa
U of the Incarnate Word
U of West Florida
U of WI, Parkside
Virginia State U
VA Union University
Wayne State College (NE)
Westchester U of
    Pennsylvania
West Liberty State College
WVA State College
WVA Wesleyan College
Western OR University
Western State College (CO)
Western WA University
Wheeling Jesuit University

TRACK
OUTDOOR
DIVISION III

Adrian College
Albion College
Albright College
Alfred University
Allegheny College
Alma College
Amherst College

Anderson University (IN)
Augsburg College
Augustana College (IL)
Aurora University
Babson College
Baldwin-Wallace College
Bates College
Beloit College
Benedictine University (IL)
Bethany College (WVA)
Bethel University
Bluffton College
Bowdoin College
Brandeis University
Bridgewater College (VA)
Bridgewater State College
Buena Vista University
Buffalo State College
Cabrini College
CA Institute of Technology
CA Lutheran University
CA State U, Hayward
Calvin College
Capital University
Carleton College
Carnegie Mellon University
Carroll College (WI)
Carthage College
Case Western Reserve U
Catholic University
Central College (IA)
Centre College
Christopher Newport U
City College of NY
Claremont McKenna-Harvey
    Mudd-Scripps Colleges
Coe College
Colby College
Colby-Sawyer College
College Misericordia
College of Mt. St. Joseph
College of Wooster
Colorado College
Concordia
    College–Moorhead
Concordia University (IL)

Concordia University (WI)
Connecticut College
Cornell College
Defiance College
DE Valley College
Denison University
DePauw University
DeSales University
Dickinson College
Earlham College
Eastern CT State U
Eastern Mennonite U
Elizabethtown College
Elmhurst College
Emmanuel College (MA)
Emory University
Fisk University
Fitchburg State College
Franklin & Marshall College
Franklin College
Frostburg State U
Gallaudet University
George Fox University
Gettysburg College
Goucher College
Greenville College
Grinnell College
Grove City College
Gustavus Adolphus College
Gwynedd-Mercy College
Hamilton College
Hamline University
Hanover College
Hartwick College
Haverford College
Heidelberg College
Hendrix College
Hiram College
Hope College
Howard Payne University
Hunter College
Illinois College
IL Wesleyan University
Ithaca College
John Carroll University
Johns Hopkins University

Juniata College
Kean University
Keene State College
Kenyon College
Knox College
Lawrence University
Lebanon Valley College
Lehman College, City U of NY
Lewis and Clark College
Lincoln University (PA)
Linfield College
Loras College
Luther College
Lynchburg College
Macalester College
Manchester College
Marietta College
Martin Luther College
MA Institute of Tech
McDaniel College
McMurry University
Medgar Evers College
Messiah College
Methodist College
Middlebury College
Millikin University
Milwaukee School of Engineering
Mississippi College
Monmouth College (IL)
Montclair State U
Moravian College
Mount Union College
Muhlenberg College
Muskingum College
Nazareth College
NE Wesleyan University
NJ City University
NY City College of Tech
New York University
North Central College
North Park University
Oberlin College
Occidental College
Oglethorpe University

Ohio Northern University
Ohio Wesleyan University
Olivet College
Otterbein College
Pacific Lutheran University
Pacific University (OR)
PA State U Erie, the Behrend College
Plattsburgh State U of NY
Polytechnic University (NY)
Pomona-Pitzer Colleges
Principia College
Ramapo College
Rensselaer Polytechnic Insti.
Rhode Island College
Rhodes College
Richard Stockton College (NJ)
Ripon College
Roanoke College
Rochester Institute of Tech
Rose-Hulman Institute of Tech
Rowan University
Rust College
Rutgers, The State U of NJ, Camden
Saint Mary's U of MN
Salem State College
Salisbury University
Simpson College
Southern Vermont College
Southwestern U (TX)
Springfield College
St. John's University (MN)
St. Lawrence University
St. Norbert College
St. Olaf College
State U College–Brockport
State U College–Cortland
State U College–Fredonia
State U College at Geneseo
State U College–New Paltz
State U College–Brockport
State U College–Oneonta
State U of NY–Farmingdale

State U of NY–Oswego
Stevens Institute of Tech
Stillman College
Sul Ross State U
Susquehanna University
Swarthmore College
The College of NJ
Thiel College
Trinity College (CT)
Trinity University (TX)
Tufts University
U.S. Coast Guard Academy
U.S. Merchant Marine Acad.
Union College (NY)
U of Chicago
U of Dallas
U of Dubuque
U of La Verne
U of Mary Washington
U of MA, Dartmouth
U of Puget Sound
U of Redlands
U of Rochester
U of Southern ME
U of St. Thomas (MN)
U of the South
U of WI, Eau Claire
U of WI, La Crosse
U of WI, Oshkosh
U of WI, Platteville
U of WI, River Falls
U of WI, Stevens Point
U of WI, Stout
U of WI, Superior
U of WI, Whitewater
Upper IA University
Ursinus College
Wabash College
Wartburg College
Washington & Jefferson College
Washington and Lee U
Washington U–St. Louis
Wesleyan University (CT)
Westfield State College
Westminster College (PA)

Wheaton College (IL)
Wheaton College (MA)
Whittier College
Whitworth College
Widener University
Willamette University
William Paterson U of NJ
Williams College
Wilmington College (Ohio)
WI Lutheran College
Wittenberg University
Worcester Polytechnic
  Institute
Worcester State College
York College (NY)
York College (PA)

VOLLEYBALL
DIVISION I

Ball State University
Brigham Young University
CA State U, Northridge
George Mason University
Harvard University
IN U-Purdue U, Fort Wayne
Long Beach State U
Loyola University (IL)
Ohio State U
Pennsylvania State U
Pepperdine University
Princeton University
Quincy University
Rutgers, State U of NJ,
  New Brunswick
Sacred Heart University
Saint Francis U (PA)
Stanford University
U of CA, Irvine
U of CA, Los Angeles
U of CA, Santa Barbara
U of Hawaii–Manoa
U of Southern CA
U of the Pacific

VOLLEYBALL
DIVISION II

Dallas Baptist University
East Stroudsburg U of
  Pennsylvania
Lees-McRae College
Lewis University
Mercyhurst College
NJ Institute of Technology
Queens College (NY)
Southampton Campus of
  Long Island University
U of CA, San Diego
U of Findlay
U of New Haven
U of Puerto Rico, Bayamon
U of Puerto Rico, Cayey
U of Puerto Rico, Mayaguez
U of Puerto Rico, Rio
  Piedras

VOLLEYBALL
DIVISION III

Baptist Bible College
Bard College
Bernard M. Baruch College
Brooklyn College
City College of NY
Clarke College
College of Mt. St. Vincent
D'Youville College
Eastern Mennonite U
Elms College
Emmanuel College (MA)
Endicott College
Hilbert College
Hunter College
Johnson and Wales U
Juniata College
Lasell College
Lehman College, City U of
  NY
MA Institute of Tech
Medaille College

Medgar Evers College
Milwaukee School of
  Engineering
Mount Ida College
NJ City University
NY City College of Tech
New York University
Newbury College
Palm Beach Atlantic U
Philadelphia Biblical U
Polytechnic University (NY)
Ramapo College
Rivier College
Roger Williams University
Springfield College
State U College–New Paltz
Stevens Institute of Tech
U of CA, Santa Cruz
U of La Verne
Vassar College
Villa Julie College
Wentworth Institute of
  Tech
Yeshiva University
York College (NY)

WATER POLO
DIVISION I

Brown University
Bucknell University
George WA University
Harvard University
Iona College
Long Beach State U
Loyola Marymount U
Pepperdine University
Princeton University
Santa Clara University
St. Francis College (NY)
Stanford University
U.S. Air Force Academy
U.S. Naval Academy
U of CA, Berkeley
U of CA, Irvine
U of CA, Los Angeles

U of CA, Santa Barbara
U of Southern CA
U of the Pacific

WATER POLO
DIVISION II

Brigham Young U, HI
Chaminade University
Gannon University
Mercyhurst College
Queens College (NY)
Salem International U
Slippery Rock U of PA
U of CA, Davis
U of CA, San Diego

WATER POLO
DIVISION III

CA Institute of Technology
CA Lutheran University
Chapman University
Claremont McKenna-
    Harvey Mudd-Scripps
    Colleges
Connecticut College
Grove City College
Johns Hopkins University
MA Institute of Tech
Occidental College
PA State U Erie, the
    Behrend College
Pomona-Pitzer Colleges
U of CA, Santa Cruz
U of La Verne
U of Redlands
Washington and Jefferson
    College
Whittier College

WRESTLING
DIVISION I

American University
Appalachian State U

Arizona State U
Birmingham-Southern
    College
Boise State University
Boston University
Brown University
CA Polytechnic State U
CA State U, Bakersfield
CA State U, Fresno
CA State U, Fullerton
Campbell University
Central MI University
Clarion U of Pennsylvania
Cleveland State U
Columbia University
Cornell University
Davidson College
Delaware State U
Drexel University
Duke University
Duquesne University
East Carolina University
Eastern IL University
Eastern MI University
Edinboro U of PA
Franklin & Marshall College
Gardner-Webb University
George Mason University
Harvard University
Hofstra University
IN University, Bloomington
Iowa State U
James Madison University
Kent State U
Lehigh University
Lock Haven U of PA
Michigan State U
Millersville U of PA
North Carolina State U
Northern IL University
Northwestern University
Ohio State U
Ohio University
Oklahoma State U
Old Dominion University
Oregon State U

Pennsylvania State U
Portland State U
Princeton University
Purdue University
Rider University
Rutgers, State U of NJ,
    New Brunswick
Sacred Heart University
Slippery Rock U of PA
Stanford University
State U of NY–Binghamton
The Citadel
U.S. Air Force Academy
U.S. Military Academy
U.S. Naval Academy
U at Buffalo, the State U
    of NY
U of CA, Davis
U of IL, Champaign
U of Iowa
U of MD, College Park
U of Michigan
U of MN, Twin Cities
U of MO, Columbia
U of NE, Lincoln
U of NC at Greensboro
U of NC, Chapel Hill
U of Northern IA
U of Oklahoma
U of Oregon
U of Pennsylvania
U of Pittsburgh
U of TN at Chattanooga
U of Virginia
U of WI, Madison
U of Wyoming
UT Valley State College
VA Military Institute
VA Polytechnic Institute &
    State University
Wagner College
WVA University

WRESTLING
DIVISION II

Adams State College
American International
   College
Anderson College (SC)
Ashland University
Augustana College (SD)
Carson-Newman College
Central MO State U
Central WA University
Chadron State College
CO School of Mines
Fort Hays State U
Gannon University
Kutztown U of PA
Mercyhurst College
MN State U Mankato
MN State U Moorhead
North Dakota State U
Northern State U
San Francisco State U
Shippensburg U of PA
South Dakota State U
Southern IL U–Edwardsville
Southwest MN State U
St. Cloud State U
Truman State U
U of Central OK
U of Findlay
U of Indianapolis
U of MN, Morris
U of NE at Kearney
U of NE at Omaha
U of NC at Pembroke
U of Northern CO
U of Pittsburgh, Johnstown
U of Puerto Rico, Bayamon
U of Puerto Rico, Mayaguez
U of WI, Parkside
West Liberty State College
Western State College (CO)

WRESTLING
DIVISION III

Albright College
Augsburg College
Augustana College (IL)
Baldwin-Wallace College
Baptist Bible College
Bridgewater State College
Buena Vista University
Case Western Reserve U
Centenary College (NJ)
Central College (IA)
Coe College
College of Mt. St. Joseph
Concordia
   College–Moorhead
Concordia University (WI)
Cornell College
DE Valley College
Elizabethtown College
Elmhurst College
Gallaudet University
Gettysburg College
Heidelberg College
Hunter College
Illinois College
Ithaca College
John Carroll University
Johns Hopkins University
Johnson and Wales U
King's College (PA)
Knox College
Lakeland College
Lawrence University
Loras College
Luther College
Lycoming College
MacMurray College
Manchester College
Maranatha Baptist Bible
   College
MA Institute of Tech
McDaniel College
Menlo College
Messiah College

Millikin University
Milwaukee School of
   Engineering
Montclair State U
Mount Union College
Muhlenberg College
Muskingum College
New York University
North Central College
Norwich University
Ohio Northern University
Olivet College
Pacific University (OR)
Plymouth State College
Rhode Island College
Rochester Institute of Tech
Roger Williams University
Rose-Hulman Institute of
   Tech
Simpson College
Springfield College
St. John's University (MN)
St. Olaf College
State U College–Brockport
State U College–Cortland
State U College–Oneonta
State U of NY–Oswego
State U of NY Maritime
   College
The College of NJ
Thiel College
Trinity College (CT)
U.S. Coast Guard Academy
U.S. Merchant Marine
   Academy
U of Chicago
U of Dubuque
U of Scranton
U of Southern ME
U of WI, Eau Claire
U of WI, La Crosse
U of WI, Oshkosh
U of WI, Platteville
U of WI, Stevens Point
U of WI, Whitewater
Upper IA University

Ursinus College
Wabash College
Wartburg College
Washington and Jefferson
    College
Washington and Lee U
Waynesburg College
Wesleyan University (CT)
Western New England
    College
Wheaton College (IL)
Wilkes University
Williams College
Wilmington College (Ohio)
Worcester Polytechnic
    Institute
Yeshiva University
York College (PA)

Appendix 5

Mixed Sports

These lists identify institutions that offer specific sports, as well as in which division the sport competes. Go to their websites for complete information.

CROSS-COUNTRY
DIVISION III

Centenary College (NJ)
Greenville College

EQUESTRIAN
DIVISION III

Bridgewater College (VA)
Colby-Sawyer College
Roger Williams University
U of Mary Washington

FENCING
DIVISION I

Lafayette College

FENCING
DIVISION II

NJ Institute of Technology

GOLF
DIVISION II

Johnson C. Smith U
U of the Sciences in
  Philadelphia
Virginia State U

GOLF
DIVISION III

Centenary College (NJ)
Claremont McKenna-
  Harvey Mudd-Scripps
  Colleges
D'Youville College
Endicott College
Hilbert College
Johnson and Wales U
Roger Williams U
U of Southern Maine

RIFLE
DIVISION I

Duquesne University
Mercer University
Morehead State University
Murray State University
North Carolina State U
Ohio State U
TN Technological U
U.S. Air Force Academy
U.S. Military Academy
U.S. Naval Academy
U of Akron
U of Kentucky
U of Memphis
U of MO, Kansas City
U of Nevada
U of TN at Martin

Wofford College
Xavier University

RIFLE
DIVISION II

U of Alaska–Fairbanks
U of the Sciences in
  Philadelphia

RIFLE
DIVISION III

John Jay College of
  Criminal Justice
MA Institute of Tech
MA Maritime Academy
Norwich University
U of Wisconsin, Oshkosh
Wentworth Institute of
  Tech

SWIMMING
DIVISION II

Adelphi University

TENNIS
DIVISION III

PA State Berks-Lehigh
  Valley College

TRACK INDOOR
DIVISION II

Adelphi University

TRACK INDOOR
DIVISION III

Greenville College

TRACK OUTDOOR
DIVISION II

Adelphi University

TRACK OUTDOOR
DIVISION III

Greenville College

Index

A

Academic requirements, 35–36
Academics, 33–41
"America's Best Colleges," 18
Athletic Tender, 102–103
Award Letter, 98–99

C

Combination financial aid, 23
Communications Log, 68
Contact information for
  colleges, 163
Contacts, 37
Cover letter, 56–57

D

Division III institutions, 121–129
Documents, critical, 71–78
  ACT/SAT scores, 76
  Application form, 72
  CSS profile, 74
  Financial Aid Estimator, 77
  Free Application for Federal
  Student Aid (FAFSA), 72
  High-school transcript, 75
  Institutional Financial Aid
  Application form, 77
  NCAA Clearinghouse form, 77
  Student Aid Report (SAR), 75

E

EFC#, 75, 81
Equivalency Sports, 113
  Baseball, 119
  Basketball, 118
  Football, 117
  Equivalency Limits for Division I
  Sports, 114
  Equivalency Limits For Division
  II Sports, 115
Evaluations, 37

F

Free Application for Federal
  Student Aid (FAFSA), 19, 72
Full-ride athletic scholarships, 23

G

GAP, 81
Goal setting, 26–30

H

Head-count sports, 113
Hope Tax Credit, 21

I

Information for Financial Aid
  Recipients form, 100

L

Letter of Intent, 105

M

Men's sports by division, 275
Minority student athletes, 33
Mixed sports by division, 339

N

NAIA Eligibility Rules, 38–39
NAIA's *A Guide for the College-Bound Athlete,* 79
NCAA Guide for the College-Bound Student-Athlete, 13, 83
NCAA violations, 8–9
Negotiation, 107–112, 141–147

O

Organization, 67–69

P

Partial athletic scholarships, 23
Pell Grants, 23
Planning, 149–151
   Freshman Year, 149
   Junior Year, 150
   Senior Year, 151
   Sophomore Year, 150
Profile, 43–46
Athletic statistics to include, 46–53

R

Recruiting myths, 5
Resources, 159
   Books, 162
   Recruiting service, 162
   Websites, 161

S

SAR (Student Aid Report), 75
Sleazy recruiting tactics, 95–96

Statement of Educational Purpose, 101
Student loans, 20–22

T

Tables, Statistical Inventory, 159–161
   Approximate Number of Student Athletes by Division, 159
   NCAA Men's Sports Sponsorships, 160–161
   NCAA Women's Sports Sponsorships, 159–160

U

Ultimate Recruiting Seminar, 11, 84

V

Videotape, 59–60
Visiting the college, 83–85
   Questions to ask, 87–91

W

Williams, Doug 10
Women's sports by division, 205

About the Author

Without athletics, Dion Wheeler would never have graduated from UW–La Crosse. Growing up in an institution for dependent boys, he was an average student in high school. But a young coach inspired him to both exploit his athletic ability and to take his education seriously, as they were the foundation upon which he would "prepare for the future." And so he did.

Education and athletics have been the motivators of his time. Despite a few interruptions to experience the business world, he has taught and coached at every level: grade school, high school, and college. He has been a presenter and instructor at business, athletic, recruiting, and education seminars and has occasionally been accused of being a motivational speaker.

In addition to his recruiting experience—fourteen years at the high-school level and eleven years at the college level—he managed the recruitment of his two (now grown) children, who were both successfully recruited. One by a Division I state university, the other by a Division III private college. One was an All-American, the other's career was cut short by injury.

His ownership of a college prospect recruiting service was the experience where the final piece of the recruiting puzzle fit. There he exposed, and often negotiated for, academically and athletically qualified prospects to coaches of nearly every sport around the country. His unique grasp of the recruiting process from every angle has prepared him to write this powerful guide.

Dion is retired and lives with his wife, Dianne, in Plainfield, Illinois.